Transnational Indians in the North American West

Connecting the Greater West Series
Sterling Evans, Series Editor

Transnational Indians in the North American West

Edited by Clarissa Confer, Andrae Marak, and Laura Tuennerman

Foreword by Sterling Evans

Texas A&M University Press
College Station

First edition

This paper meets the requirements of ANSI/NISO Z39.48-1992 (Permanence of Paper).
Binding materials have been chosen for durability.
Manufactured in the United States of America

Library of Congress Cataloging-in-Publication Data

Transnational Indians in the North American West / edited by Clarissa Confer, Andrae Marak, and Laura Tuennerman; foreword by Sterling Evans. — First edition.
pages cm — (Connecting the greater west series)
Includes bibliographical references and index.
ISBN 978-1-62349-326-4 (cloth: alk. paper) —
ISBN 978-1-62349-327-1 (ebook)
1. Indians of North America. 2. Transnationalism—North America.
I. Confer, Clarissa W., 1965– editor. II. Marak, Andrae M. (Andrae Micheal), editor.
III. Tuennerman, Laura, 1966– editor. IV. Series: Connecting the greater west series.
E77.2.T73 2015
970.004'97—dc23
2015012117

To transnational peoples—and to those who study them

Contents

Illustrations, Maps, and Tables

Illustrations

Maps

Tables

Foreword

In your hands is the fourth book in the new Connecting the Greater West Series, and I believe you will see how *Transnational Indians in the North American West* is a perfect fit for this series of books. This collection of scholarly works seeks to explore the changing and growing ways that historians and others are coming to view "the West"—the American West, northern Mexico, western Canada, parts of the Pacific Rim, and the borderlands between these regions. As such, the series includes books on transnational history, borders and borderlands, immigration, environment and agriculture, and indigenous negotiations of bordered regions—the theme especially pertinent for this particular edited volume. Historians Clarissa Confer, Andrae Marak, and Laura Tuennerman have worked well to compile and edit *Transnational Indians in the North American West*, and without doubt you will see how each essay within this volume works so well to address this important and oft-neglected aspect of North American Native American history. As the editors note on the dedication page, this book is about and for "transnational peoples and to those who study them."

The introduction and twelve chapters that follow, written by scholars from across this transregional West, deal with a variety of different aspects of western Native history in a broad range of themes across time and space. The essays range from the Spanish colonial period in the Southwest to themes of imperialism and neo-liberalism in Indian country today. Some of the chapters explore how Native peoples negotiated changing national boundaries as they came to live in borderland regions between Mexico and the United States or the United States and Canada. Others examine internal boundaries within nation states; how Indian reservations (in the United States) or reserves (in Canada) have created their own bordered regions and how Native peoples have negotiated these frontier zones of interaction at a particular time or over time. Case studies presented within deal with internal borderlands in Nevada, Oklahoma, the Canadian Prairie Provinces, and "Seriland" in the northern Mexico state of Sonora. In all of these instances, there is a great deal of movement of peoples as North American Indians or First Nations became fluid societies between nation-states and across different types of borders. As Andrae Marak and Gary Van Valen explain in their introduction to the volume, "shifting borders and alliances" came to characterize these indigenous North Americans' way of life and political economies, which was all part of the "long process of colonialism" across time in the West.

Readers will see, then, that these essays represent new ways of understanding indigenous borderlands in North America. No one size fits all here; sometimes borders restricted indigenous movement and lifeways, but other times Native peoples capitalized on them, using them in creative ways, including for cultural preservation. Borders inherently imply the boundaries between nation-states, and thus the authors here do not dismiss the role of these more political entities and how they have affected various indigenous peoples in the West. Rather, in some noteworthy ways, many Native peoples underwent a kind of "de-nationalization" process. Evidence presented here on this theme includes questions of nationality and citizenship, forms of resistance to nation-state governments, and how Indians were not mere passive victims to statist policies, as indigenous points of view were made known at grassroots levels. But none of these themes is forced into a borderlands structure. Instead, as good borderlands history should be, they are woven into the narratives of the contributed chapters, integrated uniquely into the larger story that each historian is telling here.

Proudly for the Connecting the Greater West Series, *Transnational Indians in the North American West* is one of the first books anywhere to deal with Native Americans in borderland regions. It will therefore be of interest and use for historians of the American West, the Canadian West, the Mexican North, Native America, and borderlands, as well as for anthropologists, geographers, and sociologists interested in this important and emerging field of study. The volume will be an important addition to classes for any and all of these subjects and areas of study. The first place scholars, students, and others interested in this field should begin is with Marak's and Van Valen's excellent introduction. It perfectly sets up the volume's goals and objectives and frames the study in what borderlands scholars will find a highly useful analysis of how we should understand Native peoples in borderlands places.

—Sterling Evans
General Editor, Connecting the Greater West Series

Acknowledgments

Because this edited volume has taken several years to move from an idea to a finished product, there are many people that we need to thank. First, at California University of Pennsylvania: the Department of History and Political Science, the College of Liberal Arts, and the Faculty Professional Development Center provided us with research funds and professional space to take up this project. A special thanks goes out to Cindy Speer, who makes all of our jobs easier. At Indiana University–Purdue University Columbus, we would like to thank the faculty and staff who attended presentations on the indigenous borderlands and provided important feedback. This includes Anna Carmon, Jim Clack, Terry Dibble, Doug Gardner, Julie Goodspeed-Chadwick, Ryan Neville-Shepard, Lisa Siefker Bailey, Katherine Wills, and Aimee Zoeller. We would also like to thank Vicki Kruse for her assistance and support. Governors State University has also provided important support. We would especially like to thank Reinhold Hill, Sandi Kawanna, Nancy McDaniel, and Sabrina Slocum.

A number of people have read portions of the edited volume and provided meaningful feedback. We would like to thank Sharon Bailey Glasco, Marc Becker, Steve Bunker, Gerry Cadava, Elaine Carey, George Díaz, Jay Dwyer, Paul Eiss, Ramón Gutiérrez, Paul Jentz, Ben Johnson, David Rich Lewis, Stephen Lewis, Hong-Ming Liang, María Cristina Manzano Munguía, Eric Meeks, Justin Quinn Olmstead, Margaret Power, Teresa Prados-Torreira, Carlos Salomon, Brenden Rensink, Jonathan Reynolds, Jason Ruiz, Jeffrey Sheperd, Jim Tallon, Gary Van Valen, and Ellie Walsh.

Texas A&M University Press has been very supportive of this edited volume. Our thanks go out to Sterling Evans for his willingness to entertain the underlying ideas of this edited volume. Mary Lenn Dixon, now retired, also served as a major supporter and helped us bring this idea to fruition. We could not have been more delighted than to have Jay Dew take up our project when Mary Lenn retired. He has been both extremely supportive and very professional.

Tracy Ellen Smith and Ted Avila, our cartographers, did excellent and timely work in spite of a major relocation in the midst of the project. Gary Van Valen designed the map of the locations of the indigenous groups of the

North American West between the eighteenth and twenty-first centuries. In addition, we want to thank the individual authors for sticking with the project even though it took quite a long time to bring it all together and make it whole.

Most importantly, we would like to thank our families for their love and support: John, Angie, Flannery, Delaney, Rowan, Scott, Elyse, and Megan.

Transnational Indians in the North American West

Introduction

Transnational Indians of the North American West

Andrae Marak and Gary Van Valen

As the year 1815 began, Juan Antonio Ignacio Baca reached the height of his political career when the elders of New Mexico's Cochiti Pueblo handed him the cane of office that came with the title of Pueblo Governor. A Pueblo Indian man, he had also been recognized as a Spanish citizen and had helped manage a Spanish election in the previous year. However, Baca took the wrong side in a land dispute and was overthrown and expelled by a rival faction within Cochiti later in 1815. He found a new home at Zia Pueblo and later at Jemez Pueblo, and lived long enough to see sovereignty over New Mexico pass from Spain to Mexico in 1821 and from Mexico to the United States in 1848.

Baca's case demonstrates the difficulties scholars can encounter when trying to frame Native American history within national history. Does Baca's story form part of the national history of Spain, Mexico, or the United States? Or does it belong to the stateless (but locally autonomous) Nations of Cochiti, Zia, or Jemez? Clearly, Baca was part of all of these national and local histories. Thus, he is an example of the need to approach native history through a transnational framework.

As transnational histories cannot be defined by the boundaries of modern nation-states, another geographic unit of analysis must be chosen. In the west-central part of the continent of North America, we can conceive of a region (as others have) spanning the nation-states of Canada, the United States, and Mexico. Although its national components may be better known to Canadians and Americans as the West and to Mexicans as *el Norte*, we shall refer to this transnational region as the North American West in order to emphasize certain historical similarities.[1] Arid or semi-arid climates predominate, with the notable exception of the Pacific Northwest.[2] The North American West was a last frontier of colonization for all three nation-states, which were centered in more humid agricultural regions, and it only came completely under national control during the late nineteenth century. The North American West was the last part of temperate North America to host independent native societies, and the nation-states mostly left these peoples in parts of their homelands—especially as they were largely unable to continue the (principally US) practice of Indian removal given that they did not have anywhere else to remove them to.[3] Thus, the history of the region must always include the descendants of its original inhabitants.[4]

History has had to compete with myth, which has always exercised a profound influence on our understanding of this region. One set of myths views the North American West as a stage for the maximum expression of freedom and individualism. Canadians, Mexicans, and Americans have long conceived of the North American West as free from government-imposed constraints, in a sense borderless. The mythical West of wide open spaces, unlimited economic potential, and unfettered social structure—if only it could be subdued—helped to shape nineteenth- and twentieth-century North American societies as well as the policies adopted by the Canadian, US, and Mexican federal governments, all of which were situated great distances from the region.[5] Lawrence Culver argues that modernizers, developers, and speculators promoted the US West as a place that offered "leisure as a permanent way of life," in what we might call the boosterism version of the West. This version of the West differs from that envisioned by Frederick Jackson Turner, who promoted the idea of a transformative frontier experience that "turned Europeans into Americans," where "English-speaking white men were the stars of his story," in the words of Patricia Limerick. Nevertheless, both versions imagined an empty land or an already pacified people in the region that need not be taken into account.[6]

Another set of powerful myths of the North American West centers on the area's native people, that is, when they were taken into account. Outsiders have tended to lump all native people into a single, unified group with such diverse labels as *indios, naturales, indígenas*, American Indians, Native Americans, aboriginals, First Nations, or Indigenous peoples, which often obscures their varied and complex societies. When not speaking about a particular people, Nation, or tribe, "Indigenous" is a useful category because it refers to people who are native to a particular area and who have been colonized.[7] In recognizing that these people have come under colonial rule, we also recognize that Indigenous people had to deal with newcomers who had the power to reshape societies. This inequality in power mirrors the "long processes of colonialism and encounter" as the "national projects of Mexico and the United States" and Canada, which impacted Indigenous people who already lived there.[8] The inequality in these power relations allowed colonizers to promote primitivist myths of Indigenous people, contrasting them to their own societies for good or for ill. Indigenous people were thus depicted

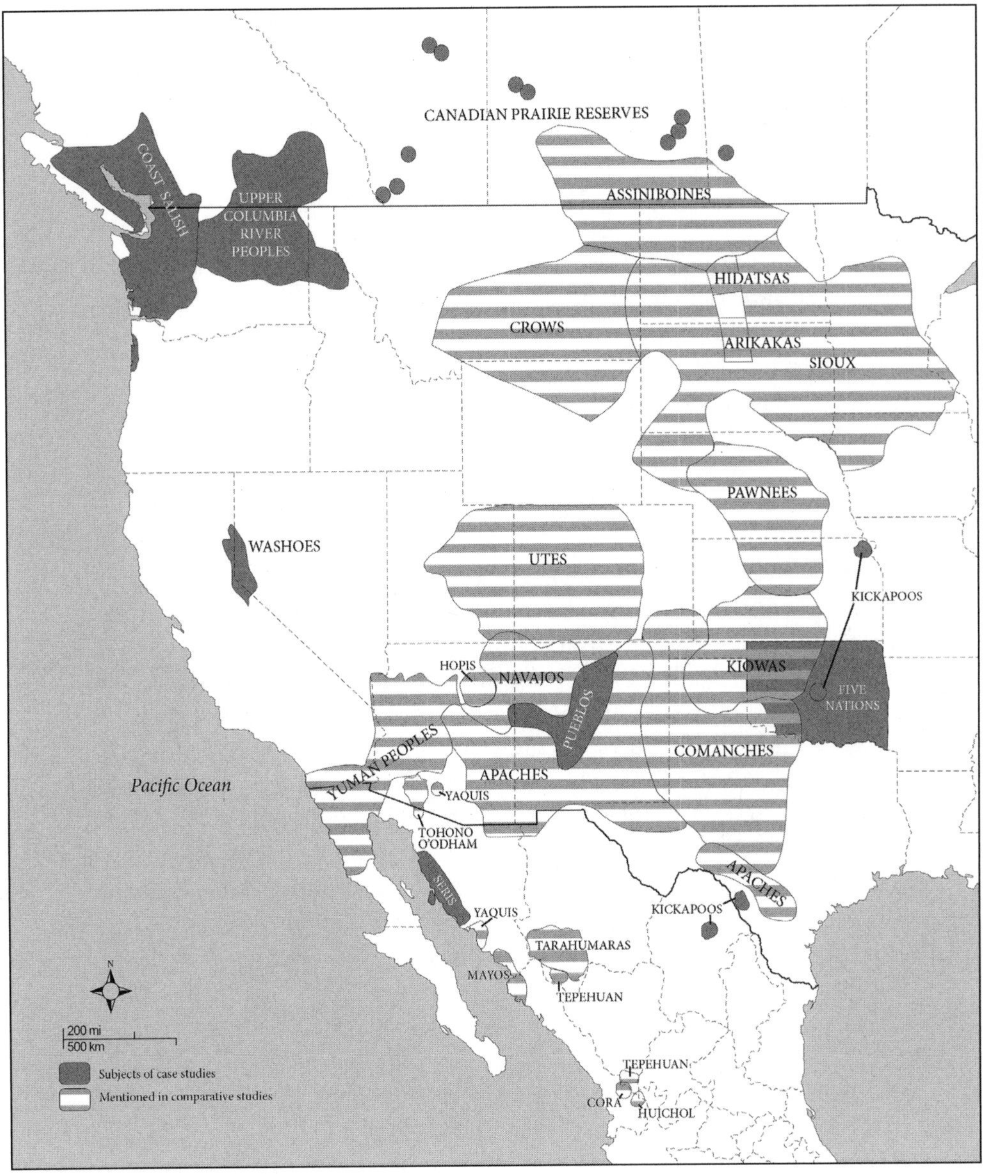

Locations of Indigenous groups of the North American West included in the case studies and comparative studies in this volume. The territories shown include a mixture of original lands and later reserved lands held by these peoples at various times between the eighteenth and twenty-first centuries. Map by Tracy Ellen Smith and Ted Avila.

either as noble savages living a simple life in tune with nature or as barbaric primitives condemned to eventual evolutionary extinction.[9]

Throughout the nineteenth and early twentieth centuries, the North American West remained a place of shifting boundaries and allegiances. Boundaries came in all forms—political, economic, and social. They could be imposed, if only on paper, by international agreements like the national US-Canadian and US-Mexican boundaries.[10] It was especially at the edges of empires and the liminal frontier spaces of newly created nation-state boundaries that Nations found it most necessary to "define and control" their borders, as Alan Taylor notes:

> By asserting and displaying political difference at a boundary, regimes consolidate the allegiance and identity of their citizens or subjects within. Loose borders make for weak nations or empires. But attempts to make and to control borders inevitably invite resistance by local people who resent restrictions.[11]

It was also at the edges of empires, however, that local actors had the most power to undermine and/or reinterpret the will of the nation-state; in other words, they could use a plethora of tools of resistance to undermine regime consolidation.[12] As Benjamin Johnson and Andrew Graybill argue, "Borderlanders . . . also used nation states and their boundaries for their own purposes and sought to forge nations that reflected their own identities."[13]

Like other borderlanders, Indigenous people were sometimes able to minimize the impact of—and in some cases, to capitalize on—these new nation-state boundaries.[14] For example, the Tohono O'odham, whose ancestral homeland was cut in half as a result of the Gadsden (or La Mesilla) Purchase of 1854, were not even aware of the new border and, for an extended time after its establishment, simply ignored its existence. Over time, as the border hardened, it evolved into an artificial barrier (in the eyes of the Tohono O'odham) that needed to be protested and navigated both through legal means and through simple refusal to obey laws they deemed as unfair.[15] In fact, Geraldo L. Cadava goes so far as to claim that, outside of "national security operations that have received lavish funding," both the US and Mexican governments engaged in an active "disinvestment in the border region as a whole."[16] And even though 9/11 resulted in further national security investments, an increased hardening of the border, and added restrictions, many members of the Tohono O'odham Nation are still informally allowed to cross the border.[17] Long before 9/11, some members of the Tohono O'odham Nation learned to use the border as leverage to extract greater resources and investments out of the Mexican federal government. For example, in the late 1920s Antonio Bustamante, the Tohono O'odham governor of Pozo Verde, Sonora, used the US investment in schooling on the then Papago Reservation and the Mexican government's fear of US cultural imperialism along the border to convince Mexico's Education Ministry to establish a local primary school. However, this leverage had its limits. When Bustamante later pushed for a monetary investment in Pozo Verde similar to that north of the border, Mexican officials decided that they might not have enough resources to please the Tohono O'odham and wrote them off as a lost cause.[18]

The Tohono O'odham experience was not entirely unique. Members of a wide range of other Indigenous groups—among them the Delaware, Kickapoo, Seminole, Apache, Kiowa, Comanche, Pima, Nez Perce, Sioux, and Iroquois—have also advantageously used international boundaries. For example, they evaded "various threats of pursuit, persecution, and prosecution" by tapping into the usual unwillingness of those tracking them, to cross international borders.[19] The Comanche were arguably most successful when a border supposedly ran through their territory (c. 1710–63, 1803–48, and 1861–65), and the Apache resisted imperial domination the longest because they could cross the US-Mexican border. Other Indigenous groups successfully used the border to play competing trading companies off against each other, engage in contraband running, or undermine government-sponsored monopolies.[20] As Brenden Rensink demonstrates, however, governments could also leverage international borders. The United States government did so by stoking Montanans' fears of the Cree to (re) establish its sovereignty in a region over which they had only intermittent control.[21] Several of the chapters in this volume address the role of international borders in Indigenous experience. Kristin Hoganson traces the history of the Kickapoo across the US-Mexican border, and Michael Marker examines how US and Canadian education policies impacted Coast Salish people on both sides of the border. Clarissa Confer's chapter deals with the residents of Indian Territory who found themselves on a new international border drawn by the Civil War, and Gary Van Valen's chapter discusses the transnational Pueblo individual mentioned at the beginning of this introduction. Neither the residents of Indian Territory nor the Pueblos had to physically migrate in order to experience different national sovereignties.

Despite the fact that many of these borders have been created only relatively recently, we often conceive of Indigenous people as belonging to particular nation-states, even though they preceded those nation-states or empires or have passed from the jurisdiction and rule of one nation-state to another. For example, just as what is now the US Southwest was once considered the North of New Spain and Mexico, what is now the US Northwest was once claimed by four nation-states or empires and dominated by the Hudson's Bay Company. Johnson and Graybill warn us of the teleological approach to history which "assume[s] the inevitability of the modern map" and suggest that we interrogate borders and investigate "[w]ith what other ways of organizing people and space did they come into conflict, and how were these resolved?"[22] One way to do this is to adopt a bottom-up, denationalized approach that avoids centralizing histories written from the point of view of Mexico City; Washington, DC; and Ottawa.[23] Such a transnational approach recognizes that although Canada, the United States, and Mexico all adopted governing strategies based on liberalism, the seizure of Indigenous lands, and the assimilation of Indigenous peoples (as unequals) into mainstream culture, as well as had similar mythologies about the North American West, their individual histories (and those of the peoples within their borders) were simultaneously uniquely shaped by local forces and by transnational governmental and nongovernmental forces that spanned localities and (by definition) nation-states. Accordingly, Pekka Hämäläinen and Samuel Truett argue that we need to

> adopt an approach that shows how imperial and national powers interpenetrated smaller (regional, local) scales without necessarily dominating them. Such an approach would destabilize distinctions between core and periphery and would challenge the convention of using territorialized spaces of empires and nations as points of departure.[24]

They go on to say, "Approaching events and processes from the borderlands, we see how imperfectly the fledgling heirs to empire imposed their modern logic of incorporation and control on those they claimed as citizens and subjects."[25] In fact, as historian Rachel St. John notes, the United States-Mexico border itself "began as a means for the" two nations "to claim territory they had yet to conquer."[26] That is not to say that nation-states (and empires) are not important. Tyler Stoval is correct in stating, "The essence of transnational and global history is not the absence of the nation [or empire], but rather a critical interrogation of its relationship to other levels of the human experience."[27] This suggests that a transnational approach is not enough. As suggested by María C. Manzano-Munguía in this volume, if we are to truly analyze the nation-state and its relationship to other ways of organizing people and space, we will need to begin adopting a grassroots approach, writing history from the point of view of Indigenous people and Indigenous Nations within (and across) nation-states, even if that means a "multiplicity and fragmentation" of our historical narratives.[28]

Nation-states created internal boundaries as well as national boundaries. In the United States and Canada, federal agencies drew arbitrary boundaries around resources like forests or lakes.[29] More importantly, every colonizing power restricted Indigenous landholding and created borders around natives' remaining lands. Spain was the first colonizing power to do so, and although the lands of colonial *pueblos de indios* in New Spain were legally protected, they were essentially equivalent to later American reservations or Canadian reserves.[30] Many of the legal boundaries affecting native people in the US and Canada were created by government attempts to restrict Indigenous people to reservations or reserves.[31] These reservations attempted to create a "hard-and-fast line separating Indians on the inside from whites and Indians on the outside."[32] And although Mexico abolished the legal separateness of Indians upon achieving independence from Spain, Andrae Marak's chapter in this volume demonstrates that Mexican officials steeped in the values of the US-Mexico border region also adopted a de facto reservation approach vis-à-vis the Seri Indians in the early twentieth century.

Like elsewhere in the Americas, Indigenous people in Mexico, Canada, and the United States faced a narrow range of choices against the onslaught of what Florencia Mallon has called "an abstract, generic, 'one-size-fits all' concept of citizenship rooted in European liberalism" that only granted them autonomy at the cost of "segregation, isolation, and poverty" or citizenship at the cost of their cultural rights and self-identity.[33] Liberalism, a compilation of ideas from the Enlightenment, theoretically aimed to replace societal groups with different and unequal legal privileges with a nation of individuals given equal treatment under the law. Liberal governments were to protect property rights, individual freedom, and religious freedom. First put into practice in the age of Atlantic Revolutions, liberalism conceived of people as citizens rather than subjects. But by undermining old loyalties to monarchs and state religions, liberal reforms helped create nationalism—a new loyalty to a group of people like oneself. Nationalism required cultural homogeneity and led to an increased desire for the assimilation of minority lands and peoples. So ironically, liberal states were also nationalistic states that denied property rights, individual freedom, and religious freedom to Indigenous peoples. These states extended the promise of equal citizenship but required Indigenous people to give up their culture in exchange. Even when natives adhered to the liberal ideal of *individual* property, Matthew Makley, Ian Stacy, and Kristin Hoganson all show that property rights were not respected by whites when it was Indian property. Liberals also had a tendency to blame individuals for a failure to advance and prosper on a supposedly level playing field of equal opportunity, so according to Marker, the Canadian government believed "that the need for welfare and residential placement was not a product of economic circumstances, but of parental moral shortcomings."

Hence, Indigenous people would long struggle over issues of nationality and citizenship: "Native people who had long identified themselves on the basis of their ties to places and kinship groups struggled to assert their rights in a new national context in which citizenship was an important source of power and privilege."[34] As Van Valen's chapter shows, Spain began experimenting with liberalism in the North American West as early as 1813. Soon after, independent Mexico began theoretically treating Indians as equal citizens, and José Angel Hernández points out that Mexican colonization policies for the North always included plans to settle Indians, often officially favoring them over foreigners. However, the full application of liberal policies only came in the later nineteenth century, and these policies tended to deprive Indians of land through their fixation on individual landownership and their demand that landownership be proven with legal documents. In Mexico, under the *Ley Lerdo* of 1856 and the *Ley de Colonización y Deslinde de Terrenos Baldíos* of 1883, the liberal undermining of corporate Indigenous identity worked hand in hand with the auctioning off of so-called "vacant lands," depriving many Indigenous people of their ancestral lands and patrimony.[35]

In the United States, the General Allotment (Dawes) Act of 1887 served simultaneously to open up Native American lands to outsiders and prepare their people for citizenship. Lawmakers believed that the law, which divided up reservation lands and distributed them to tribal members as individuals while leaving any "excess" lands for non-Natives, would end Native American dependency on the government even as it imbued Natives with "industry, hard work, and thrift."[36] As Frederick Hoxie has suggested, the Dawes Act "assumed that landownership, citizenship, and education would alter Indigenous cultures, bringing them to 'civilization.'"[37] In fact, in addition to attempts to change their culture, Indigenous people were often falsely portrayed as "agriculturally unskilled" so as to further make the case that white people should be given access to Indigenous lands because only white people could put the land to its proper use.[38] The allotted lands set aside for Indigenous people were to be held in trust by the federal government for twenty-five years while Natives underwent a state-led civilizing process. But even the "excess" lands created by allotment were often not enough to sate the desires of newly arrived non-Indian homesteaders, land speculators, and railroad interests, who convinced the government to create exceptions to the twenty-five-year grace period.[39]

In Canada, the Manitoba Act of 1870 and the Indian Act of 1876 served to protect the lands and resources of First Nations people even as they opened up "excess" lands to outsiders. These acts neither prevented the continued harassment of Indigenous people by Anglo-Canadian troops nor rectified the long delays in establishing Indian Reserves for First Nations people, but they did provide the basis for Anglo settlement on former Indigenous lands.[40] As Tony Ward notes in this volume, when Indigenous people did finally gain access to reserves, the Crown still "owned all reserve lands, holding it in trust for the Indians, whose legal status was that of minors." Although Canada never made a law like the Dawes Act, Ward indicates that in 1887–96, under orders given by Prime Minister John A. Macdonald to Indian Commissioner Edgar Dewdney in 1886, its Department of Indian Affairs assigned farm tracts to individual Indians within reserves; declared the rest a "surplus," which it sold to settlers; and kept the profits. Furthermore, Yale Belanger shows that liberalism in its most recent incarnation of neoliberalism tends to perpetuate colonial relationships, for although gaming was promoted as a way to aid First Nations' development, it actually aids the provincial government and outside investors to a large degree, and allowed the provincial government to expand its gaming bureaucracy and exert power over First Nations for the first time. In sum, then, these internal boundaries within nation-states often (purposely) played an important role in restricting the options available to Indigenous people, whether in Canada, the United States, or Mexico.

Despite such prejudicial policies, the contributors to this volume show that Indigenous people were not passive victims, but rather actively sought out ways to promote their best interests. In Ward's chapter, Indians requested farm animals and tools when making treaties, and initially tried to become competitive farmers. The Upper Columbia River groups studied by Stacy acted in the fur trade and adopted Christianity, pastoralism, and settled agriculture, all before they were put on reservations. Their relations with whites involved talking back, fighting, objecting to moving off the land, negotiating, and protesting the size and location of the reservation. The Five Nations investigated by Confer exercised agency with an emphasis on sovereignty. They participated in the politics of the day by choosing sides in the Civil War, and sided with South for economic reasons; they retained autonomy in supplying troops to the South, and Chickasaws and Choctaws claimed US forts as their own and encouraged men to enlist to defend their Nations (not the South as a nation); and Native political reasons prevailed when the Cherokees chose the South, and were more important than the wider political situation of North versus South. Hoganson demonstrates that mobility was a form of resistance for the Kickapoo, who migrated in stages from the Detroit area to Mexico. Belanger illustrates First Nations' agency with the activism of F. O. Loft, who asked the British king for equal treatment in Canada and promoted pan-Indianism by organizing a League of Indians of Canada. He also shows that First Nations willingly adopted farming and ranching, chose to promote gambling, and also chose to negotiate with Alberta instead of the federal government to get "the best deal possible with a foreign power."

Although outsiders like to conceive of Indigenous groups as internally peaceful, unified, and communally oriented, several contributions to this volume provide ample evidence of individual agency. Stacy presents us with Spokane Garry, an Indigenous Christian evangelist trained in a Manitoba mission school. The societies studied by Van Valen and Confer were beset by factional disputes, and individuals such as Juan Antonio Ignacio Baca, Stand

Watie, and the brothers Chilly and Daniel MacIntosh stand out as political opportunists who put their own interests first. And individual white opportunists played a role in Indian politics as well, so that the theme of the "white chief" surfaces more than once. Marak illustrates how the Seri dealt with whites who assumed the right to lead them, from the Mexican hacendado Pascual Encinas to the Americans Roberto Thomson and the "white chief" Edward H. Davis. Stacy discusses the "white Indian chief" George Harvey, and Confer demonstrates that a white Confederate, Colonel Douglas Cooper, led Indian troops and escalated the conflicts within Indian territory.

Many native groups took actions that followed the letter of nation-states' laws, while also defeating the nation-states' broader plans for assimilation. Many of the bands studied by Ward chose their land not for "civilized" farming, but for traditional hunting and trapping. The Washoes in Makley's chapter used the Dawes Act to choose allotments in pine nut lands rather than irrigable farmlands, turning its assimilationist goals on their head. Similarly, Marker finds that Coast Salish parents used the boarding school in Salem, Oregon, as a safe haven from persecution in public schools, thus using an originally assimilationist institution to preserve native culture.

In the North American West, boundaries sometimes matter and sometimes do not. The concept of a North American Western region itself crosses international borders. State policies toward Indigenous people have been transnational: reserved land, wardship under a national government, liberalism, land seizure, assimilation, the use of "show Indians," artifact collection, boarding schools, and gaming have all been applied in two or all three of the nation-states. In this commonly accepted view, a transnational approach deals with histories that transcend the borders of modern nation-states.

To the contributors to this volume, transnationalism can be expressed in various and perhaps unexpected ways. One thing that they have in common is an approach that takes Indigenous claims to nationhood seriously and thus allows for a broader interpretation of the transnational. To Dirk Raat, transnationalism relates to post-processual archaeology reconnecting with Braudelian, dependency, and world-system approaches to history so that archaeologists look beyond the local context to investigate long-distance interactions between peoples. Manzano-Munguía and Makley link it to the New Western history, which depicts the West as more than just a place for Anglo men and includes Indians as well as immigrants and women. Marak points out that Seri territory was transnational because the same land was claimed by both the Seri and Mexico. The fact that Indigenous people came to form nations within nations (usually as wards of nation-states) automatically makes their lived experience transnational. The contributors to this volume cite cases of movement between the Indian and non-Indian worlds, and between different Indian groups. Indians left their reserved lands—and hence crossed into other Nations—to work, hunt, fish, gather, practice ceremonies, raid, make allies, negotiate treaties, pursue legal cases, and seek out education. Some of these activities took Indigenous people across the borders of nation-states as well. Manzano-Munguía, Van Valen, and Confer all deal with "forced transnationalism," in which natives are forced to adapt to changing jurisdictions imposed by nation-states. Even natives who remained on reserved lands were transnational, for as Ward notes, the reserves did not completely "belong" to Indians; the nation-state's government owned and controlled almost everything, and different laws applied to people on and off reserves.

Indigenous people are members of local communities by birth, and many choose to remain part of one and to maintain a local sense of identity. Yet even under the most oppressive policies of nation-states, the native peoples of the North American West have never been entirely constrained by borders. If every myth contains a kernel of truth, then the myth of the North American West as borderless is, in a sense, true when seen from the perspective of Indigenous people. It is clear that Indigenous history can no longer be depicted as local and isolated; rather, scholars must simultaneously show the importance of the local and involvement in the wider world. As the contributions to this volume show, the scholars who write about Indigenous history in the North American West are also learning to look beyond borders.

Notes

1. Scholars in a variety of disciplines have found it useful to cross the boundaries of modern nation-states in western North America, with the term "North American West" appearing in recent years. See Terry G. Jordan, *North American Cattle Ranching Frontiers: Origins, Diffusion, and Differentiation* (Albuquerque: University of New Mexico Press, 1993); Terry G. Jordan et al., *The Mountain West: Interpreting the Folk Landscape* (Baltimore: Johns Hopkins University Press, 1996); Anne F. Hyde, *Empires, Nations, and Families: A History of the North American West* (Lincoln: University of Nebraska Press, 2011); Richard White and John M. Findlay, *Power and Place in the North American West* (Seattle: University of Washington Press, 2012); Nayan Shah, *Stranger Intimacy: Contesting Race, Sexuality and the Law in the North American West* (Berkeley: University of California Press, 2012); Susan G. Clark and Murray B. Rutherford, eds., *Large Carnivore Conservation: Integrating Science and Policy in the North American West* (Chicago: University of Chicago Press, 2014); and Susan E. Gray and Gayle Gullett, eds., *Contingent Maps: Rethinking Western Women's History and the North American West* (Tucson: University of Arizona Press, 2014).

2. Historians of the US West have long viewed aridity as a defining characteristic of their portion of this transnational region; see Walter Prescott Webb, *The Great Plains* (New York: Grosset and Dunlap, 1931); Donald Worster, *Rivers of Empire: Water, Aridity, and the Growth of the American West* (New York: Oxford University Press, 1992); and Patricia Nelson Limerick, *The Legacy of Conquest: The Unbroken Past of the American West* (New York: W.W. Norton and Company, Inc., 1987).

3. Exceptions include the US removal of the Chiricahua Apache to Florida, Alabama, Oklahoma, and the Mescalero Reservation in southeastern New Mexico, and the Indian removal practiced against the Yaqui by the regime of Mexican President Porfirio Díaz. See Bertha P. Dutton, *American Indians of the Southwest* (Albuquerque: University of New Mexico Press, 1983), 111; John Kenneth Turner, *Barbarous Mexico* (Chicago: Charles H. Kerr & Company, 1911); Manuel Balbás, *Recuerdos del Yaqui: Principales episodios durante la campaña de 1899–1901* (Mexico, D.F.: Sociedad de Edición y Librería

Franco Americana, S.A., 1927); and Alfonso Fabila, *Las Tribus Yaqui de Sonora: Su cultura y anhelada autodeterminación* (México: Departamento de Asuntos Indigenas, 1940).

4. Patricia Limerick regarded "the persistence of natives" as a defining characteristic of the US West and noted "the presence of most of the nation's Indian reservations" there. See Limerick, *The Legacy of Conquest* 30, 179.

5. Many works deal with North American Western myths of individualism and boundless opportunity as well as a common North American Western resentment against perceived exploitation by national core regions. For Canada, see George F. G. Stanley, "The Western Canadian Mystique," in *Prairie Perspectives*, ed. David P. Gagan (Toronto: Holt, Rinehart and Winston, 1970); Richard Allen, ed., *A Region of the Mind* (Regina: University of Saskatchewan, Canadian Plains Study Centre, 1973); John W. Bennett and Seena B. Kohl, "Characterological, Strategic, and Institutional Interpretations of Prairie Settlement," in *Western Canada Past and Present*, ed. A. W. Rasporich (Calgary: McClelland and Stewart West, 1975); and J. F. Conway, *The West: The History of a Region in Confederation* (Toronto: James Lorimar & Co., 1983). For the United States, see Frederick Jackson Turner, *The Frontier in American History* (New York: Henry Holt and Company, 1920); Earl Pomeroy, "Toward a Reorientation of Western History: Continuity and Environment," *Mississippi Valley Historical Review* 41 (March 1955); R. Hofstadter & S. M. Lipset, eds., *Turner and the Sociology of the Frontier* (New York: Basic Books, 1968); and Limerick, *The Legacy of Conquest*. For Mexico, see Carl O. Sauer, "The Personality of Mexico," *Geographical Review* 31 (July 1941): 353–64; Miguel León-Portilla, "The Norteño Variety of Mexican Culture," in *Plural Society in the Southwest*, eds. Edward H. Spicer and Raymond H. Thompson (New York: Weatherhead Foundation, 1972); Barry Carr, "Las peculiaridades del Norte Mexicano," *Historia Mexicana* 22 (January–March 1973); and Edgard Mason, *México y sus mexicanos* (México: Ed. Posada, 1990).

6. See Culver, "Promoting the Pacific Borderlands: Leisure and Labor in Southern California, 1870–1950," in *Land of Necessity: Consumer Culture in the United States—Mexico Borderlands*, ed. Alexis McCrossen (Durham, N.C.: Duke University Press, 2009), 168; Turner, *The Frontier in American History*; and Limerick, *The Legacy of Conquest*, 20–21. Carlos A. Schwantes notes that although Oregon and Washington were depicted and imagined differently than British Columbia, both were understood as places where "enterprising and industrious" immigrants could make a living through their own labor. See Schwantes, *Radical Heritage: Labor, Socialism, and Reform in Washington and British Columbia, 1885–1917* (Caldwell, Idaho: Caxton Press, 1994), 8. In fact, the US West has long depended on massive and disproportionate investments and spending from the federal government, even as non-Indigenous settlers made claims of self-sufficiency and self-reliance. See, for example, Limerick, *The Legacy of Conquest*, 87–89. Environmental historian Donald Worster argues that WWII resulted in the dominance of the US military-industrial complex. See Worster, *Under Western Skies: Nature and History in the American West* (Oxford: Oxford University Press, 1992), 10–11. Northwestern Mexico was similarly portrayed as a region in need of subdual. The earliest non-Indigenous arrivals, including conquistadores and Jesuit missionaries, characterized the area as "inhospitable and barbarous." See María Luz Cruz-Torres, *Lives of Dust and Water: An Anthropology of Change and Resistance in Northwest Mexico* (Tucson: University of Arizona Press, 2004), 30. The nineteenth-century Mexican government provided lands and local political autonomy to colonists who agreed to pacify and defend the borderlands against local Indigenous people. See Júrgen Buchenau, *Plutarco Elías Calles and the Mexican Revolution* (Lanham, Md.: Rowman and Littlefield, 2007), 7–8; and Ana María Alonso, *Thread of Blood: Colonialism, Revolution, and Gender on Mexico's Northern Frontier* (Tucson: University of Arizona Press, 1995). Interestingly, the settlers of European descent along the US-Canada border often had more in common with each other than they did with the people who dominated their governments in Washington, D.C., and Ottawa; this largely resulted from the fact that many of the immigrants who settled in Canada were "from the United States." See Walter N. Sage, "Geographic and Cultural Aspects of the Five Canadas," *Report of the Annual Meeting* (Canadian Historical Association, 1937): 33, http://id.erudit.org/iderudit/290003ar; Bruno Ramírez and Yves Otis, *Crossing the 49th Parallel: Migration from Canada to the United States, 1900–1930* (Ithaca, N.Y.: Cornell University Press, 2001), ix; James Laxer, *The Border: Canada, the US and Dispatches From the 49th Parallel* (Mississauga, Ontario: Doubleday Canada, 2003); and Paul F. Sharp, *Whoop-Up Country: The Canadian-American West, 1865–1885* (Norman: University of Oklahoma Press, 1973 [1955]), 3–4. See also, Benjamin H. Johnson and

Andrew R. Graybill, eds., *Bridging National Borders in North America: Transnational and Comparative Histories* (Durham, N.C.: Duke University Press, 2010), 11; and Walter N. Sage, "Some Aspects of the Frontier in Canadian History," *Report of the Annual Meeting* (Canadian Historical Association, 1928): 62–72, http://id.erudit.org/iderudit/300064ar. Schwantes notes that in both Washington and British Columbia, the high number of European migrants who maintained their connections with northern and western Europe created unique cross-border similarities. See Schwantes, *Radical Heritage*, 13–14. William G. Robbins argues that although there are both geographic and cultural divides in the Pacific Northwest (and a great diversity of opinion about them), there are good grounds to argue for a distinct regional culture that spans the US-Canada border. See Robbins, "Introduction," in *Regionalism and the Pacific Northwest*, eds. William G. Robbins, Robert J. Frank, and Richard E. Ross (Corvallis: Oregon State University Press, 1983), 1–9. See also Robin W. Winks, "Regionalism in Comparative Perspective," in *Regionalism and the Pacific Northwest*, 13–36; and Judith Austin, "Desert, Sagebrush, and the Pacific Northwest," in *Regionalism and the Pacific Northwest*, 129–47.

7. Indigenous communities, peoples, and Nations have been defined by the United Nations as "those which, having a historical continuity with pre-invasion and pre-colonial societies that developed on their territories, considered themselves distinct from other sectors of the societies now prevailing in those territories, or parts of them. They form at present non-dominant sectors of society and are determined to preserve, develop and transmit to future generations their ancestral territories, and their ethnic identity, as the basis of their continued existence as peoples, in accordance with their own cultural patterns, social institutions and legal systems." From *Study of the Problem of Discrimination against Indigenous Populations*, UN Doc. E/Cn.4/Sub.2/1986/ 7Add.4, para.379 (1986), quoted in *Indigenous Peoples and Democracy in Latin America*, ed. Donna Lee Van Cott (New York: St. Martin's Press, 1995), 23–24, n.3. See also UN Secretariat of the Permanent Forum on Indigenous Issues, "The Concept of Indigenous Peoples," (Background Paper to Workshop on Data Collection and Disaggregation for Indigenous Peoples, New York, US, 19–21 January 2004) UN Doc PFII/2004/WS.1/3, http://www.un.org/esa/socdev/unpfii/documents/workshop_data_background.doc.

8. Johnson and Graybill, *Bridging National Borders*, 8.

9. The idea of the noble savage arose as early as the late fifteenth century, when Christopher Columbus told the Spanish Crown that Indigenous people were "marvelously timorous" and would therefore be easy to enslave and in the early sixteenth century when Bartolomé de las Casas's *Apologética Historia Sumaria* defended Indigenous people as living in a "terrestrial paradise." See Columbus's Letter to King Ferdinand of Spain, describing the results of the first voyage, http://xroads.virginia.edu/~hyper/hns/garden/columbus.html. We quote de las Casas from Charles C. Mann, *1491: New Revelations of the Americas before Columbus* (New York: Alfred A. Knopf, 2005), 13. One reason that this myth was perpetrated was to advance a Lockean argument that enhanced European claims to land. See Allan Greer, "Commons and Enclosures in the Colonization of North America," *American Historical Review* 117 (April 2012): 365–86. Indigenous people have also advanced this claim for their own political purposes, especially as a response to the depredations committed by early anthropologists. See Paul Jentz, "From the Pristine Myth to the Pleistocene Overkill to the 'Quantitative Global Analysis of the Role of Climate and People in Explaining late Quaternary Megafaunal Extinctions,'" paper presented at the Third Annual Midwest World History Association Conference, Grand Rapids, MI, August 5, 2012. One of the main purveyors of the Pristine Myth is Vine Deloria Jr.; see "Anthros, Indians, and Planetary Reality" in T. Biolosi and L. Zimmerman, *Indians and Anthropologists: Vine Deloria, Jr., and the Critique of Anthropology* (Tucson: University of Arizona Press, 1997); *God is Red* (New York: Grosset and Dunlap, 1973); and *Red Earth, White Lies, Vol. 1: Native Americans and the Myth of Scientific Fact* (Golden, Colo.: Fulcrum Publishing, 1997). Another such is Russell Means; see *Where White Men Fear to Tread: The Autobiography of Russell Means* (New York: St. Martin's Press, 1995). This is not meant to deny the fact that many Indigenous groups did exploit "the landscape in a way that maintained species population and diversity" or that "dietary security, not the maximization of crop yields, was the most important element of Native American subsistence." See Ted Steinberg, *Down to Earth: Nature's Role in American History* (New York: Oxford University Press, 2002), 16–17. Daniel Murphree has examined the "othering" of Indigenous people that resulted in their being viewed as backward and doomed to extinction. See "Race and Religions on the Periphery: Disappointment and Missionization in the Spanish Floridas, 1566–1763," in *Race, Nation and Religion in the Americas*, eds. Henry Goldschmidt and Eliza-

beth McAlister (Oxford: Oxford University Press, 2004), 35–59. See also Gary Nash, "The Image of the Indian in the Southern Colonial Mind," *William and Mary Quarterly* 29 (April 1972): 197–230; and J. M. Blaut, *The Colonizers Model of the World: Geographical Diffusionism and Eurocentric History* (New York: The Guilford Press, 1993), 11–30. Many borderlands anthropologists, both amateur and professional, adopted this vision of Indigenous people. For examples dealing with just the Seri Indians, see Edward H. Davis, "Secrets of the Desert," in *Edward H. Davis and the Indians of the Southwest United States and Northwest Mexico: A harvest of photographs, sketches and unpublished manuscripts of the indefatigable collector of artifacts of these border Indians*, eds. Charles Russell Quinn and Elena Quinn (Downey, Calif.: Elena Quinn, 1964), 61; Roberto Thomson as told to H. H. Dunn, "Sons of the Stone Age: The Seri—Modern Mexico's Most Savage Indians," *Travel* 56 (April 1931); Dane and Mary R. Coolidge, *The Last of the Seris: The Aboriginal Indians of Kino Bay, Sonora, Mexico* (Glorieta, N.M.: The Rio Grande Press, Inc., 1979 [1939]); W. J. McGee, *The Seri Indians, Extract from the Seventeenth Annual Report of the Bureau of American Ethnology* (Washington, D.C.: Government Printing Offices, 1898); and Charles Sheldon, *The Wilderness of the Southwest: Charles Sheldon's Quest for Desert Bighorn Sheep and Adventures with the Havasupai and Seri Indians* (Salt Lake City: University of Utah Press, 1993). Finally, mission Indians in Spanish California were often depicted as easily malleable, whitewashing the physical and sexual coercion often required to subdue them and stripping them of their agency. See Carey McWilliams, *Southern California: An Island on the Land* (Salt Lake City: Peregrine Books, 1943); William Deverell, *Whitewashed Adobe: The Rise of Los Angeles and the Remaking of Its Mexican Past* (Berkeley: University of California Press, 2004); and Phoebe Kropp, *California Vieja: Culture and Memory in a Modern American Place* (Berkeley: University of California, 2006).

10. As Amy S. Greenberg notes, John Russell Bartlett, the American commissioner of the US-Mexico Boundary Commission, and his replacement, William H. Emory, who, in conjunction with Mexican general Pedro García Conde, was tasked with establishing the US-Mexico border after the Mexican-American War of 1846 to 1848, found the borderlands region to be barren and lacking the attributes "that would enable a 'civilized' domestic life." See Greenberg, "Domesticating the Border: Manifest Destiny and the 'Comforts of Life' in the US-Mexico Boundary Commission and Gadsden Purchase, 1848–1854," in *Land of Necessity: Consumer Culture in the United States-Mexico Borderlands*, ed. Alexis McCrossen (Durham, N.C.: Duke University Press, 2009), 89. Perhaps not surprising either, the Tohono O'odham, whose lands the new border bisected, took no notice of the Boundary Commission or the new official border; see David Rich Lewis, *Neither Wolf Nor Dog: American Indians, Environment, and Agrarian Change* (Oxford: Oxford University Press, 1994), 135; and Bernard Fontana, "History of the Papago," in William C. Sturtevant (gen. ed.) and Alfonso Ortiz (vol. editor), *Handbook of North American Indians*, vol. 10 (Washington, D.C.: Smithsonian Institution, 1983), 140.

11. Alan C. Taylor, *The Divided Ground: Indians, Settlers, and the Northern Borderland of the American Revolution* (New York: Vintage Books, 2006), 7. This need to "define and control" does not end when empires and nation-states are no longer young. Reece Jones notes that the post–Cold War creation of border walls falls most heavily along areas with high levels of economic inequality and cultural difference, not as a result of legitimate national security risks. See Jones, "Why Build a Border Wall?" *NACLA Report on the Americas* 45 (Fall 2012): 70–72.

12. Andrae Marak and Laura Tuennerman, *At the Border of Empires: The Tohono O'odham, Gender and Assimilation, 1880–1934* (Tucson: University of Arizona Press, 2013), 2, 145.

13. Benjamin H. Johnson and Andrew R. Graybill, "Borders and Their Historians in North America," in *Bridging National Borders in North America: Transnational and Comparative Histories*, eds. B. H. Johnson and A. R. Graybill (Durham, N.C.: Duke University Press, 2010), 23. See also, Elaine Carey and Andrae Marak, "Introduction," in *Smugglers, Brothels, and Twine: Historical Perspectives on Contraband and Vice in North America's Borderlands*, eds. E. Carey and A. Marak (Tucson: University of Arizona Press, 2011), 4–5.

14. For examples of non-Indigenous people undermining the intent of faraway national policy makers by capitalizing on the border, see Rachel St. John, "Divided Ranges: Trans-border Ranches and the Creation of National Space along the Western Mexico-U.S. Border," in *Bridging National Borders in North America*, eds. B. H. Johnson and A. R. Graybill, 116–40; and S. Deborah Kang, "Crossing the Line: The INS and the Federal Regulation of the Mexican Border," in *Bridging National Borders in North America*, eds. B. H. Johnson and A. R. Graybill, 167–98.

15. Guadalupe Castillo and Margo Cowan, *It Is Not Our Fault: The Case for Amending Current Nationality Law to Make All Members of the Tohono O'odham Nation United States Citizens, Now and Forever* (Sells, Ariz.: Tohono O'odham, Executive Branch, 2001). On the transition of borderlands to borders, see Jeremy Adelman and Stephen Aron, "From Borderlands to Borders: Empires, Nation-States, and the Peoples in Between in North American History," *American Historical Review* 104 (June 1999): 814–41.

16. Geraldo L. Cadava, "Borderlands of Modernity and Abandonment: The Lines within Ambos Nogales and the Tohono O'odham Nation," *The Journal of American History* 98 (September 2011): 383.

17. John Dougherty, "One Nation, Under Fire," *High Country News*, February 19, 2007, http://www.hcn.org/issues/340/16834.

18. Marak and Tuennerman, *At the Border of Empires*, 139–41; and Andrae Marak, *From Many, One: Indians, Peasants, Borders, and Education in Callista Mexico, 1924–1935* (Calgary: University of Calgary Press, 2009), 105–32. David G. McCrady notes that the Sioux used the same approach in figuring out whether the United States or Canada would grant them access to better lands. See McCrady, *Living with Strangers: The Nineteenth-Century Sioux and the Canada-American Borderlands* (Lincoln: University of Nebraska Press, 2006), 3. This practice of playing two or more colonizing empires off against each other is reminiscent of the ideas purported by Richard White, *The Middle Ground: Indians, Empires, and Republics in the Great Lakes Region, 1650–1815* (Cambridge: Cambridge University Press, 1991).

19. Brenden Rensink, "The Transnational Immigrant-Refugee Experience of Mexican Yaquis and Canadian Chippewa-Crees in Arizona and Montana," *Journal of the West: American Indians and the Borderlands of the West*, eds. Andrae Marak and Laura Tuennerman, 48 (Summer 2009): 12–13; and McCrady, *Living with Strangers*, 3.

20. McCrady, *Living with Strangers*, 3–4; William Kates, "Mohawks, Feds Have Different View of Smuggling Case," *Associated Press*, November 6, 1998; Estanislao Oziewicz, "Border Pipeline," *Globe and Mail*, December 11, 1998, A7; and Hogue, "Between Race and Nation," 61–66.

21. Brenden Rensink, "Cree Contraband or Contraband Crees? Early Montanan Experiences with Transnational Natives and the Formation of Lasting Prejudice, 1880–1885," in *Smugglers, Brothels, and Twine: Historical Perspectives on Contraband and Vice in North America's Borderlands*, eds. Elaine Carey and Andrae Marak (Tucson: University of Arizona Press, 2011), 24–43.

22. Johnson and Graybill, *Bridging National Borders in North America*, 2.

23. Carey and Marak, *Smugglers, Brothels, and Twine*, 2; and Truett and Young, "Making Transnational History: Nations, Regions, and Borderlands," in *Continental Crossroads: Remapping US-Mexico Borderlands History*, eds. Truett and Young (Durham, N.C.: Duke University Press, 2004), 8.

24. Pekka Hämäläinen and Samuel Truett, "On Borders," *The Journal of American History* 98 (September 2011): 352.

25. Ibid., 359.

26. St. John, *Line in the Sand*, 5.

27. Tyler Stoval, "Civil Rights Meets Decolonization: Transnational Visions of the Struggle for Racial Equality in France and America," *World History Bulletin* 26 (Spring 2010): 27.

28. Quote from Manzano-Munguía. For examples, see Pekka Hämäläinen, *The Comanche Empire* (New Haven, Conn.: Yale University Press, 2008); Andrés Reséndez, *Changing National Identities at the Frontier: Texas and New Mexico, 1800–1850* (Cambridge: Cambridge University Press, 2005), 197–236; Jeffrey P. Sheperd, *We Are An Indian Nation: A History of the Hualapai People* (Tucson: University of Arizona Press, 2010); Brian DeLay, "Independent Indians and the U.S.-Mexican War," *American Historical Review* 112 (February 2007): 35–68; and David J. Weber, *Bárbaros: Spaniards and Their Savages in the Age of Enlightenment* (New Haven, Conn.: Yale University Press, 2006).

29. For example, parts of the ancestral lands of the Tohono O'odham were set aside for the Organ Pipe National Monument and as a firing range to train US military personnel.

30. Spanish officials interpreted laws on Indian lands differently in different jurisdictions. In territory subject to the Audiencia of Mexico, Indian lands included a town site (*fundo legal*), farmland divided among community members (*tierras de repartimiento*), communal pasture and forest (*ejido*), and lands that could be rented to outsiders (*propios*); in practice, ejido lands could be farmed, grazed, or distributed among community members. In territory subject to the Audiencia of Guadalajara, the term *fundo legal* was used for all community lands, and the term *ejido* was not used, and towns were

to receive a site one league long. Near Guadalajara and in Sonora, this was interpreted as one square league with the town in the center, but in New Mexico, communities got four square leagues centered on the town's church or cemetery cross. See Michael T. Ducey, "Liberal Theory and Peasant Practice: Land and Power in Northern Veracruz, Mexico, 1826–1900, in *Liberals, the Church, and Indian Peasants: Corporate Lands and the Challenge of Reform in Nineteenth-Century Spanish America*, ed. Robert H. Jackson (Albuquerque: University of New Mexico Press, 1997), 70; Cynthia Radding, *Wandering Peoples* (Durham, N.C.: Duke University Press, 1997), 358–59; and William B. Taylor, "Cochití Lands and the Disputed Sale to Luis María Cabeza de Baca, 1805," in *Pueblo de Cochiti Lands Bill: Hearing Before the Select Committee on Indian Affairs, United States Senate*, 98th Cong. (1984), 44–45.There were about 4000 *pueblos de indios* in the viceroyalty of New Spain. During the Bourbon Reforms, Crown officials tried to control the finances and land use of Indigenous villages. See Dorothy Tanck de Estrada, *Pueblos de indios y educación en el México colonial, 1750–1821* (Mexico City: Centro de Estudios Históricos, El Colegio de México, 1999).

31. Alaska Natives were, for the most part, treated differently than their counterparts in the United States and Canada, as the vast majority of them were not placed on reservations. The US government created one reservation in 1891 and a series of reserves that did not have the same status as reservations in 1936. Regardless, the United States still adopted policies that served the same ends as reservations. Upon acquiring Alaska from Russia in 1867, the United States granted "to them (Indigenous people) title to a portion of the lands which they occupied, to extinguish the aboriginal title to the remainder of the lands by placing such lands in the public domain, and to pay the fair value of the titles extinguished." Even then, the policy of paying Indigenous people for "unused" lands was often dishonored in the breach. See *Do Alaska Native People Get Free Medical Care? And other frequently asked questions about Alaska Native issues and cultures* (Anchorage, Ala.: University of Alaska Anchorage and Alaska Pacific University, 2008), 21, 59. Historian Carroll Smith-Rosenberg argues that the United States constructed its own self-image through a sustained program of violence against "Others." This included "a commitment to rapid western expansion, racial separation and removal, and, when it seemed necessary, the extirpation of Native American peoples." See Smith-Rosenberg, *The Violent Empire: The Birth of an American National Identity* (Chapel Hill: The University of North Carolina Press, 2010), 239. Noted ethnohistorian Edward H. Spicer notes that reservations themselves grew out of the practice of Indian isolation and were meant to maintain sufficient "peace for Anglo expansion." See Spicer, *Cycles of Conquest: The Impact of Spain, Mexico, and the United States on the Indians of the Southwest, 1533–1960* (Tucson: University of Arizona Press, 1997 [1962]), 345. Sharp notes that both the United States and Canada deployed resources to control illegal transnational contraband and Indigenous peoples as a means of making the US-Canada border region ripe for settlement by European descendent homesteaders. See Sharp, *Whoop-Up Country*, 78–106, 122–32.

32. David A. Chang, "Borderlands in a World at Sea: Concow Indians, Native Hawaiians, and South Chinese in Indigenous, Global, and National Spaces," *The Journal of American History* 98 (September 2011): 390.

33. Florencia Mallon, "Indigenous Peoples and Nation-States in Spanish America, 1780–2000," in *The Oxford Handbook of Latin American History*, ed. Jose C. Moya (Oxford: Oxford University Press, 2011), 282, 289.

34. St. John, *Line in the Sand*, 8.

35. Mario García, *Desert Immigrants: The Mexicans of El Paso, 1880–1920* (New Haven, Conn.: Yale University Press, 1981), 34; John H. Coatsworth, "Measuring Influence: The United States and Mexican Peasantry," in *Rural Revolt in Mexico: US Intervention and the Domain of Subaltern Politics*, ed. Daniel Nugent (Durham, N.C.: Duke University Press, 1998), 68; Emilio Kourí, "Interpreting the Expropriation of Indian Pueblo Lands in Porfirian Mexico: The Unexamined Legacies of Andrés Molina Enríquez," *Hispanic American Historical Review* 82, (February 2002): 69–117; and Robert H. Holden, *Mexico and the Survey of Public Lands: The Management of Modernization, 1876–1911* (DeKalb: Northern Illinois University Press, 1994).

36. Lewis, *Neither Wolf Nor Dog*, 16.

37. Frederick Hoxie, *A Final Promise: The Campaign to Assimilate the Indians, 1880–1920* (Lincoln: University of Nebraska Press, 2001), 74–78. Following Jacob Torfing, we would argue that cultural hegemony is complete when the dominant "discourse of norms, values, views, and perceptions" has

been adopted by oppressed people, a process that has never been completely achieved. See Torfing, *New Theories of Discourse: Laclau, Mouffe, and Zizek* (London: Blackwell, 1999), 302; and Gary Gerstle, "A State Both Strong and Weak," *American Historical Review* 115 (June 2010): 779–85. Nonetheless, the state has been able, through both public and private actors, to deeply penetrate people's daily lives. See William J. Novak, "The Myth of the 'Weak' American State," *American Historical Review* 113 (June 2008): 752–72. One means of preparing Indigenous people for "civilization" was the outing system, which generally placed Indigenous girls in white homes as servants, but in some locations also included the placement of Indigenous men and boys. In conjunction with the Dawes Act, outing was viewed as a means of stripping Indigenous people of their lands by preparing them for a different life. See Victoria K. Haskins, *Matrons and Maids: Regulating Indian Domestic Service in Tucson, 1914–1934* (Tucson: University of Arizona Press, 2012), 19–20.

38. Susan Sleeper-Smith, *Indian Women and French Men: Rethinking Cultural Encounters in the Western Great Lakes* (Amherst: University of Massachusetts Press, 2001), 96.

39. Hoxie, *A Final Promise*, 70–71; Stuart Banner, *How the Indians Lost Their Land: Law and Power on the Frontier* (Cambridge: Harvard University Press, 2005); Janet A. McDonnel, *The Dispossession of the American Indian, 1887–1934* (Bloomington: Indiana University Press, 1991); and Fergus M. Bordewich, *Killing the White Man's Indian: Reinventing Native Americans at the End of the Twentieth Century* (New York: Anchor Books, 1996), 121–25.

40. Michel Hogue, "Between Race and Nation: The Creation of a Métis Borderland on the Northern Plains," in *Bridging National Borders in North America: Transnational and Comparative Histories*, eds. Benjamin H. Johnson and Andrew R. Graybill (Durham, N.C.: Duke University Press, 2010), 63–66.

Chapter 1

The Indigenous Southwest as Mesoamerica's Northern Frontier

Mexico, Harmony, and the Quincunx*

W. Dirk Raat

Until recently, the academic discipline of the New Archaeology has largely thought of the people of the American Southwest in small-scale, regional, ahistorical, and cross-cultural processual terms.[1] Changes in contemporary historiography, especially the rise of a new world or global history (and world-system analyses), are now affecting archaeological (and anthropological) thinking, and the result is a historically oriented sociology and archaeology of the Indigenous Southwest that views regional groups in continental and even hemispheric terms. Thus the impact of Mesoamerica in general and western Mexico in particular on the American Southwest is becoming a common topic of current archaeological studies.

The concern of this essay will be first to summarize briefly these historiographical trends, then argue generally for the Mesoamerican (and western Mexican) connection, and finally illustrate the same by an example taken from the history of ideas, that is, a pattern known as a *quincunx* with four points or objects at each corner of a square or rectangle and a fifth one in the middle.

The quincunx, a constant and recurring theme in the history of Mesoamerica and the Greater Southwest (northern Mexico and the American Southwest), is a design derived from the ideas of cardinality and harmony. It is expressed in quincuncial form as a five-part arrangement. For cardinality this means a circular movement through four directions to reach a fifth point that completes the rotation. When the movement around a point of axis is finished, the process has completed a harmonious whole. These ideas

* An abbreviated version of this article appeared in the electronic journal *History Compass*. See W. Dirk Raat, "World History, MesoAmerica, and the Native American Southwest," in *History Compass* 10/7 (2012), 10.1111/j.1478–0542.2012.00857.x.

of cardinality, harmony, and the quincunx will be explored and developed in a later context, after a historiographical introduction and a survey of the Mesoamerican connection.

The New Archaeology Rediscovers History

After World War II, historians started to move world history away from the traditional concerns of an Oswald Spengler or Arnold Toynbee, who sought to write universal histories, establish grand designs, and postulate underlying laws, toward a new global history that would be thematically focused on recurring processes like migration (including ecological imperialism or migration as a biological phenomenon), colonization, warfare, and religious expansion; or on cross-cultural patterns like the spread of disease and epidemics, trading networks, urbanism, food and culinary practices, gender or technology.

Of all works, Fernand Braudel's magnum opus, *Civilization and Capitalism, 15th–18th Century*, was a major departure in historical writing and marked the beginnings of the new world history. Braudel's disciple, the sociologist Immanuel Wallerstein, argued that regions peripheral to the European core were linked together in a world-economy that shifted resources and wealth from the poorer nations to northwestern Europe from the sixteenth century onward. Wallerstein's three-volume study was collectively known as *The Modern World System.*[2]

Janet L. Abu-Lughod looked at long-distance trade in the late medieval period in her work entitled *Before European Hegemony: The World System A.D. 1250–1350.*[3] Needless to say, with the possible exception of Frank's later works, these studies were highly Eurocentric.[4]

Historians soon began to expand the European center. Marshall G. S. Hodgson put the world of Islam in a global context in *The Venture of Islam*, and Ross E. Dunn in *The Adventures of Ibn Battuta: A Muslim Traveler of the 14th Century* showed that world history was not simply a European matter, but an Afro-Eurasian affair.[5] Yet the main thrust of global history historiography was Old World—Europe, Asia, and Africa. Until recently, the Americas, including the American Southwest, did not have its own global historian.[6]

The scholar who did the most to make the transition from the Old World to the New World and abrogate the boundaries between Western and non-Western history was anthropologist Eric R. Wolf in *Europe and the People Without History*. Wolf studied the expansion of Mesoamerica into the American Southwest and the Mississippian world; the Iberians in America, particularly the attempts at extracting wealth from Peruvians and Mexica Indians; as well as the fur trade in North America.[7]

The "others" of the non-Western world finally had their perspectives vocalized, and these new voices would continue to be heard by a new generation of sociologists, anthropologists, and archaeologists studying the people of the Greater Southwest. These scholars include the sociologist Thomas D. Hall, the anthropologist Carroll L. Riley, and the archaeologist Stephen H. Lekson.

In Hall's narrative, nonstates were as worthy of note as states, peripheries as important as cores, and Indians as significant as Hispanics and Anglo-Americans.[8]

Riley too expanded the chronology in *Becoming Aztlan: Mesoamerican Influence in the Greater Southwest, AD 1200–1500*, and *The Frontier People: The Greater Southwest in the Protohistoric Period.* Riley argued against the "processualism" of the New Archaeology and for historical methodologies, the ideas of diffusion and migration, and the Mesoamerican influences on the socioreligious life of ancient and modern Southwesterners.[9]

The "anti-process" process reached its height with the publication of *A History of the Ancient Southwest* by Stephen H. Lekson in 2008. For Lekson, the Anasazi (ancient Colorado Plateau peoples), Hohokam (located in the Phoenix basin and southern Arizona), and Mogollon (east central Arizona and west central New Mexico) were not "atomistic isolates," but societies interconnected with each other and the larger North American world. His intent is to frame southwestern events in the political context of the Mississippi Valley and Mesoamerica. Shifting away from the micro scales of humanistic history and the scientism of the New Archaeology, but building on the hard work of these pioneer disciplines, Lekson has moved New Archaeology toward the new world history with his narrative of the ancient Southwest.[10]

Migration, Mexico, and the Mesoamerican Connection

Archaeologists and anthropologists are revising their views every day concerning the amount and types of cultural diffusion and/or migration that took place between central Mexico and the Greater Southwest in prehistoric times. Because much of the evidence is cursory, the same artifacts may support opposing theories of "external influence" versus "localism," and similarities in shards, for example, between Mesa Verde and Paquimé, may be used to support migration or trade (or both) as the form of contact. In looking for cultural contacts between ancient Mexico and the prehistoric Southwest, linguistic trails, migration patterns, transportation routes, trade (commercial exchanges), tribute, architecture, dietary habits, and religious themes should be studied.

For example, archaeologist David Wilcox has discovered a Mexican-Hohokam trade route that he has named the Tepiman Connection, a series of geographical sites joined by related Uto-Aztecan languages. This connection may have eased the flow of ideas as well as commerce between the Hohokam and cultures from Mexico. From West Mexico came maize, canal and irrigation technology, clay figurines and cremation burial rituals, ball courts, Mesoamerican motifs on shell arm bracelets, parrot effigy pottery, architectural forms and layouts (especially household plans, patio groups, and courtyard groups), pyrite mirrors, and copper bells—all imported by Hohokam or Mesoamerican traders. The Hohokam Canon, comprised of ideas, beliefs, and practices from West Mexico, came north from the Pacific Coast and the Gulf of California, through the Hohokam entrepôt at Gila Bend, as well as along the San Pedro/Sonora River systems and the Santa Cruz/Altar/Magdelena/Concepción River network. Hohokam priests very easily could have apprenticed themselves to religious organizations in Mexico, and upon completion of their training brought back artifacts and ideas, including ball courts (of which there were over two hundred between 750 A.D. and 1200 A.D.) and their meaning, as symbols of their new status.[11]

Maize probably arrived from Mexico in the Southwest around 1500 B.C. with the migration of Uto-Aztecan peoples who propagated the seeds. Their water management skills permitted the spread of cultivation throughout the Southwest, first in the low desert country of the Hohokam, and later on the northern Plateau from 500 B.C. to A.D. 500. The Hohokam canal system eventually became the largest and most complex in North America. Because the Hohokam developed an expertise in hydrology and water management, it is likely that some of their advanced ideas returned to Mexico. It is now known that Palenque excelled in water pressure technology by 750 A.D., as did many other central Mexican sites. Thus, the Greater Southwest was not simply a passive receptor of Mexican ideas and commodities, but an active one that sent concepts, including ideas about sophisticated hydraulic engineering techniques, as well as precious stones, medicinal herbs, pine nuts, acorns, bison skins, slaves, and commercial goods, to Mexico.[12]

These Uto-Aztecan-speaking groups connected the western deserts and West Mexico. By 1000 B.C., desert villages consisted of small pit houses around a common plaza. In 400 A.D., there were perhaps as many as a hundred of these farming villages established near small streams where the inhabitants were irrigating their crops with water from simple ditches. Three centuries later the Hohokam had established the largest irrigation system in the Americas, with large towns situated next to massive canals.[13]

The model for much of this urban development came from the largest city in Mesoamerica, Teotihuacán, a city known to the peoples of the Southwest. There were also other smaller cities that could inspire urbanism, including Teuchitlán in western Mesoamerica—a kind of Uto-Aztecan homeland. The emerging leaders of the Hohokam found their inspiration from their Mexican counterparts and very quickly developed private residences, known as Big Houses, near central plazas, which distinguished them from others with less wealth and power. Like Teotihuacán, but on a smaller scale, from the Big Houses came the bureaucratic managers (perhaps priests and politicians) who manned the councils and committees that ran a hydraulic society. Between 750 A.D. and 1150 A.D., ball courts were established on earthen-mound plazas, displacing but not replacing the Big Houses.[14]

The rapid spread of ball courts and burial rituals followed creeks and rivers upstream into the Western Plateau and into the Mimbres region south of the Mogollon Rim. After 1150, the Hohokam fell apart as Plateau populations moved into the deserts and the upper Gila and Salt Rivers. While Plateau people were moving south into the Mogollon uplands, the Mogollon populations, including the Mimbres, were spilling out into the New Mexican and Chihuahua Deserts. With the huge floods that hit the Salt River between 1357 and 1384, and the great flood of the Gila River in 1420, the Hohokam heartlands were abandoned.[15]

As for the eastern Plateau peoples, the Anasazi (or Ancestral Pueblos), the evidence is overwhelming that migration, flux, and movement of peoples from various directions was the rule rather than the exception. The era of Chaco florescence is usually placed between A.D. 900 and 1150 (Pueblo II), with Chaco reaching its peak in the eleventh century A.D. as the hub of a massive, pan-Southwest pilgrimage. At this time it was composed of Great Houses, Great Kivas, and black-on-white pottery. It attracted travelers from miles away, who very likely followed huge causeways that had ceremonial sites on them leading all the way to Chaco Canyon. Chaco may have had several functions at this time, from economic center and military headquarters to political hub and religious capital. Or these various functions may have changed from generation to generation. In any case, the Chaco area was a major urban core that rivaled many of the cities of Mesoamerica at that time, so much so that some scholars have suggested that Mesoamerican migrants traveled thousands of miles to establish this "Teotihuacán of the high desert."[16]

Chaco started to decline in the early part of the twelfth century A.D. A change in the climate, especially drought, and social conflict were probably the main culprits. But contrary to common belief, Chaco did not collapse. It continued on, with private and family residences replacing the large ceremonial palaces of the past. Many of those who moved followed causeways that radiated out from the Chaco Great Houses and Great Kivas to buttes and landmarks in several directions. Most moved along the ceremonial path called the Great North Road that went for 50 miles and connected Pueblo Alto in Chaco to the San Juan River in the north. There the Animas River flows into the San Juan, and it was along this tributary that individuals built the city of Aztec a hundred years after the peak of Chaco. In what appears to have been a conscious effort at continuity, these founders developed a new locus of power that imitated the architecture and function of Chaco. It was as if Chaco picked up and moved 50 miles due north![17]

During the thirteenth century A.D., migration continued from Chaco and Aztec to southwestern Colorado, especially to Mesa Verde and Sleeping Ute Mountain. This was a time of large pueblos, towers, and cliff dwellings. Orange ware ceramics appeared in the Four Corners area and the Kayenta region of northeast Arizona. Then, around 1300 A.D., these sites were abandoned. There is evidence of wholesale murder and cannibalism at Sleeping Ute, with fire destroying much of the area. Similarly, the cliff dwellings at Mesa Verde and Kayenta were left behind. Mesa Verde produced no tree ring dates after 1280, and Kayenta was deserted by A.D. 1290. Both were affected adversely by changes in the climate: first the Great Drought, then falling water tables, and finally eroded lands.[18] Most of the movement was from north to south.

In the fourteenth century, a new technology of using coal instead of wood to fire pottery appeared. The new technology, involving higher temperatures and greater oxidization during firing, meant that the pottery created was of an egg-yolk hue. These yellow ceramics began to appear further south of Mesa Verde and Kayenta. People were moving from north to south. In effect, Antelope Mesa, near what would become the sixteenth century Hopi town of Awat'ovi, became the principal pueblo that attracted migrants like never before. It was probably no coincidence that the katsina religion was established at Antelope Mesa in the fourteenth century, a "pull" factor as important as the "push" factors of climate and drought. In any case, it was in these northeastern Arizona mesas that the two halves of Anasazi culture came together, with eastern Mesa Verde people joining their western cousins from Kayenta.[19]

As the fourteenth century progressed, new sites appeared even further south, first along the margin of ponderosa pines and deep canyons of the Mogollon Rim in east-central Arizona, then later at Bonita Creek in southeast Arizona. The Mogollon Highlands became the locus of a melting pot fusing outsiders and locals. Thirteen major cliff dwellings were built here. The exterior adobe walls appear to be more the result of Hohokam techniques from the low desert than that of Anasazi northerners. Yet the adjacent masonry was definitely Anasazi. Ceramic styles were a fusion of patterns from Mimbres further south and Kayenta to the north. Anasazi was being transformed into Salado, and Salado culture was expanding in all directions into the Colorado Plateau and Mexico.[20]

Further south at Bonita Creek in southeastern Arizona, a ceremonial cache containing religious objects has been uncovered. It was brought to Bonita Creek from Kayenta and is similar in content and style to caches excavated in southern Utah and northeast Arizona. A migratory path was being forged, going from north to south, from the Four Corners through southeastern Arizona, to the Sierra Madre of Mexico.[21]

The most significant archaeological site in northern Mexico is Paquimé. It lies adjacent to Casas Grandes, nestled in the eastern hills of the Mexican Sierra in northwestern Chihuahua. Here are the ruins of over two thousand rooms, several hundred of which were excavated by the American archaeologist Charles Di Peso.[22] From earlier beginnings, Paquimé became a crucial trading center in the thirteenth century that reached its height in the fifteenth century A.D. Full-scale warfare hit the city around 1450 A.D., with each house being sacked and the town being fully destroyed. Only 300 plus years earlier, it had been an important commercial center, breeding turkeys for communities in the southwest and exchanging turquoise from Chaco and Hohokam shells and Anasazi puma skins for copper bells and macaws from the Toltec *pochteca*, or merchant traders, of Tula in Hidalgo. As for migrants at Paquimé, some dare assert a relationship with Chaco and the American Southwest.

To assert that Paquimé and Chaco had anything to do with each other is to earn the wrath of several generations of American archaeologists. One of the deadly sins of Southwest archaeology is to suggest a connection between two communities separated in time by hundreds of years and in space by over 400 miles. One theory that will get you excluded from the coffee klatches at most southwestern universities is the so-called Chaco Meridian hypothesis (originated by archaeologist Steve Lekson), in which it is noted that a 400-mile line following the 108th meridian connects Chaco (and for that matter, Aztec) with Paquimé, and that that reality is not simply coincidental, but the result of a planned migration of individuals from Chaco who used the same navigational feats to chart a route to Paquimé that had produced the causeways around Chaco.[23]

In spite of the hysteria that the Meridian hypothesis produces in New Archaeologists, some aspects of the hypothesis are worth examining. First, contrary to what contemporary observers might think, distances did not matter to the ancient peoples of the Southwest. For example, the Spanish conquistadores explored and established an urban frontier throughout the hemisphere in less than a hundred years, and most of these explorations were accomplished with the aid of Indian guides. Southwesterners, like the Polynesians, traveled between societies over vast distances. People in the Hohokam area knew about the Anasazi, and vice versa, and both were influenced by events in Mesoamerica.[24]

Hopi clan histories recount origins deep in Mexico at the Red City of the South known as Palátkwapi. Some Hopi spokesmen associate the Red City with the ancient Maya city of Palenque in Chiapas, whereas others suggest that it was Paquimé near Casas Grandes. Navajo oral traditions speak of a divine gambler, named Nohoilpi, who first lived in Chaco Canyon before travelling to Mexico and from Mexico to the Southwest. The Navajo story of creation says that after "The People entered the Fifth World the Sun ascended to the zenith and then stopped," demanding a human life be sacrificed before the Sun would move again—a story with parallels to Mesoamerican human sacrificial rites. These oral traditions may have some historicity, and while they may suggest to some that Hopis and Navajos migrated to the Southwest from Mexico, a more conservative interpretation would be that these people knew about their Mexican neighbors and that Hopi and Navajo rites, ceremonies, and legends were constructed with this knowledge in mind.[25]

Again, whereas scholars in the 1980s had excavated around 400 miles of ancient roadways, by the 1990s the network had increased to over 1000 miles. These were mostly linear roads up to 30 feet wide and linking several trading networks and regional outliers of the Chaco people.[26] Coincidence or not, a straight line runs along the 108th meridian from Casas Grandes in the south to Chaco and Aztec in the north. Any group (or several generations of migrants) travelling along that line would notice the continental divide crossing it about five or six times, and would not find the hike too difficult.

In addition, the outer limits of the Chaco outlier may have been as much as 150 miles, with roads leading from present-day Blanding in southeastern Utah to the Chaco center, and from the Chuska Mountains in eastern Arizona to Chaco, or from Chaco to the southwest near Gallup and Peach Springs. Paquimé's outlier extended north to Redrock and Pueblo Viejo in the Mimbres region. Outliers represented trading networks and had regional connections with one another. These roads were transportation networks as well as paths for migrants and, as such, benefited the entire redistribution system by which trade items went back and forth to and from Mexico.[27]

Finally, with the political anarchy and social conflict that developed after 1050 A.D., the Chaco elite, divided by a philosophical schism between cardinal and solstitial groups, initially struggled with each other and the commoners who lived in pithouses lining the southern side of the Chaco Valley. By 1125 or later the cardinal faction headed south. Elites and commoners, as well as residents in the Big Houses in the outliers, pushed south, forcing whole villages out of the Mogollon uplands onto the lower desert, and desert peoples into Chihuahua. With the fall of Tula in 1150 A.D., Mesoamerican princes came north. It is not unlikely that Plateau peoples and ideas mixed with their Mesoamerican counterparts to create the greatest city ever built in the Southwest—Paquimé in the Casas Grandes Valley.[28]

However, in spite of the controversy surrounding the Meridian hypothesis, some similarities between Chaco, Aztec, Mesa Verde and Paquimé should be noted. First, the Great Kivas in Chaco and Aztec contained huge stone disks beneath their ceiling timbers. One can find similar disks in Paquimé. Around Chaco, Aztec, and Paquimé, there are T-shaped portals at every turn, as well as similarities in hilltop architecture. In both Chaco and Paquimé, one discovers bird feathers galore, along with fire signals and pre-Columbian roads. Similar images can be found in the designs on Paquimé pottery and floor stones at Mesa Verde. These are comparable to icons on cliff paintings in Hovenweep in Utah and inscriptions on rock art at Antelope Mesa in northern Arizona. Finally, similarities between Mesa Verde pottery and shards from Paquimé should be noted. These latter could be evidence of north–south migration or long-distance exchange, or both.

If the theory that migrants between 1050 and 1150 A.D. formed a continuous trail from the Four Corners to Casas Grandes is correct, then it would not take much evidence to suppose that the cultural road continued down the Sierra Madre to present-day Durango (ancient La Quemada, a Toltec outpost) and Hidalgo (site of ancient Tula). From Tula the Toltecs traded north, west, and south, carrying Quetzal bird feathers from Guatemala, rubber from the Gulf Coast, shell ornaments from southern Arizona, and turquoise from Chaco.[29]

Certainly, as indicated above, trade and tribute items, like migrants, went back and forth between northern Mexico and the American Southwest. Without commenting on the various models used by archaeologists to determine whether trade goods represent international commerce or simply are examples of a local prestige exchange network, several observations can be made. Today archaeologists are studying pottery interconnections between Paquimé and northern areas. The Paquimé–Mimbres–Tularosa–Zuni ceramic connections suggest several contacts between these areas. Mesa Verde shards have been found in Paquimé, indicating that trade went from the northern Anasazi region to northwestern Mexico. Also, Mesoamerican chocolate has been found in Mesa Verde. In addition, the black-on-white, tall cylindrical vessels excavated in Chaco Canyon have been found to have unique chemical traces only found in chocolate. Chocolate beans, which do not grow in the desert, must have been introduced from the south. The amount of goods unearthed at Chaco suggests a tributary society in which more goods came in than went out. Some of these items were of local origin, such as the turquoise used by Chaco elites imitating their Mesoamerican cousins. Other articles were of foreign origin, such as copper bells forged either in Mexico or Ecuador and the tropical bird feathers that may have come from Central America. Clay figurines and pottery designs at the Hohokam sites in southern Arizona testify to northern Mexican influences.[30]

The people of the Mogollon culture not only traded pottery with the Anasazi, but the differences between the Pueblo languages of Keresan (spoken by the Pueblos that live along an east–west axis from Cochiti near Santa Fe to Acoma in western New Mexico) and Tanoan (discourse used by most eastern pueblos that run on a north–south axis along the Rio Grande from Taos in the north to Isleta, south of Albuquerque) might have evolved from differences between Mogollon and Anasazi.[31]

Another Mesoamerican influence was the relationship between the Mexican water god, Tlaloc, and the Pueblo katsinas. Although they may have an earlier history (associated with the coming of maize), no katsina images have been found prior to 1325 A.D., when masked beings appeared on pottery in the Mogollon Rim area. By 1350, katsina likenesses appeared on rock art in the Rio Grande Valley, the Zuni country, and the middle Little Colorado River areas. Northern Mexico, especially the Casas Grandes area, was very likely the focal point for the development of the katsina style, a style that travelled either up the San Pedro River Valley or up the Rio Grande through the Mimbres and Salado areas. As archaeologist E. Charles Adams has declared, "As to the origin of the <katsina> cult . . . Most recent archaeological evidence has authorities in agreement that the source is Mexican."[32]

The katsina phenomenon was a religion centered on hundreds of supernatural intercessors, or katsinam, who dwelled in the sacred mountains and negotiated with the gods to bring crops, health, and water. These spiritual intermediaries, sometimes associated with departed ancestors, interacted with humankind during a ceremonial calendar that began with the winter solstice and ended after the summer solstice. As suggested earlier, the katsina religion was very likely a "pull" factor that attracted people from Utah and the Colorado plateau to the mesas of northeast Arizona. It provided a religious rationale and a unifying force for some migratory people facing the chaos and uncertainty of an unfriendly climate and the hazards of hostile peoples and geography.[33]

Katsina motifs are found in rock art, on pottery, and as paintings in Kuaua and Pottery Mound murals (both Kuaua and Pottery Mound are located in the Upper Rio Grande Valley). In modern Zuni and Hopi villages, wall murals are found on kiva and non-kiva walls, as well as wooden dolls carved from cottonwood roots. Today the religion is very strong in the western pueblos like Hopi, Zuni, Acoma, and Laguna, and likely does not exist at all in the Tiwa-speaking groups of the Rio Grande (or at least the religion is well hidden from western views). Katsinam are very similar to Mesoamerican Tlaloques, that is, the children of Tlaloc. Like the Pueblo katsinam of the Southwest, they too dwell in the clouds atop isolated mountains and bring rain and thunder to the people. Tlaloc iconography, abundant in Mesoamerica, is also found in the rock art and pottery decoration of the Southwest, especially among the Mogollon peoples.[34]

Before exploring the Mesoamerican quincunx, some final examples of the Mesoamerican connection must be mentioned. The Mexican origins of many contemporary southwestern Indian traits can be recognized, including the *cacique* structure of Pueblo political organization; the cooperative agriculture of modern economic systems; and the technologies of cotton weaving and jewelry production, including the use of semiprecious stones, shell, coral, jet, and obsidian. But the most dominant heritage is religious syncretism, a characteristic of Náhuatl speakers in central Mexico, the Sierra Madre groups (such as Huichol, Cora, Tepehuan, Tarahumara, Mayo, and Yaqui), the plateau Pueblos, and the Papago, or O'odham, people of southwestern Arizona.[35]

Central to Papago religious thinking is the idea of the Water Serpent, or *corúa*. The *corúa* is a large snake that lives in springs and protects the local people. If you kill it, the spring will dry up, and the locals will lose their spiritual protector. *Corúa* means "boa constrictor" in the O'odham language and is derived from the Yaqui word meaning a "large, thick snake." The root *co* means "snake" in many Uto-Aztecan languages, and the same root appears in the Aztec word *quetzalcóatl*, the feathered serpent deity associated with wind and water. This Water Serpent lore of nineteenth- and twentieth-century Sonora and southern Arizona is widespread throughout Mesoamerica.[36]

Native Christianity in O'odham culture is known as "God Way" or "Saint Way" (*santo himdag*), or Sonoran Catholicism to non-O'odham writers. The spirit of *santo himdag* is reflected in the religious architecture of the Tohono O'odham Nation, and the best way to experience "Saint Way" is by visiting an O'odham chapel. Built without the approval or assistance of the Franciscans, the Papago Chapel is designed to meet the local spiritual needs of the people who live in relatively isolated, small villages. Franciscan mission churches and chapels have large areas where priests and religious specialists administer sacraments, and the congregation prays and participates in religious ceremonies. The O'odham Chapel, on the other hand, is a small building, always facing east, designed to store sacred and holy objects. It is part of a larger complex that lies outside adjacent to the chapel, where one can find a dance floor, an enclosure for musicians, and a feast house and cooking area under a ramada where people can cook and eat. The holy objects and images inside the chapel protect the health of the community, and outside, the community is involved in ritual processions, dancing, music making, and feasting.[37]

To many scholars this type of architecture suggests a non-Western, Mesoamerican origin. For example, folklorist James S. Griffith notes that "it sounds highly reminiscent of the temple structures [Aztec temples] of pre-Columbian Mesoamerica . . . Outside the structures . . . priests and populace danced, sang, marched in processions, feasted, and performed public rites, which in the case of the Aztecs, included human sacrifice." And ethnologist and field historian Bernard Fontana speculates "that the Papago notion of religious space . . . is a cultural survival reflecting the Papagos' Aztec roots."[38] And, along with religious architecture, a central tenet of Mesoamerican religious and intellectual thinking was the quincunx pattern.

The Mesoamerican Quincunx

In surveying the various surviving elements of Indigenous thought in Mesoamerica, the quincunx stands out as one of the more important aspects of the Mexica (Aztec) and Maya mind-set. In simplest terms, the quincunx is an arrangement of five objects in a square or rectangle, one at each corner and one in the middle. This was the design of the Mesoamerican calendar, and this pattern is found more than fifty times on the Aztec Calendar Stone. It was also a design found in nature. For example, in botanical terms the quincunx is an arrangement of five petals or leaves in which two are interior, two are exterior, and one is partly interior and partly exterior.

Laurette Séjourné, the deceased French archaeologist and ethnologist (d. 2003), argued that the quincunx was the stylized representation of a Mesoamerican pyramid, with the four corners at the base and the center at the apex. It was symbolic of the idea of four primordial elements redeemed by a unifying center. She called it the Law of the Center, in which the Fifth Sun, as the center point, prevented the splitting apart of opposing forces. To emphasize her point, she quoted the famed Mexican anthropologist and Aztec scholar Alfonso Caso, who, in his book *El Pueblo del Sol*, emphasized that the "fundamental idea of the four cardinal points and the central area

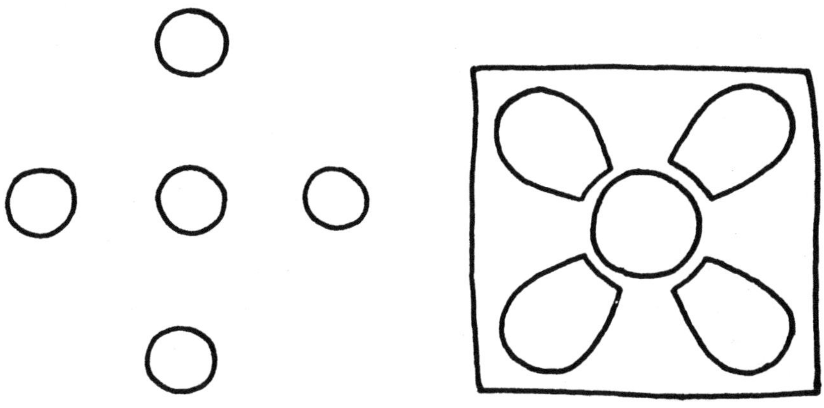

A. B.

(A) The five points in a cross or quincunx. (B) Five points enclosed in a square. In this form, the symbol occurs more than fifty times on the Aztec calendar.

which forms the fifth or central area is found in all the religious expressions of the Aztec people."[39]

Frances Karttunen, in discussing the survival of the traditional Mesoamerican view of the world, speaks of the quincunx in terms of cardinality. It is a counterclockwise "rotation through four <cardinal> points to reach a fifth state that completes the count or rotation." This rotation, according to Karttunen, is fundamental to Mesoamerican counting systems, calendars, rituals, and literary forms.[40]

Unlike the decimal pattern used in the West, in which numbers are based on units of ten, Mesoamerican counting was a vigesimal system based on units of twenty. These units of twenty were arranged into four groups of five, with each group consisting of one through four cardinal points followed by the fifth number. This vigesimal system of counting was used to calculate space/time in the Mesoamerican world, whether the sacred round of the 260-cycle year, the solar calendar of 365 years, or the calendar round that combines day names from both calendars to arrive at a 52-year cycle (a Maya century). This method of counting also included what scholars called the Long Count, an era-based calendar that started with the mythical beginning of the cosmos and, using multiples of twenty, was supposed to end on December 23, 2012, at which time the Long Count cycles were supposed to return to the symmetry of the beginning.[41]

The ritual calendar of 260 days consisted of twenty day names that were associated with the four cardinal points and were placed in five sets of four days each. The numbers one to thirteen were associated with the twenty day names (13 × 20 = a 260-day cycle). The solar year was made up of eighteen of these twenty-day periods, plus a nineteenth month of five days called *Uayeb*, for a total of a 365-day cycle (18 × 20 = 360 + 5 = 365 days). Although similar to the European calendar of the same era, like the sacred round, this calendar is a count of whole days running in a limitless progression without any adaptation to the fractional remainder of the actual solar year. The days and numbers themselves ordered time and space into an endless succession, reflecting both the natural cycles of the movements of the moon, the planets (especially Venus), and the constellations, as well as the symmetries intrinsic to the numbers themselves (e.g., the activity of counting in twenties). The succession of days measuring time and space fell into quadrants, each with a color and location.[42] This latter was true throughout the Americas.

The Nahua (i.e., speakers of Náhuatl) cosmological ideal involved a belief in the existence of four separate worlds that preceded the present era, the age of the Fifth Sun. In the Toltec version, the First Sun was called 4-Water and was destroyed by the gods with floods. As the myth states, "the water carried away everything. The people were changed into fish." Then the Second Sun was founded and its name was 4-Tiger. Then the sky was crushed, and when it became dark the people were eaten by the tigers, and the earth was destroyed by earthquakes. The Third Sun sign was 4-Rain-of-Fire, and the world was destroyed by fire. The Fourth Sun was 4-Wind. Its destruction came when winds destroyed the sun and the people were turned into monkeys. The present age is the Fifth Sun and 4-Movement is its sign. The world will be destroyed by earthquakes, and there will be hunger.

The last verse from the ancient Náhuatl manuscript known as *Anales de Cuauhtitlán* is worth quoting:[43]

> This Sun, its name 4-Movement,
> this is our Sun, in which we now live,
> and this is his sign,
> where the Sun fell in fire
> on the divine hearth,
> there in Teotihuacán.
> Also this was the Sun
> of our prince of Tula,
> of Quetzalcóatl.

This was the Sun, our prince of Tula, of Quetzalcóatl—the Plumed Serpent, Venus, the Morning Star, and 4-Movement.

Interestingly enough, the Nahua cross of Quetzalcóatl is identical to the petroglyph of the "Maltese Cross" excavated at the Hohokam site in Snaketown, Arizona. At a rock outcropping in South Mountain Park in Phoenix, there is another Hohokam cross. In the early dawn hours, one can see the cross, a symbol for Venus, while at the same time if one glances above the cross and the outcropping, the planet Venus is well in view. In another Hohokam site in Pinal County, Arizona, a swastika-like design with round instead of angular bends has been discovered by rock art specialist Ekkehart Malotki. Outlined crosses on petroglyphs found at El Tecomate in Sinaloa are similar to crosses in Tula that represent Quetzalcóatl under the designation "The Morning Star" or "Venus." Similarly, rock art in the Hopi mesas shows symbols for crosses that are akin to the petroglyphs at Snaketown. In introducing the reader to the Hohokam culture and its rock art, Malotki suggests that "many characteristics of the culture suggest strong influence, if not actual immigration, from Mesoamerica."[44]

From the evidence of petroglyphs and pictographs in the rock art of Mexico and the American Southwest, the Quetzalcóatl legend or myth was widespread throughout the Indigenous areas of the Greater Southwest. Like the Quetzalcóatl crosses, the symbol for Venus in Teotihuacano and Mayan hieroglyphic writing, as well as the various Nahua versions of the glyph for *movement*, are all in the shape of the quincunx.[45]

A.

B.

(A) Cross of Quetzalcóatl. (B) Hieroglyphs for *movement*.

As is well known, *quetzal* refers to the national bird of Guatemala, distinguished for its golden-green and scarlet plumage. The bird is so rare and the plumes so valued that the word *quetzalli* came to mean "precious." *Cóatl* is the Náhuatl word for "snake" or "dragon," as well as "twin." Thus, the translation of Quetzalcóatl is usually either Plumed Serpent or Precious Twin. Not so well known is that fact that in Mesoamerica there were many Quetzalcóatls at different places and times. For example, the Plumed Serpent was also called *ehecacóatl*, that is, wind snake or whirlwind. Swastikas (which are also quincunxes) found on Hohokam pottery, Pee Posh ceramics, Yavapai baskets, and Navajo sand paintings are often construed as representing whirlwinds.

The Quetzalcóatl story is well known. Tula is the place where the earth-bound serpent had feathered wings and learned how to escape the earth by flying. The Feathered Serpent was born of divine origin and succumbed to evil. Tempted by Tezcatlipoca (the Smoking Mirror), Quetzalcóatl committed the sins of vanity, drunkenness, and incest. Ashamed of his behavior, he abandoned Tula and went to the east coast, where he took on a costume of feathers and ascended the heavens in a ball of fire. Materiality was transcended as he became Venus, the Morning and Evening Star. It was Quetzalcóatl's breath or wind that kept the sun moving and prevented it from being captured by inertia and plunging into the darkness of earth.

Without accepting the somewhat *spiritualist* interpretation of Séjourné, or succumbing to the Gnostic and occult view that matter is evil, it should be noted that the Quetzalcóatl myth contains a unifying symbol that harmonizes opposites: heaven and earth, water and fire (burning water), day and night, good and evil, morning and evening star (Venus), matter and spirit. It is a universal expression of the ideas of death and resurrection; god becomes man, and man becomes god. It should not be surprising that this myth would appeal to Anglo-Europeans and American Indians alike, or that the mythology (in part or whole) would motivate individuals in the American Southwest as well as Mexico.[46] Whether this was due to cultural diffusion and/or migration or independent invention (or parts of both) will be discussed in a later context.

The Mesoamericans made no distinction between time and space. They thought in terms of space/time. The Maya viewed the world as a sacred place, and like their European counterparts, organized space according to philosophical and religious principles. Allegorical illusions were used in which the physical landscape reflected the parallel, unseen Otherworld (*Xibalba*) in which Maya shaman-kings could pass. The human plane was depicted as a flat disc floating in a primordial sea. The four cardinal directions served as a grid for the surface of the world. The principal axis of this Middleworld was the path of the sun from east to west. Each cardinal point was associated with a direction, a color, a special tree, and rituals. East was red and was associated with the birth of the sun. North was white, the abode of the North Star. West, the dying place of the sun, was black. South, the right-hand side of the sun, was yellow. This global model was concentric as well as quadrangular, with the four cardinal points seen in relationship to the center. The world tree plunged through the center—roots in the Underworld, trunk in the Middle World, and branches soaring to the heights of the Otherworld. The geography (or cosmography) of human beings was connected to the Otherworld along the World Tree axis, a center symbolized by the interior of the Maya temple and materialized through rituals in the person of the Maya king.[47] Once again is seen the phenomenon of the quincunx.

Other forms of the application of cardinality and the quincunx can be seen in Mesoamerican ritual observations, civil administration, and even literary forms. In Indigenous rituals, the cardinal directions are always honored by offerings of sprinkled water, puffs of smoke, animal blood, and the like. This is true even outside of Mesoamerica, for example, the Tarahumaras (Rarámuris) of the western sierra of Chihuahua. When a burial party of Tarahumara men enters a cemetery ground, they complete a counterclockwise circuit of a large cross erected there, turning at each of the four sides.[48] Further north, Arizona Yaqui (or Yeome) from Sonora speak about the unusual floor plan of their Catholic chapel that is in the shape of a Greek cross by saying its four arms represent "the four sacred directions," a notion not likely in the minds of the local Catholic clergy.[49] Generally speaking, Hopi and Pueblo tribes, as well as O'odham- and Yuman-speaking peoples and other groups that have been in the Greater Southwest for millennia, have ample correspondences with Mesoamerica such as quadripartite social structures, fourfold division of pottery decoration, counterclockwise movements, and multiple creations.

As for civil administration, the Mayas of Yucatán rotated civil and religious duties through four community groups, an early practice that was continued during the Spanish colonial era. For the Nahuas, historian James Lockhart has demonstrated that social organization was divided into cellular and quadripartite groups with rotating responsibilities. Finally, groups of four are important for Indigenous literature. Many Mesoamerican poems are written in four verses that rotate around a common theme.[50]

Diffusion, Migration, and/or Independent Invention?

It is obvious that the ideas of cardinality and harmony, communicated with quincuncial symbols, were and are important for Mesoamerican thought. It has also been suggested that these ideas, especially the quincunx, were not foreign to the area north of Mesoamerica in what historians refer to as the Gran Chichimeca (Greater Southwest). Before identifying some of the Mesoamerican traits found in the Gran Chichimeca, the issue of cultural contacts, diffusion, and independent invention needs to be addressed.

If, as will be argued here, that cardinality and the quincunx were as typical of Indigenous thought in the Greater Southwest as they were in Mesoamerica, the question remains as to why this is the case? Was it due to cultural diffusion and/or migration from Mexico, or is the quincunx a universal symbol that has appeared among most cultures at most times and places in the world? The latter is certainly the case when comparing medieval Europe with classical Maya America.

In medieval Europe one of the most common ways of rendering the earth was through the *mappae mundi* of which over a thousand have survived, including the so-called T-O map. Like other European maps of that time, this map was schematic and presented the world as an allegorical statement in which material images represented theological truths. Here, the world was depicted as a flat disc surrounded by an ocean sea forming the O shape. The O was internally divided by a T, with east at the top. The stem of the T represented the Mediterranean, separating Europe from Africa. The crossbar of the T formed the waters stretching from the Don River to the Nile along the Black Sea and the Aegean. Jerusalem, representing the medieval Christian ideal of the terrestrial paradise of the Garden of Eden, was in the center. All maps were oriented with east (*Oriens*) at the top, the direction of the rising sun, with other directional points being *Septentrio* (north), *Occidens* (west), and *Meridies* (south).[51]

Some interesting comparisons can be made between the medieval T-O map and the Maya model of the world. As indicated earlier, both were mythic maps that viewed the earth as a sacred place. Again, both schemas fuse cardinality with religious symbols, with east, the rising sun, at the top of the map. Because of ethnocentrism, both thinkers placed their most important religious image in the center of the map—Jerusalem for the medieval monk,

The World Tree for the Maya priest. And these schemas form a quincunx pattern, a universal design found in art and nature and in a variety of ways, from Roman coins, English literary works and New England farmhouses, to Teotihuacán frescos and Hohokam crosses. Ethnocentrism and human nature explain the similarities between two cultures coexistent in time but separated in space by a vast ocean, with little evidence of cultural diffusion before 1492 A.D.[52]

Another example that argues for independent invention is that of the humoral theory of medicine. The great physician Galen, who lived in the Roman Empire between A.D. 130 and 201, argued that an individual maintained health as long as the four humors of blood, yellow bile, black bile, and phlegm remained in a state of equilibrium. All four humors had to balance each other in order to develop the fifth state of harmony and health. The humoral theory of health held sway in medical circles until the English physician William Harvey challenged it with his discoveries about the circulation of blood in the seventeenth century.[53] Thus, the Europeans had their own quincuncial theories that had a history as long as or longer than that of the Mexicans and Mayas in Mesoamerica, based on a theory independent of the ideas of Aztec priests and Maya kings.

Again, another example of quincuncial thinking can be found in the Buddhist and Hindu veneration of Mount Kailas in Tibet. There it is believed that Mount Kailas is the epicenter of the universe, the source of life itself created by God and blessed by the Buddha. From the foot of Mount Kailas, the four rivers that nourish the world—the Indus, Ganges, Sutlej, and Brahmaputra—have their origins, with each one rising from a cardinal point.[54]

With the above qualifications in mind, it should be remembered that although the quincunx appears to be universal throughout world history, the specific form it takes in any one locale may be due to diffusion and/or migration. It is not the five-part pattern of the quincuncial crosses and swastikas that are found in the rock art of the Southwest that is important, but the meaning the people attach to these patterns and symbols. The meaning of the petroglyphs can only be hinted at, but contemporary Indigenous rituals and ceremonies can indicate what something signifies or its inner importance in both a moral and psychological sense. The critical idea is the Mesoamerican notions of harmony and cardinality expressed in quincuncial form, symbolic of four primordial elements redeemed by a unifying center. Unlike the examples cited above of the quincunx in Europe, there was no physical, and very little cultural, space between the Greater Southwest and Mesoamerica. People in Hohokam knew about the Pueblos of the plateau, and both groups were aware of happenings, events, and ideas in Mesoamerica, including the "Law of the Center."

Cardinality, Harmony, and the Quincunx in the Greater Southwest

Mesoamerican traits, especially the ideas of cardinality, harmony, and the quincunx, are found in abundance in the Greater Southwest. The quincunx, in particular, can be discovered as an icon on rock art (carvings on petroglyphs and paintings on pictographs), in pottery designs, as patterns in sand paintings and weavings, or jewelry motifs and basketry figures. The rock art of the Greater Southwest contains quincuncial symbols for feathered serpents, crosses, stars, and swastikas. Symbols for feathered serpents (Quetzalcóatl figures) are pan-American in that they are found throughout the Americas, including Mesoamerica (early Olmec as well as the more recent Aztec images), the eastern woodlands, at Chaco, and again Paquimé.

Petroglyphs as crosses, as indicated before, are quincunxes, and as such the cross at El Tecomate in Sinaloa, Mexico, is similar to symbols in Tula and elsewhere that represent Quetzalcóatl as either the "Morning Star" or "Venus," just as Snaketown crosses are identical to the so-called "cross of Quetzalcóatl" found at Teotihuacán. Rock art that symbolizes stars can also be called quincunxes, especially the aforementioned cross or star of El Tecomate, the design of the Sky God in Hopi shields, or Hopi clan symbols (the Star Clan).[55]

For the Hopi, the symbol for migration is the swastika, an icon seen in rock art, on basketry, and in ceramics throughout the Southwest. The symbol represents four arms whirling round and round, guiding the eye to a focal point in the center. After years of wandering, the Hopi clans finally found their way to the one center of the universe in the Hopi mesas! The swastika, which has been around for thousands of years in the Old World and the New, is an ancient Indian design found throughout the Southwest and has been discovered on old Hohokam pots, modern Navajo rugs, and contemporary Papago (O'odham) baskets. For the O'odham, it represents "the wheel of life" in constant motion, with its four arms being birth, youth, maturity, and death.[56]

Early Hohokam artifact styles include ceramics, especially simple bowls, which display the quincunx. These bowls have four-part, bilaterally symmetrical designs that are identical to West Mexican dishes from sites in Zacatecas and Guanajuato, as well as styles found in Mesoamerica.[57] Examples of quincuncial designs in the artifacts of Indigenous Arizona curated at the Heard Museum in Phoenix, Arizona, include an Apache silver pin identical to the "Maltese Cross" from Snaketown; Yavapai baskets, most of which had crosses on them called *cruzados* by the Spanish; Catholic-Yaqui symbols on clothing and textiles; as well as the crosses, mountains, and storm patterns woven into Navajo rugs.

In following the historical development of quincuncial rituals, the trail initially leads to and from Mesoamerica proper, along the east coast of Veracruz and across central Mexico, to the west coast of northwestern Mexico and the Greater Southwest. In the fifteenth century, the Gran Chichimeca (or Greater Southwest) was composed of various regional "provinces," or culture areas, for example, the Little Colorado Province of northeastern Arizona, the Desert Province of southwestern Arizona, the Serrana Province of Sonora and northwestern Mexico, or the Rio Grande Province of New Mexico. The entire Greater Southwest functioned as an interacting whole with not only trade networks but also sociopolitical and religious ties.[58]

Because the Serrana contained several statelets or chiefdoms that lay across the major northern route from Mesoamerica to the upper Southwest, and were known to the conquistadores, they were the nodal points in the redistribution network that attracted that first generation of European visitors. In the eighth and ninth centuries, the primary routes ran through Sonora to southern Arizona (the Hohokam country). By 1500 A.D., secondary routes ran either up the Yaqui River to the Mimbres area of New Mexico or up the Fuerte River and along the Rio Conchos-Rio Grande Rivers across Chihuahua to the Colorado Plateau (circumventing the Hohokam). These then were the routes along which rituals, beliefs, and ceremonies travelled in both pre-Hispanic and early modern historic times.[59]

In reconstructing the movement of quincuncial ceremonies, one intriguing clue can be found in the ritual dance and music of the Totonacs of Totonocapan. It is here where the ritual of the "Voladores of Papantla" takes place. The ritual of the *volador* (meaning "he who flies") was performed originally throughout much of Mexico and extended to the Tzutujil Maya of Guatemala and as far south as Nicaragua. And it was very likely the Totonacs who carried the dance and its meaning to the Huichols of north central Mexico and the Greater Southwest. Today the ritual of the volador is performed throughout Mexico and the American Southwest, from Mexico City to Austin, Texas.

Although some writers consider the rite sacred to Quetzalcóatl, the Morning Star, it most likely originated as a prayer to Xipe Totec, the God of fertility. This rite was a petition for the return of water and rain so that the soil could be nourished, allowing the crops to grow.[60]

Before concluding this essay, two more examples will be illustrated, that of the Chiricahua Apache and the Navajo (or Diné). As for the Chiricahuas, the critic might argue that the selection of these Athapaskan-speaking tribes is a strange choice as they are supposedly recent newcomers to the Southwest. It should be remembered that these people have been in Mexico at least since the seventeenth century (some archaeologists suggest much earlier dates for pre-Athapaskan speakers) and that their traditional homeland included parts of the Chihuahua desert and the northern Sierra Madre with its intersecting trade routes to and from Mexico. Throughout the early modern period, the Chiricahuas were raiding, fighting, living, and trading with Mexicans, Pueblos, and O'odham speakers. As late as the 1880s, the Chiricahuas were on the western Chihuahua plains, first pushing the Tarahumaras further west into the canyonlands of the Sierra Madre, and then fighting the Mexican and US Armies. There were plenty of chances for contact between Mexican Indians and Apaches that could lead to cultural exchanges.

Finally, the Navajo, apart from some Indigenous characteristics, derive most of their culture from Spanish, Mexican, Anglo, and Pueblo sources. Spaniards brought the churro sheep, wheat, and the peach orchard; the Mexicans contributed silver smithing; and Anglo traders introduced synthetic dyes and wool. Pueblos gave the Navajo the vertical loom, weaving techniques, Zuni inlay methods of jewelry making, matrilineal customs, and some katsina-like religious figures. In other words, the bulk of the Navajo's physical and intellectual life was inherited from old Mexico by way of the Spanish, Mexican, and Pueblo peoples. In the mountains of eastern Arizona and western New Mexico, a ritualistic dance was being performed by various Apache groups, including the Western Apaches and the Chiricahuas of southeast Arizona. This dance too follows a quincuncial pattern, consisting of four Mountain Spirit Dancers or Crown Dancers representing the cardinal points (known as *gaans* to the Western Apache) in conjunction with a fifth dancer, the clown or Grey One.

They are best known, however, for their participation in what is probably the most important ceremony for the Apache, the Sunrise Dance, the rite of passage for an Apache girl entering womanhood. Not only is this four-day ceremony a rite of transformation for the adolescent girl but a ritual that Apaches consider profound for its importance in reasserting traditional Apache values. One of the most important holy beings for the Apaches is White-Painted Woman, the first woman of creation. In the Sunrise Ceremony, the young girl literally is transformed into White-Painted Woman (or White Shell Woman), just as the Crown Dancers "become" the sacred mountain spirits. The conclusion of the ceremony involves a community blessing bestowed upon the group by White-Painted Woman that assures harmony, cohesiveness, and regeneration (the life force) for the entire band or clan.

The Mountain Spirit Dancers and the Grey One perform each evening during the four-day Sunrise Ceremony. The dancers, their bodies painted black with either zigzag designs or four-pointed stars (a quincunx) on their chests, wear black hoods over their heads and faces (like those worn by Navajo *Yei*). The gaan regalia include the wearing of an elaborate wood superstructure on the top of the head, not unlike the "tablitas" of Hopi katsinam.[61]

According to Philip Cassadore, an Apache authority on the Sunrise Ceremony, Athe Gaan are predictable, stable. The foundation of the world rests on them. The Grey One is unpredictable. He represents chance that comes into a person's life. With the predictable and unpredictable together there is equilibrium, balance. One needs to have strength, balance, to face the unpredictable in life."[62] The four Mountain Spirit Dancers, each representing a cardinal point, and the clown in the center, guarantee to the community the harmony and cohesiveness necessary for the community to survive.

A final example of the quincunx in the American Southwest relates to the nature of the Navajo value system and creation story. The Navajo place great value on peace, contentment, and harmony. The word that most often embraces these ideas is *hózhó*, usually translated as "beauty." But the term is more inclusive than that and should be thought of as a philosophical and religious goal. The meaning of life is to attain *hózhó*, perfect *hózhó*, and to regain *hózhó* when it is lost through a violation of rules or taboos. Navajo ceremonialism is designed to attain and retain *hózhó*—meaning balance, wholeness, togetherness, peace, beauty, health, and harmony.

In the creation story that tells how the Navajo came to be, although details may vary from clan to clan, the world was created four times before the present, or fifth, era. All of the preexisting worlds were destroyed when disharmony destroyed *hózhó*. As the creatures in these four worlds evolved, from insects, animals, and birds, to humans, they took the form of the *Yei*—supernatural forces or spirits. When disharmony destroyed the Fourth World, the humans emerged in the Fifth World, also called Earth Surface World or Glittering World.[63]

The surface of the Glittering World follows the pattern of the quincunx. The point of emergence (located geographically in the mesas southeast of present day Farmington, New Mexico) is a cosmological hogan and locus surrounded by sacred mountains on four sides in which the *Yei* as mountain spirits dwell.[64] According to the legend, when the humans emerged into the Glittering World, they were instructed to found the first four Navajo clans. The spirit doing the instruction was the greatest of the Navajo *Yei*, Changing Woman. Her sons, the Twin Heroes, must slay the Monsters of the Fourth World in order to make the Fifth World safe for human occupancy. More importantly, it is Changing Woman who teaches the Navajo how to avoid the disharmony that destroyed the Fourth World and how to restore *hózhó*, or harmony, to the Surface World.[65]

Navajo weaving traditions express these creation story themes and the idea of *hózhó*; Storm pattern weavings from the Shiprock area are an example. The Storm pattern rug contains motifs and symbols that represent four sacred mountain spirits, cardinal directions, a universal center (a "storm" house, or hogan), and other essential aspects of *hózhó*.[66] So it is that the quincuncial world view of the Navajo contains a belief system in which all

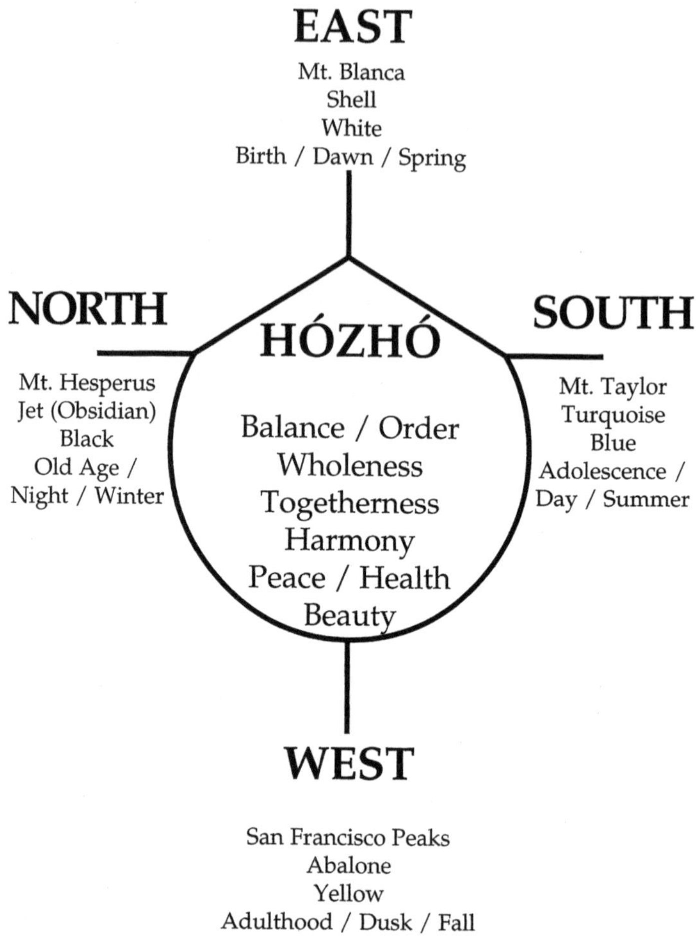

Navajo cosmogram.

the sacred colors, winds, directions, precious shells and stones, life cycles, sunrise and sunset, and seasons must follow the order of the universe to assure harmony and balance.

CONCLUSION

This essay has argued that archaeological thinking has recently been influenced by world history trends and that many archaeologists, anthropologists, and southwestern historians have begun to think in continental, and sometimes even hemispheric, terms. A result of the new thinking has been a developing awareness of the "Mesoamericanization" of the northern frontier, a process that began in 200 A.D. and intensified right up to the first European intrusion.

The interconnectedness of these areas was reflected in mining (especially of gem-quality turquoise), long-distance commerce and trade, manufacturing, and endemic warfare, along with ceremonialism and religion. It should be remembered that a thousand years ago there were river valleys and fluvial systems that supported huge populations and major transportation networks.[67]

Given the astronomical importance of the heavens, these pre-Hispanic peoples were sky watchers who created calendars out of the movement of the sun, studied the solstices, and were able to easily calculate true north and the other cardinal points. The different clans and lineages of the Hohokam and Pueblo had astronomical leanings.[68] When one considers the various ancient dwellings that existed along the 108th meridian, and the importance of cardinality, the Chaco Meridian hypothesis does not seem so outlandish.[69] Finally, the central message of this essay is that the patterns of Indigenous thought of the Greater Southwest, historical and contemporary, are similar in form and content to those of Mesoamerica. The basic elements of these thought patterns consist of cardinality, harmony, and the quincunx. Obviously, quincunx designs might be similar in form but differ in content. This could certainly be the case for much of the rock art of the Southwest. And as noted, it could always be the case that similarities in thought are the results of coincidence, randomness, or independent invention. Similar cultural traits may at times be due to the fact that mankind experiences universal phenomena, especially considering the seemingly common patterns of the seasons and astronomical activity. And there is biology that gives to all humanity a human nature. But it is also the case that certain human activities can be learned and passed on not only to the next generation but to adjacent generations in nearby locations. Certainly historical diffusion, migration, and cultural contacts took place between Mexico and the American Southwest, and these exchanges not only involved material goods but ideas and technologies as well. The most likely explanation of the origin of many Indigenous patterns of thought in the American Southwest, especially the quincunx, is northern Mexico and Mesoamerica.

Notes

1. These developments in the archaeology of the ancient Southwest are narrated by Chaco specialist and iconoclast Stephen H. Lekson in *A History of the Ancient Southwest* (Santa Fe, N.M.: School for Advanced Research, 2009), esp. 105–11, 144–50, 179–89, and 218–25.

2. Wallerstein's three volumes shared the same title and publisher: *The Modern World System I* (New York: Academic Press, 1974), *The Modern World System II* (1979), and *The Modern World System III* (1989). The first volume treated the sixteenth-century world economy; the second, the period from 1600–1750; and volume three, the second era of capitalist expansion after 1750. For Frank, see "The Development of Underdevelopment," *Monthly Review* 18 (1966): 17–31.

3. Janet L. Abu-Lughod, *Before European Hegemony: The World System A.D. 1250–1350* (New York and Oxford: Oxford University Press, 1989).

4. Janet Lippman Abu-Lughod surveys the historiography of global history, including the problem of Eurocentrism, in "The World System in the Thirteenth Century: Dead-End or Precursor?" in *Essays on Global and Comparative History*, ed. Michael Adas (Washington, D.C.: American Historical Association, 1993). For Eurocentrism, see J. M. Blaut, *Eight Eurocentric Historians* (New York and London: The Guilford Press, 2000); and Peter Gran, *Beyond Eurocentrism: A New View of Modern World History* (Syracuse, N.Y.: Syracuse University Press, 1996).

5. Ross E. Dunn, *The Adventures of Ibn Battuta* (Berkeley and Los Angeles: University of California Press, 1989).

6. A possible exception might be the brief study by Felipe Fernández-Armesto, *The Americas: A Hemispheric History* (New York: Modern Library, 2003). The book does lack depth, and coverage of precontact America, especially the Greater Southwest, is limited and erroneous (e.g., on p. 44 the author locates Casas Grandes in Sinaloa instead of Chihuahua). Another recent trend that goes far beyond the Afro-Eurasian region and the normal perimeters of world history is "Big History." See, for example, the work by David Christian known as *Maps of Time: An Introduction to Big History* (Berkeley and Los Angeles: University of California, 2004), in which world history is treated on an unprecedented scale from the Big Bang to the present day. The scale is not only expansive, but the methodologies are diverse, ranging from cosmology and geology to archaeology and environmental studies.

7. Eric R. Wolf, *Europe and the People Without History* (Berkeley and Los Angeles: University of California Press, 1982).

8. Thomas D. Hall, *Social Change in the Southwest, 1350–1880* (Lawrence: University of Kansas, 1989).

9. Carroll L. Riley, *Becoming Aztlan: Mesoamerican Influences in the Greater Southwest, AD 1200–1500* (Salt Lake City: University of Utah Press, 2005) and *The Frontier People: The Greater Southwest in the Protohistorical Period* (Albuquerque: University of New Mexico Press, 1987). The quotation is from p. 1 of *Becoming Aztlan*. For purposes of this discussion, see the work by J. Charles Kelly entitled "Mesoamerica and the Southwestern United States," in *Handbook of Middle American Indians, Vol. 4: Archaeological Frontiers and Connections*, ed. Gordon F. Ekholm and Gordon R. Wiley (Austin: University of Texas Press, 1966), 95–110. The classic work by Charles C. Di Peso is *Casas Grandes: A Fallen Trading Center of the Gran Chichimeca*, vols. 1–3 (Dragoon, Ariz.: Amerind Foundation, 1974).

10. Lekson, *A History of the Ancient Southwest* (Santa Fe, N.M.: School for Advanced Research, 2008); see esp. pp. 3–9. Lekson quotes from Bentley's *The New World History* (2002), 3, and the Wolf quotation is from the aforementioned *Europe and the People Without History*, 9. In addition to Bentley and Wolf, Lekson derives many of his ideas from some of the following world historians: Janet L. Abu-Lughod, Christopher Chase-Dunn, and Thomas D. Hall, "World-Systems in North America (1998); David Christian, *Maps of Time* (2004); Philip Curtin, *Cross-Cultural Trade in World History* (1984); Jared Diamond, *Guns, Germs and Steel* (1997); Felipe Fernández-Armesto, *The Americas*; Andre Gunder Frank, *The World System* (1993); Patrick Manning, *Navigating World History* (2003); William H. McNeill and J. R. McNeill, *The Human Web* (2003); Arnold Toynbee, *A Study of History*, 10 vols. (1934–1961); and Immanuel Wallerstein, *The Modern World System* (1974). For a survey of recent archaeological studies that focus on Mexican influence in the American Southwest, see David R. Wilcox, Phil C. Wiegand, J. Scott Wood, and Jerry B. Howard, "Ancient Cultural Interplay of the American Southwest in the Mexican Northeast," *Journal of the Southwest* 50 (Summer 2008): 103–71.

11. John P. Andrews and Todd W. Bostwick, *Desert Farmers at the River's Edge: The Hohokam and Pueblo Grande* (Phoenix, Ariz.: Pueblo Grande Museum, 2nd ed., 2000), 57. See also David Wilcox and Charles Sternberg, *Hohokam Ballcourts and Their Interpretation* (Tucson, Ariz.: Arizona State Museum, Anthropology Series no. 160, 1983), 25, 76.

12. Stephen Lekson, *A History of the Ancient Southwest*, 39–47. See also Charles Q. Choi, "Ancient Mayas Likely Had Fountains and Toilets," *Live Science.com* (Dec. 23, 2009); and reporting on "hydro-archaelogy" by Kirk French and Christopher Duffy in the *Journal of Archaeological Science* (Dec. 16, 2009).

13. Lekson, *A History of the Ancient Southwest*, 226–27.

14. Ibid., 227–31.

15. Ibid., 230–32, 241, 243.

16. Craig Childs, *House of Rain: Tracking a Vanished Civilization Across the American Southwest* (New York: Little, Brown and Company, 2006), 24–25.

17. Ibid., 91.

18. Ibid., 250.

19. Ibid., 256–57. The spelling "katsina" rather than the more common "kachina" is the preferred use here. Because the Hopi language has no "ch" sound, *kachina* is not used by the Hopi. The plural of *katsina* is *katsinam.*

20. Ibid., 317–19.

21. Ibid., 347–48.

22. See note 13, Di Peso, *Casas Grandes.*

23. Lekson, *A History of the Ancient Southwest,* 242–46. See also Childs, *House of Rain,* 392–97.

24. Lekson, 9.

25. Lekson, 246, 327, n.53. Also see Frank Waters, *Book of the Hopi* (New York: Penguin Books, 1977), 67–71 and Raymond Friday Locke, *The Book of the Navajo* (New York: Kensington Publishing Corp., 2010), 79–85.

26. Worth consulting on Chaco roads is Margaret Senter (Gretchen) Obenauf, "The Chacoan Roadway System" (M.A. thesis, University of New Mexico, May 1980). This source was cited by David Rothberg, "The Mysteries of Chaco Canyon" (Ketoh Presentation: Phoenix, Ariz., Heard Museum, November 2008), 17, 18.

27. Rothberg, 16–18; Lekson, *Ancient Southwest,* 131.

28. Lekson, 234–46.

29. Childs, *House of Rain,* 395–96.

30. Timothy G. Baugh and Jonathon E. Ericson, "Trade and Exchange in a Historical Perspective," in *The American Southwest and Mesoamerica: Systems of Prehistoric Exchange,* ed. Baugh and Ericson (New York: Plenum Press, 1993), 3–20. See also Childs, *House of Rain,* 19.

31. Allan Hayes and Carol Hayes, *The Desert Southwest: Four Thousand Years of Life and Art* (Berkeley, Calif.: Speed Press, 2006), 56.

32. E. Charles Adams, *The Origin and Development of the Pueblo Katsina Cult* (Tucson: University of Arizona, 1991), 21–22, 93, 99. The quotation is from 21.

33. David Roberts, *In Search of the Old Ones: Exploring the Anasazi World of the Southwest* (New York: Simon & Shuster, 1996), 102.

34. Adams, *Origin and Development,* 29, 47, 93; Childs, *House of Rain,* 420–23, 459.

35. Carroll L. Riley, *Becoming Aztlan,* 200–3.

36. James S. Griffith, *Beliefs and Holy Places: A Spiritual Geography of the Pimeria Alta* (Tucson and London: The University of Arizona Press, 1992), 3–13.

37. Ibid., 75–86. Also see Bernard L. Fontana, *Of Earth & Little Rain: The Papago Indians* (Tucson: University of Arizona Press, 1989), 123–27.

38. Griffith, 86; Fontana, 127.

39. The quotation is from Alfonso Caso, *El Pueblo del Sol* (México: Fondo de Cultura Economíca, 1953), p. 21. See Laurette Séjourné, *Burning Water: Thought and Religion in Ancient Mexico* (Berkeley, Calif.: Shambhala, 1976), 89–90.

40. Frances Karttunen, "After the Conquest: The Survival of Indigenous Patterns of Life and Belief," *Journal of World History* 3 (Fall 1992): 242–45.

41. Karttunen, 212; Linda Schele and David Freidel, *A Forest of Kings: The Untold Story of The Ancient Maya* (New York: William Morrow, 1990), 77–84.

42. Schele and Freidel, 78–81.

43. Miguel León-Portilla, *Pre-Columbian Literatures of Mexico* (Norman: University of Oklahoma Press, 1969), 37.

44. The quotation is from Ekkehart Malotki, *The Rock Art of Arizona: Art for Life's Sake* (Walnut, Calif.: Kiva Publishing Co., 2007), 138. For the Hohokam swastika, see Malotki, 145. For the petroglyphs at Snaketown, the Hopi Mesas, and El Tecomate, see Alex Patterson, *A Field Guide to Rock Art Symbols of the Greater Southwest* (Boulder, Colo.: Johnson Books, 1992), 76–77, 163. A photograph of Venus and the rock outcropping at South Mountain can be found in Frank Zullo, "It was a Dark Night . . . ," *Arizona Highways* (January 2010): 30–31.

45. Séjourné, 96–97.

46. See both Burr Cartwright Brundage, *The Fifth Sun: Aztec Gods, Aztec World* (Austin: University

of Texas Press, 1991), 102–3, 107–8; and Frank Waters, *Mexico Mystique: The Coming Sixth World of Consciousness* (Chicago: Swallow Press, 1975), 125–26.

47. Schele and Freidel, 66–67. See also W. Dirk Raat, "Innovative Ways to Look at New World Historical Geography," *The History Teacher* 37 (May 2004): 286–87.

48. William L. Merrill, *Rarámuri Souls* (Washington, D.C.: Smithsonian Institution, 1988), 164.

49. Griffith, 98–99.

50. Kartunnen, 243–44.

51. Raat, "Innovative Ways to Look at New World Historical Geography," 286–87.

52. Ibid., 287.

53. Sherwin B. Nuland, a review of *Passions and Tempers: A History of Humours* by Noga Arikha in "Bad Medicine," *The New York Times Book Review* (July 8, 2007): 12.

54. Colin Thubron, "On Tibet's Holy Mountain," *The New York Review of Books* (March 10, 2011): 25–27.

55. Patterson, *A Field Guild to Rock Art Symbols*, 76–77, 163, 191.

56. Childs, *House of Rain*, 260; Terry DeWald, *The Papago Indians and Their Basketry* (Tucson, Ariz., 1979), 41.

57. Randall H. McGuire and Elisa Villapando C., "The Hohokam and Mesoamerica," in *The Hohokam Millennium*, ed. Suzanne K. Fish and Paul R. Fish (Santa Fe, N.M.: School for Advanced Research, 2007).

58. Carroll L. Riley, *The Frontier People*, 7–14.

59. Ibid., 7, 76–77.

60. "Los Voladores" (http://www.earthdancer.org/TradeDays/flyers.html).

61. W. Jackson Rushing III, *Alan Houser: An American Master <Chiricahua Apache, 1914–1994>* (New York: Harry N. Abrams, Inc., 2004), 45–46.

62. As quoted by Rushing in Ibid., 4. Another quincuncial ritual is the child moccasin ceremony. For a description, see Peter Aleshire, *The Fox and the Whirlwind* (New York: John Wiley & Sons, Inc., 2000), 19.

63. Irvin Morris, *From the Glittering World: A Navajo Story* (Norman: University of Oklahoma Press, 1997), 3–15.

64. The association of colors with the cardinal directions is typical of Indigenous peoples, even though the colors change among groups. For Mesoamericans, red, the fiery color of the sun, is usually east. All Pueblos, like their cousins the Navajo, couple white with east, while only the Tiwa speakers of Picuris have color associations identical to the Navajo. For color associations, see Edward P. Dozier, *The Pueblo Indians of North America* (Long Grove, Ill.: Waveland Press, 1970), 205.

65. Ernie Bulow, *Navajo Taboos* (Gallup, N.M.: Buffalo Medicine Books, 1991), 14–15.

66. As quoted by Ann Lane Hedlund, "A Turning Point: Viewing Modern Navajo Weaving as Art," in *American Indian Art Magazine* (Spring 2011): 75.

67. Phil C. Weigand, "Continuity: The Pre-Hispanic Background for Mining, Trade, and Warfare in Northern Mexico and the Southwestern United States," *Journal of the West* 47 (Summer 2008): 11–16.

68. For Hohokam astronomy, see the chapter "Saluting the Sun: A Hohokam Calendar," in Todd W. Bostwick, *Landscapes of the Spirits* (Tucson: University of Arizona Press, 2002), 173–203.

69. George Johnson, "Scientist Tries to Connect Migration Dots of Ancient Southwest," *New York Times*, June 30, 2009, D1.

Chapter 2

"Forced Transnationalism" among Indigenous People across Borderlands

Mexico and the United States*

María Cristina Manzano-Munguía

> *I do not consider myself Canadian. I was born in the USA and I do not consider myself American. I am Seneca Nation and our nationhood precedes both the US and Canada . . .*
>
> Elder Dan Smoke, Seneca Nation (interview with Dan Smoke, 2013)

The American West meant the domain for Anglo-Saxon men to experience freedom, adventure, wilderness, and free access to land and resources. However, Indigenous people, immigrants, and women recounted and contested the multiple and fragmented stories of the West. Consequently, the revised histories of the American West included, but were not limited to, Indigenous people, miners, Western cowboys, the Chinese, the mythic heroes, and women in the frontier.[1] Within a Turnerian perspective, the westward expansion of the United States of America fulfilled Manifest Destiny and provided access to free land for economic development or progress.[2] It also promoted the belief that Indigenous peoples of North America

* An earlier version of this chapter was presented at the "Transnational American Studies" 58th Annual Conference of the German Association for American Studies, University of Regensburg, Regensburg, Germany, in 2011. I am grateful for the comments and suggestions from those who attended the workshop, especially from Dr. Brigitte Georgi-Findlay, and also those from Dr. Karl Hele, who engaged in a substantial manner with an earlier version. A special thanks to Helen Abraham, Oneida Nation, and Elder Dan Smoke, Seneca Nation, for their thoughtful comments and contributions. A very special thank-you for their thoughtful comments and endless support to our editors, Clarissa Confer, Andrae Marak, and Laura Tuennerman. I am also grateful to the two anonymous reviewers who provided insightful comments on the initial manuscript. Nonetheless, I am responsible for the views and interpretations expressed in this chapter.

were incompetent in terms of land use and self-government, and thus the solution was to civilize these "*primitives* in the name of progress."[3]

In contrast, Klein noted that westward expansion represented the locale for conflict between Europeans and Native Americans.[4] As Limerick accurately noted, Indigenous people were also "influential players" in *La Frontera*, or the Borderland.[5] Consequently, this population also influenced the complex pattern of social relations in the area where "trade, violence, conquest, and cultural exchange punctuated and shaped life in the borderlands,"[6] Following this line of inquiry, I realize the need to further explore the forced transnational experience among Indigenous people across borderlands.[7]

From an anthropological approach, the concept of transnationalism encompasses the processes experienced by immigrants who build and support multiple aspects of their relations between their point of origin and their settlement.[8] Basch, Glick Schiller, and Szanton Blanc propose an overarching framework that includes the experiences of multiple transmigrants who create and sustain economic, social, political, and cultural relationships between their home community and host country.[9] This theoretical framework, however, falls behind when being transnational is the forced outcome of territorial annexation due to conflict.

Therefore, this chapter will explore the forced transnational experiences of Native Nations across political borderlands during the second and third quarters of the nineteenth century. Here, being transnational meant an imposition from above and the product of territorial annexation due to conflict rather than the outcome of socioeconomic and political relationships between the home and host countries of Indigenous peoples. For many Native Nations, using and relating to their territories meant crossing international political borderlands or forced transnationalism. For example, after the Treaty of Guadalupe Hidalgo, some Native Nations experienced forced transnationalism while using and relating socially, economically, and politically to their Indigenous territories across the United States and Mexico.

Specifically I will look at how Indigenous nationhood and territory give strength to conceptualizing Indigenous forced transnationalism across political borderlands. Under my lens, raiding was a transnational activity once the political border between Mexico and the United States was enacted and imposed by outside forces on the Apache Nations, Comanche Nations, Navajo Nations, and so forth.[10] In the end, I will attempt to explore whether being "transna" as Helen, a First Nation Oneida articulated, could be the other way to construct and understand grassroots perspectives on contemporary Indigenous transnationalism. Thus, the general purpose of this chapter is to add flexibility to the concept of transnationalism while creating and enforcing grassroots epistemologies, keeping in mind that this work is in progress and is more suggestive than conclusive. Before launching into further details, a discussion on transnationalism is necessary.

(De)Constructing Transnationalism

Transnationalism encompasses the study of immigrants and their complex relations between their home country/territory and their new settlement. Since its inception in the 1990s, the concept seems quite problematic given its variability to cover a wide collection of activities and individuals.[11] To give some consistency while framing transnational studies in multiple settings, Basch et al. proposed four premises: First, transnational migration included the analysis of global relations between capital and labor; second, it was a process whereby migrants created social fields (through socioeconomic and political relations) that crossed national boundaries. Third, the perception and analysis of transnationalism can be limited by social science concepts that blend physical location, culture, and identity; and fourth, transmigrants are confronted and engaged in the processes of nation building of two or more nation-states in which their "identities and practices are configured by hegemonic categories . . . that are deeply embedded in the nation building processes of these nation states."[12] Whereas the first set seems quite resourceful in framing transnationalism among Indigenous peoples across borderlands, the latter is quite constraining.

It is my contention that framing the study of transnationalism within the context of nation-states is not always feasible. Indeed, the recurrence of being transnational within the context of stateless nations is gaining ground in the study of Indigenous communities across the world. This fluidity has been thoroughly elaborated by Duany in his studies of the stateless nation of Puerto Rico. The strong sense of Puerto Ricanness across the borders between the island and the United States has been present since colonization.[13] His framework of transnationalism undermines the traditional anchoring model of social actors engaging with and confronting two or more nation-states. So Duany's nation-to-nation framework is also applicable for Native Nations in the United States, Mexico, and Canada. Indigenous Nations expand their overarching identities beyond the national frame of their communities, territory, and life across and beyond these North American countries. Indeed, they are "nations within nation-states [and] they are neither autonomous nor sovereign."[14]

After exploring the narrations of nationhood among the Kahnawake Mohawk First Nation in Canada, Simpson proposes that nationhood is a process shaping social relations, sensational deposits, and desires both personal and collective. It is neither objective nor randomly practiced.[15] Her theoretical proposition is useful in understanding the complexities and fragmentations of these processes known as nationhood. It is then feasible to connect with Anderson's concept of nation-ness as imagined in political and cultural terms and intrinsically restricted and sovereign.[16] To a certain extent, Indigenous nationhood is also objectified through its special status condition within a nation-state, which includes a group of complementary, contested, and decisive levels of authority. Band and tribal governments also exercise significant control over Indigenous people living on reserves that constructs and facilitates their national status. Indigenous nationhood is an assertion of Native self-determination voiced through a sense of belonging to a specific tribe, even if individuals possess multiple and mixed identities both imagined and real.

Following Valaskakis, Indigenous Nations should avoid the reconstruction of their hybrid histories as narratives that build single stories of a particular heritage and a shared sense of experienced culture, identity, sacrifice, and empowerment. Rather, she proposes the emphasis of multiplicity in narrating stories of displacement, wars, adoptions, and intermarriages that create "narrative histories."[17] Good examples are Brooks and also Hämäläinen's seminal work on the Indigenous Nations in the Southwest borderlands. The latter scholar emphasizes the political mechanism forming joint councils that projected a unified front of opponents and supporters.[18]

Scholars have lately revised the complexity and fluidity of Indigenous Nations' histories by emphasizing their intertribal warfare for territorial expansion with neighboring nations, including confrontations with Spain, France, Mexico, England, and the United States.[19] This illuminating path of research brings new lines of inquiry that complicate the assumption that Indigenous Nations contended alone or with neighbors for "honor, plunder, captives, and above all hunting grounds."[20] For instance, Richard White elaborates upon intertribal warfare between the Sioux Nations and other Nations of the Northern Plains (such as the Crows, Pawnees, Hidatsas, Assiniboines, and Arikaras), as well as the Euro-American settlers before and after the Laramie Peace Conference of 1851, where conflict was recognized as the outcome of "two expanding powers—the United States, and the Sioux and their allies," and not the armed resistance of Indigenous people being directed by the US expansion.[21] At the same time, there is an ongoing recognition of the historical fluidity, porosity, and agency of Indigenous Nations and of the political power, tribal interests, and loyalties that drive their warfare affairs. Thus, major improvements have been achieved in reconstructing their stories.[22] Territorial expansion is central to conceptualizing Indigenous forced transnationalism and framing how Native Nations crossed and continue to cross political borderlands needs further exploration.

In Between: Crossing Borderlands

The Southwest expansion for settlers meant access to resources, land, capital, and labor. As Hurtado suggests, in California, "[N]ative household[s] subsidize[d] incipient capitalism even as the [N]ative economy [was] being replaced."[23] Land, resources, and labor were the landmarks that involved symbiotic relationships among and between settlers and Indigenous peoples in Indigenous territories.[24] Indigenous territories encompassed the current states of Nevada, Colorado, Wyoming, Utah, New Mexico, Arizona, a portion of Kansas, and California that were usurped by the United States through warfare with Mexico during the Mexican-American War from 1846 to 1848.[25]

For the United States, the Treaty of Guadalupe Hidalgo (1848) not only meant gaining the Southwest but also creating a blurred line for Indigenous people's territories across the political borderlands. Here, territory is neither a commodity nor a permanent and fixed construct where human beings "are the owners of it," but rather Indigenous constructions of fluid and inconsistent areas for social relations and practice.[26] After the Treaty of Guadalupe Hidalgo, for many Indigenous Nations, such as the Apaches, Navajos, Comanches, and Utes, using and relating to their territories meant crossing international political borderlands or forced transnationalism. In other words, Indigenous Nations experienced forced transnationalism while using and relating socially, economically, and politically within their Indigenous territory across political borderlands.[27] Conceptualizing Indigenous Nations as stateless-nations is fundamental in understanding their forced transnational experiences.

Indigenous Nations as Stateless Nations

The United States recognized Native tribes as "domestic dependent Nations" once settlement and other principles of civilization were exhibited, as was the case with the Five Civilized Nations, which included the Cherokee, Creek, Choctaw, Chickasaw, and Seminoles.[28] The following excerpt illustrates the principles that framed these Nations

> . . . with national boundaries, national constitution, and national political institutions rooted in American democracy but also reflecting Indian traditions. On fertile, well-watered lands blessed also with timber, coal, and other resources, the people took up individual homestead. They farmed . . . [and] set great . . . classroom learning, and during the 1850s they developed public school systems . . . They readily embraced Christianity and welcomed Methodist, Presbyterian, and Baptist missionaries . . . and looked for leadership to an extraordinary gifted elite native and mixed-blood alike . . .[29]

On the one hand, this Eurocentric framework of nationhood is also applicable to the Southwest Pueblos Nations who settled and practiced agriculture.[30] On the other hand, the concept of nationhood is not applicable to nomadic Indigenous people who practiced intertribal warfare affairs and war–peace relationships with colonists; rejected Hispanic culture and Christianity; and conducted trading, enslaving, and raiding activities in the American West and deep into Mexico.[31] Even if we consider these Indigenous tribes as nomads, they are also stateless-nations, and their framework for constructing this nationhood is neither Eurocentric nor circumscribed in modernity. Instead, it is based on Indigenous principles that some Native scholars have been advocating in the past several years.[32]

The ongoing contention of constructing the notion of nation and nationhood as blurred, contingent, and always undergoing processes of redefining themselves with political effects seems quite resourceful.[33] It is even more applicable if we consider these nations as culturally constructed and understood as "agenc[ies] of ambivalent narration[s]."[34] It is precisely this ambiguous narrative that the federal government [referring to Canada but also applicable to the United States] uses to recognize Indigenous Nations in terms of their heritage as "culturally distinct, historically continuous, and politically separate on the basis of different decrees: treaties, land grants, statutes, executive or administrative orders, past practice, or current criteria."[35] All these issues are relevant, but what frames the nationhood of Indigenous people from non-Western paradigms? I think both Sunseri (Oneida First Nation in Ontario, Canada) and Simpson (Mohawk Kahnawak First Nation in Quebec, Canada) provide grassroots paradigms on the conceptualization of Indigenous Nations based on their own experience and research.[36] From both ends, nationalism can be traced before colonialism by looking at how individuals connect to each other through multiple and fragmented lines of descent (including adoption). Moreover, their tribe/nation membership is also constructed through their cultural, spiritual, and political identities, and their land represents another binding mechanism.[37] Nomadic, semi-nomadic, and settled Indigenous tribal Nations fall within this Indigenous paradigm of nationhood and are relevant for their inclusion in transnational studies.[38] The practice of transnational economic and warfare activities such as raiding, among *Naciones errantes* (hostile Indian Nations), represents a prolific area for exploring the forced transnational experience of Indigenous people across borderlands.[39]

The Praxis of Raiding

Although Indigenous people engaged in activities such as raiding, trading, enslaving, stealing, and gift giving, these practices transcended Western understandings of them. As Hämäläinen noted, the Comanches "understood [trade] as a form of sharing between relatives either real or fictive[,] . . . considered theft a legitimate way of rectifying short-term imbalances in resource distribution[, and] . . . killed, waged war, and dispossessed other societies . . . to extract vengeance and to appease the spirits of their slain kin through enemy bodies."[40] I think these grassroots understandings of Indigenous practices are not only relevant to understanding the Comanches' worldviews but to other Indigenous Nations' economic, political, and sociocultural practices. Therefore, intermittently these nations dwelling in what they considered their territory conducted intertribal warfare, trade, and sociocultural interchange that "punctuated and shaped life in the borderlands."[41]

The following scenario described by Weber illustrates the violence, negotiation, and shifting conditions for settlers, Indigenous Nations, and travelers who lived in the Southwest borderland:[42]

> [P]obladores who enjoyed harmonious relations with one group of Apaches or Comanches might have their livestock stolen by members of another band, or even by individuals from a friendly group of Indians . . . [They] slaughtered or ran off livestock, destroyed or appropriated crops, and rendered mining a risky occupation. They captured women and children and killed men. Everywhere, travelers felt unsafe, even near sizable cities such as Chihuahua. Indeed, *once outside a Mexican settlement, the traveler for all practical purposes entered Indian territory* [emphasis added]. Some Apaches, who had learned Mexican ways from years of close contact, even collected taxes on occasion from persons traveling between New Mexico and Sonora, and kept abreast of events by reading mail that they appropriated from couriers.[43]

This "Land of War," or the Southwest, embodied a fragile region where peace treaties between Indigenous Nations, the Spanish, the Mexican, and later the Anglo settlers provided short-term solutions to long-term problems.[44] As Hämäläinen notes, "the European imperialism not only stalled in the face of indigenous resistance; it was eclipsed by indigenous imperialism":[45]

> Throughout the Mexican era, officials reported raids from the East by Comanches, Kiowas, Pawnees, Jicarillas, and other bands from the Plains, but the most unrelenting damage to New Mexico settlements between 1821 and 1846 came from Navajos to the west. Of Athapaskan origin, as were Apaches, these semi-nomadic agricultural and pastoral people had resisted the Franciscans' attempts to plant missions among them and remained completely independent . . . After [a] peaceful interlude . . . [1805], Navajo raids on the Mexican and Pueblo settlements in the Rio Grande Valley resumed in 1818. Navajos drove off livestock, appropriated crops, and carried off captives.[46]

> Comanches and Lipans raided Laredo, Revilla, and other villages along the Rio Grande for horses and captives, sometimes plunging south of the valley to attack the wealthy haciendas in Tamaulipas, Nuevo Leon, and Coahuila . . . Then, however, the raids into Mexico slowed down. In 1822, Comanches signed a national treaty in Mexico City and a provincial treaty in San Antonio and for a while refrained from raiding Mexican settlements.[47]

Indeed, by the first quarter of the nineteenth century, these relations turned for the worst. The Comanche Nations and other Indigenous Nations practiced "transnational networks of violence and exchange," which in turn stimulated the exchange of people, goods, and ideas across "ecological, ethnic, and political boundaries."[48] On the one hand, some Comanche Nations in conjunction with Kiowa allies restored warfare in the 1820s, and riding from the Great Plains conducted raids (including Indigenous slave raiding) in ranchos located in the Northeastern part of New Mexico and Texas, as well as the Mexican states of Coahuila, Durango, Chihuahua, and Nuevo Leon. By the 1840s, some Comanches reached the states of Zacatecas and Queretaro; the latter is located 135 miles North of Mexico City.[49] On the other hand, the Apaches who lived in tribes or Nations such as the Chiricahuas, Lipan, Jicarillas, Mimbres, and Mescaleros, stretched their territories from Texas to Arizona and Mexico.[50] Some of the powerful Apache Nations—the Mogolloñes, Mimbreños, Chiricahuas, Tontos, and Coyoteros, whose territory encompassed the mountains of eastern Arizona and western New Mexico—raided the western part of Sonora. The Mogolloñes and other Gileños also raided Chihuahua and Durango.[51]

According to Weber, there are no grassroots manuscripts explaining the reasons that drove these Indigenous Nations to conduct raids throughout various territories.[52] Nonetheless, scholars have emphasized the relevance of oral history in reconstructing Indigenous histories, albeit contested by Indigenous people and scholars.[53] For instance, Hämäläinen elaborates a semi-grassroots approach by using historical and ethnohistorical methods to interpret, understand, and reconstruct Comanches' histories. As he puts it, "I have prioritized accounts that recount even in a mutated form, Comanche voice—while keeping in mind that that voice is recorded through a cultural colander and it belongs often to a privileged headmen."[54]

Despite the aforementioned constraints, Weber is able to spell out an overarching framework that explains raiding practice among Indigenous Nations. First, raiding was a defense mechanism against injustice or threat provoked by outsiders such as the "seizure of Indian captives . . . the buying and selling of Indian men, women and children . . . to work in households."[55] These events contributed to Navajo and Ute raids in New Mexico and in Sonora by Apaches and Yumans. Second, raiding was the product of intertribal warfare history in the region. For instance, the Sioux Nations, or the "Mojave and Yuma traditions of warfare" and raiding practices, related to religious beliefs even before European colonization.[56]

Third, raiding meant the access to resources and food supplies intertwined with the socioeconomic and political relations among and between Native Nations and Spanish, Mexican, and Anglo settlers. As St. John notes, the Apaches and other hostile Indigenous Nations represented a threat to Spanish, Mexicans, and Anglo settlements due to their raids on cattle that fed on "borderlands grasses" or to their desire to access "horses" or "horse meat."[57] Another example relates to the on-going trade that included material goods and human beings between Indigenous Nations and Anglo traders. As Weber states, it benefitted both ends: "Indians raided Mexican settlements [by] taking livestock and even human captives that could be traded to the Americans for more arms and munitions, as well as whiskey and other goods."[58] This synergy of trading relationships between and among hostile Indigenous Nations, Mexicans, Spanish, and American settlers continued and even intensified in turbulent moments across the borderlands.

Hämäläinen's work illustrates quite well the aforementioned shifting conditions and complexities for raiding. Indeed, Comanche Nations raided as early as 1710 in order to acquire their first horses; by the second quarter of the eighteenth century, it was the solution to obtaining horses for domestic use and captives for exchange from Apache Nations located in the South. By 1865, the Comanche Nations exploited the chaotic aftermath of post–Civil War Texas and "forged a transnational raiding-and-trading network."[59] They also expanded their raiding into Mexico as a strategy of protection and reducing counterattacks into Comanchería:

> Large-scale raiding resumed in 1825 and 1826. Accompanied by Kiowas and apparently guided by Mexican captives, western and eastern Comanches sent several war parties to the south [Mexico]. From there on, the raids escalated steadily, eventually engulfing much of northern Mexico . . . They seized control of Apache war trails from Matamoros to northern Chihuahua, forcing the Lipans and Mescaleros to shift their raiding operations west, south, and north.
>
> There was still another upsurge of raiding activity in 1840 and 1841 when large-scale war parties struck deep into Mexico, and soon the Comanche raiding network covered much of Chihuahua, Coahuila, Nuevo Leon, Tamaulipas, Durango, Zacatecas, and San Luis Potosi.[60]

Under my lens, raiding seems a rhizomatic activity in which Indigenous Nations stretched back and forth throughout their territories while using and relating to them (socially, economically, politically, and culturally), even if this meant crossing politically constructed borderlands (Indigenous, Mexican, and American).[61] After the Mexican-American War, Indigenous Nations continued to raid, but now their activity entailed crossing political borderlands imposed by two nation-states that neither addressed their concerns nor asked for their input. To put it simply, using and relating to their territories through raiding meant, for many Indigenous Nations, being transnational, and was an imposition from above.

Forced Transnationalism

General Kearny, an American general who took possession of New Mexico in August of 1846, stated, "From the Mexican Government you [have] never received protection. The Apaches and [the] Navajos come down from the mountains and carry off your sheep, and even your women, whenever they please. My government [the United States] will correct all this."[62] Apache raided settlements on both sides of the border and crossed back and forth between the Mexican and the American side. Despite the fact that the land seemed depopulated when the Treaty of Guadalupe Hidalgo ratified the political boundary line between Mexico and the United States, Indigenous Nations were physically distributed in New Mexico and Arizona by 1848:

> [T]he most populous Native American [Nations] living in the region were the Pueblos, Navajos, and Apaches. The eastern Pueblos lived in villages along the Rio Grande in New Mexico and spoke the languages Keres, Piro, Tiwa, Towa, Tewa, and Tano. Farther to the west were the Zuñi Pueblo—just to the east of the New Mexico border with Arizona—the Hopi villages, located on three mesas in northern Arizona . . . In the land between the Rio Grande Pueblos and the Hopis and Zuñis lived the Athapaskan-speaking Navajos. . . . The Apaches, also Athapaskan speaking, lived in northeastern New Mexico and in southwestern New Mexico and southeastern Arizona and Sonora (Mexico). The western Apaches were culturally more similar to the Navajos than were the more northern, Plains-influenced Apache groups, they were organized into bands, and they farmed but also relied on raiding into Sonora and Chihuahua to supplement their food supply.[63]

By 1860, only ruins and desolate cattle remained. What used to be a welcoming trade relationship with raids and counterraids between Indigenous Nations and settlers turned out to be, as mentioned earlier, a bloody war rather than a war–peace relationship.[64]

Even though David Meriwether, the third territorial governor, tried to solve the problem through treaty negotiations and reserve implementation, both proved to be a complete failure. In addition, intertribal warfare escalated as the Pueblo Nations and New Mexico settlers witnessed for over fifteen years how the Apache, Ute, and Navajo Nations continued to raid, despite help from the United States (US) army and New Mexicans. The total toll amounted to from two to three hundred deaths and approximately one million dollars of property lost in cattle, mules, horses, and sheep. The peace promise once made by US authorities, like the one made by general Kearny, was more utopian than real. Even with the "three thousand soldiers and five Indian agents work[ing] hard to make the promise come true, but the end was nowhere in sight and the toll continued."[65]

Despite this grim scenario, St. John argues that US officials (e.g., Boundary Commissioners) envisioned the renaissance of the ranching economy in the borderland under the United States control.[66] In other words, this state project had two driving objectives: to exercise control over the borderlands by ceasing Apache, Comanche, and other Indigenous Nations raiding activities and to connect this region to markets in the United States.[67] Thus, the process of creating borderlands pastoral economy was indeed a bloody business that included, but was not limited to, violent confrontations and displacements of Indigenous Nations from their territories, the establishment of ranches as "productive pastoral landscape[s]" through private property, access to water resources, and building the transcontinental railroad.[68]

For instance, by the period from 1882 to 1886, the United States and Mexican authorities agreed to cooperate in campaigns that drove Apaches to their reservations and allowed their persecution across either side of the border. As Dilworth emphasizes, a more fluid process of negotiation also took place in the United States, where some interests and needs were met at both ends: the Apache and the Anglo-American settlers/ranchers.[69] This process of giving and taking in negotiations could be interpreted, as White noted, as "the middle ground" between the Anglo-Americans and Indigenous Nations.[70] For instance, some Apache Nations allowed ranching and mining activities on their lands in exchange for payments made by Anglos; however, the Civil War (1861) altered these dynamics.[71] The following excerpts illustrate why it was almost impossible to terminate something that hostile Indigenous Nations enjoyed, as Utley interpreted, "the best of two worlds" both at peace and at war:

> The Kiowas Nations and Comanches continued to enjoy their double standard of peace on the Arkansas and bloody war against the Frontier settlers of Texas....[72]

> Each year on the Arkansas they [Kiowas Nations and Comanches Nations] received $10,000 worth of presents, including guns and ammunition, and each year they killed and plundered in Texas as they had always done. As Texas Agent Robert Neighbors complained in 1855 $10,000 would not pay for the

> property [. . .] these same Indians had stolen in Texas during the preceding three months. . . .[73]

> There were still thousands of Comanches on the plains . . . when large-scale raiding began anew in 1854, all seemed chaos. Some Comanche rancherías fragmented into small parties that struck settlements across Texas, while others raided into Mexico, skirting Fort Clark on the Nueces . . . Comanches raided the Delawares, Choctaws, and Cherokees in Indian Territory and were in turn raided by them . . . They raided the Kickapoos and Seminoles but at times also teamed up with them to form multiethnic raiding gangs[; and] plundered Apache rancherías along the Rio Grande but used Mescalero rancherías as way stations to Mexico.[74]

By the late nineteenth century, the ranching economy boomed through the synergy of multiple yet entwined processes: the decrease of Apache raiding, the arrival and settlement of new ranchers, and railroad usage. The railroad included the Southern Pacific Railroad (1880), which transported "hundreds of thousands of cattle" to other US locations.[75] Despite the ranching economy effect, Kiowas, Comanches, and other Indigenous Nations adapted to circumstances and constraints while continuing with their traditional activities of using and relating with their territories. In order to survive, and as Limerick accurately notes, many Indigenous Nations had to accommodate to the changing conditions, and at the same time, they kept their Indigenous traditions alive.[76]

The "bloody process"[77] escalated when the Union launched warfare to exterminate the Apache Nations for preserving the service of the overland mail, and by 1871 the United States confined Apache Nations to reservations.[78] In southwestern New Mexico and central Arizona this represented another solution to border raiding and to putting an end to the nomadic, violent, and savage life of "hostile Indians."[79] Settlement and farming were supposed to turn them into peaceful and "assimilated" Indians, even though this process of removal was both highly contested and negotiated. The removal of Indigenous Nations from their Southwest territories into reserved land was also a painful process that included, but was not limited to, negotiation (e.g., signed treaties), resistance, and death. Moreover, the removal or "extermination" of Indigenous Nations was viewed as necessary in the name of civilization and/or to protect US citizens.[80] For instance, in 1878 approximately five thousand Apache were displaced to San Carlos Reservation or San Carlos Apache Nation, located on the Gila and San Carlos Rivers in Arizona. Others resisted by not moving to the Rez. Despite Indigenous people's interest in establishing peaceful relations with the Anglos, settlers intruded on reservation land to "mine deposits of copper, silver, and gold and to farm."[81] Resistance escalated through confrontations, and the Chiricahua leader, Geronimo, is a good example. In 1882, he left the San Carlos Nation and joined, along with his followers, Victorio, the Mimbreño leader in Mexico. For four years, Geronimo and his hostile followers attacked Anglo settlers and the United States army, until 1886, when he surrendered to General Nelson A. Miles and was sent to prison in Florida.[82]

Despite the increasing number of Indigenous people who experienced forced displacement through the reservation system across the US–Mexican border, their nomadic life persisted, including their indigenous constructions of territory and nationhood.[83] Indigenous Nations neither vanished nor remained the same; rather, they continued to "build their own collective subjectivities and social boundaries in a politicized process that expresse[d] not only their resistance but also their cultural continuity."[84] Precisely this pattern of "persistence and change"[85] is what Indigenous Nations experienced while conveying overarching social relations and activities such as raiding, trading, hunting, gathering, warfare, farming, ceremonial burial, and trading grounds, which were practiced in porous territories where they found themselves within a "forced transnational" context between themselves, Mexico, and the United States. My argument, thus far presented clearly, gives force to create new epistemologies about transnationalism across the Mexican and American borderlands.

New Epistemologies: TransNa

Truett and Young stated that being a resident of the Mexican North (as well as the American South and American North) in the modern age meant to be entwined in the "web of transnational relationships" where "statesmen, entrepreneurs, and capitalists in the United States and Mexico made laws, investments, and transnational alliances to facilitate the flow of technology, capital, and workers across the border."[86] The modern and postmodern "web of transnational relationships" must also include contemporary Indigenous Nations as well. The latter are caught between their Nations and the nation-states of Mexico, United States, and Canada. For some Indigenous people, being transnational across political borderlands might entail being "FirstNa" or "TransNa," as Helen Abraham articulated while thinking about her experiences of migration as an Oneida Nation member:

> I was born here in London, [Ontario] in [the] Victoria Hospital. My family moved out of the reserve [she is referring to the Oneida Nation settlement located in Southwestern, Ontario, Canada] in 1959 and [her parents] decided to live their life for God. My dad went to bible school in Minnesota for some

> years. We were out [of the] reserve for about 7 years maybe. . . . We were seven [and] we all moved back in 1969 but then my two older brothers decided they didn't like it and moved back to Canada. They were older 14 or 15 maybe. All my relatives live on reserve, except for my Mom and Dad [they passed away]. I have two brothers and a younger sister living there [Oneida Nation].
>
> I was four when we moved [to the Oneida settlement] and I didn't know anybody, not even my own family when we moved. . . . So coming back and moving forward was really, really different. I went to the school on the reserve and it was like . . . "the new kid."[87] (Helen Abraham, interview 2013)

She currently goes back and forth from Canada to the United States to visit her relatives, to attend community and religious events, and for educational purposes. So when someone asks her "Where are you from?" she says, "I'm displaced" . . . "a FirstNa" [Nation] or "TransNa" [Nation]. Her "transnationalism" is the outcome of migration experiences similar to other stories that I have previously addressed.[88] I think her grassroots contribution to transnationalism is illuminating given that theory is meaningless without the empirical data. Her thoughts encourage my research to continue this line of analysis and to think about "TransNa" as contemporary Indigenous Nations' experiences of transnationalism across Mexico, the United States, and Canada.

CONCLUSION

The experiences of "forced transnationalism" by Apache Nations, Comanche Nations, and Navajo Nations, among others, demand our attention for understanding the fragmentation, complexity, and porosity of political borderlands where Indigenous Nations within nation-states experienced not only change but continuity in using and relating with their own territories. My work not only expanded the overarching meanings of transnationalism but added flexibility to the concept and noted the urgency for crafting theoretical constructs from grassroots perspectives, even though these might entail multiplicity and fragmentation. It is my hope that the aforementioned argument will encourage further refinements and critiques that will lead to a better understanding of Indigenous Nations and transnationalism across borderlands. This book includes the fruitful contributions from Indigenous and non-Indigenous scholars and communities that might significantly redefine the current epistemologies that we use in our attempts to explain the complexities of human experiences, histories, and transnationalism. My emphasis on Indigenous "forced transnationalism" is an attempt to complicate the current model of transnationalism studies and to search for alternative grassroots frameworks.

Notes

1. Richard White, "Frederick Jackson Turner and Buffalo Bill," in *The Frontier in American Culture: An Exhibition at the Newberry Library*, August 26, 1994–January 7 1995, ed. James Grossman (Los Angeles, Cal.: University of California Press, 1994), 52; Patricia Nelson Limerick, "The Adventures of the Frontier in the Twentieth Century," in *The Frontier in American Culture: An Exhibition at the Newberry Library*, August 26, 1994–January 7 1995, ed. James Grossman (Los Angeles, Cal.: University of California Press, 1994), 67–102; and "Turnerians All: The Dream of a Helpful History in an Intelligible World," *American Historical Review* 100 (1995), 697–716. See also Brigitte Georgi-Findlay, *The Frontiers of Women's Writing: Women's Narratives and the Rhetoric of Westward Expansion.* (Tucson, Ariz.: The University of Arizona Press, 1996); Albert Hurtado, *Indian Survival on the California Frontier* (New Haven, Conn.: Yale University Press, 1988); Mary Ellen Jones, ed., *The American Frontier: Opposing Viewpoints* (San Diego, CA: Greenhaven Press, 1994); Mary Lawlor, "The Fictions of Daniel Boone," in *Desert, Garden, Margin, Range: Literature on the American Frontier*, ed. Eric Heyne (New York: Twayne Publishers, 1992), 29–43; Patricia Nelson, *The Legacy of Conquest: The Unbroken Past of the American West* (New York: W.W. Norton & Company, 1987); Richard Slotkin, "Nostalgia and Progress: Theodore Roosevelt's Myth of the Frontier," *American Quarterly* 33 (1981), 608–37; Robert Utley, *The Indian Frontier of the American West 1846–1890. Histories of the American West* (Albuquerque: University of New Mexico Press, 1984); and White, "Frederick Jackson Turner and Buffalo Bill," 7–65.

2. Turner (1893) gave closure to the expanding American Frontier, where images of "taming" wilderness through civilization and democracy were consistent with his depiction of the west [Frederick Jackson Turner, *The Frontier in American History* (Lavergne, Tenn.: CreateSpace, 1920)]. However, more than giving closure, the "Frontier thesis" meant economic expansion, settlement, opportunity, dispossession, and tension [for a well-elaborated Turnerian and borderland theory, see Phil Bellfy, *Three Fires Unity: The Anishnaabeg of the Lake Huron Borderlands* (Lincoln: University of Nebraska Press, 2011); Kerwin Lee Klein, *Frontiers of Historical Imagination: Narrating the European Conquest of Native America, 1890–1990* (Los Angeles: University of California, Press, 1997); Limerick, "The Adventures of the Frontier" and "Turnerians All"; and Frederick Jackson Turner, "The Significance of the Frontier in American History," in *The Frontier in American History* (1920).

3. Leah Dilworth, *Imagining Indians in the Southwest: Persistent Visions of a Primitive Past* (Washington, D.C.: Smithsonian Institution Press, 1996), 6; and White, "Frederick Jackson Turner and Buffalo Bill," 12–13. In addition, "Progress came to be seen [by whites] as rise from savagery to civilization" (Utley, *The Indian Frontier of the American West*, 333).

4. Klein, *Frontiers of Historical Imagination*, 7.

5. Limerick, "The Adventures of the Frontier," 90. For details on the concept of *La Frontera*, see Gloria Anzaldua, *Borderlands La Frontera: The New Mestiza*, 3rd ed. (San Francisco: Aunt Lute Books, 2007); and Bellfy, *Three Fires*, for details on Native people in the borderlands, specifically in the Lake Huron borderlands area.

6. Limerick, "The Adventures of the Frontier," 90.

7. I use the term *political borderlands* to refer, in principle, to State-driven projects of crafting "borderlands" from above, but with the premise in mind that the material and social processes involved in crafting these borders were also from below. These processes were conducted in a much more fluid, contentious, blurred, and transnational manner, as this study intends to demonstrate. Some scholars have emphasized the diversity of social actors in borderland studies of the United States, Mexico, and Canada. This model deconstructs the "single nation–based inquiry model" for studying borderlands and highlights borderlands as porous, contentious, blurred, and transnational. Benjamin Johnson and Andrew Graybill, "Introduction: Borders and Their Historians in North America," in *Bridging National Borders in Northern America*, eds. Benjamin Johnson and Andrew Graybill (Durham, N.C.: Duke University Press and the William P. Clements Center for Southwest Studies, Southern Methodist University, 2010), 1–29; Samuel Truett and Elliott Young, eds., *Continental Crossroads: Remapping U.S.-Mexico Borderlands History* (Durham, N.C.: Duke University Press, 2004). The aforementioned model for studying borderlands is quite different from the "Boltonian borderlands" studies [John Francis Bannon, *The Spanish Borderlands Frontier, 1513–1821* (New York: Rinehart and Winston, 1970); and

Herbert E. Bolton, *The Spanish Borderlands: A Chronicle of Old Florida and the Southwest* (New Haven, Conn.: Yale University Press, 1921)]. The latter framed and constructed national borderland histories beyond the British Empire and eastern North America, and yet he constrained the area of study to the "Spanish colonial project" (Johnson and Graybill, "Introduction: Borders and Their Historians," 4). By doing so, the "Boltonians" excluded the Canadian, Chicana, and Indigenous Nations borderland studies. See, for instance, Anzaldua, *Borderlands La Frontera*; Bellfy, *Three Fires Unity*; Benjamin Johnson and Andrew R. Graybill Johnson, eds., *Bridging National Borders in Northern America*. For an ample critique on Bolton and Turner's work, see Alberto Hurtado, "Parkmanizing the Spanish Borderlands: Bolton, Turner, and the Historians World," *Western Historical Quarterly* 26 (1995): 149–67; and David Weber, "Turner, the Boltonians, and the Borderlands," *American Historical Review* 91 (1986): 66–81.

8. Raine Bauböck, *Transnational Citizenship: Membership and Rights in International Migration.* (Brookfield: Edward Elgar Publishing Company, 1994): 20.

9. Linda Basch, Nina Glick Schiller, and Cristina Szanton Blanc, *Nations Unbound: Transnational Projects, Postcolonial Predicaments and Deterritorialized Nation-States* (London: Routledge, 1994), 7.

10. The "transnational (or trans-imperial) networks of violence and exchange" were practiced not only by the Comanche Nations but also by other Indigenous Nations, who "moved goods [e.g., commerce, gift exchanges, pillaging, tribute extracting], ideas, and people [e.g., slave raiding, ransoming, adoption] across ecological, ethnic, and political boundaries." Pekka Hämäläinen, *Comanche Empire* (New Haven, Conn.: Yale University Press, 2008), 8.

11. Lloyd Wong and Vic Satzewich, "Introduction: The Meaning and Significance of Transnationalism" in *Transnational Identities and Practices in Canada*, eds. Vic Satzewich and Lloyd Wong (British Columbia: University of British Columbia Press, 2006), 2. For an ample discussion on transnationalism, see Thomas Faist, "Transnationalization in International Migration: Implications for the Study of Citizenship and Culture," *Ethnic and Racial Studies* 23 (2000): 189–222; Michael Kearney, "The Local and the Global: The Anthropology of Globalization and Transnationalism," *Annual Review of Anthropology* 24 (1995): 547–65; Peter Kivisto, "Theorizing Transnational Immigration: A Critical Review of Current Efforts," *Ethnic and Racial Studies* 24 (2001): 549–77; Diana G. Palmerín Velasco, " (Re)pensar el género y el transnacionalismo en el estudio de la migración: una propuesta basada en la experiencia vivida y la subjetividad," en *Debates sobre Transnacionalismo*, Coordinado por Velia Cecilia Bobes, Versión Kindle (México, D.F.: Facultad Lationamericana de Ciencias Sociales [FLACSO], 2013); Alejandro Portes, "Introduction: The Debates and Significance of Immigrant Transnationalism," *Global Networks* 1 (2001): 181–93; and Alejandro Portes, Luis Guarnizo y Patricia Landolt, "The Study of Transnationalism: Pitfalls and Promise of an Emergent Research Field," *Ethnic and Racial Studies* 22 (1999): 217–37.

12. Basch, Glick Schiller, and Szanton Blanc, *Nations Unbound Transnational Projects*, 8.

13. Jorge Duany, *Blurred Borders: Transnational Migration between the Hispanic Caribbean and the United States* (Chapel Hill: The University of North Carolina Press, 2011), and *The Puerto Rican Nation on the Move: Identities on the Island and in the United States* (Chapel Hill: The University of North Carolina Press, 2002).

14. Following Valaskakis (2005), I use the term *Native Nations* in order to talk about tribes and/or bands in North America. To a certain extent, it also pertains to the legal "recognition" of these Nations by the federal governments in the United States and Canada. Gail Guthrie Valaskakis, *Indian Country: Essays on Contemporary Native Culture* (Waterloo, Ontario: Wilfrid Laurier University Press, 2005). See also Jose Barreiro, *Thinking in Indian: A John Mohawk Reader* (Golden, Colo.: Fulcrum Publishing, 2010). For another critique on sovereignty, see Taiaiake Alfred, *Peace, Power and Righteousness: An Indigenous Manifesto* (Oxford: Oxford University Press, 1999).

15. Audra Simpson, "Paths Toward a Mohawk Nation: Narratives of Citizenship and Nationhood in Kahnawake," in *The Indigenous Experience: Global Perspectives*, ed. Roger Maaka and Chris Andersen (Toronto, Ontario: Canadian Scholar's Press Inc., 2006), 176, 185.

16. Anderson, Benedict, *Imagined Communities: Reflections on the Origin and Spread of Nationalism*, rev. ed. (London: Verso, 2006), 7, 12.

17. Valaskakis, *Essays on Contemporary Native Culture*, 214–15; and Alfred, *Peace, Power and Righteousness*, 47. See also Taiaiake Alfred, *Heeding the Voices of Our Ancestors: Kahnawake Mohawk Politics and the Rise of Native Nationalism* (Toronto, Ontario: Oxford University Press, 1995); Barreiro, *Think-*

ing in Indian; Renya Ramirez, *Native Hubs Culture, Community, and Belonging in Silicon Valley and Beyond* (London: Duke University Press, 2007); James Brooks, "Life Proceeds from the Name: Indigenous People and The Predicaments of Hybridity," in *Clearing a Path: Theorizing the Past in Native American Studies*, ed. Nancy Shoemaker (London: Routledge, 2002); Glen Sean Coulthard, *Facing the Challenge of Freedom: Dene Nationalism and the Politics of Cultural Recognition*, Unpublished Master Thesis (Victoria, B.C.: University of Victoria Indigenous Governance Program, 2003); and Simpson, "Paths Toward a Mohawk Nation."

18. James F. Brooks, *Captives and Cousins: Slavery, Kinship and Community in the Southwest Borderlands* (Chapel Hill: University of North Carolina Press, 2001); and Hämäläinen, *Comanche Empire*, 279.

19. See Brooks, *Captives and Cousins*; Limerick, *The Legacy of Conquest*; Peter Mancall and James Merrell, eds., *American Encounters: Natives and Newcomers from European Contact to Indian Removal 1500–1850* (London: Routledge, 2000); William McLoughlin, "Cherokee Anomie, 1794–1810: New Roles for Red Men, Red Women, and Black Slaves," in *American Encounters: Natives and Newcomers from European Contact to Indian Removal 1500–1850*, 452–76; Hämäläinen, *Comanche Empire*; Theda Perdue, "Cherokee Women and the Trail of Tears," in *American Encounters: Natives and Newcomers from European Contact to Indian Removal 1500–1850*, 527–40; Weber, *The Mexican Frontier*; Richard White, *The Middle Ground: Indians, Empires, and Republics in the Great Lakes Region, 1650–1815* (New York: Cambridge University Press, 1991); and Richard White, "The Winning of the West: The Expansion of the Western Sioux in the Eighteenth and Nineteenth Centuries," in *American Encounters: Natives and Newcomers from European Contact to Indian Removal 1500–1850*, 541–62.

20. Utley, *The Indian Frontier of the American West*, 11; see also Hämäläinen, *The Comanche Empire*.

21. White, "The Winning of the West," 556.

22. See, for instance, Brooks, *Captives and Cousins*; Hämäläinen, *The Comanche Empire;* White, *The Middle Ground* and "The Winning of the West."

23. Hurtado, *Indian Survival on the California Frontier*, 9.

24. See Jack Forbes, *Columbus and Other Cannibals: The Wetiko Disease of Exploitation, Imperialism and Terrorism* (New York: Seven Stories Press, 2008).

25. See Weber, *The Mexican Frontier*, for an ample understanding of the Mexican Frontier.

26. Lina Sunseri, *Being Again of One Mind* (Vancouver: University of British Columbia Press, 2010), 25.

27. For Indian territoriality, see Bethel Saler and Carolyn Podruchny, "Glass Curtains and Storied Landscapes: The Fur Trade, National Boundaries and Historians," in *Bridging National Borders in Northern America*, eds. Benjamin Johnson and Andrew Graybill (Durham: Duke University Press and the William P. Clements Center for Southwest Studies, Southern Methodist University, 2010), 292. See also Patricia Albers and Jeanne Kay, "Sharing the Land: A Study in American Indian Territoriality," in *A Cultural Geography of North American Indians*, eds. Thomas E. Ross and Tyrel G. Moore (Boulder, Colo.: Westview Press, 1987), 47–91; Leroy Little Bear, "Aboriginal Paradigms: Implications for Relationships to Land and Treaty Making," in *Advancing Aboriginal Claims: Visions/Strategies/Directions*, ed. Kerry Wilkins (Saskatoon: Purich, 2004).

28. Utley, *The Indian Frontier of the American West*, 59, 125. In 1830, President Jackson enforced the policy of removal, originally promoted by Thomas Jefferson through the Indian Removal Act, which "authorized the President to negotiate cessions of Indian Land in the East and transportation of native peoples west of the Mississippi." Perdue, "Cherokee Women and the Trail of Tears," 527. See also Alfred Cave, "Abuse of Power: Andrew Jackson and the Indian Removal Act of 1830," *Historian* 65 (2003): 1330–53. Thus, Native Nations experienced the painful and deathly process of removal, or walking the "Trail of Tears," from their eastern territories to the western region beyond the Mississippi River to the "Indian Territory" or, as Utley stated, to the "Permanent Indian Frontier." Utley, *The Indian Frontier of the American West* 84; Len Green, "Trail of Tears from Mississippi Walked by our Choctaw Ancestors," *Bishinik* (1995): 4, http://web.archive.org/web/20080604005108/http://www.tc.umn.edu/~mboucher/mikebouchweb/choctaw/trtears.htm, accessed June 5, 2011; and Perdue, "Cherokee Women and the Trail of Tears."

29. Utley, *The Indian Frontier of the American West*, 59–60.

30. Utley, *The Indian Frontier of the American West*, 58.

31. Dilworth, *Imagining Indians in the Southwest*; Hämäläinen, *Comanche Empire*; Rachel St. John, "Divided Ranges: Trans-Border Ranches and the Creation of National Space along the Western

Mexico-U.S. Border," in *Bridging National Borders in Northern America*, eds. Benjamin Johnson and Andrew Graybill Durham (Durham, N.C.: Duke University Press and the William P. Clements Center for Southwest Studies, Southern Methodist University, 2010): 116–40; Weber, *The Mexican Frontier*, 83; and Utley, *The Indian Frontier of the American West.*

32. Alfred, *Peace, Power and Righteousness* and *Heeding the Voices*; Simpson, "Paths Toward a Mohawk Nation"; Barreiro, *Thinking in Indian*; Bruce Clark, *Native Liberty, Crown Sovereignty: The Existing Aboriginal Right of Self-Government in Canada* (Quebec: McGill Queens University Press, 1990); Doug George-Kanentiio, *Iroquois Culture & Commentary* (Santa Fe, N.M.: Clear Light Publisher, 2000); Patty Loew, *Indian Nations of Wisconsin: Histories of Endurance and Renewal* (Madison: Wisconsin Historical Society Press, 2001); Sunseri, *Being Again of One Mind*; Valaskakis, *Essays on Contemporary Native Culture.*

33. Partha Chatterjee, *The Nation and Its Fragments: Colonial and Postcolonial Histories* (Princeton: Princeton University Press, 1993); Duany, *Puerto Rican Nation on the Move*; Nestor García Canclini, *Culturas Híbridas: Estrategias para Entrar y Salir de la Modernidad* (Mexico City: Grijalbo, 1990).

34. Homi Bhabha, ed., *Nation and Narration* (London: Routledge, 1990), 3.

35. Valaskakis, *Essays on Contemporary Native Culture*, 23. As Elder Dan Smoke, Seneca Nation, expressed, "We are all Treaty People . . . we have to educate the Canadian and American public that we are all Treaty People" (personal communication, 2012).

36. Sunseri, *Being Again of One Mind;* Simpson, "Paths Toward a Mohawk Nation." See also Kiera Lander, "Women and Blackfoot Nationalism," *Journal of Canadian Studies* 35 (2000): 35–60; Valaskakis, *Essays on Contemporary Native Culture.*

37. Sunseri, *Being Again of One Mind.*

38. Despite Spanish and Mexican authorities conferring the status of nations to errant people in the Mexican Frontier, Weber (*The Mexican Frontier*) fails to provide further elaboration and critique of his Western model of nationhood where "neither Apaches nor Comanches [nomadic and hostile Indians] possessed a central political structure or functioned as a unit or a "nation." On the other hand, Hämäläinen emphasizes precisely the political structure of the Comanches (see Hämäläinen, *Comanche Empire*, for details). See also Valaskakis, *Essays on Contemporary Native Culture*, 214.

39. Utley, *The Indian Frontier of the American West*; Weber, *The Mexican Frontier*, 83. One self-imposed limitation in my analysis is the exclusion of California and Texas. For borderland studies in these areas, see Miguel Angel Gonzalez-Quiroga, "Conflict and Cooperation in the Making of Texas Mexico Border Society, 1840–1880," in *Bridging National Borders in Northern America*, eds. Benjamin Johnson and Andrew Graybill (Durham, N.C.: Duke University Press and the William P. Clements Center for Southwest Studies, Southern Methodist University, 2010), 33–58; Hurtado, *Indian Survival on the California Frontier*; Benjamin Johnson, "The Plan de San Diego Uprising and the Making of the Modern Texas-Mexican Borderlands," in *Continental Crossroads Remapping U.S.-Mexico Borderlands History* (Durham, N.C.: Duke University Press, 2004): 273–98; Raul Ramos, 2004. "Finding the Balance: Bexar in Mexican/Indian Relations," in *Continental Crossroads: Remapping U.S.-Mexico Borderlands History* (Durham, N.C.: Duke University Press, 2004), 35–66; and David Weber, *The Mexican Frontier 1821–1846: The American Southwest under Mexico* (Albuquerque: University of New Mexico Press, 1982).

40. Hämäläinen, *Comanche Empire*, 15.

41. Limerick, "The Adventures of the Frontier," 90.

42. Bannon, *The Spanish Borderlands*; Hurtado, *Indian Survival on the California Frontier*; Ramon Gutierrez, *When Jesus Came, the Corn Mothers Went Away: Marriage, Sexuality, and Power in New Mexico 1500–1846* (Stanford, Calif.: Stanford University Press, 1991); Limerick, "The Adventures of the Frontier"; Weber, *The Mexican Frontier*; Richard White, *"It's Your Misfortune and None of my Own": A New History of the American West* (Norman: Oklahoma University Press, 1991). See Brooks, *Captives and Cousins*, for an ample study on borderlands cross-cultural economy of the southwest related to "kinship slavery," violence, and servitude. Neither Indigenous peoples nor the settlers had the power to rule one over the other.

43. Weber, *The Mexican Frontier*, 87.

44. Weber, *The Mexican Frontier*, 83.

45. Hämäläinen, *Comanche Empire*, 1.

46. Weber, *The Mexican Frontier*, 92.

47. Hämäläinen, *Comanche Empire*, 220.

48. Hämäläinen, *Comanche Empire*, 8.

49. Weber, *The Mexican Frontier*, 86.

50. Weber, *The Mexican Frontier*, 86. Military and political alliances among Indigenous Nations were complex endeavors. For instance, the Comanches and Utes bound their alliance through intermarriage and kinship ties, which proved useful, whereas the Utes encountered ongoing wars with the Navajos over "raiding and trading privileges in northern New Mexico," as Hämäläinen noted (*Comanche Empire*, 24).

51. Utley, *The Indian Frontier of the American West*, 20.

52. Weber, *The Mexican Frontier*.

53. See for instance, Jennifer Brown and Elizabeth Vibert, eds., *Reading Beyond Words: Contexts for Native History* (Peterborough, Ontario: Broadview Press, 2003); Julie Cruikshank, "Oral History, Narrative, Strategies, and Native American Historiography: Perspectives from the Yukon Territory, Canada," in *Clearing a Path: Theorizing the Past in Native American Studies*, ed. Nancy Shoemaker (London: Routledge, 2002), 3–28; and Peter Kulchyski, Don McCaskill, and David Newhouse, eds., *In the Words of Elders: Aboriginal Cultures in Transition* (Toronto: University of Toronto Press, 1999).

54. Hämäläinen, *Comanche Empire*, 13.

55. Weber, *The Mexican Frontier*, 94; see also Gutierrez, *When Jesus Came*.

56. White, *The Middle Ground*; and Weber, *The Mexican Frontier*, 94.

57. St. John, "Divided Ranges: Trans-Border Ranches," 119; Weber, *The Mexican Frontier*, 94.

58. Weber, *The Mexican Frontier*, 95.

59. Hämäläinen, *Comanche Empire*, 39, 320.

60. Hämäläinen, *Comanche Empire*, 220–21.

61. Gilles Deleuze and Felix Guattari, *A Thousand Plateaus*, translated by Brian Massumi (London and New York: Continuum, 1980).

62. Utley, *The Indian Frontier of the American West*, 30. See also Ralph Twitchell, *The History of the Military Occupation of the Territory of New Mexico from 1846 to 1851* (Ithaca, N.Y.: Cornell University Press, 2009).

63. Dilworth, *Imagining Indians in the Southwest*, 10–11.

64. St. John, "Divided Ranges: Trans-Border Ranches," 120; Utley, *The Indian Frontier of the American West*, 81.

65. Utley, *The Indian Frontier of the American West*, 58.

66. St. John, "Divided Ranges: Trans-Border Ranches."

67. St. John, "Divided Ranges: Trans-Border Ranches," 121.

68. St. John, "Divided Ranges: Trans-Border Ranches," 119. See also Grenville Goodwin and Keith Basso, *Western Apache Raiding and Warfare* (Tucson, Arizona: University of Arizona Press, 1971).

69. Dilworth, *Imagining Indians in the Southwest*, 12.

70. White, *The Middle Ground*.

71. Dilworth, *Imagining Indians in the Southwest*, 12.

72. Utley, *The Indian Frontier of the American West*, 122.

73. Utley, *The Indian Frontier of the American West*, 61.

74. Hämäläinen, *Comanche Empire*, 309.

75. St. John, "Divided Ranges: Trans-Border Ranches," 121.

76. Limerick, The Legacy of Conquest.

77. St. John, "Divided Ranges: Trans-Border Ranches," 119.

78. Dilworth, *Imagining Indians in the Southwest*, 12.

79. Dilworth, *Imagining Indians in the Southwest*; Edward H. Spicer, *Cycles of Conquest: The Impact of Spain, Mexico, and the United States on the Indians of the Southwest, 1533–1960* (Tucson, Arizona: University of Arizona Press, 1962).

80. Howard Lamar, "From Bondage to Contract: Ethnic Labor in the American West, 1600–1890," in *The Countryside in the Age of Capitalist Transformation: Essays in the Social History of Rural America*, eds. Steven Hahn and Jonathan Prude (Chapel Hill, N.C.: University of North Carolina Press, 1985); Richard Slotkin, *The Fatal Environment: The Myth of the Frontier in the Age of Industrialization, 1600–*

1890 (Middletown, Conn.: Wesleyan University Press, 1985); Utley, *The Indian Frontier of the American West.*

81. Dilworth, *Imagining Indians in the Southwest,* 12.

82. Dilworth, *Imagining Indians in the Southwest,* 13; Francis Paul Prucha, *The Great Father: The U.S. Government and the American Indian* (Lincoln: University of Nebraska Press, 1984), 652.

83. Keith Basso, *Wisdom Sits in Places* (New Mexico: University of New Mexico Press, 1996); Dilworth, *Imagining Indians in the Southwest*; Gutierrez, *When Jesus Came*; St. John, "Divided Ranges: Trans-Border Ranches"; and Saler and Podruchny, "Glass Curtains and Storied Landscapes."

84. Valaskakis, *Essays on Contemporary Native Culture,* 212.

85. Limerick, *The Legacy of Conquest,* 189.

86. Truett and Young, "Introduction," *Continental Crossroads Remapping,* 9.

87. Personal communication and interview, 2006, 2008. See Sunseri, *Being Again of One Mind,* for a detailed history on the Oneida Nation; See James Cliffton, *A Place of Refuge for All Time: Migration of the American Potawatomi into Upper Canada 1830–1850* (Ottawa: National Museum of Canada, 1975); and Roger Nichols, *Indians in the United States and Canada: A Comparative History* (Lincoln: University of Nebraska Press, 1998).

88. "First Nations in Canada: An Emerging Form of Transnationalism," paper presented at the Annual Meeting of the American Anthropological Association (AAA), Four Points Sheraton and Marriott Hotels, New Orleans, Louisiana, 2010.

Chapter 3

In Search of Juan Antonio Ignacio Baca, a Pueblo Participant in the Shifting Politics of Nineteenth-Century New Mexico*

Gary Van Valen

In the North American West, the first native peoples to be colonized by a European power lived in what is now northern Mexico and the US Southwest. The colonizing power, the Spanish, called them Indians (*indios*) and their towns, *pueblos*. Under Spanish rule, the people we now call the Pueblo Indians of New Mexico retained local ethnicities while participating in a much wider world. Pueblos crossed all kinds of boundaries by interacting with non-Indians as well as other Indians; by leaving Indian land and culture for Spanish society, either temporarily or permanently; by becoming bilingual; or by forming new groups with hybrid identities. During the nineteenth century, boundaries crossed *them*, and they were forced to adjust to new realities as New Mexico passed from Spanish to Mexican to United States jurisdiction. This chapter is an attempt, using evidence from both recorded oral histories and government documentation, to uncover the life story of a Pueblo individual who lived all of these experiences.

Memories of Something Big

In 1880, the Swiss-American ethnographer and archaeologist Adolph Bandelier began several years' work in New Mexico's Cochiti Pueblo and its surroundings. Although he was principally concerned with ancient ruins and current culture, his Cochiti informant, Juan José Montoya, occasionally offered information on the pueblo's more recent history. On October 24, 1880, Montoya told Bandelier of a tradition of internal dissention during Mexico's struggle for independence from Spain. According to Montoya:

* Research for this chapter was funded by the University of New Mexico's Latin American and Iberian Institute through a Richard E. Greenleaf Visiting Library Scholar Award, and by the University of West Georgia through a Research Travel Grant. I would like to thank both institutions for their generous support.

> [A]t that time (1819) there were two parties in the pueblo. One of them, infected by the uprising of the Mexicans against Spain, sought the rights of citizenship, and sold many of their lands to Mexicans; therefore the Mexican population of Cochiti. Three years previous, the first fever epidemic occurred, and there was great strife in the pueblo. Both parties sent delegates to Guadalajara, where the matter was settled . . .[1]

On April 12, 1882, Montoya again spoke about the same subject, with additional detail on the identity of the two "parties":

> [T]hose of the Estufa of "Shyu-amo" were always against the Pueblo, and that in consequence of it, there had been constant squabbles between them and the "Tanyi." . . . The former went to Mexico to secure the citizenship of the Pueblo, still he says it was in the times of Spain. The latter sent a delegation also, who reached the City of Mexico after the former had already ret'd home. The citizenship was revoked, but in the meantime the Mexicans had already occupied the lands near Peña Blanca, and the Pueblo was split up.[2]

Cochiti Pueblo as it appeared in 1879–80. "View of Cochiti Pueblo, New Mexico." Credit: J. K. Hillers, Courtesy Palace of the Governors Photo Archives (NMHM/DCA), negative number 002493.

Juan José Montoya, Cochiti governor and informant to Adolph Bandelier. Detail from "Juan José Montoya and daughter Adelaido Montoya, Cochiti Pueblo, New Mexico." Credit: George C. Bennett, Courtesy Palace of the Governors Photo Archives (NMHM/DCA), negative number 002490.

The Shyu-amo represent the Sho'ame, or Turquoise people, and the Tanyi are the Dañi, or Pumpkin people. These moieties or kiva groups traditionally organized dances, held meetings in kivas (called *estufas* in Spanish), and often (but not always) alternated offices annually in the pueblo government. Montoya was a Pumpkin member and, perhaps not surprisingly, claimed that his moiety had acted for the good of the pueblo.

Juan José Montoya's accounts reflect a memory of something big, of internal political turmoil linked to the granting of citizenship and of appeals made to higher authorities in Mexico. He interpreted this turmoil in terms of moiety politics without naming any individuals. Thirty years earlier, however, other oral traditions circulated concerning the same events at Cochiti that do mention a specific person.

In April 1852, John Greiner, the Acting Superintendent of Indian Affairs in the United States' recently acquired territory of New Mexico, became concerned over the actions of a certain Cochiti man. Greiner received reports from several different pueblos that this man was traveling among them. On April 2, the governor and another man from San Ildefonso Pueblo told Greiner that "the mischivious [sic] Indian who is among the pueblos, has gone to the Rio Abajo." On April 4, Carlos Vigil of Tesuque Pueblo named the man as "Antonio Baca the Indian from Cochiti" and claimed that Baca had "said nothing bad" at Tesuque.[3] On the same day, Greiner wrote to Indian agent Spruce M. Baird at Albuquerque "requesting him to see the Indian Juan Antonio Baca, who is among the Pueblos and ascertain what he is about," saying, "He needs watching closely—there is some devilment afoot."[4] On April 9, people from San Ildefonso told Greiner they had seen the man, whom they now called Ignacio Baca, and on the following day they offered to bring Baca to Greiner by force. Greiner refused, saying, "I can see him when he comes of his own accord."[5]

Finally, on April 12, Greiner received a detailed account of Baca's past and present activities from Pablo Romero of Taos Pueblo, which included the following:

> Pablo had heard when he visited Cochiti that this said Baca had been the ruin of that pueblo by his bad conduct, *[sic]* He had when governor of Cochiti about thirty years ago made a trip to old Mexico and when he returned pretended to have all authority to judge cases, and succeed[ed] in making a great deal of money off the pueblos of Santo Domingo and his own, some of the principal men resolved to find out the truth went to Old Mexico, and found his pretensions false.
>
> He was then expelled from the Pueblo of Cochiti he is looked upon as a great rascal . . .[6]

The information obtained by Greiner suggests that one man's actions lay behind the internal political turmoil remembered by Juan José Montoya in the 1880s. That man's full name was most likely Juan Antonio Ignacio Baca, although no one referred to him by all of his names at once. The accounts of Pablo Romero and Juan José Montoya agree that Cochiti Pueblo was divided by some political issue and that both sides took their cases to higher authorities in Mexico. Taken together, these recorded oral accounts from the 1850s and 1880s reflect a memory that something important had occurred in Cochiti around the transition from Spanish to Mexican rule, either in 1819 by Bandelier's estimate, or around 1822 in Greiner's account. The next question is, can documentary sources help clarify what happened and establish the exact date of these events?

The Historical Background

Documentation surviving from New Mexico's colonial period, although sometimes lacking in certain details, provides a coherent picture of politically active Pueblos with their own governments. The Spanish allowed the Pueblos to choose their own officials annually. Officials such as Pueblo governors (usually called by the diminutive *gobernadorcillos* to distinguish them from the Spanish provincial governor), war captains, *fiscales* (church assistants), and their respective lieutenants, appear in documents dealing with relations between Pueblos and the wider society. Although anthropological studies have shown that the religious leaders, called *caciques* by the Spanish, were the highest authority, they seldom appear in the documentation, as they did not handle relations with the Spanish government. Spanish documents more frequently refer to *principales*, Indian men regarded as "principals," or important men, in their pueblos. Ethnographic studies indicate that several pueblos, including Cochiti, have a council of principales made up of former governors, war captains, and fiscales. The council, as a reservoir of political experience, acted as an advisory body to the cacique.

During over two centuries of Spanish rule (1598–1680 and 1693–1821), Pueblos learned how to navigate the bureaucracy for their own interests. They knew that Spanish laws formally protected their land and water rights and provided for a *protector partidario de indios* to help them bring legal processes against Spaniards. Each pueblo was guaranteed its "league," meaning four square leagues of land centered on its church or cemetery cross, and Pueblos expected the local authorities to defend their rights.[7] When local Spanish officials failed to dispense justice, Pueblos commonly appealed to the provincial governor or to even higher authorities in Mexico against them. As a result, these officials could be put on trial for their misbehavior, as when Juan Antonio Baca, *Teniente de Justicia Mayor* (deputy justice) of the Rancho de Peña Blanca, was tried in September 1808 for intercepting a letter of complaint that Santo Domingo Indians had sent to the minister at Cochiti.[8] This Juan Antonio Baca (1783–1835) was the son of Luis María Cabeza de Baca (1754–1833), the Spanish hacendado of Peña Blanca, and should not be confused with the Cochiti man Juan Antonio Ignacio Baca.[9]

In addition to frequently pressing their legal claims, the Pueblos even helped choose their protector partidario at least once through political activism. In 1810, Juan José Quintana of Cochiti wrote to the *comandante general* of the *Provincias Internas Occidentales* (Western Interior Provinces) in the name of all of the Pueblos to request that Felipe Sandoval be named protector partidario. Quintana's understanding of the Spanish bureaucracy was imperfect: the comandante general in Chihuahua was the New Mexican governor's superior, but the protector partidario was subject to and appointed by the Audiencia (high court) of Guadalajara. Nevertheless, the audiencia agreed with the Pueblos' choice and named Sandoval protector after the comandante general forwarded Quintana's letter.[10] Quintana's activism takes on added significance when we realize that the office of protector partidario of New Mexico had been vacant since 1716, so that Quintana essentially had to discover that the position existed before petitioning that it be filled. As a result of the reestablishment of the office, the number of known legal cases involving Pueblo lands increased from only one in the 1770–1810 period to fourteen in the decade from 1810 to 1820.[11]

Recent research sheds some light on the complexity of Pueblo-Spanish relations. James Brooks and Tracy Brown have emphasized that ethnic identities were not timeless and that not all Pueblos were conservatives fighting to maintain tradition. Many Pueblos became at least partially Hispanized and joined settlements of either *genízaros* (Indians separated from their original communities) or Hispanos (who were generally called *vecinos* or *paisanos* in the documents). Some *ladinos* (Indians fluent in Spanish) left their pueblos permanently; some moved away but maintained ties; and some continued to reside in pueblos. Brown has even delineated a category of "Indian vecinos," meaning Indians who left their pueblos; adopted private landholding, the Spanish language, and Christianity; and gained legal recognition as vecinos. Given their experience with Spanish society, ladinos and Indian vecinos were the Pueblo individuals most likely to be politically active and to appear in Spanish documentation. Juan José Quintana of Cochiti was just such a person; he is identified as Indian in some documents and as vecino in others.[12] Juan Antonio Ignacio Baca must have been another: identified as Indian, serving as governor, and able to present a legal claim before higher Spanish authorities in Mexico. His name suggests some kind of relationship with the Spanish Bacas of Peña Blanca, and he could well have been the godson or even the mestizo son of one of the male members of that family.

The Spanish colonial system proved to be remarkably stable. After their final acceptance of Spanish rule in the 1690s, most Pueblos found that they could work within the Spanish system and solve their problems using Spanish law. The internal strife that later oral sources say beset Cochiti around 1819 or 1822 was not symptomatic of a stable colonial order, but rather of the upset of that order. As Juan José Montoya explicitly linked this strife to the granting of citizenship, we need to examine how the idea of citizenship, and the revolutionary liberal philosophy that promoted it, came to New Mexico.

The Spanish Liberal Reforms

In 1808, the Spanish Empire was thrown into turmoil when Napoleon deposed the Spanish king and placed his own brother on the throne. Although some Spaniards collaborated with the French, others resisted in the mountains or sought the protection of the British navy in the port of Cádiz. In the absence of a legitimate king, Spanish reformers called on representatives from the empire to form a congress, the Cortes of Cádiz, which assembled on September 24, 1810. The influence of the revolutionary idea of equality soon became apparent. On March 24, 1811, the Cortes decreed creoles (American-born Spaniards) and Indians to be equal to European Spaniards. On March 18, 1812, the Cortes produced the Constitution of Cádiz, which promoted the ideals of what would soon be termed liberalism. According to its Article 18, all those with ancestry on both sides from the Spanish dominions, and residing in those dominions, would be Spanish citizens. Europeans born in Spain or the Spanish colonies became citizens, as did Indians and mestizos, but people with any African ancestry were excluded in a maneuver intended to reduce representation of the colonies in favor of Spain itself.[13]

In further reforms, the Cortes promoted liberal ideas of political participation and private landownership. Its decree of May 23, 1812, required all towns of one thousand or more people to elect *ayuntamientos* (municipal governments headed by an *alcalde*). The decree of November 9, 1812, ordered the division of lands near pueblos among individual Indians, but not existing community lands and private lands. An exception was made when a pueblo's community lands were large and the population small, when up to one-half of community lands could be divided. The Cortes desired private landownership as a means to promote individual initiative and turn land into a commodity that could be bought and sold. The same decree also ended personal service (forced labor) requirements for Indians. The Cortes provided for a system of indirect representation through a series of elections in which all adult male citizens could vote. First were parish elections, where voters would choose *compromisarios* (delegates), *escrutadores* (scrutineers), and a secretary. The compromisarios would elect one or more parochial electors. Later, parochial electors would meet to elect a *partido* (district) elector, and partido electors would meet to elect a provincial *diputado* (deputy).[14]

New Mexico under the Constitution of Cádiz

In New Mexico, the Constitution of Cádiz was in effect from 1813 to 1815 and again from 1820 to 1822, with the restored absolutism of King Ferdinand VII in between. Mexico gained its independence from Spain in August 1821 and operated under the Constitution of Cádiz until the next year. As the recorded oral histories suggest dates of 1819 or 1822 for the turmoil at Cochiti, one might expect that it was linked to either the second implementation of the Constitution of Cádiz or to Mexican independence. In 1820–21, pueblo governors were renamed *alcaldes de barrio*. Spanish officials questioned whether Pueblos still needed a protector, and Pueblos expressed disapproval of Felipe Sandoval's successor as of 1817, Ignacio Sánchez Vergara.[15] The government called elections, which did not take place until after news arrived of the independence of Mexico. Independence was decided upon in central Mexico, and its announcement in New Mexico in September 1821 caused barely a ripple beyond the official celebration held in Santa Fe on January 6, 1822, during which Tesuque Indians danced on the plaza.[16] Elections took place in January 1822, following the Cádiz rules, and there are indications of political activism by the leaders of the pueblos of San Juan, Socorro del Sur, and Isleta del Sur in the same year.[17] The elected ayuntamiento of Cochiti experienced some turmoil between June and August of 1822, when the provincial government replaced its alcalde, called new elections due to local protests and "popular resistance" to the interim alcalde, and finally ordered the election of a new alcalde and the reinstatement of the previous year's other ayuntamiento members. However, the participants appear to have been Hispano vecinos of the Cochiti district rather than Pueblo Indians, and the documentary records are silent regarding Cochiti Pueblo itself.[18]

Therefore, we must consider the possibility that Bandelier's date of 1819 could be slightly off and that Pablo Romero's statement in 1852, that the events in Cochiti occurred "about thirty years ago," could be interpreted as meaning "at least thirty, but not as much as forty years ago." Additionally, Juan José Montoya linked memories of factional disputes to other events: a fever epidemic, which must have been the smallpox epidemic of 1816, and the destruction of Pueblo religious images by the Catholic priest in 1819. In 1880, Montoya told Bandelier that the first fever epidemic (1816) was followed by the destruction of the "idols" and party disputes (both in 1819), and a second fever epidemic (1820). But in 1882, Montoya said that the party disputes came first, followed by the 1816 epidemic and then by the 1819 surrender of "idols."[19] We should also remember that Montoya's account of citizenship granted and then revoked fits the pattern of a first implementation of the Constitution of Cádiz in 1813 and of its suppression by order of Ferdinand VII in 1815. With that in mind, let us examine how the Pueblos were affected by the Constitution of Cádiz from 1813 to 1815.

After receiving news of the new constitution in 1813, New Mexicans began to implement its provisions regarding the election of ayuntamientos and the election of provincial diputado through lower elections. These provisions were designed more for Spain and its more populous colonies than for a frontier province like New Mexico. Pueblo Indians were one quarter of the population and should have been quite prominent now that they were considered equal citizens. At first glance, we find that ayuntamientos often bore the names of pueblos, and parochial elections were often held at pueblos. Nevertheless, Spanish vecinos dominated the political processes. If ayuntamientos were named after pueblos, it was because they were nucleated settlements whose people could help meet the required population of one thousand. But vecinos lived in dispersed settlements around and between pueblos, and it was they who controlled the ayuntamientos. And if parochial elections were held at pueblos, it was because parishes were where Catholic priests lived, and most priests in New Mexico were assigned to pueblos.

Quite a bit of documentation survives on the series of elections that led to the choice of provincial diputado in 1814. Based on the guidelines of Cádiz, the government called elections in which voters would be those reputed as Spanish, pure Indians, and mestizos who did not violate any laws; those of African origin were barred from voting. As no one really knew how many people in New Mexico had African ancestors, a junta in Durango determined New Mexico's eligible population (for purposes of representation) by discounting half of its mestizo population. The right of Indians to participate was unquestioned.[20]

In the partido of Alameda, the parish of Sandia held elections on January 30, 1814, and chose sixteen compromisarios, including "Juan Roque Natural." From other sources we know that his name was Juan Roque Perico; "Natural" shows that he was considered Indian, but Tracy Brown uses him as an example of a late colonial Indian vecino. San Felipe held elections on February 6, and all eleven compromisarios had Spanish names. The twenty compromisarios that Cochiti elected on February 13 included Antonio Baca and Josef Quintana, almost certainly referring to Juan Antonio Ignacio Baca and Juan José Quintana, though neither was identified as Indian. All the parochial electors chosen were Hispanos (including the Spanish Juan Antonio Baca for Cochiti parish), and the partido elector they chose on February 15 was also Hispano.[21] So, Pueblo participation in the electoral process of Alameda partido was limited to three men, unless some of the Spanish-surnamed individuals were Indian and not identified as such. Each of the three had one foot in the Hispano world as ladinos or Indian vecinos, and none of them rose above compromisario.

Limited Pueblo participation was the rule throughout New Mexico as it was in Alameda partido. At Taos and Jemez, there was no apparent Indian participation. At Taos, although Spanish vecinos and Pueblos all heard the constitution read to them, only Spanish vecinos voted for compromisarios (again, unless some of the Spanish-surnamed individuals were Indian). Tesuque witnessed the most Pueblo participation when Spanish vecinos and Pueblos met to choose five compromisarios, three of whom were Pueblo.

Nevertheless, they elected a Spanish vecino parochial elector, and the electoral junta of Santa Fe partido ultimately rejected him, saying that Tesuque didn't have the necessary number of vecinos to hold elections and that the man they had elected was not old enough to serve anyway.[22]

Disputes at Cochiti

And what of the disorders at Cochiti intimated in the oral histories recorded by Greiner and Bandelier? A letter that Comandante General Bernardo Bonavía (in Durango) sent to Interim Governor Pedro María de Allande on October 20, 1815, provides some tantalizing information. According to Bonavía, the Cochiti Indian Juan Antonio Ignacio had personally presented him with a complaint about Allande's removal of the pueblo governor and other elected officers. Bonavía told Allande that "if the variation you made in the governor and other officers of said pueblo is certain, proceed at once to restore to the exercise of those duties those individuals elected for them by the same natives." The comandante general continued, saying that the interim governor should not have deposed the pueblo officials, even if there was good cause, without consulting him first. On December 18, Allande wrote his response in the margin: "Juan Roque and Toribio were put in possession of their jobs, and receipt and compliance were acknowledged to the comandante general."[23]

Although the document does not state that Juan Antonio Ignacio Baca himself was governor of Cochiti, it is evident that he "made a trip to old Mexico," as Pablo Romero said in 1852. If, as Romero's account indicates, Baca had been expelled as governor, then Allande must have worked with a faction in Cochiti that was interested in removing him. Allande then restored only two minor officials in December 1815, knowing that new officials would be chosen for the New Year anyway. If the comandante general even noticed that Baca had not been reinstated, Allande could then claim that his legitimate term as pueblo governor had ended.

If Baca submitted a written letter of complaint to Bonavía, it has unfortunately not survived in the archives, so we know no more than what Bonavía wrote. The documents do not make clear why Baca was removed from office and expelled. In the language of Juan José Montoya, it was probably for actions that were deemed to be "against the Pueblo." Montoya's accounts mention the selling of land by Turquoise people to Mexicans (Spanish vecinos) as the cause of strife within the pueblo. A possible way to combine this information with what we know from other sources is to assume that Baca was a member of the Turquoise moiety (the problems with this assumption will be discussed below) and that he sold Cochiti lands to Hispanos while governor. If Juan Antonio Ignacio Baca was indeed a relative or ally of the Spanish Bacas of Peña Blanca, we might expect that he would have

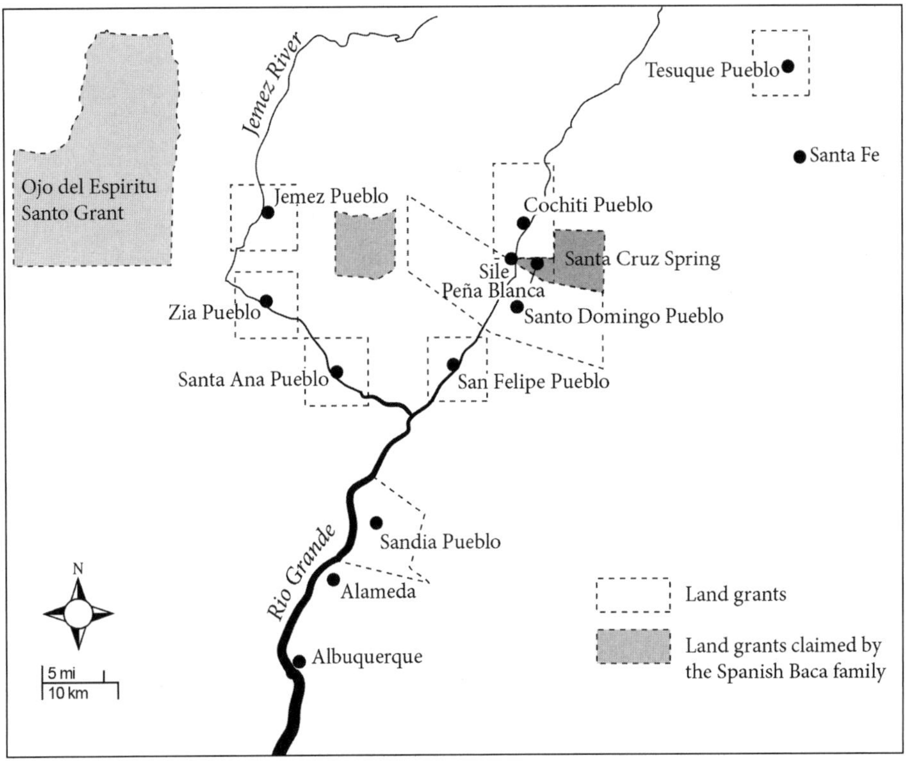

The Near World of Cochiti Pueblo. Boundaries of Santa Cruz Spring are approximate, based on Taylor, "Cochití Lands and the Disputed Sale to Luis María Cabeza de Baca," 69–77. Boundaries of other land grants are those determined by the United States government; other interpretations as to their extent under Spanish and Mexican rule are possible. Map by Tracy Ellen Smith and Ted Avila.

facilitated the transfer of land to them. Spanish documentation reveals that a land dispute between Cochiti and Spanish vecinos was indeed underway in 1815.[24] The source of the dispute was a sale of land at Peña Blanca by Cochiti Indians to Luis María Cabeza de Baca in 1805. In 1812, the protector partidario Felipe Sandoval (who had been proposed for his position by Juan José Quintana) filed a claim for the land on behalf of Cochiti, and Governor José Manrique ordered Cabeza de Baca to leave the land without compensation. When Cabeza de Baca appealed to the comandante general, his claim to the land was denied. Nevertheless, he remained on the land and even acquired part of another land grant in September 1812, further hemming in Cochiti land to the west.[25]

As Cabeza de Baca refused to leave the disputed land, Sandoval began to press Cochiti's case again in 1815. On March 14, 1815, Juan Antonio Baca wrote from Peña Blanca to New Mexico governor Alberto Maynez that he had received an order from "*el justicia deste partido*" (the local alcalde) that he and his father Luis María should not touch the land beyond Cochiti's boundary marker, which the alcalde Juan José Gutiérrez had built at the direction of Governor Manrique a few years earlier. Juan Antonio Baca claimed that Manrique later ordered the boundary moved back to where an earlier alcalde, José de Miera, had located it. As the Spanish Bacas had houses and farmland within the disputed territory, Juan Antonio claimed that if they were forced to move, they would demand four thousand pesos in compensation.[26]

According to Juan Antonio Baca, the Pueblo claim had been advanced by "the Indian Quintana of Cochiti." Baca then stated:

> Lastly, sir, in order to know about the unfounded presentation of the Indian Quintana, I went to the gobernadorcillo of said pueblo, and he says: that he neither knows anything nor has to ask for anything; neither do the people of his pueblo meddle in anything, only Quintana; and his partisans are those of the entanglements by which, year by year and day by day, the aforementioned Quintana keeps them embroiled.[27]

"The Indian Quintana" was undoubtedly Juan José Quintana, who thus appears as the leader of one faction at Cochiti in 1815. Having helped secure the position of protector partidario for Felipe Sandoval in 1810, Quintana now used his relationship with the protector to advance Cochiti land claims against the family of Luis María Cabeza de Baca, which had been in the vicinity since at least 1799. Because all evidence points to Juan Antonio Ignacio Baca being the Cochiti governor during the first half of 1815, then he was the gobernadorcillo mentioned above. It was thus Juan Antonio Ignacio Baca who led the opposing faction, refusing to support the legal action against the Spanish Bacas while also characterizing Quintana and his followers as troublemakers. Quintana's faction then worked with Allande to secure the gobernadorcillo's removal by mid-1815, at which point Juan Antonio Ignacio Baca took his appeal to Durango.

Juan Antonio Ignacio Baca may well have allowed Spanish vecinos to acquire Cochiti land, perhaps supported by the new liberal laws on landownership after 1813. The most incriminating document is a statement of July 10, 1815, in which Cochiti officers Juan Roque and Ignacio affirmed that the land sale to Cabeza de Baca had been made willingly and with the consent of the pueblo.[28] We know that Juan Roque and Juan Antonio Ignacio Baca were both deposed sometime before October 20, presumably in response to such declarations of support for Cabeza de Baca. Still, the oral histories that preserved memories of 1815 came from sources critical of Baca and his faction. It is worth noting that Spanish documents provide no proof that the Cochiti Baca actually transferred land to the Spanish Bacas, but only that he supported the Spanish Bacas' claims against the reclamations of Quintana. But among Pueblos, even the suspicion of alienating land could result in negative commentary and harsh punishment of an alleged offender, as Jemez Pueblo historian Joe Sando has pointed out in the treatment of his own grandfather.[29]

The land dispute continued for five more years. On April 15, 1815, the neighboring pueblo of Santo Domingo entered the fray by requesting the measurement of their league, together with one hundred *varas* (yards) of land they had purchased, which apparently also overlapped Cabeza de Baca's land at Peña Blanca. The Santo Domingos asked to be allowed to seek justice at another tribunal if refused.[30] On April 26, Governor Maynez ordered Cabeza de Baca to move off the contested property, which caused the hacendado to petition the governor for a grant of land at Ojo del Espiritu Santo, west of Jemez Pueblo, on May 23, "being compelled to withdraw my animals to avoid difficulties with the Quintarsas [i.e., Quintanas] Indians." Maynez granted Cabeza de Baca's request the next day, probably hoping that he would leave the disputed land to the Pueblos. Despite being put in possession of the Ojo del Espiritu Santo on June 14, Cabeza de Baca continued the legal fight by appealing to Comandante General Bonavía, who ordered on October 20 that he be allowed to remain at Peña Blanca until the dispute was resolved.[31] Juan José Quintana and other Cochiti Indians then took their case to the Indian protector of Durango. Protector José Joaquín Reyes argued Cochiti's case against Cabeza de Baca's lawyer, Rafael Bracho, but the court in Durango decided that the Audiencia of Guadalajara was the proper venue for further litigation—quite correctly, because New Mexico had been placed clearly under the jurisdiction of Guadalajara in 1779.[32]

Yet there was some misunderstanding of jurisdictions among Cochiti people, for five representatives of the pueblo traveled to Mexico City to present their case before the Audiencia of Mexico's General Indian Court (*Juzgado General de Indios*) on September 26, 1816. These five men (Antonio Quintana, Santiago Coris, and others recorded simply as Manuel, Domingo, and Francisco) convinced Dr. José Blas Abadiano y Jasso, the audiencia's defense attorney for the Indians, to take up their case. On February 8, 1817, Abadiano y Jasso sent a letter asking the governor (whom he mistakenly believed was still Maynez) to provide either the Indians or their protector with documentation of land transfers conducted by Joaquín del Real Alencaster, the governor of New Mexico in 1805–08. According to Abadiano y Jasso, Alencaster had sold the rancho of Sile to the Ortiz family and had given Captain Anacleto Miera Pacheco an order to sell another rancho (Peña Blanca) to Luis María Cabeza de Baca. Maynez forwarded this letter to Protector Sandoval on September 27, unaware that Sandoval had died in December 1816.

Someone (probably Governor Allande) responded to Abadiano y Jasso on December 17, 1817, that he had already sent the documents to Guadalajara.[33]

The fact that appeals were being made to two different audiencias in the same case gives some indication of the seriousness with which it was pursued. Abadiano y Jasso's letter gives a clue to which Cochiti faction had appealed to him. The defense attorney referred to "the Protector that was named for them by the Comandancia General," even though the protector was named by the Audiencia of Guadalajara. As we know that Juan José Quintana mistakenly believed that the comandante general appointed the protector in 1810, it seems that he communicated this misconception to the defense attorney through the Cochiti representatives. As Charles Cutter points out, Antonio Quintana may have been a relative of Juan José Quintana. Like Juan José, Antonio was a ladino, for he knew Spanish well enough to not need an interpreter.[34]

The Audiencia of Guadalajara began to deal with Cochiti claims by late 1816. On December 31, Dr. Francisco Antonio de Landa ordered Governor Maynez to measure the leagues of both Cochiti and Santo Domingo Pueblos because of litigation over the sites of Sile, Peña Blanca, and Santa Cruz Spring. On January 16, 1817, the audiencia's fiscal (the court attorney who also acted as Indian protector) addressed the claims of the *común* (commonwealth) of Cochiti. One was that the sale of the rancho of Peña Blanca to Luis María Cabeza de Baca be nullified because it was located within the pueblo's four square leagues or *fundo legal.* Another was for the return of the Santa Cruz Spring site (outside the fundo legal to the east) that had been purchased by Cochiti in 1744 but had later come into Cabeza de Baca's possession. The fiscal requested that the high court ask the governor of New Mexico to forward all relevant documents pertaining to Cochiti, Peña Blanca, and Santa Cruz Spring. On January 31, the Audiencia of Guadalajara asked Governor Allande to send them the documents.[35] On May 10, Maynez (as interim governor) appointed a commission of Spanish vecinos to measure the Cochiti and Santo Domingo leagues, and also named Vicente Villanueva to act as protector in place of the late Felipe Sandoval. The commission did its work between May 12 and 17, and Maynez remitted the entire case file to Guadalajara on May 31.[36]

In his report to Guadalajara on May 31, 1817, Interim Governor Maynez stated that the Indians of Santo Domingo and Cochiti now had quiet and peaceful relations with Antonio Ortiz and Luis María Cabeza de Baca, after trying to take the Spanish vecinos' property, "as their deceased protector partidario, Don Felipe Sandoval, had inclined them to that."[37] In Maynez's view, Sandoval had instigated the Pueblo land reclamations, which then fell apart following the protector's death. Nevertheless, the Audiencia of Guadalajara decided against Cabeza de Baca in August 1817, after the fiscal listed all of

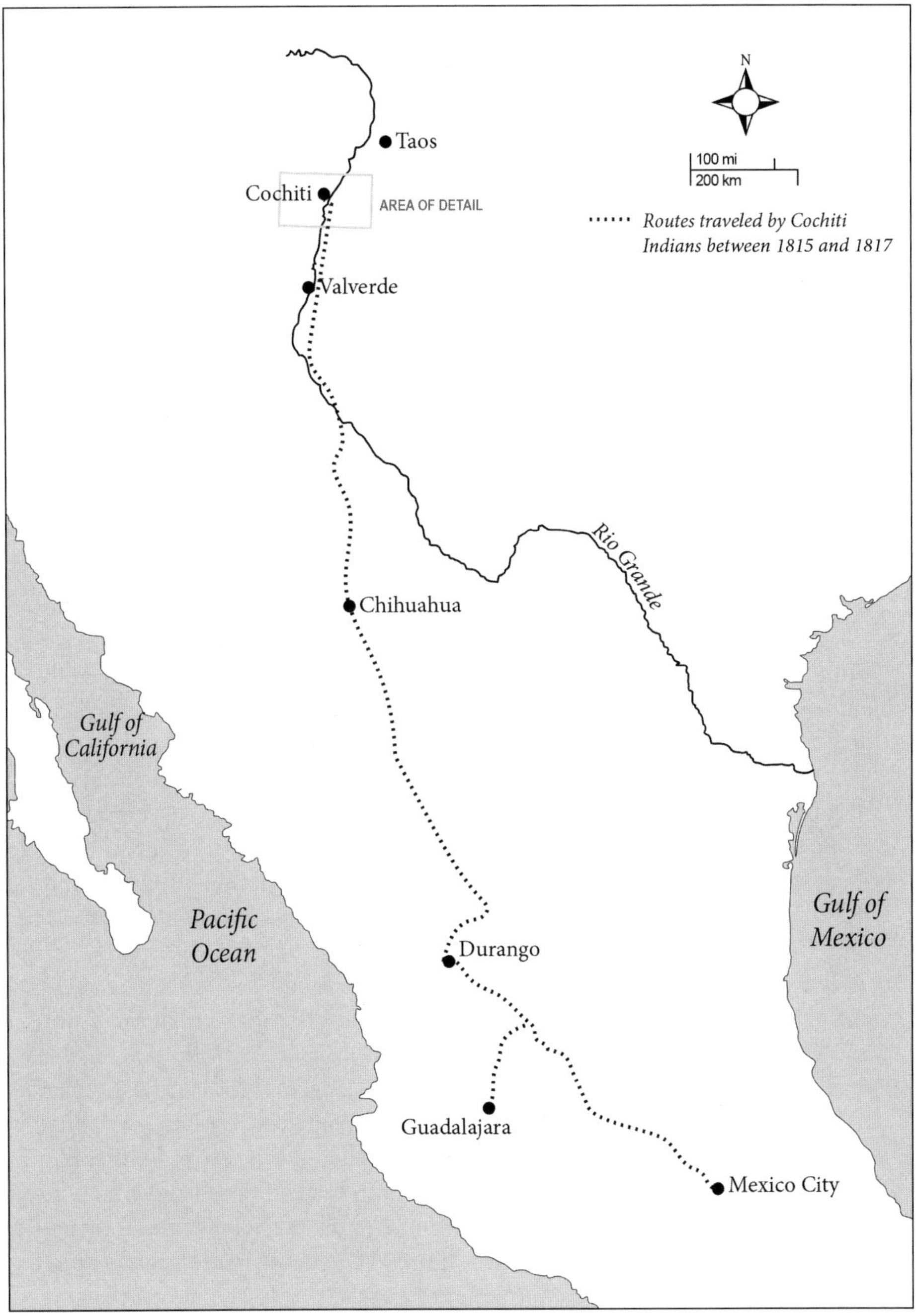

The Wider World of Cochiti Pueblo. Higher authorities that supervised New Mexico included the Comandante General in Chihuahua or Durango and the Audiencias of Guadalajara and Mexico City. Map by Tracy Ellen Smith and Ted Avila.

the ways that he had violated the law in his acquisition of Indian land. After Cabeza de Baca failed to appear before the audiencia, the court made a final decision in January 1819 that Peña Blanca and Santa Cruz Spring should be returned to Cochiti.[38] On February 27, 1819, the high court told Governor Facundo Melgares to charge Cabeza de Baca 192 pesos 7 reales for costs to the audiencia caused by the land case against Cochiti. Melgares responded on October 18, 1819, that he would collect the money and send it to Guadalajara. The convoluted land dispute finally drew to a close when Melgares wrote on June 19, 1820, that Cabeza de Baca could not raise the cash to pay these costs and had instead delivered eight mules to Santa Fe's military detachment. The treasury of Durango then deducted money originally designated for Santa Fe in order to pay the audiencia.[39]

It appears that the audiencia left Ortiz in possession of Sile. And although it found against Cabeza de Baca in the cases of both Peña Blanca and Santa Cruz Spring, for some reason Cochiti never learned of this decision at the time, and the hacendado was allowed to remain in possession of both places. William B. Taylor suggests that Luis María's son Juan Antonio Baca was still a local official and could have intercepted inconvenient correspondence to Cochiti as he did with Santo Domingo in 1808, while Cutter cites the change from Spanish to Mexican government as a possible reason for this lapse in enforcement.[40] In addition, warfare between New Mexicans and Navajos broke out in 1818, and Juan José Quintana was killed by Navajos and buried at Cochiti on December 9, 1821.[41] With the moving force behind Cochiti land reclamations no longer present, it is not surprising that Luis María Cabeza de Baca was able to remain on the disputed land. Perhaps Cochiti was too weak to go on fighting for justice after the smallpox outbreaks of 1816 and 1820, for according to Juan José Montoya, "These two epidemics destroyed the pueblo."[42]

Juan José Montoya's accounts lack the strict focus on land issues present in the Spanish legal documents, and instead offer interpretations from a Cochiti perspective. Therefore, a word must be said about the role of the Pumpkin and Turquoise moieties in the crisis of 1815. Montoya told Bandelier that the Turquoise people had sought citizenship and sold land to Mexicans, and that the Pumpkin people managed to get citizenship revoked but could not recover the alienated land. As Juan Antonio Ignacio Baca led the faction that refused to take part in the reclamations against the Spanish Bacas, while Juan José Quintana and his followers pressed the pueblo land claims against them, it would be logical to assume that Baca led the Turquoise people and Quintana led the Pumpkin people. However, Charles Lange's ethnography of Cochiti gives the moiety affiliations of officers and society members during the mid-twentieth century, and every person with the surname Quintana is identified as Turquoise. Esther Schiff Goldfrank noted nine Turquoise

Quintanas and two Pumpkin Quintanas during her fieldwork in 1921–22, but the latter two were both women who had joined the Pumpkin moiety through marriage. As moiety membership and surnames are both inherited from one's father, it is likely that Juan José Quintana was also Turquoise. To maintain that the turmoil of 1815 was essentially a conflict between moieties would then require Baca to be Pumpkin, which would completely reverse the claims of Juan José Montoya. To identify both Quintana and Baca as Turquoise would negate the whole idea of factionalism based on moieties. And although people inherit moiety membership from their fathers, custom allows them to switch sides either temporarily or permanently, making it impossible to know the affiliations of the two protagonists of 1815 for sure.[43]

We cannot deny the possibility that moiety-based factions were behind the conflicts of 1815, especially since a later division between Progressives and Conservatives developed overtones of moiety conflict because the majority of Progressives came from the Pumpkin people.[44] Even so, none of the evidence allows us to understand the role of moieties in 1815 unequivocally. It may be that Montoya projected the emerging Progressive–Conservative conflict of his own time back onto earlier events. Also, as anthropologist Robin Fox points out, the moieties "represent a ritual division of labour which serves the ends of community," so that kiva groups are supposed to cooperate harmoniously in ceremonies for the good of the whole pueblo, not engage in political disputes that disrupt the community. Instead, Fox found one dispute in twentieth-century Cochiti to be based not on moiety, but on two rival family groups.[45] Thus, the 1815 factions seem more likely to have been based around Juan José Quintana and his relatives and Juan Antonio Ignacio Baca and his relatives (possibly including the Spanish Bacas) than on the Turquoise and Pumpkin moieties.

Finally, we must address some of the details in Pablo Romero's account, which states that Juan Antonio Ignacio Baca's pretensions to act as judge for both Cochiti and Santo Domingo, and the profits he made as judge, caused some of the principales to expose him and expel him from Cochiti. As none of this is confirmed by the existing Spanish documentation, we could assume that the oral tradition reflects, in a confused way, memories that Cochiti and Santo Domingo had acted together in the land dispute, that Baca had been expelled from Cochiti for his perceived support of the Spanish vecinos, and that he had "made a trip to old Mexico." But there may be something more behind Romero's version, for Juan Antonio Ignacio Baca came to power during a period when changes in local government were being enacted. If we take Romero's account at its word, Baca claimed authority over both pueblos unjustly after a trip to Mexico, perhaps through a forged document. Alternately, Baca could have been delegated new powers by a Spanish ayuntamiento. Whether he had claimed or was given extra powers under the

Constitution of Cádiz, they would have been revoked after Ferdinand VII returned to power in Spain. On December 28, 1814, the king issued an order to reestablish the old forms of local government, which was pronounced in Mexico on July 20, 1815.[46] If this news reached New Mexico in August or September, it could have provided Baca's enemies with a reason to depose him and enough time for Baca to lodge his complaint in Durango on October 20. But given the lack of Spanish documentation and the antagonistic nature of the account that Romero heard in Cochiti, we may never know the whole story.

The Later Life of Juan Antonio Ignacio Baca

What became of Juan Antonio Ignacio Baca after his expulsion from Cochiti in 1815? A letter from Alcalde of Jemez Ignacio Sánchez Vergara to Governor Allande on September 12, 1816, provides information on his whereabouts and proves that he was indeed expelled from Cochiti. Sánchez Vergara wrote that an Indian named Antonio was living at Zia Pueblo and had encouraged the people to complain when the alcalde's cattle damaged a cornfield. Sánchez Vergara told the interim governor that Antonio "is one of the conclave of troublemakers [*reboltosos*] of Cochiti, and the cause of many disorders [*revolturas*] in his pueblo; for which I beg Your Lordship to give him your reprehension, and [tell him] to not meddle in his pueblo, nor with its officials, because he goes around meddling with everything, and in this presentation and in all others, he doesn't even care why."[47] Once again, Baca's enemies painted him as a troublemaker. Yet it is obvious that Baca, as a ladino with experience in the Spanish legal system, was trying to help the people of Zia defend their rights. Although he could have left Pueblo society and lived among Hispanos as a genízaro or an Indian vecino, Baca preferred to continue living as an Indian in an Indian pueblo. His actions in 1816 certainly allow us to question whether a man who defended Indian property at Zia would have sold Indian property to Spanish vecinos at Cochiti.

Our next documentary record of Juan Antonio Ignacio Baca shows that although he was no longer at Zia, he had made his home in another Indian pueblo. An 1830 census from the archives of the Archdiocese of Santa Fe lists him as Antonio Baca (age 60), living at Jemez Pueblo with his wife Lucía (age 50) and his children José (age 25) and Francisca (age 20). The 20-year-old widow Teresa Baca, listed in the next entry as living with her 5-year-old daughter Juana María, may well have been a daughter or daughter-in-law of Juan Antonio Ignacio Baca.[48] Far from the roguish character depicted in other documents, Baca appears here as a family man. He may have founded a large family at Jemez. Thirty-eight Bacas, identified as Indian and distributed among ten households, are listed at this pueblo in the United States Census of 1860.[49]

The final reference to the later life of Juan Antonio Ignacio Baca comes from the account that Pablo Romero of Taos gave to John Greiner in 1852, which is worth quoting at length:

> He [Romero] states that the Indian from Cochiti (Baca) had visited Taos Pueblo, and said that the Colonel at Valverde had appointed him chief over all the pueblos in the Territory; and he was now on a visit to all the pueblos for the purpose of getting the Pueblos to volunteer to go into the United States in proof of what he said he carried coat and epaulett[e]s given him by the officer at Valverde.
>
> As the Taos people were well acquainted with all my [Greiner's] views in this respect they placed no confidence in any thing he said, Baca said he had visited all the pueblos in [the] Territory ex[c]ept Picuris, and he was on his road there, on Sunday April 4 when he intended to come to Santa Fé to see the superintendent. . . .
>
> Baca when questioned closely by the Pueblos of Taos why he was meddling in these matters, said he was well paid for it by the colonel of Valverde, and he visited all the pueblos in order to show that he earned his money.[50]

Romero presented Baca as an old scoundrel who had not changed his habits in thirty years. Just as he had fraudulently claimed authority from the Spanish government to act as judge over two pueblos, now he maintained that the new United States government had appointed him chief of all the pueblos.

The reason the aged Baca even appears in Greiner's reports is that he became a cause of concern during the still fluid and transitional early years of the United States government in New Mexico. American officials like Greiner knew they were a small minority in an alien land whose people did not necessarily want them there. With the killing of Governor Charles Bent by Hispanos and Pueblos only five years in the past, Greiner feared that Baca was exhorting the Pueblos to join the Hispanos and Comanches in a vast conspiracy to return New Mexico to Mexican rule. Whatever Baca was trying to do, it was for his own benefit, as the Pueblo-Hispano-Comanche conspiracy never existed. And if he toured the pueblos as a roguish opportunist, he was not the only one in these early, uncertain years of United States rule. In 1854, Víctor de la O of Chihuahua, Vicente Avilucea, and Ramón Sánchez traveled among the Pueblos and exploited their need to prove land rights to the new regime by selling the so-called "Cruzate grants," which were later proven to be forgeries.[51]

In his younger years, Juan Antonio Ignacio Baca tried to obtain benefits by appealing to higher authorities in Mexico. As Peter Whiteley has shown, Tesuque principales did something similar by traveling to Washington, D.C., in 1852. Baca, by then over eighty years old, could not hope to make such a journey. Instead, he traveled to Valverde, where Colonel Edwin V. Sumner had established Fort Conrad in 1851.[52] Receiving his coat with epaulets as a gift from the colonel, Baca then set off to impress the other Pueblos with the authority he claimed to have been granted. What did the old man hope to achieve, traveling around in his US Army coat? Romero's account shows that a version of history originating with Juan José Quintana's faction, which presented Baca as a troublemaker and a traitor, was still current among the Pueblos. Perhaps Baca saw this journey as his last opportunity to reclaim a position of respect and leadership that he had lost in 1815. If so, he was unsuccessful, and Greiner's report is the last that we hear of him.

Conclusion

Juan Antonio Ignacio Baca was a fascinating individual whose life, until now, has been overlooked by professional historians. In the context of this volume, he represents an example of a transnational Indian because he moved between the Pueblo and Spanish worlds, among several pueblos, and from Spanish, to Mexican, and to United States sovereignty during his life. Centuries of Spanish rule resulted in the creation of groups of transnational Indians designated as ladinos or Indian vecinos. Both Baca and his rival, Juan José Quintana, were in this sense transnational, as they were both fluent in Spanish and equally capable of engaging in internal pueblo politics, the emerging Spanish liberal system of elections, or the legal appeals process that led to higher tribunals in Mexico. Researching the life of Juan Antonio Ignacio Baca is an exercise in connecting the dots: the evidence is fragmentary and requires that suppositions be made that could be proven wrong should more detailed sources come to light. Nevertheless, the sources available represent an ethnohistorian's dream, for having both recorded oral history and government documentation allows us to approach Baca from more than one perspective and to include Native American voices.

The oral tradition and the Spanish documentation coincide at least partially. We have seen how both sources attest to a factional struggle in Cochiti at a time when Spain granted and then rescinded Indian citizenship. According to both type of sources, the turmoil involved a land dispute with Spanish vecinos and resulted in both sides taking their cases before higher authorities in Mexico. Even so, the oral traditions are not important just for the few details that can be corroborated with government documentation, but for the Native American view of history that they provide. Juan José Montoya's comments to Bandelier provide a wonderfully Cochiti-centric view of history. He understood that the two Cochiti moieties made the Spanish grant and revoke citizenship as part of their dispute, not that Spanish politics in the wake of Napoleon's invasion had generated this political experimentation. Similarly, he presented a military expedition against the Comanches that was probably led by the Mexican government as a purely Pueblo endeavor, and pointed out that "the Mexicans wore their hair long like the Indians" until the 1820s, with no reference to European hairstyle trends.[53]

Most importantly, the oral traditions point to things that have heretofore gone unnoticed in the government sources. Most of the "dots" which I have attempted to connect—individual Spanish documents, and Greiner's and Bandelier's reports—have been known to historians for the last one hundred years. Scholars have written about Cochiti's land dispute with Luis María Cabeza de Baca several times, but always as a black and white struggle of Pueblo Indians versus Spanish vecinos. Historians have focused solely on the paperwork generated by Cochiti's legal struggles partly because colonial land and water disputes remain very relevant in present-day New Mexico, so that colonial cases are frequently revisited as part of modern legal processes. But relying exclusively on Spanish documents leads to the conclusion that land was the only important issue. This approach also reduces a complex society to the one-dimensional role of plaintiff in a case in the Spanish legal system.

We have long known that Spanish colonial society was by no means monolithic and that the interests of the Spanish government and the vecinos were not necessarily the same. The oral histories recorded by Greiner and Bandelier show us that Pueblo society similarly was not always unified. There were factional disputes within Cochiti in the early nineteenth century, and they made such an impression that they were remembered as late as 1882. The accounts of Juan José Montoya and Pablo Romero are valuable because they tell us what Pueblos thought were the important events in their own history. That history points to societies actively engaged in balancing the interests of individuals and the community. Pueblos remembered the turmoil of 1815 not primarily for the loss of land, but rather as a time when something even more important was threatened—a community's harmony. The maintenance of community harmony was sometimes not an easy task, and the dispute in which Juan Antonio Ignacio Baca figured so prominently shows that the words of a former Cochiti council member (told to Charles Lange around 1950) can be applied equally as well to 1815: "Anyone who thinks that everything in an Indian pueblo is all calm and co-operation just simply doesn't know anything about pueblo politics."[54]

Notes

1. Charles H. Lange, *Cochiti: A New Mexican Pueblo, Past and Present* (Albuquerque: University of New Mexico Press, 1990), 14. Compare *The Southwestern Journals of Adolph F. Bandelier, 1880–1882*, eds. Charles H. Lange, and Carroll L. Riley (Albuquerque: University of New Mexico Press, 1966), 167.

2. Lange, *Cochiti*, 194. Compare Lange and Riley, *The Southwestern Journals of Adolph F. Bandelier*, 263.

3. Annie Heloise Abel, "The Journal of John Greiner," *Old Santa Fe* 3 (July 1916), 191.

4. Ibid., 192; Peter Whiteley, "Reconnoitering 'Pueblo' Ethnicity: the 1852 Tesuque Delegation to Washington," *Journal of the Southwest* 45 (Autumn 2003), 455. Greiner's letter to Baird is mistakenly

identified as a letter to Colonel Edwin V. Sumner in *The Official Correspondence of James S. Calhoun while Indian Agent at Santa Fe and Superintendent of Indian Affairs in New Mexico*, ed. Annie Heloise Able (Washington: Government Printing Office, 1915), 519; and Francis Stanley, *E. V. Sumner, Major-General, United States Army (1797–1863)* (Borger, Texas: Jim Hess Printers, 1969), 157.

5. Abel, "The Journal of John Greiner," 193.

6. Ibid., 194.

7. Herbert O. Brayer, *Pueblo Indian Grants of the "Rio Abajo," New Mexico* (Albuquerque: University of New Mexico Press, 1938), 8–16; G. Emlen Hall and David J. Weber, "Mexican Liberals and the Pueblo Indians, 1821–1829," *New Mexico Historical Review* 59 (January 1984), 5–6.

8. Spanish Archives of New Mexico (hereafter SANM) II, R. 16, Fr. 611–629, September 3–September 13, 1808.

9. Fray Angélico Chávez, *Origins of New Mexico Families: A Genealogy of the Spanish Colonial Period*, revised edition (Santa Fe: Museum of New Mexico Press, 1992), 152–53; J. J. Bowden, "Luis María Cabeza de Baca Grant," accessed at New Mexico Office of the State Historian site http://dev.newmexicohistory.org/filedetails.php?fileID=24833 on December 17, 2012.

10. SANM II, R. 17, Fr. 52–53, Nemesio Salcedo to Interim Governor of New Mexico, 21 March 1810; Fr. 116–17, letter of Governor of New Mexico, May 31, 1810; Fr. 179–80, Letter of Vicente Alonzo Andrade, Fiscal and Protector General de Indios of Audiencia of Guadalajara, August 20, 1810.

11. Ross H. Frank, review of *The Protector de Indios in Colonial New Mexico, 1659–1821*, by Charles R. Cutter, *American Indian Quarterly* 13 (Summer 1989), 291.

12. James F. Brooks, *Captives & Cousins* (Chapel Hill: University of North Carolina Press, 2002); Tracy Brown, "Tradition and Change in Eighteenth-Century Pueblo Indian Communities," *Journal of the Southwest* 46 (Autumn 2004), 463–500; SANM II, R. 17, Fr. 52–53, Nemesio Salcedo to Interim Governor of New Mexico, March 21, 1810; and SANM II, R. 17, Fr. 477, Petition of Juan José Quintana, José Archibeque, Antonio, and Felipe, Indians of Cochiti, February 3, 1812.

13. David J. Weber, *The Mexican Frontier, 1821–1848: The American Southwest under Mexico* (Albuquerque: University of New Mexico Press, 1982), 16–17; Constitución de Cádiz de 1812, accessed at Biblioteca Virtual Miguel de Cervantes on April 30, 2012.

14. SANM II, R. 20, Fr. 196, Royal decree of 22 April 1820 (republication of Cortes' decree of 9 November 1812); Hall and Weber, "Mexican Liberals and the Pueblo Indians," 8–10; Constitución de Cádiz de 1812.

15. SANM II, R. 20, Fr. 486–88, José Manuel Salazar to Governor Facundo Melgares, December 25, 1820; SANM II, R. 20, Fr. 667–74, Governor Facundo Melgares to Excelentísima Junta de Provincia, April 18, 1821; SANM II, R. 18, Fr. 836–39, Mariano Mendiola Velarde to Audiencia of Guadalajara, June 21, 1817; and Mexican Archives of New Mexico (hereafter MANM), R. 1, Fr. 1184–97, Complaints of San Juan Pueblo against their Father Mariano Sánchez Vergara, March 1822.

16. Hall and Weber, "Mexican Liberals and the Pueblo Indians," 5.

17. MANM, R. 1, Fr. 1157–58, Ayuntamiento of Socorro and Isleta [del Sur] to Diputación Provincial, 18 September 1822; and MANM, R. 1, Fr. 1184–97, Complaints of San Juan Pueblo against their Father Mariano Sánchez Vergara, March 1822.

18. MANM, R. 42, Fr. 20–21, *Journal of the Diputación Provincial*, June 29, 1822; Fr. 31, *Journal of the Diputación Provincial*, July 10, 1822; Fr. 48–49, *Journal of the Diputación Provincial*, August 29, 1822. For the previous year's membership, see SANM II, R. 20, Fr. 927–28, Ayuntamiento of Cochiti to Fray Manuel Bellido, September 29, 1821.

19. Lange, *Cochiti*, 14, 194; Lange and Riley, *The Southwestern Journals of Adolph F. Bandelier*, 167, 263. For the 1816 smallpox epidemic, see Henry F. Dobyns, "Disease Transfer at Contact," *Annual Review of Anthropology* 22 (1993): 283.

20. SANM II, R. 20, Fr. 401–08, Letter of Alejo García Conde, July 5, 1820.

21. SANM II, R. 17, Fr. 846–54 (including Acta de elección de parroquia of Pueblo of Sandia, January 30, 1814; Acta de elección de parroquia of Pueblo of San Felipe, February 6, 1814; and Acta de elección de parroquia of Pueblo of Cochiti, February 13, 1814); SANM II, R. 19, Fr. 659–61, Testimony of Juan Roque Perico, April 17, 1819; Brown, "Tradition and Change in Eighteenth-Century Pueblo Indian Communities," 479. Luis María Cabeza de Baca served as escrutador in the Cochiti parochial elections.

22. See SANM II, R. 17, Fr. 869–70, February 8, 1814; Fr. 873, February 13, 1814; and Fr. 880–81, Febru-

ary 14, 1814 for Taos. See SANM II, R. 17, Fr. 874–75, February 15, 1814; and Fr. 876–79 for Jemez. See SANM II, R. 17, 886, February 6, 1814; and Fr. 887–90 for Tesuque.

23. SANM II, R. 18, Fr. 252–53, Comandante General Bernardo Bonavía to Interim Governor Pedro María de Allande, October 20, 1815.

24. Previous treatments of this land case include Ralph Emerson Twitchell, *The Spanish Archives of New Mexico*, vol. 1 (Cedar Rapids: The Torch Press, 1914), 360, 372–73, 432–35; Brayer, *Pueblo Indian Grants of the "Rio Abajo,"* 111, 116–22; William B. Taylor, "Cochití Lands and the Disputed Sale to Luis María Cabeza de Baca, 1805," in *Pueblo de Cochiti Lands Bill: Hearing Before the Select Committee on Indian Affairs, United States Senate*, 98th Cong. (1984), 31–78; and Charles R. Cutter, *The Protector de Indios in Colonial New Mexico, 1659–1821* (Albuquerque: University of New Mexico Press, 1986), 1–2, 88–93.

25. Taylor, "Cochití Lands and the Disputed Sale to Luis María Cabeza de Baca," 52, 57–58.

26. SANM I, R. 6, Fr. 1655–1656, Juan Antonio Baca to Governor Alberto Maynez, March 14, 1815.

27. Ibid.

28. Taylor, "Cochití Lands and the Disputed Sale to Luis María Cabeza de Baca," 57, 59 n.60.

29. Joe S. Sando, *Nee Hemish: A History of Jemez Pueblo* (Albuquerque: University of New Mexico Press, 1982), 74–75.

30. SANM II, R. 18, Fr. 42, Fray Antonio Caballero to Governor Alberto Maynez, April 13, 1815.

31. Cutter, *The Protector de Indios in Colonial New Mexico*, 89; Taylor, "Cochití Lands and the Disputed Sale to Luis María Cabeza de Baca," 59; "New Mexico—Private Land Claim of the Heirs of Luis Maria C. de Baca," in 36th Cong., 2nd Sess. (1861), House of Representatives Ex. Doc. No. 58, 2–5.

32. Cutter, *The Protector de Indios in Colonial New Mexico*, 89–91; and Charles R. Cutter, "La Real Audiencia del norte de la Nueva España: Historia de un proyecto frustrado," in *Memoria del X congreso del Instituto Internacional de Historia del Derecho Indiano*, vol. 1 (Mexico City: Escuela Libre de Derecho and Universidad Nacional Autónoma de México, 1995), 280.

33. Cutter, *The Protector de Indios in Colonial New Mexico*, 1–2, 91–92; Taylor, "Cochití Lands and the Disputed Sale to Luis María Cabeza de Baca," 59; SANM I, R. 6, Fr. 1660–1662, Dr. José Blas Abadiano y Jasso to Alberto Maynez, Feb. 8, 1817 and Alberto Maynez to Felipe Sandoval, Sept. 27, 1817; and SANM I, R. 6, Fr. 844, Letter to Dr. José Blas Abadiano y Jasso, Dec. 17, 1817.

34. SANM I, R. 6, Fr. 1660–1662, Dr. José Blas Abadiano y Jasso to Alberto Maynez, Feb. 8, 1817; Cutter, *The Protector de Indios in Colonial New Mexico*, 91; and Taylor, "Cochití Lands and the Disputed Sale to Luis María Cabeza de Baca," 61.

35. SANM I, R. 6, Fr. 1664–66, Pedimiento and auto of Rafael Cuentas, Jan. 31, 1817; and Taylor, "Cochití Lands and the Disputed Sale to Luis María Cabeza de Baca," 54.

36. SANM I, R. 6, Fr. 1667, Report of Interim Governor Alberto Maynez to Audiencia of Guadalajara, May 31, 1817; and Taylor, "Cochití Lands and the Disputed Sale to Luis María Cabeza de Baca," 62.

37. SANM I, R. 6, Fr. 1668–69, Report of Interim Governor Alberto Maynez to Audiencia of Guadalajara, May 31, 1817.

38. Taylor, "Cochití Lands and the Disputed Sale to Luis María Cabeza de Baca," 62–65.

39. SANM II, R. 19, Fr. 1027–28, Governor Facundo Melgares to Audiencia of Guadalajara, Oct. 18, 1819; SANM I, R. 6, Fr. 1071–1072, Governor Facundo Melgares to Audiencia of Guadalajara, June 19, 1820; and SANM I, R. 6, Fr. 1063, Sergeant Santiago Abreu to Governor Facundo Melgares, July 18, 1820.

40. Taylor, "Cochití Lands and the Disputed Sale to Luis María Cabeza de Baca," 66; and Cutter, *The Protector de Indios in Colonial New Mexico*, 92.

41. Weber, *The Mexican Frontier, 1821–1848*, 11; and Harrison Lapahie Jr., "Navajo Timeline, Mexican Era: 1821–1847," accessed at http://www.lapahie.com/Timeline_Mexican_1821_1847_Btfm.cfm, December 5, 2012.

42. Lange, *Cochiti*, 14.

43. Lange, *Cochiti*, 273, 310, 390, 447–514; and Esther Schiff Goldfrank, *The Social and Ceremonial Organization of Cochiti* (New York: Kraus Reprint Corporation, 1964), 114–15, genealogy III.

44. Ibid., 30–31, 312, 391–92.

45. Robin Fox, *The Keresan Bridge: A Problem in Pueblo Ethnology* (London: The Athlone Press, 1967), 61–63, 116–18. The twentieth-century factionalism centered on Cochiti's two rival baseball teams.

46. SANM II, R. 17, Fr. 1105, Bando of Viceroy Félix Calleja, July 20, 1815, publishing King Ferdinand VII's cédula of December 28, 1814.

47. SANM II, R. 18, Fr. 708–10, Alcalde Ignacio Sánchez Vergara to Interim Governor Pedro María de Allande, Sept. 12, 1816.

48. Virginia Langham Olmsted, *Spanish and Mexican Censuses of New Mexico, 1750–1830* (Albuquerque: New Mexico Genealogical Society, Inc., 1981), 268.

49. *1860 U.S. Census, Population Schedule*, Jemez, Santa Ana, Territory of New Mexico. NARA microfilm publication M653, roll 716, 73–74, 77, 83, Washington, D.C.: National Archives and Records Administration, n.d. Accessed via Ancestry.com, April 30, 2012.

50. Abel, "The Journal of John Greiner," 194.

51. See Sandra K. Mathews-Lamb, "The 'Nineteenth Century' Cruzate Grants: Pueblos, Peddlers, and the Great Confidence Scam?" (Ph.D. diss., University of New Mexico, 1998).

52. Whiteley, "Reconnoitering 'Pueblo' Ethnicity," 437–518; and T. M. Pearce, *New Mexico Place Names: A Geographical Dictionary* (Albuquerque: University of New Mexico Press, 1965), 58.

53. Lange and Riley, *The Southwestern Journals of Adolph F. Bandelier*, 158, 162.

54. Lange, *Cochiti*, 194.

Chapter 4

"Indios Bárbaros" and the Making of Mexican Colonization Policy after Independence

From Conquest to Colonization*

José Angel Hernández

This chapter examines how the demographic and strategic position of Indios Bárbaros, immigrants, migrant Indians, and Mexicans north of the Rio Grande influenced the direction and ultimate implementation of immigration-cum-colonization policies after Mexican independence. Many intellectuals of the era argued that one of the primary reasons for dramatic US economic growth and aggressive westward expansion was the arrival of European immigrants—a global phenomenon on which Mexico also sought to capitalize. But, unlike its neighbors, Mexico received few of these immigrants because of restrictive policies influenced by botched colonization schemes, lower wages, three Spanish expulsions, and religious intolerance against non-Catholics. Mexican colonization policy fluctuated between inclusion and exclusion, but ultimately these early trials and tribulations became the basis for a series of laws that would ultimately give preferential treatment to Mexicans willing to settle and colonize the frontiers of the Republic.

These conclusions contradict a view in the immigration and colonization historiography that suggests these policies were implemented solely to "whiten" the populations like those in the United States, Argentina, or Brazil. Aside from emerging in a period that witnessed the movement of millions of people across the globe, Mexico's immigration policies emerged in large

* The article is based in part on the following piece: José Angel Hernández, "From Conquest to Colonization: Indios and Colonization Policies after Mexican Independence," in *Mexican Studies/Estudios Mexicanos*, vol. 26, no. 2 (Summer 2010), pp. 291–322.

part as a way to incorporate the majority of the Indigenous populace into the larger "Mexican family," but also as a way to "Mexicanize" communities outside of state control like those residing on the frontiers of Tejas, Alta California, and Nuevo Mexico. The botched colonization project of Stephen F. Austin in Texas in the early 1820s—a project that set in motion the confrontation between Mexico and the United States in 1846—forever altered not only the politics of colonization in Mexico but the very way in which Mexican national identity was imagined. Populations along the newly independent nation's frontiers, many of whom had been neglected for generations under the Spanish Empire, were now being courted to thwart European and Euro-American immigrants making their way toward Texas and the frontiers of the two republics.

Nineteenth-Century Mexican Immigration Policies and Indios Bárbaros

In the years that followed independence from European rule and in the exuberance of defeating their one-time colonizers, the young nations of the Americas sought to throw off the yoke of colonialism while also inviting the migration and settlement of Europeans. This effort to attract European immigrants in the aftermath of American and Mexican independence coincided with a period of global mass migrations that lasted for about a century. Historian José Moya asserts that the movement of Europeans that began modestly after the end of the "Latin American wars of Independence[,] gathered steam after mid-century, reached massive proportions after the 1870s, and lasted—with a pause during WWI—until the Great Depression" was unprecedented: "[N]othing resembling this massive movement had ever happened before anywhere on the planet, and nothing similar has happened since."[1]

Scholars of this particular period in world history, however, contend that most researchers who discuss world migrations often ignore the larger pattern of movements across the globe occurring at the exact same time. These critics argue that African and Asian migrations are ignored and "when mentioned, are usually described only as indentured migration subject to the needs of Europeans or as peasants fleeing overpopulation pressures." As such, historian Adam McKweon reminds us that along with the millions of Europeans coming to the Western hemisphere after several Latin American nations gained their independence, 48 million to 52 million Indians and southern Chinese migrated to southeast Asia, the Indian Ocean, and the South Pacific; and 46 million to 51 million Russians and northeastern Asians migrated to points in Manchuria, Siberia, Central Asia, and Japan. In short order, the period between 1846 and 1940 witnessed the global migration of 160 million individuals, and thus Latin America become one site of these multiple settlements.[2]

There was also a direct correlation between the number of immigrants accepted by a particular nation and its economic production. Thus, to cite Moya once more, "It is no coincidence that the four most important receivers of European immigrants in the nineteenth century (the United States, Canada, Argentina and Brazil) also became the four most important recipients of British investment and the four fastest growing economies in the Western Hemisphere." The link between a booming economy and European immigrants was not lost on the Mexicans of the 1820s as they witnessed how a vast majority of those individuals would eventually settle in the United States, further spurring that nation to project an expansionist policy. Migrants and immigrants provided the demographic conditions for US expansionist policy, which required more territory to settle the millions that were arriving. By the time of the global Great Depression of 1929, the United States had received the vast majority of these European immigrants, whereas Mexico was only able to attract between 1 and 3 percent of the total.[3]

Why did Mexico receive so few immigrants while other locales became important sites for European settlements? What was problematic about Mexican immigration and colonization policies that prevented or impeded the migration of Europeans, particularly as compared to the policies of Brazil and Argentina? Did the ideology of Mexican colonization policy concern itself more with domestic issues to the detriment of those of an international nature? How did expulsions, low wages, a large Indigenous population, unfertile and unsurveyed lands, and thwarted colonization schemes affect subsequent colonization policy? Why did Europeans prefer the United States, Canada, Argentina, and Brazil to Mexico, and how did the Mexican government respond?

The following attempts to provide answers to these multiple questions by arguing that Mexico's colonization policies need to be evaluated not simply in terms of failure or success but also as legal vehicles intended to encourage the incorporation of certain groups of people into the nation of Mexico and to discourage the incorporation of others.[4] Potential immigrants not only had to deal with lower wages, unsurveyed landscapes, "administrative disorder," and unclear guidelines regarding colonization, but then also had to contend with Mexican nativism surrounding the ambiguity of foreign colonization, especially after 1836 and 1848. Moreover, the official Mexican ideal of *mestizaje* that articulates a painful, if invented, community of miscegenation has conveniently overlooked the nation's violent practices of expulsions and exclusions that ultimately contributed to a hostile environment for European settlement. In this regard, although much of the historiography on Mexican immigration policy has made an argument for whitening analogous to that of Brazil or the United States, this sort of language was never codified into law. An examination of this historiography reveals that the origins of this argument date to the post-WWII period, when scholars sought to solidify a critique of the *ancien* régime of Porfirio Díaz by painting it as despotic, pro-American, and thus anti-Mexican. In this regard, immigration and colonization policy in this early period seems more in line with the political thinking that Claudio Lomnitz drew attention to in his study of Mexican national culture, in which he argued that writings on "Lo Mexicano" constitute a "racial ideology of Mexicaness [that] can be understood as a qualified (but not absolute) critique of Westernization and imperialism."[5]

Intellectuals at various times in the nation's history had called for the "whitening" of Mexico, but immigration policies that favored Europeans over Mexicans and Indians were never adopted.[6] On the contrary, Mexican immigration policy simultaneously permitted both the settlement of Euro-Americans in Texas and the expulsion of Spaniards from Mexico. Following the Mexican-American War, the 1848 decree that instituted the Department of Colonization specifically banned Euro-American colonists from immigrating to Mexico. Otherwise, settlement in Mexico was open to the entire world.[7] By the time the 1883 Land and Colonization Law was passed, coupled with the experience of foreign invasions and repeated episodes of filibustering along the northern frontiers, immigration policy favored Mexicans in the United States over other potential immigrants to Mexico. Unlike more overt attempts at whitening—as in the examples of Cuba, the Dominican Republic, Brazil, or the United States—Mexico's immigration policies emerged in large part as a way to incorporate the Indigenous populace into the larger "Mexican family" but also as a way to Mexicanize communities outside of state control. Immigration policy was conceived and contested in the context of a very substantial Indigenous population and then evolved to a policy that eventually placed Mexicans in the United States at the top of the immigration pyramid.

Attorney and Asian American studies professor Bill Ong Hing provides a number of answers to the question of what immigration policies can tell us about national identity in his 2004 study *Defining America Through Immigration Policy*. The inclusion or exclusion of particular peoples via immigration and colonization policies are "interactive frames" by means of which intellectuals and politicians could shape national identity in postcolonial Mexico.[8] Ong Hing points out, "Immigration policies are not simply reflections of whom we regard as potential Americans, they are vehicles for keeping out those who do not fit the image and welcoming those who do."[9] Mexican nationalism, as it oscillated between exclusion and inclusion, "went from excluding Spaniards in the early Independence movement, to including them at Independence, to excluding them again, all in a very short lapse of time."[10] This is why immigration policies cannot be examined statically, but as policies that change over time and in accordance with the social and political context of the day. Such policies articulate a number of facets regarding national identity when espoused, and they (immigration laws, decrees, and policies) deserve to be analyzed in their own right as primary documents.

Certainly, political and economic concerns were of more interest to post-independence politicians and military officials, whose main unease was the territorial integrity of the nation and the looming threat of US and European expansion into its defined borders. Indios Bárbaros of the northern frontier regions, *fronterizos*, as well as migrant Indians, came into the purview of post-independence colonization policies that attempted through force and coercion to "amalgamate" independent Indian nations that had been resisting certain aspects of US and Mexican westernization-cum-modernization for at least three centuries. Immigration and colonization policy in Mexico after independence, in contrast to the prevailing historiography, was not so much concerned with "whitening" as it was with incorporating independent Indians and subsequently creating a buffer zone against US and European encroachments.

Independence and the Promise of Empire: Indios and Intellectuals

Independence in Mexico, as in most Latin American nations, was an historical watershed. When speaking of the transformation of Spanish American nationalism during this period, historian and anthropologist of Mexico Claudio Lomnitz argues that post-independence statehood in Spanish America "forced deep ideological changes, including a sharp change in who was considered a national and who a foreigner, a redefinition of the extension of fraternal bond through the idea of citizenship, and the relationship between religion and nationality and between race and nation."[11] Thus, all persons now born in Mexico were considered equal when Agustín de Iturbide's government "solved the so-called Indian problem by ending legal proscriptions for Indians and making them citizens."[12] With the issue of citizenship theoretically resolved, Mexicans imagined themselves as independent and on the way to full-fledged participation in the larger community of nations.

During the First Constituent Congress in 1821, those behind the first effort to implement a colonization policy believed that Mexico was in an "era that will change the face of the earth . . . putting commerce at the center of the nations among us in Anáhuac as the balancing point between Europe and Asia."[13] The authors of this document—among them some of the most important political and intellectual figures of the period—shared a vision of Mexico assuming a more prominent role in world history as the continent that would serve as the meeting point between the East and the West.[14]

Reinscribing their own historical trajectory back to the so-called discovery of the New World as the gateway to the East, these men now inverted that historical moment whereby Mexico–Anáhuac was to be the meeting point between two other civilizations. In his recommendations to the first independent government, Simón Tadeo Ortiz de Ayala made note of the fact that:

> The physical situation of the Mexican empire offers invaluable advantages, considered with regard to its communications and the remainder of the civilized world. Situated in an isthmus bathed by the Pacific and Atlantic oceans, the old empire of Anahuac seems destined to exercise a large influence on the political events that agitate the large nations. The government of the empire can communicate with Europe in five weeks, in six with Asia, and in three with both Americas (North and South America).[15]

This perception of Mexico as an equal partner and a middleman in world history rested in part on the belief that immigrants would help facilitate, but not control, this coming prosperity. European immigrants, aside from being conduits for commerce and trade, would also help to break down the "wasteful hacienda system" by increasing the population of the country and forcing the breakup of the large landholdings concentrated in the hands of the few, according to these same authors.[16]

The confidence of postcolonial Mexican intellectuals was further fueled by the publication of Alexander Von Humboldt's (1769–1859) studies of the continent, in which he too incorrectly declared that the wealth of New Spain lay in its rich and abundant lands. His influence on the intelligentsia is evident from an examination of Ortiz de Ayala's *Resumen de la estadística del imperio mexicano, 1822*, which refers explicitly to the "wise baron."[17] According to Von Humboldt's observations, "Those who know the interior of the Spanish colonies from the vague and uncertain notions hitherto published will have some difficulty in believing that the principal sources of the Mexican riches are by no means the mines, but in agriculture which has been gradually ameliorating since the end of the last century."[18] The distinction that was overlooked was not so much the largesse of the territory, but the lack of arable land to irrigate and grow accordingly.

Much of Mexico's available land in the post-independence period, it would later be articulated, was not arable land, but land located either in deserts along the northern frontiers or in extreme tropical locales along the eastern and southern coasts of the Republic. More important, and as Raymond Craib reminds us, much of the territory was not fully surveyed.[19] True as this may have appeared to Humboldt, the bounty and promise of Mexico's fertile lands were seen as the ideal incentives for "energetic, industrious, and liberal-minded Europeans" to colonize in the country. Moreover, the intellectuals and politicians of post-independence Mexico believed that the wealth derived from mining during the colonial period would continue to increase.[20] Various expulsion orders against Spaniards, many of whom were middlemen and of the commercial class, did little to ameliorate the dire economic situation after independence.

This optimism of the Mexican intelligentsia also had its roots in the colonial period, growing out of the conception of "New Spain" as the jewel of the Iberian world[21] that had supplied that world with great riches in the form of bullion, crucial for the rise of the cash economy, and had also contributed the food staples that would eventually bring about the "demographic revolution" in Europe.[22] The large and ever-increasing shipments of silver to Europe and the myths of Mexico's untapped wealth, perpetuated by the writings of Von Humboldt, further bolstered the idea that Mexico would simply have to open its doors to Europe, and the teeming millions would soon come rushing in.[23] Mexican intellectuals and politicians envisioned a republic composed of small yeoman farmers cultivating small plots of land; inevitably they would become part of the world economy and thus hasten the economic development of the nation as a whole. But unlike the United States, Argentina, or Brazil, much of Mexico's arable land was claimed in one form or another by the hacendado class. The "land-tenure system," as Victor Bulmer-Thomas argues, "revolving as it did around the plantation, the *hacienda*, the small farm, and communal Indian lands, was barely affected."[24] In the case of Mexico, a disproportionate amount of available land was not yet surveyed, difficult to work, or located along the frontiers of the republic that were still very much under the control of various independent Indigenous groups, something worth discussing at length.

For most Mexican politicians and intellectuals, the model for parceling out lands to those willing to colonize frontier regions was based partly on their young and expanding neighbor to the north. Mexico, however, developed a different policy toward the indigenes than that of the United States.[25] When discussing the sheer geographical challenge that the Mexican territories represented for these post-independence intellectuals, Ortiz de Ayala could only conclude, after calculating the size of Mexico compared to its concentrated population: "This proves the necessity of adopting the system of the United States, peopling the most depopulated areas with the surplus of inhabitants of some provinces."[26] Based on statements like this, many historians have concluded that Mexicans were quick to accept many aspects of the United States as a model for their own nation "[because] it was evident that the ease with which the United States altered and accepted immigrants had paid off handsomely," according to one view.[27] But the US example would not be followed to the letter because the formulation of and ideology behind Mexico's colonization policy ostensibly reflected Mexico's particular social and cultural milieu. Ortiz de Ayala qualifies his earlier praise of the US system by stressing that Mexico should not "imitate in this part that of our neighbors."[28] And compared to that of the United States, Mexican demography enjoyed a larger Indigenous population.

In the decades prior to the wars of independence, the population of Mexico—and several regions in Central and South America—was predominantly Indigenous. These differing demographics are, in my estimation, important in analyzing why such different policies would be established. Take the estimates of New Spain's population in 1793 that two scholars of colonial Mexico offer the reader: of a population of 3.8 million, approximately 2.3 million were considered "Indian," or around 61 percent of the total.[29] Scholars examining the population statistics for the years between 1810 and 1821 differ with regard to the total population but find essentially the same percentage for the Indigenous population. Historian Eric Van Young states that during this period there were approximately 6.1 million inhabitants in New Spain, of which 3.7 million were Indian, or about 60 percent.[30] Thus the majority of the population was Indigenous during this period and would remain so until well into the nineteenth century. With a population composed primarily of Indigenous peoples, the demographic reality on the ground necessarily provided the reference point for most legislation dealing with the makeup of the population following the wars for independence. This legislation entailed, in some form or fashion, the acceptance of Mexican hegemony or the targeted extermination of indigenes by colonists and other allies of the state.[31]

These ideas shared a long trajectory going back to the colonial period, and the rupture of the wars for independence provided another opportunity to settle unresolved issues. Other historians of Mexico have argued along these same lines, and noted historian William B. Taylor believes that "the Post Independence period brought massive impersonal changes to peasant life, comparable in scale to the sixteenth-century political revolutions, epidemics, resettlement programs, religious conversion, and labor and tax systems that resulted from Spanish colonization."[32] Laws enacted to eliminate the communal property holding of Indigenous peoples "opened the way to the alienation of village lands." Moreover, "the process of dismemberment began in the late 1820s and reached its peak . . . when the Liberals attempted to integrate Indians into national society by dissolving their communal life."[33] Lomnitz expands on this observation in pointing out that "[t]he ideological, legal, and physical assault on communal village lands and other Indigenous community institutions such as hospitals, public political offices, schools, and the management of community chests began in the first years of Independence."[34]

The dissolution of communal life was a tactic of the state to incorporate those who had resisted the imposition of alternative modes of citizenship, like Indios Bárbaros and independent Indians. Among the laws that can be cited as instrumental in the process of incorporating the Indigenous populations of Mexico into the larger "social organism" were those dealing with the question of colonization of and immigration to Mexico, to which we now turn.[35]

European Immigration, 1821–1900

At a more hemispheric level that follows our global approach, one scholar of Latin America argues that intercontinental immigration between 1824 and 1924 totaled "52 million individuals. Some 72% of these set out for the U.S., while 21% departed for Latin America and only 7% for Australia," according to Magnus Mörner. Of the 11 million immigrants who settled in Latin America, 5.5 million (50 percent) settled in Argentina, and 36 percent settled in Brazil, leaving the other Latin American nations only 14 percent of all other European immigrants. By contrast, Mexico received a mere 3 percent of the Latin American total by Mörner's estimates.[36] José Moya's excellent study *Cousins and Strangers, Spanish Immigrants in Buenos Aires, 1850–1930*—which covers a period four years earlier and eight years later—offers us some different numbers worth considering. According to his research, Europeans who migrated to various destinations between 1820 and 1932 totaled 56,183,000. In contrast to Mörner's total, Moya suggests that of the 56 million Europeans who emigrated, 13.4 million made their way to Latin America. In his calculations, the number of European immigrants to Mexico is half of one percent, just 270,000 by 1932.

Of the 13.4 million Europeans who immigrated to Latin America between the 1820s and the 1930s, estimates are that almost 60 percent eventually settled in Argentina. Moya's study of Spanish immigrants to Argentina has not only generated some new numbers and statistics but has also revolutionized the manner in which historians approach the question of transnational migrations to and from the Americas.[37] Between 1820 and 1932, Moya estimates, Argentina received 6.5 million immigrants, coming in second to the United States, which took in 32.5 million immigrants, or five to one. Third was Canada, with 5 million immigrants for the same period.

The larger percentage of immigrants to the United States was due to its geographical location, fertile lands, liberal land and immigration policies, higher wages, and a relatively low population density of Indigenous peoples—a population that usually served to compete with incoming immigrants for wage labor. Argentina too offered higher wages than did Mexico during this period and did little to finance the travel costs of immigrants. Mexico would neither subsidize European immigrants to any significant degree nor raise wages for their sake.

The connection between a high concentration of land after independence and increased wages is something that previous economic historians have noted. Historian Victor Bulmer-Thomas argues, for instance, "The durability of the land-tenure system and the domestic capital markets implied that no drastic changes could be made in labor relations or in the operation of labor markets."[38] Countries more apt to adopt and adapt to global markets were also those that offered higher wages to potential immigrants seeking to earn better money abroad. Timothy J. Hatton and Jeffrey Williamson note in their *longue durée* analysis of global immigration during this period, "Undoubtedly, the major incentive for emigration was the large difference between wages in the country of origin and those in the country of destination."[39] Wages in Mexico and "the Mexican economy stagnated throughout the first half of the nineteenth century . . . and it was not until the second half of the nineteenth century that the economy once again began to grow, slowly at first throughout the 1860 s and 1870 s, then accelerating during the final decades of the century," according to Enrique Cárdenas.[40]

And although legislation favoring some groups over others is perhaps not as important for some scholars, I would argue that it is crucial for understanding the question of national identity as it relates to the demographic composition of the country. Besides, what better way to analyze how a nation imagines itself if not by the very people who compose it? Legislation may not always be able to control who arrives in the country, but it certainly speaks volumes as to what kind of people are initially desired. Early ideas about immigration in Argentina favored North Americans and the English, but in the end, Argentina ended up with a population that was considered "least desirable" by the likes of Juan Bautista Alberdi—the intellectual author behind Argentina's immigration policies.[41] Brazil, on the other hand, sought to replace African slave labor with industrious and pliable European immigrants but ultimately ended up abandoning colonization projects for low-wage local laborers by the 1930s.[42]

Mexico's approach was multifaceted and shaped by a large population of Indigenous groups along its northern frontiers. Fear of land loss shaped this colonization policy and forced the country to incorporate a population that could act decidedly in a battle for supremacy, and later as a "buffer zone" between the center and periphery of Mexico. The difference between the three countries is the presence of the United States and the new international boundary. As the quintessential preferred location of most immigrants coming from Europe, the higher wages and more intense labor demands pulled emigrants from Mexico at a time when places like Argentina, Brazil, and Cuba were enjoying the benefits of new immigrants.

What we can say from this brief overview of European immigration to Mexico is that by 1876, between twenty-five thousand and thirty-five thousand foreigners had taken up residence since the liberalization of immigration policies in 1823. The total number of immigrants (European and otherwise) to Mexico increased to 116,527 by the end of the Porfiriato in 1910. After the Great Depression, this number more than doubled to 270,000 according to some scholars, though Mexico was in thirteenth place among the nations that received immigrants during this period, or about 2 percent of the Latin American total. By contrast Argentina received 6,501,000 immigrants, followed by Canada (5,073,000), Brazil (4,361,000), and Cuba (1,394,000).[43] In each of these countries, we can generally assume, laws were not passed that restricted immigration to those of the Catholic faith nor was legislation ambivalent about its treatment of foreign immigrants. There were no expulsion orders against Spaniards in any of these countries after independence comparable to those enacted by Mexico, nor did these countries share a border with the United States.[44] These countries, finally, offered better wages to potential immigrants.

These numbers stand in stark contrast to the numbers of Mexican laborers who migrated to the United States during the same period. For example, the 1930 US Census states that there were 1,422,533 Mexicans residing in the US Southwest while a mere 270,000 immigrants resided in Mexico, leaving a deficit in the population of 1,152,533.[45] Even during the period just prior to Porfirio Díaz taking power, the foreign population numbered between twenty-five thousand and thirty-five thousand, and the number of Mexican migrants to the United States totaled 68,399 by 1880. In other words, two Mexicans were leaving the country for every foreigner who arrived in Mexico between 1821 and 1876. After the 1870s, this disparity would increase. By 1930, upward of 5.2 Mexicans were leaving for the United States for every foreigner that arrived in Mexico. Put in another way, more Mexicans had migrated to the United States by the 1930s than Europeans had arrived in Cuba, which numbered 1,394,000 immigrants and constituted the fifth most popular destination for immigrants to the Americas.

This paradox of inviting Europeans to colonize Mexican territory and then seeing its own population migrate northward did not occur in any other Latin American country during this period. Even Francisco I. Madero, Mexico's "apostle of democracy" and the first president of the revolution, lamented the situation in his country when he pointed out in 1910 that "Mexico is the only country in all of the Americas where its nationals migrate abroad."[46] Although the contrast between European immigration to Mexico and Mexican emigration to the United States is stark, it is important to keep in mind the historical context of this paradox. To begin with, although Mexico was one of the few countries to receive immigrants during this period, it shared a border with a northern neighbor (the preferred destination for 32.5 million immigrants) that also attracted Mexican laborers from the northern states of the republic—the very region that the country had struggled to settle and colonize prior to 1848. Thus, although Mexico sought to invite European settlers, if only on paper, its own laborers were migrating north in growing numbers, a trend which would escalate under the Porfirian regime and which continues almost without pause to this very day.

Post-Independence Ideologies of Mexico: Inclusion and Exclusion

The version of the Mexican nation championed by the government of Agustin de Iturbide—the failed constitutional emperor whose administration lasted less than a year after independence in 1821—was considered the most likely to succeed in "modernizing" the country according to Western values and via symbols and rituals provided by the elite during the colonial period. Through various methods, the Indigenous populations were obligated to "accept and assimilate the cultural values they [Iturbide's government] upheld and recognized as the only possible government and nationality for the state—the Mexican nation."[47] Noted intellectual José María Luis Mora summed up the postcolonial liberal stance when he pointed out that the Farías administration that ruled in the following decades ignored the distinctions "of past years that were proscribed in constitutional law, but he applied all his efforts towards forcing the fusion of the Aztec race with the general masses; thus he did not recognize the distinction between Indians and non-Indians in government acts, but instead he replaced it with one between the poor and the rich, extending to all the benefits of society."[48]

The goal was to *transform* the Indians, who were the majority of the nation's population, into Mexicans. The government's hope was that these new citizens would convert their property into private holdings and subsequently become part of the global economy; this would enable Mexico to join the larger community of modern nations. Here the inclusion of the Indigenous population also entailed the loss of the institutional protections these communities had enjoyed during the colonial period. No longer able to rely on the large corporate holdings protected by the Spanish colonial system for three hundred years, the Indigenous peoples were expected to become private landowners who would be self-sustaining and therefore subject to state taxation and rationalization. For this reason, the immigration of Europeans—as individuals outside the "colonial constitutions" of the Mexican Indians—would assist in modernizing and rationalizing the republic.[49]

Another factor that had plagued colonial officials was the disproportionate concentration of the population in a handful of states around Mexico City. Magnus Mörner notes, "[T]he approximately seven million Mexicans who formed the population in 1821 were insufficient for a land that extended from Oregon to Yucatán and from Texas to Guatemala."[50] The presence of the state in the sparsely populated northern regions radiated outward from the center in the form of presidios, military colonies, and citizen–soldiers, while the church extended its influence via the extensive yet waning missions system.[51] Most of the population in Mexico was concentrated in areas where the presence of the state was more visible and most capable of protecting its citizens from the raids that were frequent in areas of low population density, like the north. The millions of Europeans migrating to the Western Hemisphere, it was hoped, would people the north and take up arms on behalf of "civilization."[52] Joining them in this larger national project to settle *terrenos baldíos* would be the Mexicans concentrated in the center of the country. In short, the presence of the state along its peripheries was limited, and immigration policy was therefore seen as one of the many remedies to this ongoing concern in post-independence Mexico.

Immigration debates after 1821 thus centered on two questions: whether the Mexican government should focus its energy on inviting Europeans to settle in Mexico or whether it should concentrate on what was then known as "auto-colonización" or "colonization from the interior."[53] The latter entailed the resettling of primarily an Indigenous population in locations where the inhabitants were not considered sufficiently loyal to the state. The former entailed the immigration of European settlers to sparsely settled areas in the Mexican republic, offering them lands and then Mexicanizing them. What eventually became settled law was that all subsequent colonies would be mixed with Mexican citizens, and no colony composed of foreigners would be able to settle twenty leagues from the border in order to prevent another Texas episode. The ideology of colonization in Mexico was based on a number of demographic particulars, and as a result, very different immigration and colonization policies were developed there when compared to Argentina, Brazil, or the United States. Two proposals submitted to the first Mexican Empire provide us with a detailed description of post-independence Mexico and illustrate the ideology behind the colonization policy prior to its transformation into various laws and decrees between 1821 and 1848.

Early Proposals for Colonization: From Conquest to Colonization

The most telling of these proposals was presented on December 29, 1821, to the governing junta, following independence from Spanish rule. Entitled *Dictamen Presentado a la Soberana Junta Gubernativa del Imperio Mexicano* (1821) (hereafter *Naciones Bárbaras*), this extensive document made several observations, recommendations, and other suggestions that would outline colonization policy in the coming years.[54] The policy shift in this document represents a slight departure from the colonial approach with regard to the process of colonizing—and therefore "civilizing"—the Indigenous populations of the north. According to this document, "conquest" was out of the question, and a different strategy of colonization would have to be employed along the northern corridors populated by Indios Bárbaros.

Beginning with a description of the largest of these Indigenous groups in the northern part of the republic, *Naciones Bárbaras* suggests that it is "necessary to abandon all projects of conquest" because there were not enough people to settle those lands. The first observation reflects the recognition that—both in the past and at present—there was a sheer lack of bodies to populate and guard the northern frontiers.[55] Employing an early version of cost-benefit analysis, the document noted the costly nature of conquest, suggesting the best prospects for success lay in the establishment of friendly commercial ties with those areas where such ties did not exist and in maintaining ties where they were already established:

> The punctuality in complying with the treaties and good faith in commerce are the magnetism that attracts the Indians, and by this conduct they communicate their fruits and riches, they become civilized, they acquire the better uses and customs; and they are disposed unfeelingly to embrace the religion established in the Provinces and with the inhabitants of the *reducciones* and towns that have a relationship with them. If the Empire would adopt this measure it will achieve greater profits with lower expenses comparable to those realized by the English, the French, and the Anglo-Americans.[56]

The comparison with the French, English, and Anglo-American strategies of conquest is notable and illustrates the power and influence of the Indian nations themselves. Past experience had taught the previous governments that Indigenous populations could be employed and coerced by other European powers seeking to advance their expansionist projects in the Americas.[57] The change in policy proposed in this document is that conquest be abandoned in favor of colonization, but with the same end results. We can therefore say that the strategy changed while the intention remained the same, the intention being to forcefully assimilate or acculturate independent Indians into the larger social organism.

These same concerns are voiced in another document by Tadeo Ortiz de Ayala, titled *Resumen de la estadística del imperio mexicano, 1822*, which constitutes part of a genealogy to the immigration and colonization policies that emerged in the years following independence. Influenced by the Enlightenment ideas of the day—notably the writings of Adam Smith, Alexander Von Humboldt, and Melchor Gaspar de Jovellanos—Ortiz de Ayala's attitudes toward the Indigenous populations mirrored those expressed in *Naciones Barbaras.*[58] Brief and yet erudite, *Resumen de la estadística del imperio mexicano, 1822* covers issues surrounding geography, demography, economics, sources of wealth, and problems with governmentality in the first part and then offers up suggestions for solving these issues in the second part. Here, Ortiz de Ayala provides 115 recommendations on a variety of issues including political thought, foreign policy, public education, labor, agriculture, industry, commerce, transportation, and finally colonization.[59]

With respect to the northern territories with which this chapter is most concerned, Tadeo Ortiz de Ayala remains faithful to the Enlightenment ideals that had so influenced the intelligentsia during the Bourbon reforms as he condemns the cruel treatment of the indigenes by military and ecclesiastical authorities situated along the northern frontiers.[60] His commentary is worth quoting at some length here because he suggests the same recommendations made in *Dictamen Presentado a la Soberana Junta Gubernativa del Imperio Mexicano* (1821). For Ortiz de Ayala:

> The conduct of the cruel soldiers and the ignorant missionaries of the northern borders is neither the best means to attract the innumerable nations, whom the missions of the United States solicit with other political methods for the commercial advantage and growth of that nation. It is very sad to see a continuous and costly bloodthirsty war against towns that did no wrong to begin with, *and that are called barbarian because they do not wish to be converted by force* [emphasis added], while the protestant missionaries with their charity and sweetness are able to civilize, they convince with their persuasion, gaining the friendship of innumerable peoples, to the extent that our north provinces could cause incalculable harm in times of war with that republic.[61]

The overarching concern of Ortiz de Ayala is that the indigenes be treated with a benevolent "sweetness" lest they be converted by the "protestant missionaries" who can later "cause incalculable harm in times of war with that republic [the United States]." Ortiz de Ayala advocates abandoning the previous politics of conquest in favor of a more "benevolent" and "sweet" policy of colonization as the "best means to incorporate [into the Mexican state] the numerous nations," largely in the interest of realpolitik and national security. Recognizing the resistance to Mexican hegemony, or its unsuccessful efforts to pacify these independent Indigenous groups, to add just one more detail, is also recognizing that although the tactics would change, the intention of the state would not. Whether "sweet" or "sour," the Mexican state would forcibly incorporate or decimate independent Indians.[62]

As to the question of colonization, Ortiz de Ayala discussed the importance of populating and settling a number of areas throughout the Mexican Empire within the context of his larger imaginings for the nation. These imaginings were directly tied to his main concern regarding populating the vast and rich areas of the country. According to Ortiz de Ayala:

> [T]he integrity of the national territory continues to be weak, [and] risks being lost if there is not a change in the system or an adoption of positive measures to promote its security, by means of a strong local administration that is dependent on and conciliatory towards the federal government, [and] since that frontier point embraces the interests of the entire confederacy, it is the one who should take charge of its care and custody.[63]

His preference for European immigrants is not stated in the section where he makes those recommendations. Instead, what is expressed, at least according to article 105, is the author's excitement concerning Chinese and South Indian (the word *Indu* is used) immigrants.[64] These "hard-working inhabitants," according to Ortiz de Ayala, are accustomed to the tropical climate of the Mexican coastal areas.[65] And although "foreign families" are mentioned and favored for colonization, they are mentioned within the same paragraph as "useful nationals," "military veterans," and "federal employees." In short, the question of colonization in the aftermath of independence is tied directly to the territorial integrity of the nation and hence the Indigenous populations of the republic, but within the context of the global phenomenon of transnational immigration.

Immigration Policies after Independence, 1821–1846

As with much Mexican legislation that followed independence from Spain, several significant issues remained unresolved with the conclusion of hostilities, including a number of pending cases with respect to colonization of the northern frontiers. The Spanish government had been aware for decades of the potential threats posed by the Americans, French, and Russians, so efforts to grant lands for colonization were well under way by the time of independence.[66] Although ambivalence surrounding foreign colonization was voiced as early as 1813, the increasing number of Euro-Americans in Texas compelled the Mexican government to legally address the reality at hand.[67]

The best known, and most crucial for understanding the evolution of colonization policy, was a grant awarded to Moses Austin to settle three hundred families in Texas in January of 1821. Spanish officials in Monterrey had authorized Austin to colonize what is now Texas when a number of events led to the reconfiguration of the original agreement between Austin and the fledgling Spanish government. The first was that the Mexican monarchy instituted by Iturbide fell not long afterward, thus rendering all previous contracts null and void. Second was the fact that the elder Austin died before he could act on the grant, which was taken up by his son Stephen F. Austin. The younger Austin began to lead families into Texas in mid-1822 with the knowledge of the governor of Texas at San Antonio de Bexar.

Because the Mexican government was still forming coalitions in the wake of independence, Austin opted to travel to Mexico City to confirm the specifics of his colonization plan. According to historian Andrés Reséndez, "Austin . . . spent all of 1822 and part of 1823 in Mexico City, validating a Texas land grant that the Spanish colonial government had conferred on his father."[68] By the time Austin returned to Texas, the newly independent republic had passed an updated colonization law that restructured the older law under which the elder Austin had been awarded his grant.[69] The first colonization law, however, is worth going over for the purposes of comparison with the national colonization law published a year later.

The colonization contract that approved the land grant to Moses Austin in 1821 emanated from the northern territories and was subsequently replicated in the Imperial Colonization Law of 1823. Certain features of Austin's contract became standard and were codified in federal law, illustrating the effect of peripheral and regional particularities on federal legislation. We can see in this one example of legislative borrowing the dialectical relationship between the northern territories and Mexico City. This was a legislative pattern that persisted throughout the century as the central government sought to extend its hegemony throughout the peripheries. After independence, all contracts between the Spanish government and other northern state officials were eventually nullified with the publication of the more comprehensive Imperial Colonization Law of 1823.[70] This colonization law was approved during the brief reign of Emperor Agustín I and replaced by a national colonization law a year and a half later. The Austin colony came under this law, as well as most land grants that were awarded henceforth.

Contrary to the claims of historians concerning the whitening of Mexico (similar to what occurred in Brazil or Argentina), at least according to the Imperial Colonization Law of 1823, the articles of the law do not reveal anything that would indicate this particular objective, particularly considering that the law privileged war veterans, Mexicans, and Europeans who had married Mexican women. Moreover, article 18 states that "[n]atives of the country shall have a preference in the distribution of land; and particularly the military of the 'Army of the Three Guarantees,' in conformity with the decree of the 27th of March, 1821; and also those who served in the first epoch of the insurrection." And in support of my earlier point regarding the ongoing Mexicanization of the nation, article 27 injects a third element, intended to incorporate foreigners into the nation, when it states, "Those with the foregoing qualifications who marry Mexicans will acquire particular credit for obtaining letters of citizenship."[71] This example of legislated Mexicanization, or assimilation, contradicts some of the interpretations that I discussed in the historiographical section.[72]

In effect, one could argue that this particular colonization policy not only sought to provide settlers with lands that would serve collectively as a buffer zone between Mexico and the expansionist United States, but it also sought to Mexicanize these colonists by requiring them to convert to Catholicism and later be naturalized as Mexicans. As for the Indigenous populations, it states that "[n]atives of the country shall have a preference in the distribution of land," as suggested in the *Dictamen Presentado a la Soberana Junta Gubernativa del Imperio Mexicano por la Comisión de Relaciones Exteriores en 29 de Diciembre de 1821*. In terms of what this document tells us about how the nation imagines itself, we can draw the same conclusions from it as from the Imperial Colonization Law of 1823. And despite the fact that these policies clearly illustrate a preference for Mexicans willing to colonize the northern frontier, another piece of legislation from the frontier is worth examining here in order to observe how the incorporation of the Indigenous populations was ultimately inserted into the legislative workings of colonization policy.

The Colonization Law of the State of Coahuila and Texas, 1825 is the final piece of colonization policy that we will examine in this section before analyzing the exclusionary law of April 6, 1830, which prohibited further migration of Euro-American settlers from the United States to Mexico. This law illustrates the dialectical relationship between state and federal colonization policy, particularly the inclusion of local and regional specifics that demonstrate how the Indigenous populations were incorporated into the nation via colonization policy.[73] One of the main distinctions posited by this particular colonization law is made clear by its open reference to the incorporation of "wandering tribes" of the region. According to article 19:

> The Indians of all nations, bordering on the state, as well as wandering tribes that may be within its limits, shall be received in the markets, without paying any duties whatever for commerce in the products of the country; and if attracted by the moderation and confidence, with which they shall be treated, any of them, after having first declared themselves in favor of our Religion and Institutions, wish to establish themselves in any settlements that are forming, they shall be admitted, and the same quantity of land given them, as to the settlers spoken of in the 14th and 15th articles, always preferring native Indians to "strangers."[74]

Note the double move where the law requires a declaration that favors the religion and institutions of Mexico while at the same time affirming that the colonization and settlement of the indigenes is always more preferable to that of "strangers." The two articles mentioned—the fourteenth and fifteenth—are familiar because they were written into law in previous colonization policies that we have examined.[75] It seems, therefore, that Indios Bárbaros and foreigners in this regard are "strangers" while "the Indians of all nations (read civilized) are preferred to strangers." More explicit but less talked about is the open reference to the notion of "always preferring native Indians to strangers" and the "Indians of all nations, bordering on the state, as well as wandering tribes." In this case it is evident that the inclusion of the indigenes is intended to work itself out in the form of a policy whereby the local inhabitants are eventually assimilated into the system.

The laws mentioned earlier, despite their overt preference for native Mexicans and Indigenous groups, did not have their intended effect, and soon the northern frontiers were populated with thousands of Euro-American and American settlers. Just five years after the passage of the 1830 law, the "Anglo-Texas and slave population had grown to about 24,700 inhabitants, outnumbering Mexican Texans ten to one."[76] Encouraged by the enactment of these liberal land policies, Euro-American settlers, mostly from the trans-Appalachia states of Tennessee, Missouri, Arkansas, Alabama, Mississippi, and Louisiana, entered Texas to take advantage of inexpensive land and numerous concessions afforded to potential settlers.[77]

The events that transpired thereafter, which ultimately led to the loss of Texas and the defeat of General President Santa Anna in 1836, is a topic of great interest and debate and certainly well beyond the scope of this chapter. Suffice it to say that the growing migration of these Euro-American settlers provided the structural conditions (demographically) for what later became known as the Texas Revolution of 1836. Aware of the problem posed by these settlers, the Mexican government passed a law five years earlier prohibiting further migration to Mexico, but to no avail.[78]

Toward Exclusion: Colonization Policy during the Mid-Nineteenth Century

This alarming increase in population, along with an 1828 report on frontier conditions submitted by General Manuel Mier y Terán, caused the federal government in Mexico City to implement what has become known as the Law of April 6, 1830.[79] This law, composed of eighteen articles and quite explicit in its intentions, is a project calculated to exclude foreigners from its territory, even as regional authorities argued in favor of continued migration to these areas.[80] Articles 7 and 9 are central to the process of exclusion as they testify not only to a fear of a potential takeover by these settlers but also to a national hysteria concerning foreigners; another expression of the latter phenomenon was the expulsion orders against Spaniards between 1821 and 1836, coupled with a fear that foreigners were conspiring against Mexican independence.[81]

In order to prevent Euro-American demographic dominance, the law called for the introduction of more Mexican settlers to the area. Article 7 states that "Mexican families that voluntarily want to colonize will be helped with the trip; maintained for a year, given lands and other tools for work."[82] This article of inclusion has as its counterpart one of exclusion in Article 9 in the following, "The entrance of foreigners under any pretext without being provided with a passport issued by the agents of the Republic, at the point of origin, is prohibited along the northern border."[83] The entrance of slavers was also explicitly prohibited in this law, even though the practice had been outlawed nine years earlier. The exclusion of slaves was not intended to keep out African Americans due to any racialized ideology that targeted people of African descent, but was rather a political move intended to discourage the migration of more settlers from the southern United States, many of whom were bringing slaves with them.[84] In the end, this law could not prevent the entrance of settlers who had crossed over into Mexican territory in order to colonize the northernmost regions of the republic.

What was worse, the law had the unintended consequence of inciting the colonists to rebellion, which grew into an independence movement leading to the eventual secession of Texas from the Mexican republic and its annexation a decade later by the United States. This action, as many historians in this field have already concluded, ultimately led to a break in diplomatic relations between the two countries and culminated in the Mexican-American War of 1846–1848.

But while some Europeans were being invited into the larger Mexican family, others were being asked to leave by force. Anti-Spanish sentiment had come to the surface during the wars for independence, when upward of one-eighth of the white population was violently murdered, culminating in the tragic events of the "Alhóndiga de Granaditas" in 1810.[85] The antagonism directed by Mexicans toward *gachupines* soon shifted to other European groups considered a threat to the nation. When the Mexican government passed a law in the early 1820s, reserving the right to expel any foreigner who hindered the struggle for independence, foreign governments requested assurances that their citizens had legal rights as long as they did not meddle in Mexican affairs.[86] And it was precisely this fear of European interference that eventually led to the expulsion of Spaniards on three separate occasions between 1821 and 1836, coupled, no doubt, with Spain's reluctance to recognize the independence of its former colony. Although federal expulsions did not begin until 1827, tensions had been building amid the struggle for independence.[87]

Between 1821 and 1836, five national laws and a number of state-level expulsions were implemented in order to rid the newly formed Mexican nation of its Spanish populace.[88] According to Harold Dana Sims, "perhaps a maximum figure of 10,000 might be reasonable for the *peninsular* community at Independence when the national population had reached about 6,500,000.[89] When the first expulsion took place in late December 1827, 1,823 passports were issued, and departure lists recorded 1,771 exiles. The following year, 885 *peninsulares* left on their own, followed by fifty-three servants.[90] And although strong anti-Spanish sentiment was made visible during the wars for Mexican independence, Dana Sims reminds the reader that "a substantial source of *Criollo* pro expulsionist sentiment was mercantile rivalry between Mexicans and Spaniards during a period of severe economic decline."[91]

Spaniards in Mexico, 1810–1900

Between the three mass expulsions, the National Colonization Law of 1824, and the break in diplomatic relations between the United States and Mexico in 1846, no other colonization laws or decrees of any substance were passed.[92] The case of Texas loomed large in subsequent colonization policy. This is apparent in a circular published a decade later, intended as a reminder to those who would take charge of the *Dirección de Colonización* in late 1846. According to that circular:

> [T]he only one [colonization policy] that has been established and that has prospered, is the one that rebelled in Texas, because the thought of its establishment was not for an economic or commercial venture, but for the usurpation of our territory, taking advantage of the youthful innocence with which the Republic extended its arms to all of the foreign nations without fear during the first days of its independent existence.[93]

The legislation approving the creation of a Department of Colonization in 1846 signaled the importance of having one agency manage and encourage immigration. This law was enacted during the Mexican-American War in 1846—a war that would not end for another fourteen months. It was a case of too little, too late for the inhabitants of the territories that would ultimately be lost to the United States. Until then, little would change in terms of immigration policy. Afterward, Mexican expatriates and Indians were not only specifically mentioned within the national project but also served as symbols of exclusion in other instances when the territorial integrity of the nation was threatened.

If we take into account the number of immigration and colonization laws that were passed between the war with the United States and the beginning of 1876, at least according to the *Código de colonización y terrenos baldíos de la republica mexicana*, the same pattern regarding the inclusion of the indigenes that I have outlined appears to continue.[94] Postwar immigration and colonization laws seemed to echo the sentiments of José María

Lacunza, postwar secretary of the interior, when he noted the following about immigration and colonization policies for the latter half of the nineteenth century:

> [Regarding the allotment of lands used to invite new settlers,] to liberally grant them would resemble sarcasm, if at the same time indigenous peoples, estranged from their own land, were not deserving of the prudent consideration of the Government. This long standing population should also be attended to, so that it might multiply and prosper; and its prosperity cannot be expected without an easy and abundant means of nourishing itself that, for rural inhabitants, is not possible without productive lands to work.[95]

Even as late as 1898, the great Mexican diplomat Matías Romero maintained that Indians should be converted into "active citizens, consumers, and producers." And when speaking about European immigration, he seemingly echoed these mid-nineteenth-century sentiments when he argued, "[B]efore we think of spending money to encourage European immigration to Mexico, we ought to promote the education of our Indians, which I consider the principal public need of the country."[96] In other words, the lack of European migration to Mexico would later necessitate the continued policy of forced, coerced, or implied assimilation or acculturation of the Indigenous Mexican population.

Policies favoring Europeans over Mexicans would not be part of the Porfirian project of colonization either, as I will attempt to illustrate in later chapters. The Porfirian period between 1876 and 1911 would partly reflect nationalist ideology in terms of immigration and colonization principles intended to re-implement repatriation of the frontier. Laws encouraging European immigration are almost always accompanied by references to "Mexicanization," or to incentives for incorporating Indigenous and Mexican families founded by those few European colonies.[97] New laws, especially the 1883 Land and Colonization Law, would extend invitations for Mexicans in the United States to "return to the homeland," with the most preferential treatment ever written into Mexican immigration and colonization policies during the nineteenth century. Article XVI of the 1883 law demonstrates this new agenda of Mexico's evolving colonization and immigration policies when it stipulates that "Mexicans residing in a foreign country who are desirous of establishing themselves in the uninhabited frontiers of the Republic will have the right to a free land grant, up to an extension of 200 hectares (double that of foreign immigrants) and enjoyed for fifteen years, the exemptions granted by this law."[98] In short, repatriates were allotted twice the amount of land awarded to potential European colonists and any other foreign immigrants.

Conclusion

This chapter examined post-independence immigration laws and the role of Indios Bárbaros and Independent Indians, in particular how their demographic and strategic positions influenced the direction and ultimate implementation of Mexican colonization policy throughout the nineteenth century. The conclusions reached in this chapter contradict a view in the historiography that suggests these policies were implemented to whiten the populations like those in Argentina or Brazil and as such were failures of Mexican immigration and colonization policy. Mexico's immigration policies emerged in large part as a way to incorporate the majority of the Indigenous populace into the larger Mexican family, but also as a way to Mexicanize Indigenous communities outside of state control.

Mexico liberalized its immigration policies throughout the nineteenth century, but ultimately a number of factors prevented large-scale immigration of Europeans to that country during this period of mass global movements. I suggest that three Spanish expulsions, unfertile and unsurveyed lands, restrictive immigration policies, religious intolerance toward non-Catholics, and especially low wages all served to discourage immigration from abroad. In the midst of these efforts to attract European immigrants to settle the northern frontiers, Mexico saw a process set in motion by which the loss of its northern territories resulted due to those regions being underpopulated and contested by Independent Indians. Those who eventually did inhabit those regions were Anglo-Americans and other Euro-American settlers arriving to Texas beginning in the early nineteenth century. Mexicans who remained within the ceded territories were later asked to settle the northernmost regions of Mexico in order to act as a buffer between the latter and the former. This experience would impact colonization and immigration policy thereafter. Nevertheless, European immigrants did come to Mexico during the nineteenth century, although in smaller numbers than was the case in countries such as Argentina, the United States, or Brazil. Most would not settle in government-sponsored colonies, but instead chose to live in various urban centers of the republic.

Notes

1. José Moya, "A Continent of Immigrants: Postcolonial Shifts in the Western Hemisphere," *Hispanic American Historical Review* 86 (February 2006): 1–28.

2. Adam McKeown, "Global Migration, 1846–1940," *Journal of World History* 15 (June 2004): 155–89.

3. Moya, "A Continent of Immigrants," 1–28; Magnus Mörner, *Adventurers and Proletarians: The Story of Migrants in Latin America* (Pittsburgh, Penn.: University of Pittsburgh Press & UNESCO, 1985); Jürgen Bucheneau, "Small Number, Great Impact: Mexico and Its Immigrants, 1821–1973," *Journal of American Ethnic History* 20 (Spring 2001): 23–49.

4. Bill Ong Hing, *Defining America Through Immigration Policy* (Philadelphia: Temple University Press, 2004), 2.

5. Claudio Lomnitz, *Exits from the Labyrinth: Culture and Ideology in the Mexican National Space* (Berkeley: University of California Press, 1992), 2.

6. For some examples of these varying discussions, please see Martin S. Stabb, "Indigenism and Racism in Mexican Thought: 1857–1911," *Journal of Inter-American Studies* 1 (October 1959): 405–23; and T. G. Powell, "Mexican Intellectuals and the Indian Question, 1876–1911," *The Hispanic American Historical Review* 48 (February 1968): 19–36.

7. F. de la Maza, *Código de colonización*, 386–406; Article 1, Chapter 3 of *Proyectos de iniciativa sobre colonización* stated: "[F]oreigners originating from any nation of the world will be admitted in the territory of the Republic, without the need of a passport."

8. The term *interactive frames* is borrowed from Lomnitz, *Deep Mexico, Silent Mexico*, 13–14.

9. Ong Hing, *Defining America Through Immigration Policy*, 2.

10. Lomnitz, *Deep México, Silent* México, 29. The same pattern, one could argue, holds true for North Americans who were welcomed first as *empresarios*, then excluded after the 1830s and 1848, only to be reinvited during the Porfiriato (1876–1910) before again being excluded after 1911 (especially the Mormon Exodus of 1912).

11. Ibid., 27.

12. David J. Weber, *The Mexican Frontier, 1821–1846: The American Southwest Under Mexico* (Albuquerque: University of New Mexico Press, 1982), 103.

13. José Gutiérrez de Lara, *Proyecto de Ley General de Colonización, 1822*; quoted in Burden, *La Idea Salvadora*, 54.

14. Some of these intellectuals included Manuel Mier y Terán, Antonio Cumplido, Refugio de la Garza, José Gutiérrez de Lara, Juan José Espinosa de Monteros, and Lorenzo de Zavala.

15. Simón Tadeo Ortiz de Ayala, *Resumen de la estadística del imperio mexicano, 1822, estudio preliminar*, revisión de texto, notas y anexos de Tarsicio García Díaz (México: Biblioteca Nacional, Universidad Autónoma de México, Reimprimido, 1968), 53. Original: "La situación física del imperio mexicano ofrece ventajas inapreciables, considerada con respecto a sus comunicaciones con el resto del mundo civilizado. Situado en un istmo bañado por el Pacifico y Atlántico, el antiguo imperio de Anahuac parece estar destinado a ejercer un grande influjo en los acontecimientos políticos que agitan las grandes naciones. El gobierno del imperio puede comunicarse en cinco semanas con Europa, en seis con Asia y en tres con ambas Americas."

16. Berninger's reading of Gutiérrez de Lara also makes this point. Please see "Mexican Attitudes Towards Immigration," 24–25.

17. Simón Tadeo Ortiz de Ayala, *Resumen de la estadística del imperio mexicano*, 14.

18. Humboldt does mention earlier in his study that bullion also constituted a large source of income for Europe, when he points out: "The quantity of gold and silver annually sent by the New Continent into Europe amounts to more than nine-tenths of the produce of the whole mines in the known world." See *Political Essay on the Kingdom of New Spain*, trans. John Black (New York: I. Riley, 1811), ci and 54.

19. Raymond Craib, *Cartographic Mexico: A History of State Fixations and Fugitive Landscapes* (Durham, N.C.: Duke University Press, 2004).

20. Javier Ocampo, "El entusiasmo, expresión espontánea ante el triunfo," Capitulo I en *Las ideas de un* día; el pueblo mexicano ante la consumación de su independencia (México: Colegio de México, 1969), 13–45.

21. The optimism of Mexicans was something shared by many in independent Latin America. See Victor Bulmer-Thomas, *The Economic History of Latin America Since Independence*, 2nd ed. (Cambridge: Cambridge University Press, 2003), 2.

22. Alfred W. Crosby, "The Demographic Effect of American Crops in Europe," Chapter 9 in *Germs, Seeds and Animals: Studies in Ecological History* (Armonk, N.Y.: M.E. Sharpe, 1994), 148–63. The term *demographic revolution* is also borrowed from José C. Moya, *Cousins and Strangers: Spanish Immigrants in Buenos Aires, 1850–1930* (Berkeley: University of California Press, 1998), 13–44.

23. "Mexican industry experienced a boom in the first quarter of the century that was followed by successive spurts of growth that registered an output of between 1801 and 1810 to over 200 million pesos, more than four times the amount for 1701–1710. See Burkholder and Johnson, *Colonial Latin America*, 5th ed. (New York: Oxford University Press, 2004), 149–50; also John Lynch, *The Spanish American Revolutions, 1808–1826* (New York: W.W. Norton & Company, 1973), 295–96.

24. Bulmer-Thomas, *The Economic History of Latin America*, 29.

25. Historian David Weber posits, "Throughout the Spanish American mainland by the 1790s, numerous Indigenous peoples had been incorporated rather than eliminated, and most of the Natives who still lived independently along the borders of New Spain's American empire had come to some form of accommodation with the Hispanic world, and it with them." See *Bárbaros: Spaniards and Their Savages in the Age of Enlightenment* (New Haven & London: Yale University Press, 2005), 2.

26. Ibid., 19.

27. Berninger, "Mexican Attitudes Towards Immigration," 18.

28. Ortiz de Ayala, *Resumen de la estadística del imperio mexicano, 1822*, 85.

29. Jaime E. Rodríguez O. and Colin M. MacLachlan, *Forging of the Cosmic Race: A Reinterpretation of Colonial México, Expanded Edition* (Los Angeles: University of California Press, 1990), 197.

30. Eric Van Young, *The Other Rebellion: Popular Violence, Ideology, and the Mexican Struggle for Independence, 1810–1821* (Stanford: Stanford University Press, 2001): 46–47.

31. Jorge Chávez Chávez, *Los indios en la formación de la identidad nacional* (Ciudad Juárez, Chih.: Universidad Autónoma de Ciudad Juárez, 2003).

32. William B. Taylor, *Drinking, Homicide and Rebellion in Colonial Mexican Villages* (Stanford: Stanford University Press, 1976), 146.

33. Ibid.

34. Lomnitz, "Communitarian Ideologies and Nationalism," in *Deep Mexico, Silent Mexico*, 48.

35. It should also be pointed out that the census plays a significant role in reorienting and therefore reclassifying Indigenous populations as "Mestizo." See, for instance, Alexander S. Dawson, "From Models for the Nation to Model Citizens: Indigenismo and the 'Revindication' of the Mexican Indian, 1920–40," *Journal of Latin American Studies* 30 (1998): 279–308; Anne Doremus, "Indigenism, Mestizaje, and National Identity in Mexico during the 1940s and the 1950s," *Mexican Studies/Estudios Mexicanos* 17 (Summer 2001): 375–402; for the re-shifting of Indigenous identities in Brazil, see Muriel Nazzari, "Vanishing Indians: The Social Construction of Race in Colonial Sao Paulo," *The Americas* 57 (April 2001): 497–524; for the case of Argentina, see Gastón Gordillo, "Indigenous Struggles and Contested Identities in Argentina: Histories of Invisibilization and Reemergence," *Journal of Latin American Anthropology* 8 (2003): 4–30.

36. Magnus Mörner, *Adventurers and Proletarians: The Story of Migrants in Latin America* (Pittsburgh: University of Pittsburgh Press, 1985); for studies of immigration in Chile and Argentina, see Carl Solberg, *Immigration and Nationalism, Argentina and Chile, 1890–1914* (Austin: University of Texas Press, 1970); and Moya, *Cousins and Strangers*.

37. Moya, *Cousins and Strangers*, 46–47.

38. Bulmer-Thomas, *The Economic History of Latin America*, 30.

39. Timothy J. Hatton and Jeffrey Williamson, "Migration during 1820–1920, the First Global Century," *World Economic and Social Survey* (2004), 10.

40. Enrique Cárdenas, "A Macroeconomic Interpretation of Nineteenth Century Mexico," in *How Latin America Fell Behind*, ed. Stephen Haber (Stanford, Calif.: Stanford University Press, 1997), 65–92.

41. Juan Bautista Alberdi, *Bases y puntos de partida para la organización política de la República Argentina* (Buenos Aires, 1852), 16; see also Sam Schulman, "Juan Bautista Alberdi and his Influence on Immigration Policy in the Argentine Constitution of 1853," *The Americas* 5 (July 1948): 3–17.

42. George Reid Andrews has provided an interesting case study on the changing immigration policies of São Paolo, Brazil by pointing out this change over time. Whereas early European settlements had "failed" well into the 1880s, European immigration would be privileged for four decades, only to be replaced for native Afro-Brazilians by the 1930s. See especially his Chapter 3, "Immigration, 1890–1930," in *Blacks and Whites in São Paolo, Brazil*, 54–89.

43. Moya, *Cousins and Strangers*, 46–47.

44. A recent study on Spanish expellees from Latin America during this period notes that the expulsions from the Mexican case "had a special reach and magnitude" due in large part to their numbers and to the fact that they had enjoyed privileged positions in the most key sectors of the administration, clergy, commerce, and military. See Jesús Ruiz de Gordejuela Urquijo, *La expulsion de los españoles de México y su destino incierto, 1821–1836* (Sevilla: Consejo Superior de Investigaciones Científicas; Escuela de Estudios Hispano Americanos, 2006), 227.

45. See Mark Reisler, *By the Sweat of Their Brow: Mexican Immigrant Labor in the United States, 1900–1940* (Westport, Conn.: Greenwood Press, 1976), 269; The numbers of Mexicans leaving the United States, however, does not take into account the longer history of migration to the United States since the establishment of the international boundary between the two countries. See M. Colette Standart, O.P., "The Sonoran Migration to California, 1848–1856: A Study in Prejudice," *Southern California Quarterly* 58 (Fall 1976): 333–57.

46. Francisco I. Madero, *La sucesión presidencial en* 1910. *El partido nacional democrático* (San Pedro, Coahuila, 1908), 238.

47. Chávez Chávez, "Retrato del Indio Bárbaro. Proceso de Justificación de la Barbarie de los Indios del Septentrión Mexicano y Formación de la Cultura Norteña," *New México Historical Review* 73 (October 1998): 389–424.

48. José María Luis Mora, *Obras Sueltas* (México: Editorial Porrúa, c. 1837, 1963), 1, 152–53; Quoted in Lomnitz, *Deep Mexico, Silent Mexico*, 49.

49. The term *colonial constitution* is borrowed from Lomnitz and is intended to relay the notion that Indian republics after independence were akin to a "nation within a nation" and therefore constituted particular life worlds distinct from those of the Mexican Creoles—whose culture was not exclusively European either. See *Exits from the Labyrinth*, 275.

50. Berninger, "Mexican Attitudes Towards Immigration," 19.

51. Weber, *The Mexican Frontier*, xv–xxiv.

52. Enrique Florescano states that the population for the whole northern province (Nueva Vizcaya, Sonora, Nuevo México, Coahuila, and Texas) during the 1780s was around 220,400 in a population that totaled well over 7 million. See "Colonización, ocupación del suelo y 'frontera' en el norte de Nueva España, 1521–1750," in Alvaro Jara et al., *Tierras: Expansión territorial y ocupación del suelo en América (siglos xvi–xix), Ponencias presentadas al IV Congreso Internacional de Historia Económica* (México: El Colegio de México, 1968), 43–76.

53. González-Polo y Acosta, "Colonización e inmigración extranjera," 4–7.

54. México, Junta Provisional Gubernativa, Comisión de Relaciones Exteriores. Dictámenes Números 1 y 2. Naciones Bárbaras de las Indias. Anglo-Americanos. Dictamen Presentado a la Soberana Junta Gubernativa del Imperio Mexicano por la Comisión de Relaciones Exteriores en 29 de Diciembre de 1821, Primero de Independencia. (México: Biblioteca Aportación Histórica, reprinted 1944); the extended version of this document actually entailed a more detailed foreign policy regarding Russia, Guatemala, England, and the vulnerable coastlines. For the sake of space and in order to focus on the topic at hand, I will focus on the two main focal points of this report. See Juan Francisco de Azcarate, Dictamen Presentado a la Soberana Junta Gubernativa del Imperio Mexicano por la Comisión de Relaciones Exteriores en 29 de Diciembre de 1821, Primero de Independencia (México: Publicaciones de la Secretaria de Relaciones Exteriores,1932). Located at the AHSRE, Biblioteca José María Lafragua (hereafter cited as Naciones Bárbaras de las Indias. Anglo-Americanos).

55. Florescano, "Colonización, ocupación del suelo y 'frontera' en el norte de Nueva España, 1521–1750," 43–76.

56. *Naciones Bárbaras de las Indias. Anglo-Americanos*, 12–13. Original: "La puntualidad en cumplir los tratados y la buena fe en los comercios es el magnetismo que atrae a los Indios y por estos conductos comunican sus frutos y riquezas, se civilizan, adquieren los usos y costumbres mejores; y se disponen insensiblemente para abrazar la religión establecida en las Provincias y que siguen los habitantes de las reducciones y pueblos que con ellas tienen parentesco. Si el Imperio adoptarse esta medida, con menos gastos logrará mas utilidades, como las perciben los Ingleses, los Franceses y los Anglo-Americanos."

57. Brian DeLay, *War of a Thousand Deserts: Indian Raids and the US-Mexican War* (New Haven: Yale University Press, 2008).

58. For other ideological and intellectual influences on Tadeo Ortiz de Ayala, see Tarsicio García's introduction in Tadeo Ortiz de Ayala, *Resumen de la estadística del imperio mexicano, 1822*, vii–xxvii; also Wilbert H. Timmons, "Tadeo Ortiz, Mexican Emissary Extraordinary," *The Hispanic American Historical Review* 51 (August 1971): 463–77.

59. Ortiz de Ayala's influence in colonization policy recommendations cannot be overstated. Not only were many of his ideas implemented in subsequent colonization policy, but he also headed a

number of colonization projects to Texas and in Coatzacoalcos in the years after the publication of this document. Edith Louise Kelly and Mattie Austin Hatcher, "Tadeo Ortiz de Ayala and the Colonization of Texas, 1822–1833," *Southwestern Historical Quarterly* 32 (February–April 1929).

60. Weber's recent monograph, *Bárbaros*, provides the best background to those Enlightenment ideals regarding treatment of the indigenes.

61. Ortiz de Ayala, *Resumen de la estadística del imperio mexicano, 1822*, 21. Original: "La conducta de los crueles militares y los misioneros ignorantes de las fronteras del norte, no es tampoco el mejor medio de atraer a innumerables naciones, que con otra política las misiones de los Estados Unidos solicitan, con ventajas de su comercio e incremento de la nación. Es un dolor ver una continua guerra costosa y sanguinaria contra pueblos que no agraviaron en los principios, y que llaman bárbaros porque no quieren convertirse a la fuerza, mientras que los misioneros protestantes con su beneficencia y dulzura civilizan, convencen por la persuasión, ganando la amistad de innumerables hordas, que a nuestras provincias del norte pudieran causar incalculables males en tiempo de guerra con aquella república."

62. Chávez Chávez, *Los indios en la formación de la identidad nacional*, 26–27.

63. Tadeo Ortiz de Ayala, *Resumen de la estadística del imperio mexicano, 1822*, 85. Original: "La integridad del territorio nacional sigue débil, expuesto a perderse si no se cambia de sistema y adoptan positivas medidas de fomento y seguridad, mediante una administración local fuerte y conciliante dependiente del gobierno federal, puesto que aquel punto fronterizo abrazando los intereses de la federación entera, ella es quien debe encargarse de su custodia y cuidado."

64. As noted earlier, 12 million South Asians (Indians) and Chinese migrated to various points in the globe between 1820–1930, thus suggesting that Mexican intellectuals were attuned to global migrations.

65. It is interesting to note that Alberdi specifically points out that the migrations of Chinese and South Indians would not be good for the nation. For example, "Pero poblar no es civilizar, sino embrutecer, cuando se puebla con chinos y con indios de Asia y con negros de África," in *Bases y puntos de partida para la organización política de la República de Argentina*, 18.

66. Spain opened up its lands to foreign settlement in 1820. For an example of early fears of US expansion, see Cortés, *Views from the Apache Frontier*, passim.

67. Article 10 of *Sentiments of the Nation, or Points Outlined by Morelos for the Constitution*, states, "Foreigners shall not be admitted, unless they are artisans capable of teaching [their crafts], and are free of all suspicion." English translation located in *The Mexico Reader: History, Culture, Politics*, eds. Gilbert Joseph and Timothy J. Henderson, (Durham, N.C.: Duke University Press, 2002), 189–91.

68. Reséndez, *Changing National Identities*, 65.

69. "The Mexican Colonization Laws," Document No. 23 in *Documents of Texas History*, 2nd ed., eds. Ernest Wallace, David M. Vigness, and George B. Ward (Austin, Texas: State House Press, 1994), 46.

70. Austin received his first contract from the Spanish government, but before the Imperial Colonization Law was implemented he secured another grant from the government of Coahuila y Texas. Because of the many colonization laws being passed, there was a need for a more comprehensive and practical standard. Indeed, "[w]ith no published compendium of the Mexican laws, administrative and judicial authority rested with Austin, and the result was a mix of Mexican decrees with pragmatic Anglo-American implementation." See Margaret Swett Henson, *Handbook of Texas Online*, "Anglo-American Colonization," https://www.tshaonline.org/handbook/online/articles/uma01.

71. *Codigo de colonización*, 171–76; English translation is available online at "Colonization Law Decree of 1823," http://www.tamu.edu/ccbn/dewitt/cololaws.htm#decree.

72. For example, Bucheneau argued that Mexico had no assimilation process for immigrants. See "Small Numbers, Great Impact," 23–49.

73. The translation "natives" has changed over time, but the Spanish version is less ambiguous on its meaning when it clearly states "Se atenderá con preferencia para la distribución de las tierras á los naturales del país. . . . " The term *naturales* literally translates into "naturals" and was a term first employed by the Spaniards to describe the natives of the land.

74. A copy of the English translation is available at "Colonization Law of the State of Coahuila and Texas 1825," http://www.tamu.edu/ccbn/dewitt/cololaws.htm#coahuila; a similar law to the Coahuilan legislation is the Colonization Law of Tamaulipas in 1826. See "*Decreto de 15 de Diciembre de 1826 de la Legislatura de Tamaulipas, para la colonización de extranjeros en aquel Estado*," especially article 25. In *Código de colonización*, 212–18.

75. Art. 14. To each family comprehended in a contract, whose sole occupation is cultivation of land, one labor shall be given; should he also be a stock raiser, grazing land shall be added to complete a *sitio*, and should his only occupation be raising of stock, he shall only receive a superficies of grazing land, equal to twenty-four million square bars. Art. 15. Unmarried men shall receive the same quantity when they enter the matrimonial state, and for foreigners who marry native Mexicans, shall receive one fourth more; those that are entirely single, or who do not form a part of some family whether foreigners or natives, shall content themselves with the fourth part of the above mentioned quantity, which is all that can be given them until they marry." See "Colonization Law of the State of Coahuila and Texas 1825," http://www.tamu.edu/faculty/ccbn/dewitt/cololaws.htm#coahuila

76. Reséndez, *Changing National Identities*, 22.

77. Mark E. Nackman, "Anglo American Migrants to the West: Men of Broken Fortunes? The Case of Texas, 1821–1846," *The Western Historical Quarterly* 5 (October 1974): 441–55.

78. "Decreto permitiendo la introducción de algunos géneros de algodón; destinos de los derechos que produzcan y providencias sobre colonización y comercio, Abril 6 de 1830," *Código de colonización*, 241–4.

79. See Curtis Bishop, *Handbook of Texas Online*, "The Law of April 6, 1830," https://www.tshaonline.org/handbook/online/articles/ngl01. Also Mier y Terán's report see *Texas by Terán: The Diary Kept by General Manuel Mier y Terán on his 1828 Inspection of Texas*, ed. Jack Jackson and translated by John Wheat (Austin: University of Texas Press, 2000).

80. "Decreto permitiendo la introducción de algunos géneros de algodón; destinos de los derechos que produzcan y providencias sobre colonización y comercio, Abril 6 de 1830," *Código de colonización*, 241–44.

81. See, for example, Berninger's chapter "Rhetoric and Reality," which registers a number of abuses against foreigners. "Mexican Attitudes Toward Immigration," 81–111; also for copies of the expulsion orders, see Harold Sims, *Descolonización en Mexico: El conflicto entre mexicanos y españoles (1821–1831)* (México: Fondo de la Cultura Económica, 1982), 243–56. See also "Se recomienda al Gobernador del Distrito que mande vigilar y guardar las consideraciones debidas a las personas, casas y demás propiedades de los agentes diplomáticas y consulares y súbditos extranjeros, 1833," in *Archivo Histórico de Relaciones Exteriores*, 1–1–47 [hereafter cited as AHSRE].

82. "Decreto permitiendo la introducción de algunos géneros de algodón; destinos de los derechos que produzcan y providencias sobre colonización y comercio, Abril 6 de 1830," *Código de colonización*, 241–44.

83. Ibid. Original: "Se prohíbe en la frontera del Norte la entrada a los extranjeros bajo cualquiera pretexto, sin estar provistos de un pasaporte expedido por los agentes de la República, en el punto de su procedencia."

84. Nackman, "Anglo-American Migrants to the West," 441–55.

85. Ibid.

86. "Se les dice a los comisionados de Inglaterra que los extranjeros que el Presidente puede expulsar, son los que atenten contra la Independencia o sistema de gobierno de México, 1824," AHSRE, 4–24–7070.

87. Harold Dana Sims, *The Expulsion of Mexico's Spaniards, 1821–1836* (Pittsburgh, Penn.: University of Pittsburgh Press, 1990).

88. A recent study examines the larger expulsion of Spaniards taking place throughout the Americas, so the trend went well beyond the Mexican experience. See Jesús Ruiz de Gordejuela Urquijo, *La expulsión de los españoles de México y su destino incierto, 1821–1836* (Sevilla: Diputación de Sevilla, 2006).

89. Sims, *The Expulsion of Mexico's Spaniards*, 10.

90. Ibid., 35.

91. Ibid., 18.

92. Several state laws and decrees are registered; however, they never supersede national legislation. See Sims, *The Expulsion of Mexico's Spaniards*, 37.

93. "Circular de 4 de Diciembre de 1846, recomendando la exacta observancia de las medidas que contiene el decreto expedido para el establecimiento de la Dirección de Colonización," *Código de Colonización*, 360.

94. De la Maza, *Código de colonización*, 936–45; how these inclusionary measures play out in practice, especially among the various Indigenous groups in Mexico, is beyond the scope of this book. Robert Holden comments on two different periodizations for the question of land transfer: 1846 and 1882. See *Mexico and the Survey of Public Lands: The Management of Modernization, 1876–1911* (DeKalb: Northern Illinois University Press, 1994), 7.

95. Proyectos de Colonización presentados por la junta directiva del ramo, al Ministerio de Relaciones de la Republica Mexicana en 5 de Julio de 1848 (México: Imprenta de Vicente García Torres, 1848), 17–18. Original: "Brindándoselas por concesiones liberales, se asemejaría al sarcasmo, si al mismo tiempo la gente indígena no mereciese, extraña en su propio suelo, las miradas de la consideración del Gobierno. La población antigua también debe ser atendida, para que se multiplique y prospere; y su prosperidad no puede esperarse sin medios fáciles y abundantes de alminentarse [*sic*], que para los habitantes del campo no son posibles sin tierra productiva que labrar."

96. Matías Romero, *Mexico and the United States: A Study of Subjects Affecting Their Political, Commercial, and Social Relations, Made with a View to Their Promotion*, 2 vols. (New York: The Knickerbocker Press, 1898), 76.

97. See Robert Holden, "Priorities of the State in the Survey of the Public Land in Mexico, 1876–1911," *Hispanic American Historical Review* 70 (1990), 590–92. Holden notes, "Foreign capital played a considerable—if not commanding—role in the modernizing program of the Porfirian period. Thus it was surprising to discover that in only six of the fifty-nine original concessions was there evidence in the archival record of investments by foreigners; only one concession was awarded outright to a foreigner, Luis Huller." He also states that unlike mining or railroads, "the survey of public land . . . was largely a domestic industry."

98. Secretaría de Fomento, *Memoria Presentada al Congreso de la Unión por el Secretario de Estado y del Despacho de Fomento, Colonización, Industria y Comercio de la República Mexicana. General Carlos Pacheco Corresponde á los años Trascurridos de Enero de 1883 á Junio de 1885*, 5 vols. (México: Oficina Tipográfica de la Secretaría de Fomento, 1887), I; 185–90; see also De la Maza, *Código de colonización*, 936–45.

Chapter 5

Sovereignty to Dependence

Property Rights in the Transition of Canadian Prairie Indians onto Reserves*

Tony Ward

The original inhabitants of Canada are now referred to as "First Nations," to recognize not only that they reached the continent first but also that when the first Europeans arrived, the aboriginals already formed nations. Those first people arrived in the Americas many millennia ago, and they increased to occupy the whole of the two continents, developing civilizations and cities in Central America as early as those of the Middle East. Dating their arrival is problematic, but for all relevant purposes, it is clear that they arrived many millennia before Europeans and thereby acquired a substantial degree of property rights to the land, however those rights might have been defined. The later rejection of those property rights by the incoming Europeans, and subsequent interference with even such limited rights as did persist, was a leading factor in the subsequent catastrophe that befell Indian society.[1]

The Canadian Prairies were one of the later areas occupied by Indians, due to the presence of glaciers until approximately nine thousand years ago.[2] The social and economic systems that Indians developed on the Prairies were interrelated more with those of the southern Plains in the United States than with the more eastern areas of what became Canada, though bands moved extensively across the regions.

The Indians who came to the area that is now the Canadian Prairies

* I acknowledge the helpful comments on earlier versions of this project of participants at the Canadian Network for Economic History Conference, 2005; International Congress of Historical Sciences, 2005; Canadian Economics Association, Conference, 2005; Twentieth International Congress of Historical Sciences, 2006; Canadian Network for Economic History Conference, 2006; "Homesteading Reconsidered" Conference, University of Nebraska, 2007; Asia-Pacific Business and Economic History Conference, Gakuin University, Tokyo, 2009; 15th World Economic History Congress, 2009, First World Congress of Environmental History, 2009; and also those of two anonymous referees who made very insightful comments.

hunted bison and smaller game, moving around the area in small groups, meeting perhaps annually to exchange information and mates. Bison meat and fat fed them, and the hides clothed them and formed their shelters. Bison hides, bones, and sinews were the basic building blocks of many manufactured items. Most of the time, people could feed themselves relatively easily. Steckel and Prince note that the Plains nomads were the tallest people in the world in the mid-nineteenth century, indicating good food availability.[3] A diet consisting solely of bison meat, though, would have lacked several crucial nutrients, so it was always necessary to supplement that diet.[4] Many also sustained themselves by hunting smaller game such as deer, pronghorn antelope, and other small animals, and by trapping and fishing. They also developed a greater reliance on gathering and practiced small-scale horticulture, usually planting some seeds in the spring and returning to the area in the fall to reap the produce. Meltzer suggests that a band of twenty-five families, living on bison alone, would have needed to kill five or six bison a month.[5] This was straightforward in summer, but hard in midwinter, with bison moving away and firewood being scarce. This scarcity factor probably constrained overall population numbers.

Indians hunted on foot, driving the bison over jumps or into terrain that slowed the bison enough to kill them. The innovation of the bow and arrow, about four thousand years ago, changed the effectiveness of bison hunting considerably.[6]

The Indians' relationship with land was complex, with social, economic, and religious facets. The most important characteristic of the relationship was that the Indians were mobile, although generally not fully nomadic. For millennia, their ancestors moved around, developing a deep understanding of what they could and could not do, as they travelled. They used different areas in different seasons and different climatic periods, and relied on the accumulated knowledge of their ancestors to secure their living. To the aboriginals, land was an integral part of their existence, and separating them from it destroyed a vital part of their heritage and broke up the integrity of the tribal unit.

Horses first reached the Canadian Prairies in the mid-eighteenth century and transformed Indian life.[7] A horse can outrun a bison, so the perilous hunt on foot changed into an easier and safer equestrian pursuit. The bow and arrow remained the principal hunting technology until breech-loading rifles were available in the later nineteenth century.[8]

During the same period, the environment deteriorated for the bison. Cattle ranching spread up from the southern plains, and the cattle and horses needed the same grasses as the bison. In particular, winter-feed in the river valleys became scarce, putting pressure on the bison population. Isenberg estimates that in the early nineteenth century there were between 360,000 and 900,000 domesticated horses, and another 2 million wild horses, all competing for the same grass as the bison and cattle.[9]

Europeans reached the Canadian Prairies gradually, at first as fur traders, buying the various furs produced in the northern woodlands. They did not compete in the bison hunt until later, so the main problems they brought were smallpox and whisky. By the mid-nineteenth century, the situation evolved, and Europeans began to join in the bison hunt. The market and the new technologies of horse, rifle, and the railway enabled Indians and Europeans to extract far more than the previous flow of the resource, and the stock of bison depleted rapidly. As all bands adopted the same strategy of overhunting, an open access problem arose. The cost of killing bison ultimately fell so low that it was worth killing them just for the tongue, bones, and hide, leaving the meat to rot.

When European settlers first began to arrive in the 1870s, the only private property held by Plains Indians consisted of moveable effects—clothes, tipis, horses, dogs, cooking and hunting implements, and so on. Indians did not own any stocks of resources such as bison or static areas of land. Tribes hunted over traditional areas of land, but these had become more contested when the numbers of bison fell, and competition increased over the better hunting grounds.

Many other changes such as widespread epidemic disease swept across the Prairies in the eighteenth and nineteenth centuries, killing a great proportion of the Indian population.[10] By the late nineteenth century, the Indians' options had shrunk to the point at which they were prepared to settle on the small residual areas of land that the more recent arrivals from Europe offered them. The crisis for Prairie Indians occurred relatively quickly, with the entire socioeconomic system collapsing over about thirty years, between 1870 and 1900. Indians needed an alternative source of sustenance, and settled agriculture was the obvious alternative. The "Numbered Treaties" explicitly envisaged this.[11]

If the Indians had chosen to take up farming of their own accord to make up for the loss of the bison, using their own land-use systems and their own modes of production, and if they had traded with the incoming Europeans on equal terms, their outcomes might well have been better. They were fully competent workers and knew the land and climate well, though, as noted, their previous social capital was no longer relevant. There is no reason to anticipate that under such circumstances Indians would have fared worse than incoming Europeans did. Both groups had to develop new approaches to working the semi-arid land. Oral history would have provided the Indians with greater knowledge of long-term conditions. However, the conditions imposed by the Department of Indian Affairs reduced their chances of achieving even self-sufficiency.

Bird-Tail Creek Reserve. Manitoba.

The "Numbered Treaties" were signed between Indian bands and the Canadian Government over the period 1871 to 1921. These all pressured the Indians onto reserves, dislocating them from their ancestral territories.

As the Indians relocated, their basic social organization had to evolve to cope with the new conditions. Traditionally, each band was a loose coalition under the voluntary coordination of a chief, and members came and went, moving from band to band, as it suited them. However, when they moved onto reserves, Indians had to adjust into communities that were more static. In order to qualify for Government assistance, Indians had to register on a particular reserve, and so lost their mobility.

There was no legal mechanism for subdividing reserve land because the Crown owned it and held it in trust as a unit; however, both parties wanted some form of division, for differing motives. Indians wanted to develop farms and needed some type of private ownership in order to manage the land effectively. The Department of Indian Affairs adopted the perspective that if the reserve could be carved up into pieces suitable for subsistence farming, then a large portion of the land would become surplus to the "requirements" of the reserve, and could be removed and offered to settlers. Bird-Tail Creek Reserve, Number 57, in Manitoba, is shown with such agricultural activity as existed at the time of the survey. As in most such cases, the survey and accompanying road-allowances were just super-imposed over any pre-existing Indian farming activities. Both the surveyors and the

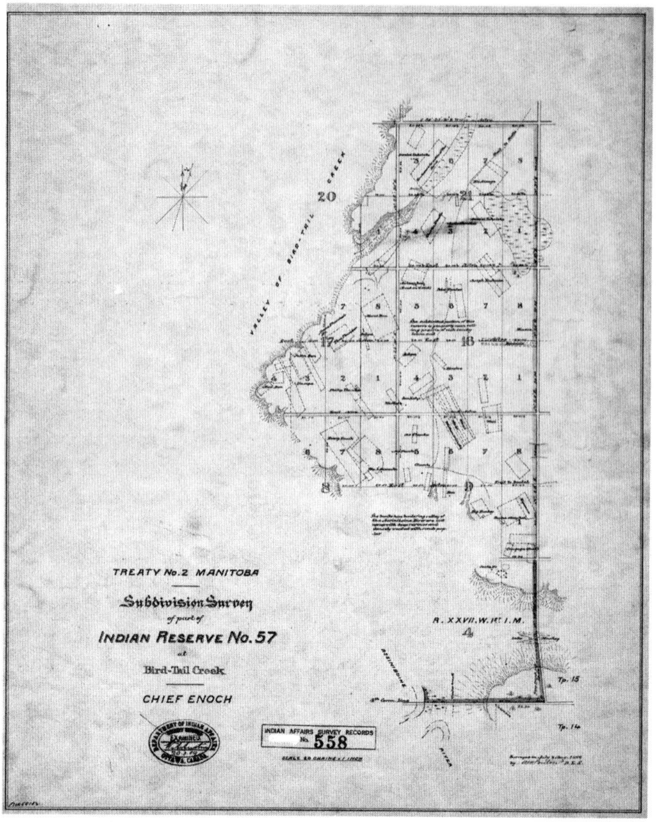

Subdivision Survey of part of Indian Reserve No. 57, at Bird-Tail Creek—Chief Enoch. Part of Tp. 15, Rge. 27, W1M. Library and Archives Canada, 540—Metro Areas, Prairie Provinces, (R12567-137-1-E). Microfiche NMC 15721, H2/540/Bird-Tail Creek (IR)/1886

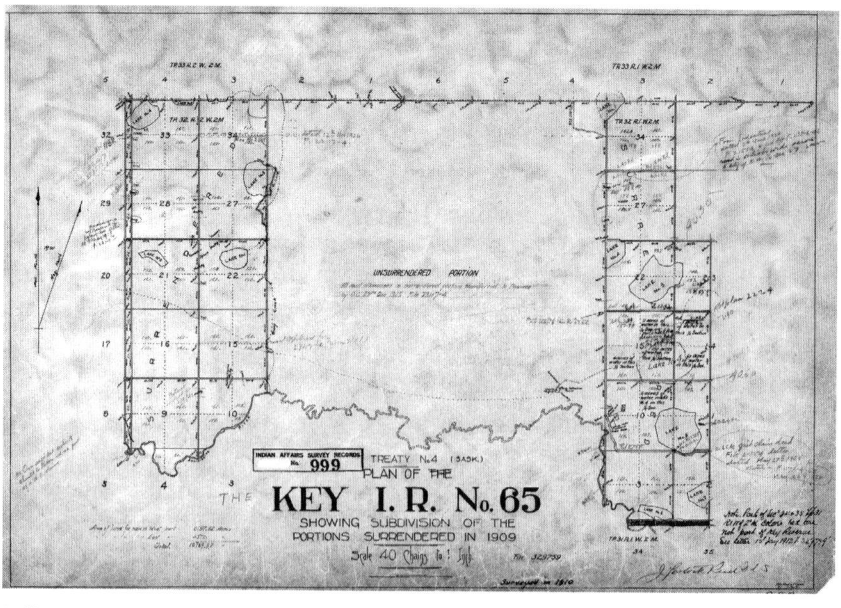

Indian Reserve Number 65, 1909. Saskatchewan Reserve NO. 65, Treaty No. 4. Plan of the KEY I.R. No. 65, showing subdivisions of the portions surrendered in 1909. Surveyed in 1910, J. Lestock Reid. D.L.S. Library and Archives Canada, Microfiche No. 8379, 13364, Record No. 2459. Open access.

Department ignored such cooperative Indian property rights as had been established. Reserve Number 65 is shown, after about half of the reserve was "surrendered." This is typical of the many such "surrenders" that took place, as Reserve Land was declared by the Department to be surplus, and sold off to "real" farmers. Even such Indian property rights as were initially accepted were in many cases subsequently retracted.

The reports of the Department of Indian Affairs between 1887 and 1896 show evidence of the subdivision of reserves. These records show the number of farms, but with no detail of the numbers of workers on each unit, and with a record only of the net area in crops, excluding any areas used for hay, pasture, or other activities. The structure of property rights on these farms is also unclear. The farmers certainly did not possess fee simple rights as we now know them, so their usage was restricted.[12]

Like the settlers, Indians faced difficult climatic conditions and undeveloped technology.[13] Indian farmers, however, faced additional constraints imposed by the antagonistic attitude of some members of the Department of Indian Affairs, and by the complicated structure of property rights on reserves. By about 1900, Indians overcame climate, technology, and the worst of the obstruction of the Department of Indian Affairs, so the remaining problems were primarily those of ill-defined property rights and the lack of capital. A few Indian farmers prospered, but the great majority failed, and Prairie Indians remain in deprivation today.

To achieve economic success in a competitive capitalist economy, which is what the Indians faced by 1880, people need clear, comprehensive property rights over productive assets. Such rights have to be explicit, and the user of any resource must have full access to and control over all inputs and outputs. Reserve Indians possessed only very limited rights. The Crown owned all reserve land, holding it in trust for the Indians, whose legal status was that of minors. Indian farmers therefore did not own the land they tried to farm, but they had only an informal usufruct, with almost none of the basic legal rights held by their neighboring settler farmers.[14] An agent of the Department of Indian Affairs had to approve any commercial transactions—buying or selling—that an Indian wanted to undertake. An economic system in which some participants face more restrictive property rights than others will inevitably yield greater benefits for those with the greater rights.

The interactions of short seasons, scarce labor, and inadequate technology held back Indians as well as Europeans.[15] After a short rush in the early 1880s in anticipation of the completion of the CPR, these problems discouraged significant European settlement until the end of the 1890s. After Krakatau erupted in 1883, severe climatic fluctuations followed for several years, shortening the growing season and further impeding the growth of grain farming. By 1900, farming technology had been adapted to suit the short summers of the Prairies. New labor-augmenting equipment enabled farmers to sow their seeds more quickly in spring and to harvest them quickly before the first frost in fall.[16]

The underlying intent of the policies of the Department of Indian Affairs was to eliminate the Indians as a social and political entity. This racist attitude was endemic in Canadian society, and is exemplified by Sir Hector Langevin MP, who, in a House of Commons debate in 1886, stated, " . . . if, by accident, an Indian should starve, it is not the fault of the Government, or the wish of the Government."[17]

Farming activities varied from place to place, with grain cultivation in Manitoba and Saskatchewan, and horse and cattle ranching in Alberta. The major commercial field crops were wheat and oats, and the most important root crop was potatoes. Indians also grew small amounts of other field and root crops, and animal husbandry was a significant source of income for Indian farms in southern Alberta. Farm incomes for both Indians and settlers were low before 1900 but increased after that, with incomes differing substantially between reserve and settler farms.

What caused that differentiation? Carter discusses a variety of factors, settling primarily on racism.[18] That was clearly an important issue, but there was another important factor, property rights, that hobbled Indians. It was not that the Indians were unfamiliar with the concepts of commercial transactions—they had been trading both with each other and with Europeans for a very long time. Nor was it a lack of interest—with the bison gone by the 1870s they were very concerned about their food supply. They also initially had enough land. The reserves were at first more than sufficient in size, though they were in some cases somewhat distant from markets.

One important issue for Prairie Indians was their circumstances at the time of signing their treaties. Loss of the bison destroyed the Indians' economic system, so negotiating the treaties took place under very unequal circumstances. The Indians had a desperate need for immediate food supplies, so they could not hold out against the pressure to sign, with its promise of immediate relief. The reports of the Department of Indian Affairs note on several occasions that Indians arriving to negotiate first had to be fed, and then they also needed to receive enough food to enable them to return to their homes. The Indians therefore had to accept whatever terms they could get.

The constraints Indians faced as they tried to farm were primarily those on inputs, including lack of expertise, climate, capital (primarily for equipment and animals), farming technology, property rights, and the loss of social capital, and also, as Carter shows, racism.[19]

They knew the land, climate, and soils intimately, but not from the perspective of commercial grain farming. The government sought to remedy that gap, and initially each reserve or group of reserves had a "home farm," where farming techniques and technologies were disseminated. Knowledge of farming technology was therefore theoretically accessible, but in practice, this assistance was not very effective because of a lack of competence and diligence on the part of the supposed experts, most of who came from very different agricultural conditions in Eastern Canada. There, farming was an extension of techniques well known from Europe. The West, in contrast, was a different climate, and new techniques to cope with the semi-arid conditions had to be developed.[20] These home farms were disbanded after 1884 due to their lack of success.

For grain farming, the main natural constraints were the short growing season and the dry climate. European settlers were able gradually to overcome this by the use of new labor-saving equipment, but not until after 1895.[21] It took time to develop the new dry-farming techniques and for the equipment to save enough labor to validate its use. Settler farming was labor scarce, which meant that the new machines were vital. Given the bad weather for most of the 1880s and early 1890s, the 1880s were also a particularly bad time for Indians to try to establish their farms.[22]

At first, land was relatively plentiful, but with the switch to intensive agriculture, and given the immature technology, physical and financial capital became more important. Prairie Indians fared badly insofar as access to capital was concerned. The only way in which they could have enhanced the small treaty payments was through retained earnings, which were rarely sufficient for significant growth. Overtly, the Department of Indian Affairs was supposed to assist the Indians in establishing a new, independent way of living, with the focus on agriculture. All the numbered treaties included, at the insistence of the Indians, the provision of implements and farm animals. Treaty Four, the Qu'Appelle Treaty, is typical, stating that:

- each family will get two hoes, one spade, one scythe, and one axe . . .
- one plow and two harrows for every ten families . . .
- also to each Chief; for the use of his band as aforesaid, one yoke of oxen, one bull, (and) four cows[23]

One collective plow for each ten families was insufficient, given that all farmers needed to plow at the same time of year. A single yoke of oxen for the entire band was far too little. A plow and a yoke of oxen were the first equipment that each European settler acquired, and they were consistently busy during the spring and fall plowing seasons.[24] A plow, harrow, seeder, reaper, and wagon were basic requirements, with a mower and a rake for hay. The timing of the farming season was so tight that without fast, high-capacity equipment, farmers could produce little more than subsistence.

Carter considers that the main problem facing reserve Indian farmers appears to have been access to these non-land inputs. This became a serious problem because of the attitudes of members of the Department of Indian Affairs. Hayter Reed, in particular, used all the powers he had at his disposal to systematically obstruct agricultural development. Reed wanted to destroy the reserve system and declared that he wanted to integrate the Indians into white society.[25]

The 1886 Report of the Department of Indian Affairs tells of the Birch River Reserve in the Pas Agency:

> This band have some splendid soil, and asked that they be supplied with a hand mill, a fanning mill, reaper and mower, and that their annuity money be kept back until these articles were paid for. I advised them not to purchase these articles until they became more experienced in agriculture, and that cradles, scythes and a hand mill would be more suitable at present, in which they concurred.[26]

It is unclear how voluntary the concurrence was, given the complete imbalance of power.

In 1889, Reed, then Indian Commissioner, announced a new "peasant" policy for Indian reserves.[27] His target was one acre of wheat, a few roots, and one or two cows, using only hand tools—a hoe, rake, sickle, cradle, and flail. This would yield a bare subsistence standard of living for the Indians, with no prospect of improvement. It would isolate them from the uncertainties of the market economy, but with a precarious existence, at the mercy of the climate.

The 1901 Report for Shoal Lake in the Pas Agency of Manitoba notes that the reserve was isolated and inaccessible, with low, poor land. "A most suitable piece of country for a reserve," where the Indians could cultivate small gardens, tend to cattle, hunt, and trap. There was "[n]o chance of outside earnings."[28]

The Sessional Papers do not list any data for the period before 1895, but it is apparent that the figures were low. The numbers increased rapidly after 1895, which accords with Carter's analysis, and this suggests that the removal of Hayter Reed had a positive effect on Indians' access to equipment. The Census does not provide us data on equipment on settler farms, so a direct comparison between settler and Indian farms is not possible. We can see how much land was under cultivation on settler farms, and the areas were initially small. The Census gives us totals, although we cannot tell how many were mature farms versus those that were just beginning to be broken in.

Overall farm sizes were initially small, largely because two critical pieces of equipment, the reaper and the gang plow, did not come into operation until between 1890 and 1900.[29] The older mower was appropriate for hay but left the cut stalks lying loose in the field, necessitating a substantial amount of labor to collect, bind, and stack the grain before the frost came, so it was not useful for grain crops. Only when a single person on a binder could cut and bind the sheaves and leave them in groups to be stooked was it possible for the labor-scarce farmer to grow commercially viable amounts of grain.[30]

Census data also include the number of reapers on specific reserves. The only increase over the period is on the Birtle Reserve—one of the few successful reserves. Other than that, there is no pattern of increase after Reed's removal in 1897, so either the capital constraint remained in place, or other reasons prevented the Indians from expanding their farms to sizes at which they needed the equipment. Racism did not disappear with Reed, and access to equipment may still have been restricted.

Another aspect of capital scarcity was the lack of infrastructure such as stores, implement dealers, gristmills, and good roads. Stuck in a low-level equilibrium, there was not sufficient volume of produce into and out of the reserves to warrant capital expenditure on these facilities, so Indians remained without the infrastructure that grew up around settler farms, helping them to prosper.

The basic approach taken by Europeans toward land rights is that of Locke, whose position was that people gained property rights to land by adding their labor to it—developing it in some way. In the mid-nineteenth century, the Prairie Indians were nomadic, moving around with the seasons and the bison, with no fixed agriculture. On that basis, the perspective of incoming Europeans was that the Indians had no ownership rights to the land, so whites could treat it as *res nullius.* This ignored the property rights that Indians had acquired over the millennia they had used the land in their diverse patterns.

Property rights have many aspects, and it is necessary to examine them as they affected Indian real property. Honoré provides an important framework of eleven standard incidents of ownership, of which eight that significantly affected Indians are discussed below.[31] These incidents are reflections of the conditions necessary for full ownership. All of these aspects of property rights assume the existence of explicit rights, rather than just physical occupation.

The most basic component of ownership is the right to possess. The owner needs to have overall control of the resource. He or she must have exclusive physical occupation, and no one can have the right to evict the owner, who furthermore can exclude others from the resource. An individual's right to possess needs the backing of a legal support system that will enforce these rules.

This fundamental aspect of ownership was completely missing from the

Indian reserves. The Department of Indian Affairs, on behalf of the Government, owned the land outright, and the Indians were occupiers with only very limited usage rights. They could not exclude other band members or members of the Department of Indian Affairs, though the Department could exclude others such as traders—in particular, whisky traders. By contrast, European settlers could acquire a 160-acre homestead for a nominal ten-dollar fee, which after a simple three-year proving-up process became their full private property. This fundamental distinction had a profound impact on the ability of Indians to exploit their reserves. They were unable to accumulate capital in land improvements, only in livestock and equipment. Indians could invest in buildings; however, they did not have the security of owning the land on which those buildings stood. Although they remained status Indians on the reserve, they could not invest in the ownership of the land itself by expanding their lands. This was a major deterrent. A principal source of capital gain for settlers was to break in their land, from which they reaped the increase in the value of that land. The value of future crops over the ensuing years determined the value of improved land, and the increased value of that land could be used as security for a mortgage to provide working capital.

For efficiency, the holder of the property right must have the unlimited right to use the resource. The only appropriate constraints are those of activities that create external effects on others. Nominally, reserve land was available only to Indians, but their right to use the land was highly constrained. A Department agent had to approve any transaction of any sort, buying or selling, with the outside economy. As Carter notes, agents frequently used this power to prevent Indians from acquiring the equipment and animals they needed for farming on anything above a trivial scale.[32] This eventually evolved into the Pass System, under which Indians could not even travel off their reserve without written permission. These restrictions severely limited the Indians' ability to exploit their reserves.

Property owners need to have the right to manage their property—the right to decide who can use the land. Theoretically, Indians had the right to carry out any activities they wanted to, but in practice the restriction that any transactions needed approval interfered with this right. Indian land and resource exploitation was therefore subject to the control of the Department of Indian Affairs, although this control was not always a problem. Some agents supported "their" Indians, encouraging reasonable farming ventures. Nonetheless, Indian rights to use resources were restricted, which would have impeded entrepreneurialism.

The Report of the Department of Indian Affairs for 1901, for the Pasquah band in the Crooked Lake agency for Qu'Appelle in the Northwest Territories noted:

> Stevenson, one of the band, got a permit to sell a carload of wheat, and when Indians can sell wheat by the carload, it is pretty good proof that the labour and expense in teaching them have not been lost. Stevenson had a seeder, a new binder, a sulky plough, a disc-harrow, a mower and a rake, two double wagons, ten heavy working horses, all private property and chiefly paid for, etc.[33]

Stevenson was doing well enough to be noteworthy, but he still had to get a permit to sell his wheat—an exceptional event for an Indian, whereas the sale of wheat in multiple carloads was normal for settler farmers.

In 1886 on the Blood Reserve in the Northwest Territories, the Report of the Department of Indian Affairs noted, "[T]here is some land uncultivated. I advised the Indians to put in more potatoes." They remarked, "What is the use, as we have lots in our cellars that we cannot sell, and more than we can eat." Given that they could not sell anything without a permit, it is not surprising that the Blood Indians were discouraged.

With exclusive property rights, the owner of the rights must receive all the income—the fruits and profits deriving from the use of the resource. He or she must also pay all costs associated with the exploitation of the resource. Under these conditions, the owner faces the appropriate incentives to put the resource to whatever usage optimizes his or her benefit. On Indian reserves, the agent had the right to control all transactions, and some used this to interfere with the band's economic activities. The agent managed the band's finances, holding the Indians' money, and thereby controlled the flow of income and expenses. Under these circumstances, the ability of the band to generate income from "their" land was significantly constrained.

A property owner must also have the right to the capital—including the power to alienate it and the liberty to consume, waste, or destroy it. For full property rights, the holder has to possess the right to alienate the resource during life or death, by way of sale, mortgage, gift, or other mode, and the power of disposition and the power of transferring title.

Indian property rights did not fulfill this criterion of having formal rights to individual areas of land. They did have individual ownership of some tools and equipment, though the Department of Indian Affairs or the band as a collective owned most such items. Indians could not alienate any of the band's land either collectively or individually.

An owner must have immunity from expropriation. Apart from bankruptcy and execution for debt, transmission of ownership must be consensual. The Government did not push Indians off reserves en masse, but they did expropriate large areas of land. Figure Two shows a typical reserve from which land was sequestered. The mechanism used was to allow an amount of land for each member of the band, without identifying specific areas. The Department then declared any land left over after the nominal allocation as surplus to the needs of the reserve, and expropriated and sold it off to settlers.

The possession of full property rights also requires that the holder should be able to determine the future disposition of the property. He or she should have the right to transmit the property to the holder's successors. Band members as a collective had a weak form of ownership of their reserve land, but they did not possess legal rights over any particular portion of the reserve. Each generation could transmit the right to live on the reserve, but not the right to any particular piece of it. Once the "surplus" land of the reserve was "surrendered," there was no land available onto which a new generation could grow.

The possession of property rights does not necessitate indeterminate possession. Various forms of property rights, such as leasehold, have finite terms. For others, the term may not be finite, but it may nonetheless be possible for others to terminate the possession, such as leasehold without fixed term. An infinite term implies transmissibility because all humans are mortal. Bankruptcy can determine some otherwise infinite terms, resulting in surrender of all property.

Reserves as a whole were established on infinite terms, and Indians were explicitly not able to mortgage the reserve land, so there was no danger of them defaulting and losing land in that manner. Restrictive laws, though, caused many Indians to lose their status, and with that went the right to live on the Reserve. The communal property right persisted, but not an individual right.

Indians had only a very limited legal interest in the land, but they did have an equitable interest. In theory then, they could have sued the Department of Indian Affairs for failure to execute the legal aspects of the trust. In practice, though, the relationship was one of highly unequal power, and the Indians did not possess the political or legal influence to pursue their interests.

Only with fee simple are all of the necessary rights fully possessed, so even European settlers did not enjoy all rights until they proved up their homesteads. Reserve Indians, however, did not fully possess any of these rights.

Any production process, such as farming, requires a number of different inputs, typically classified as land, labor, capital, energy, and so on, each of which contributes in a specific way to the production of the output. Poorly specified property rights result in an unclear distribution of the value of production. In particular, because no one owned the reserve land used for the farm, was there a return to that land? With no market, there was no explicit price, but the land was an essential factor input, and if it had been possible to sell productive reserve land, it would have commanded a price, so there was an implicit return. Who received that value?

There may have been an informal market for labor on reserves, with some workers paid fixed wages. With no one "owning" the reserve land, though, it is unclear why workers would not farm for themselves. For workers who assisted an Indian farmer, how much of the crops and animal products of the farm should have gone to each of those who worked to produce them? In many aboriginal societies, the return to land and labor was shared out in complicated ways, depending on relationships in extended families, and various other social obligations.

Overall numbers of Indians were never large—the prevailing food technology, particularly in winter, limited population density to low levels. Indians inhabited a contoured world, not a rectilinear one. *The Economist* notes: "In the flat world of maps, sharp lines show where one country ends and another begins. The real world is more fluid. People do not have borders the way that parcels of land do. They seep from place to place; they wander; they migrate."[34]

Did Indian farming fail? From a commercial perspective, few Indian farms produced a reliable surplus, but that may not have been their objective. Indians had practiced horticulture in the past, and for some, their interest was in this subsistence activity rather than market farming. Reserve agriculture got off to a very shaky start in the 1880s and 1890s. Indians tried to adapt to the new way of life, but a variety of technical and institutional constraints held them back.[35] There was continuing hardship on the reserves, with frequent food shortages. The activities of Hayter Reed were certainly problematic, but he was not the only problem faced by Indian farmers. Once Reed was gone, with improved access to equipment and with wheat markets developing, farming progressed marginally, with some Indian farms developing a surplus, albeit far smaller than those of settlers.

In the early days of Canadian Prairie farming, with only hand equipment, there were few economies of scale, and the 160 acres settlers were given were more than sufficient—most settlers farmed far less. Over time, though, the economies of scale in grain production increased as equipment improved and new seeds were developed, and settler farms expanded. As this happened, the magnitude of the problems caused by the constraints the Indians faced grew more acute, and the opportunity cost of their inability to grow increased.

An important issue was the way in which property rights on the reserves developed. Anderson and Hill observe that it is essential that property rights evolve from the bottom up. "Whether people fight over valuable resources or engage in cooperation and trade depends on how property rights are defined and enforced."[36] Robak considers that people are more likely to obey laws that they have agreed to.[37]

The structure of land ownership on reserves differed from that of land in other areas of Canada. Adhering neither to the Indian social framework internally nor to the rectilinear private property structure externally, it created a transnational space, with different peoples interacting both within and across the boundaries, and with a porous border imposing different restrictions on different people. Indians needed permission from the reserve agent to buy any seeds, animals, tools, or equipment, or to sell any produce, grain, or meat. They could, though, participate in local laboring activities such as cutting wood or helping on local farms, if they could get a pass. Their status, though, circumscribed their economic activities. Their space "belonged to" them only in a restricted sense—one that would have been unacceptable to Europeans, who came from countries from which the perhaps comparable system of feudalism was gone.

The issue of the legal subdivision of reserves is complex. In terms of neoclassical economic analysis, full individual property rights are essential for commercial success. However, that does not mean that a particular set of institutions would have worked for aboriginals, coming from their distinctive socioeconomic history. Over the millennia, Indians had evolved a set of institutions that were appropriate to their circumstances, involving communal activities and sharing institutions very different from those of the European settlers. These institutions had been adapted to the circumstances of the bison hunt and had worked well. However, the intervention of the horse, the rifle, and subsequently the markets for the output of bison hides and the "input" of alcohol had disrupted their society.[38]

It appears that, from their protestations at the constraints imposed, Indians wanted to participate in commercial farming. The Department of Indian Affairs sabotaged the early years, and the majority of Indian farms never did develop into viable large-scale operations. Some farmers gave up in frustration, and others did not start. A few prospered, but many had eventually to give up their status and move off the reserves away from the band in order to acquire the land, with its clear property rights, that they needed, thus fulfilling the stratagems of Hayter Reed.

The interrelated problems of climate and technology eased by about 1900. The forced departure of Hayter Reed reduced but did not eliminate the racist attitude of the Department of Indian Affairs. Grain prices on international markets rose, enhancing the profitability of wheat farming. A critical constraint that remained was that of property rights within the reserves. The basic structure was inappropriate to market activity. Indian farming was therefore hamstrung before it could develop.

The aggregate number of Indians was relatively small, and they had little political voice, so their needs were ignored. The primary objective of the Dominion government concerning Western Canada in the late nineteenth century was to gain political control and to build markets for the manufacturing industry of the East. Indians were in the way and had to be cleared off the land as quickly and cheaply as possible. Pushing them onto reserves, where they could eke out a subsistence living or be driven off to be assimilated, solved the problem at a minimal economic and political cost.

Notes

1. The commonplace term *Indians* will be used rather than repeating *First Nations.* The term normally includes both First Nations and Métis people.

2. David Meyer, Alwynne B. Beaudoin, and Leslie J. Amundson, "Human Ecology of the Canadian Prairie Ecozone ca. 9000 BP: The Paleo-Indian Period," in *Human Ecology of the Canadian Prairie Ecozone, 11,000 to 300 BP*, ed. B. A. Nicholson (Regina, Saskatchewan: CPRC Press, University of Regina, 2011).

3. Richard H. Steckel and Joseph M. Prince, "Tallest in the World: Native Americans of the Great Plains in the Nineteenth Century," *American Economic Review* 91 (2001): 287–94.

4. Carbohydrates were a particular problem.

5. David J. Meltzer, *First Peoples in a New World: Colonizing Ice Age America* (Berkeley: University of California Press; 2009), 3021.

6. J. V. Wright, *A History of the Native People of Canada, Vol. I (10,000 B.C. to 1,000 B.C.)* (Gatineau, Canada: Canadian Museum of Civilization, 1995); J. V. Wright, *A History of the Native People of Canada, Vol. II (1,000 BC to 500 AD)* (Gatineau, Canada: Canadian Museum of Civilization, 1999), 803. Bows and arrows had existed for far longer than this, but they only reached the Prairies about 4000 years ago.

7. A small form of horse was indigenous to the Americas, but they had all disappeared before Europeans arrived.

8. Without the innovation of the horse and rifle, the bison might well have survived. However, given those factors and the demand for hides for industrial power transmission belts, both groups hunted bison in an unsustainable manner.

9. Andrew C. Isenberg, *The Destruction of the Bison: An Environmental History, 1750–1920* (Cambridge: Cambridge University Press, 2000), 26.

10. James Daschuk, *Clearing the Plains: Disease, Politics of Starvation and the Loss of Aboriginal Life* (Regina, Saskatchewan: University of Regina Press, 2013).

11. A. Ward, "Climatic Variability and Early Prairie Farming," *Canadian Journal of Economics* 29 (April 1996), S344–48.

12. *Fee simple* is a legal term describing what in summary amounts to complete outright ownership.

13. *Ibid.* Ward, "Climatic Variability and Early Prairie Farming."

14. *Usufruct* is a legal term denoting the right to use a resource without having outright ownership.

15. F. D. Lewis, "Farm Settlement on the Canadian Prairies 1898–1911," *Journal of Economic History* 41 (1981), 517–35; K. H. Norrie, "Dry Farming and the Economics of Risk Bearing: The Canadian Prairies 1870–1930," *Agricultural History* 51 (1977), 134–48; Tony Ward, "The Origins of the Canadian Wheat Boom, 1880–1910," *Canadian Journal of Economics* (November 1994); "Farming Technology and Crop Area on Early Prairie Farms," *Prairie Forum* 20 (Spring 1995), 19–36; and A. Ward, "The Origins of the Wheat Boom: 1880 to 1910," *Canadian Journal of Economics* 27 (November 1994), 865–83.

16. A. Ward, "Farming Technology and Crop Area on Early Prairie Farms."

17. Cited in Hugh Shewell, *Enough to Keep Them Alive: Indian Welfare in Canada 1873–1913* (Toronto: University of Toronto Press, 2004), 40.

18. Carter, 1990.

19. Ibid.

20. Except perhaps for people coming from Ukraine, who were used to these conditions.

21. Ward, 1994, 1995.

22. Ward, 1996.

23. The Hon Alexander Morris, P.C. *The Treaties of Canada with the Indians of Manitoba and the North-West Territories, Including the Negotiations on Which They Are Based, and Other Information Relating Thereto* (Toronto: Belfords, Clarke & Co.), 1880. Appendix, 333.

24. Ward, 1995.
25. Carter, 1990, 16.
26. Report of the Department of Indian Affairs, 1886, 133.
27. Canada, House of Commons, Sessional Papers, 1889, vol. 23, no. 12, 48.
28. Report of the Department of Indian Affairs, 1901, 92.
29. Ward, 1995.
30. Carter, 1990, 16.
31. A. M. Honoré, *Making Laws Bind* (Oxford: Clarendon Press, 1987), 165–79.
32. Carter, 1990.
33. Report of the Department of Indian Affairs, 1901, 217.
34. *Economist* (2011), 72.
35. Carter, 1990.
36. Terry L. Anderson and Peter J. Hill, *The Not So Wild, Wild West: Property Rights on the Frontier* (Stanford, Calif.: Stanford University Press, 2004), 14.
37. Jennifer Robak, "Exchange, Sovereignty, and Indian-Anglo Relations," in *Property Rights and Indian Economies: The Political Economy Forum*, ed. Terry L. Anderson (Lanham, Md.: Rowman and Littlefield, 1992), 7.
38. Isenberg, 2000.

Chapter 6

Two Tales of the Conquest of Seriland

Pascual Encinas, Roberto Thomson, The White Chief, and the Seri Indians*

Andrae Marak

In early January of 1922, big game hunter Charles Sheldon met with a band of Seri (or Comcáac) Indians at the San Francisco de Costa Rica ranch owned by Roberto Thomson Encinas. At the ranch, Sheldon was able to contract with the Seri to take him to Tiburón Island, where he planned to hunt bighorn sheep with the Seri acting as guides. Among a great deal of laughter, merriment, and general gossiping, the Seri repeatedly approached Sheldon to ask him if, given the Seri's fierce reputation, he was afraid of coming to the island with them. Indeed, Sheldon had been repeatedly warned by local Mexicans that once he went to the island, the Seri would at the very least rob him and would more than likely kill him. It was true, of course, that the Seri could be violent. But they had reason to be. They had been engaged in on-again, off-again warfare with the Mexican government for nearly eighty years, a government that had repeatedly sought to exterminate them and that still wanted to gain control of their ancestral homeland. Their fierceness and proclivity to violence, however, should not be overstated. Between 1844 and 1904, the Seri kidnapped one Mexican and killed four others. The Mexican government, on the other hand, killed at least 250 Seris.[1] Given the unevenness of the hostilities, the Seri had reason to bolster their fierce reputation, especially if it served to limit the number of uninvited outsiders entering their ancestral

* Research support for this chapter was provided by California University of Pennsylvania, Indiana University–Purdue University Columbus, and Governors State University. I presented earlier versions of this chapter at the Western Historical Association conference, the XIII Encuentro de Historiadores de México, Estados Unidos, y Canadá, the Midwest World History Association Conference, the Rocky Mountain Council on Latin American Studies Conference, and the Newberry Seminar in Borderlands and Latino Studies. In addition, Laura Tuennerman, Teresa Prados-Torreira, Margaret Power, Ellie Walsh, Geraldo Cadava, Benjamin Johnson, and Ramón Gutiérrez have provided me with feedback. Any remaining errors are mine alone.

homeland. Charles Sheldon was an astute observer. He decided that much of what he had been told and much of what he had read about Seri savagery and violence was misleading and untrue. Commenting on the publications of famed anthropologist W. J. McGee, Sheldon said, "Much of what McGee has written about the Seris is inconsistent with what I saw. As he only saw them for a week at Rancho Costa Rica, how could he have penetrated the facts? I fear that much of what he wrote exists only in his imagination."[2]

This chapter tries to penetrate the facts by sharing two stories. The first story is how, in the late nineteenth and early twentieth centuries, the Seri Indians' ancestral homeland was really a contested transnational space because it had yet to fall under Mexican control, even though the federal and state government had long claimed sovereignty over it and had at times worked diligently to control it.[3] As part of this story, Pascual Encinas, one of the first Mexicans to settle on the Costa de Hermosillo, smack dab in the middle of the Seri's land, used violence, the threat of violence, and a combination of corporate and family patriarchy in an attempt to subordinate the Seri and convert them into potential subjects of the Mexican state. Also as part of the first story, Pascual Encinas's grandnephew Roberto Thomson Encinas, who was hired by the state of Sonora and then the Mexican government to act as an official agent in transforming the Seri into Mexican citizens and the Seri's ancestral homeland into a territory that could be fully made use of by all of Mexico's citizens, continued his great uncle's paternal practices. The second story is the way in which Thomson and his colleague Edward H. Davis, both of whom were United States citizens, supplemented these practices with a modernizing project that better reflected the practices of the broader United States–Mexico borderlands region prior to the Mexican Revolution (1910–1917) and the United States more generally than that being promoted by the post-revolutionary Mexican government.[4] In other words, Mexican government agents used borderlands/American tools in their attempts to assimilate the Seri into the Mexican nation. Hence, I argue below that the Seri's ancestral lands were a transnational space both physically and culturally. Furthermore, my adoption of a transnational framework highlights how being at the intersection of multiple borders and frontiers empowered local actors, including the Seri, in unique ways. I have argued elsewhere (with Laura Tuennerman) that it is at the edges of state power that local agents have the most impact on the implementation of national policies, and this case study further buttresses that claim.[5]

The Actors

The Seri had a population of approximately five hundred in 1844 when Pascual Encinas established a hacienda inside the boundaries of the Seri's ancestral homeland. That population dropped in half between 1855 and 1865 when

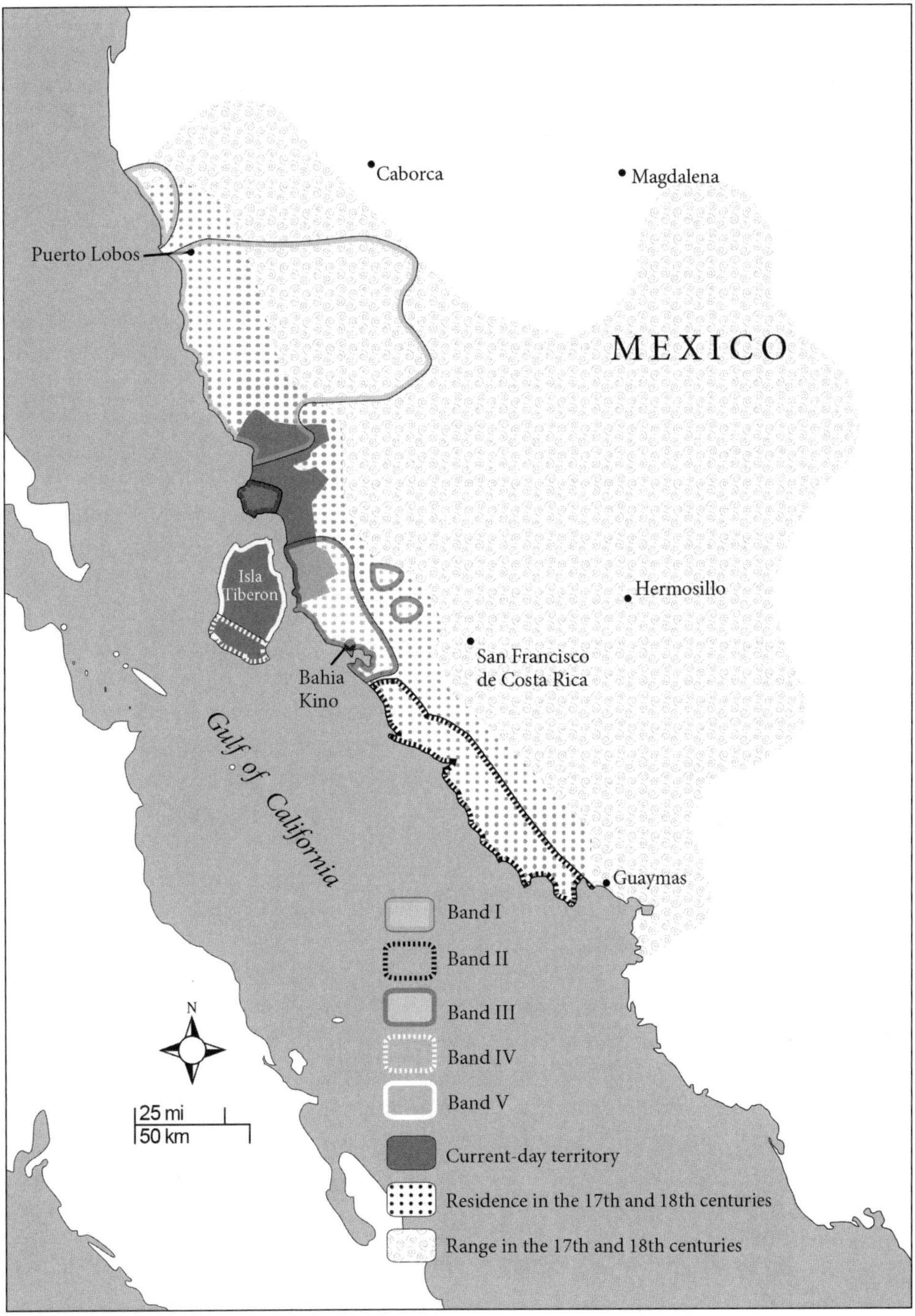

Overlapping Seri (Comcáac) and Mexican territory. The Seri's range is a conservative estimate. Map by Tracy Ellen Smith and Ted Avila.

Encincas waged war against the Seri. By the late 1930s, when the Mexican government worked with the Seri to establish a fishing commune, their population reached a near nadir of approximately 175.[6] The Seri lived in a series of geographically separate bands, each of which had its own unique culture and mutually intelligible dialect and each of which made use of different natural resources. The bands lived in temporary camps along a 4-mile-wide and 70-mile-long band of coastal desert on the Sonoran coast west of Hermosillo, stretching from Kino Bay to Desemboque, and on Tiburón Island. In addition to Tiburón Island, the Seri regularly had camps at Bahía Kino and Puerto Libertad as well as rancherías in Pozo Coyote, Las Estrellas, and San Francisco de Costa Rica. This chapter deals primarily with a group that anthropologists have identified as Band III (Seris-Tiburones).[7]

Although the coastal strip is a desert, the Bahía Kino served as a natural trap for large fish and is the breeding ground for the Pacific green turtle, which, combined with the fish, made up about two-thirds of the Seri diet.[8] In general, men did the fishing and occasionally hunted small game on the mainland and on Alcatraz and other small islands. Women and children collected mollusks as well as the fruit of succulents.[9] It was access to fresh water, and not food resources, however, that historically limited the Seri population.[10] Following the policies aimed at "incorporating independent Indians," outlined by José Angel Hernández in Chapter 4, a number of Mexican state agents tried to subordinate and modernize the Seri by promoting their Mexicanization, a process that would have required the Seri to give up their traditional way of life and permanently settle onto ranches, where they would be expected to raise cattle, farm, or hire themselves out as labor.

Pascual Encinas was a native of Tónichi, a small town in eastern Sonora and the site of a seventeenth-century Jesuit mission.[11] In 1844, Encinas and his brother Ignacio María Encinas established the hacienda San Francisco de Costa Rica in the Siete Cierras region west of Hermosillo. They drilled wells, built cattle pens, and cleared brush to plant crops. In addition, they built a small church and hired a teacher to attend to the education of their children and those of their employees. At its peak, the hacienda supported about twenty families.[12] Much like the military colonies established by the government to defend northern Mexico against the Apache threat,[13] the Mexican government supported the establishment and growth of haciendas like Encinas's through "large-scale expropriation of village" and Indigenous lands; the government hoped that haciendas like these would modernize the economy and subordinate portions of the country that were only nominally under control of the federal government.[14]

Roberto Thomson Encinas and Edward H. Davis were entrepreneurs. They collected Indian artifacts for the Museum of the American Indian (the

Heye Foundation) in New York and jointly invested in Thomson's cattle operations at the Hacienda de Costa Rica in the Seri's ancestral homeland near Kino Bay, Sonora. They were also advocates on behalf of Indigenous people. Davis styled himself as a "White Chief" and claimed that the Seri had made him a tribal medicine man, and Thomson referred to himself as the "*jefe de vigilancia de la tribu Seri* (i.e., Indian Agent)."[15] Their relationship with the Seri was complicated by the fact that Thomson and Davis were actively engaged in ranching on the Seri's ancestral homeland; had connections to the commercial fishing sector that competed with the Seri; worked on behalf of the Mexican Education Ministry (SEP), which sought to assimilate the Seri into mainstream Mexican society; and had transborder ties with US-based entities that were best served by preserving the Seri's "barbaric" culture. Further muddying the situation was the fact that Thomson was a devout Catholic and a close friend of Sonoran Bishop Juan Navarrete, a target of a state-sponsored post-revolutionary anti-clerical campaign and a veiled supporter of armed resistance against the state.[16] In fact, the Mexican government, especially in the state of Sonora, pushed its anti-church agenda through the very Education Ministry by which Thomson was employed. Hence, Thomson worked for the state even as he allied himself with local counter-state forces.

Thomson was born in 1888 in Flagstaff, Arizona, to Canadian parents of Irish descent; a major reason for his family's migration to and settlement in Sonora was their desire to practice Catholicism in a majority Catholic country.[17] He grew up speaking both English and Spanish and later learned Seri and Yaqui. His family had strong ties with other non-Hispanic local immigrants.[18] Davis was born in Brooklyn, New York, in 1862 and migrated to the San Diego area in 1885 as a means of dealing with a kidney ailment.[19] In San Diego, he came into money through land speculation and while working at a variety of jobs—farmer, rancher, "deputy county assessor . . . [and] justice of the peace"—began to collect Native American artifacts. Around 1915, he sold his first collection of artifacts to an agent for the Museum of the American Indian and then turned his home in Mesa Grande into a store, allowing local Indigenous folks to sell their "ancient arts and crafts." By 1916, he had become a purchasing agent for the Museum of the American Indian, and from then on he crossed the border into Mexico on a regular basis to purchase Indian artifacts.[20]

Mexican Nation Building

In a recent article on borderlands history, Pekka Hämäläinen and Samuel Truett argue that "greater attention to indigenous and transnational perspectives can help us map out more compelling centers for borderlands history."[21] Meanwhile, Rick A. López reminds us:

> Though recent studies have tempered the historical revisionist view of the Mexican state as Leviathan, many scholars continue to exaggerate the initiative and intentionality of the state regarding the county's [sic] postrevolutionary cultural transformation. In the movement to exalt the indigenous culture, we find that the state was actually something of a Johnny-come-lately. When it did get involved, it was at the behest of intellectuals, artists, and commercial interests who courted government support.[22]

Although López was focused on post-revolutionary Mexico, as I will demonstrate, his findings are also applicable to pre-revolutionary Mexico. I will try to honor his and Hämäläinen and Truett's insights by treating the overlapping spaces of the Seri's ancestral homeland and the Kino Bay–Costa de Hermosillo region of Sonora as a contested transnational space and by keeping in mind that pre-revolutionary and post-revolutionary state and federal officials lacked the ability to control the Kino Bay–Costa de Hermosillo region (even as they claimed sovereignty over it) and were often more reactive than proactive in advancing state and federal programs. As mentioned in the introduction, Mexico had long claimed the Seri's ancestral homeland as its own and had expended significant resources to control it. Nonetheless, the Seri's homeland continued to be a place of shifting borders and frontiers well into the twentieth century.

One of the reasons that the Mexican state was so reactive was that much of the borderlands region, extending deep into Sonora, was abandoned due to the Apache threat (and US-launched filibuster attempts) until the 1880s; hence, many parts of Sonora were transnational and contested by multiple actors.[23] The Mexican government did expend significant resources in trying to control the most economically viable regions of Sonora during the Porfiriato (1876–1911). As a result, they focused most of their efforts on eliminating the nearby Yaqui Indians.[24] As historian John J. Dwyer notes, "The Porfirians' heavy-handed policies were designed to transfer control of Yaqui lands to private interests and hasten their assimilation into mainstream mestizo culture."[25] The Costa de Hermosillo, lacking the economic potential of the Yaqui River, did not get the same level of resources, but the Porfirian state did not entirely ignore the Costa de Hermosillo either. Troops arrived in the Costa de Hermosillo to remove the Seri in hopes that local hacendados would be able to make more "rational" use of the area's resources. The government's military campaign drove the Seri (as well as some Yaqui) to seek refuge on Tiburón Island. As soon as Mexican troops left, however, the Seri returned. Lacking enough resources to maintain a permanent military occupation of the Seri's ancestral homeland, the Mexican government was forced to function through the auspices of corporate patriarchy. By this I mean the idea that "a well-ordered society was composed of well-ruled families.

Such families were governed by patriarchs who exercised power, demanded obedience, provided maintenance, and guaranteed protection."[26] Corporate patriarchy in turn was based on family patriarchy where men were owed deference and service from and sexual access to their wives in exchange for providing for them materially. Importantly, as Ana María Alonso notes in her groundbreaking *Thread of Blood*, patriarchal control of female sexuality has as much to do with domesticating women as with domesticating men because it is within the family writ large that society and the state reproduce themselves.[27] This was especially true in borderlands/frontier areas where the state had yet to fully form and societal norms were particularly contested. It was the combination of corporate and family patriarchy that defined the relationship between hacendados and resident families and allowed hacendados to consolidate power over them.[28]

Pascual Encinas embraced these values. He deemed himself worthy of deference because, in the face of great odds, his "ambition" led him to "valiantly" take "wild and virgin" lands and develop them.[29] Thomson argued that his great-uncle "Don" Pascual Encinas, even before he came to know the Seri personally in the mid-1840s, viewed it as his duty to "befriend them in order to offer them protection and prevent conflicts." Once he got to know them, Encinas granted the Seri access to local springs—water sources that he had appropriated from the Seri and were central to their semi-sedentary existence— a chapel, and a school. He also introduced them to his *tienda de raya* in hopes of tying them to his estate via debt peonage.[30] Famed anthropologist William J. McGee noted that Encinas had the "idea that he could control the Seri and gradually assimilate them into a civilized life" through a combination of work, school, and evangelization, a process that would eventually lead to the establishment of new "relations between the Indians and the colonists."[31] In other words, the Seri would become dependents of and subordinate to Encinas, and as a result, to Sonora and Mexico. Thomson recalls at least three Seri who went to school under the auspices of Encinas: Juan Astorga, who became a teacher at the hacienda's school; Fernando Kolosio, who directed the school and acted as an official interpreter between state officials and the Seri; and Juan Antonio, who acted as sacristan in the hacienda chapel and eventually ran the hacienda school.[32]

Encinas's success at subordinating the Seri and gaining untrammeled access to their ancestral lands and water sources varied over time. Thomson notes that overall few Seri attached themselves to the Hacienda de Costa Rica and that when the threat of Apache raids increased and in times of drought, large swaths of the hacienda were abandoned, and the majority of the attached Seri returned to their traditional semi-sedentary migrations.[33] This suggests that the hacienda served as a possible target for Apache raids, whereas the temporary Seri camps did not. Even more damning, McGee notes that not only did the majority of the Seri keep their distance from Encinas, but the ones that did attach themselves to his estate did so in a capricious manner, using it more to their advantage than as a means of social and cultural transformation. From the point of view of the Seri, the Hacienda de Costa Rica and its school, chapel, and store served as one additional resource to be woven into their hunter-gatherer lifestyle—a resource, however, that could be set aside when it did not meet their needs. McGee did claim that Encinas's contact with the Seri had one "positive effect"; by 1850, "perhaps the first time in their history, [the Seri] voluntarily permitted the free entry of foreigners to their territory," allowing Encinas to visit Kino Bay, Tiburon Island, and to begin planning the construction of a modern port.[34] Here we get a hint at the hopes that Encinas had for his modernizing program. By the mid-1850s, this supposed compact had broken down, resulting in open warfare that anthropologist Thomas Bowen rightly calls the "Encinas War."[35] Encinas used this period to hunt down and kill "half the Seri population" and expand his land ownership. He appropriated more Seri lands by building the Santa Ana and Libertad ranchos as extensions of his hacienda.[36] Thomson viewed this war as necessary for the "peaceful possession of his [great-uncle and grandfather's] ranch on the edge of the Sonoran desert over which the Seri roam."[37] McGee claims that by 1860, Encinas had consolidated his power enough that "the Seris saw [Encinas] as a governor whose approval was required prior to the ratification of their chief."[38] The fact that Seri elders were still bitter about the Encinas War into the 1960s suggests otherwise.[39]

Following the model of corporate patriarchy (and from the point of view of the Mexican government), it was through Encinas that the Seri expressed their "nominal loyalty to the state"; it was also through Encinas that the state's modernization program first penetrated the Seri's ancestral homeland. Encinas managed to maintain this status quo with the Seri until the late 1870s, when, Thomson claims, due to old age he was no longer able to defend the Seri frontier against renewed Seri encroachment. The truth of the matter appears to be that the Seri found it more advantageous to hunt Encinas's livestock than to work for him for wages, thus reworking Encinas's hacienda into their hunter-gatherer strategy in new ways.[40] This status quo continued until at least 1904, when Sonoran interim Governor Rafael Izábal (1900–1903) led the last formal raid against the Seri.[41] As a result of Encinas's limited successes at creating patriarchal relations with the Seri and extending the ephemeral reach of the state into the Seri's ancestral homeland, most Mexicans continued to view the Kino Bay–Costa de Hermosillo region as dangerous and off limits. McGee, for one, argued that the Seri were "the most bloodthirsty and treasonous of all the Indians of North America . . . also, their character is well known in all of Sonora, and certainly, in a general manner in all of Mexico, Arizona, and the southern part of California. The head of the military and the prefect in Sonora assured me that it would practically be suicide . . . to visit these Indians or disembark on their island without an armed guard. Furthermore, through conversations with them, I learned that all white men, Mexicans, or Indians from other tribes that come into contact with them are assassinated without the least scruples, unless they are restrained by fear [of retribution]."[42]

Davis later echoed these claims: "For centuries these nomads of the wastes have borne an evil reputation as killers and cannibals, and many an expedition to the Island for trade or exploration has never left its beautiful shores. Lured away from their boats by friendly gestures of the Indians, every last man has been killed by arrow or rifle and the expedition never heard from."[43]

As noted earlier, businessman, hunter, and conservationist Charles Sheldon had a more nuanced understanding: "I hope to go [to Tiburon Island], in spite of the advice of all the Mexicans to the contrary. They say that once the Seris get me there in their own land they will be very different and at least will rob me of everything. Should they find any cactus fruit so that they can brew a drink which makes them drunk, they may harm me."[44]

McGee, Davis, and Sheldon all agreed that the Seri's ancestral homeland was a contested transnational space. On official maps, it was part of Mexico; on the ground, much of it was controlled by the Seri.

This continued to be true into the 1920s, when Thomson took on a major role as liaison between the state and the Seri. In doing so, Thomson adopted many of the same approaches as his great-uncle Pascual Encinas, the difference being that Thomson, unlike Encinas, took on an official role (in 1923) as the liaison between the Seri and the state and federal government, whereas Encinas's connection to the state remained informal.[45] In fact, following the logic of corporate patriarchy, we might argue that in the absence of the state in the Seri's ancestral homeland, Pascual Encinas and his hacienda were the state. In any case, as López indicated more generally for post-revolutionary Mexico, the Mexican state was the Johnny-come-lately in this relationship, as it was Thomson who approached the state and offered to assist in modernizing the Seri, not the other way around.

Like his great uncle, Thomson also tried to promote Seri modernization through access to water, schooling, the chapel, and a dependent economic relationship. In 1926, Thomson, with the approval of the SEP, established a primary school in Carrizal, a mainland location in Kino Bay. The school did not work out well, so Thomson asked the SEP if he could establish a mobile school that followed the Seri's seasonal migrations. Adjusting to the Seri's needs, however, would undermine the school's purpose of transforming the Seri from semi-sedentary hunter-fisher-gatherers to sedentary farmers. Instead, the school was shifted 20 kilometers inland to Pozo Peña near San Miguel Point.[46] As for access to water, Thomson negotiated the Seri rights to a series of springs—Tecomate, La Cruz, La Higuera, El Carrizo, Pozo de Peña, and Agua Chiquita—in exchange for Seri modernization such that the Seri would become self-sustaining.[47] As in the past, the water to which they negotiated access was within the boundaries of their ancestral lands and had been appropriated by Thomson and other hacendados. In the realm of religion, given the post-revolutionary government's anti-clerical campaign, Thomson had to use subterfuge to teach the Seri Catholic catechism. Hence, it is no surprise that neither he nor his younger brother Luis ("Nene"), who took on most of the teaching duties, mentioned that Thomson's wife Sara often accompanied them to provide religious instruction.[48] Unlike Encinas, who tried to force the Seri into economic dependence through a *tienda de raya*, Thomson signed a series of contracts on behalf of the Seri that forced them into debt and into a dependent relationship with him as the go-between. This was specifically aimed at forcing the Seri to enter more fully into the cash economy and away from their subsistence livelihood. It should be noted, however, that Thomson and his associates viewed this positively. For example, in 1926 the state's head of federal education, Fernando F. Dworak, ordered Thomson to sell the fish that the Seri caught to local buyers in order to raise funds for the federal government's school and the associated permanent settlement.[49] By December, Thomson had entered into a contract with Carlos C. García and Jesús A. Ramírez, whereby García and Ramírez advanced the Seri $100 pesos in exchange for the exclusive right to buy the Seri's catch at below market rates.[50] In 1927, Dworak and Thomson arranged to have Sonora's governor, General Fausto Topete (1927–1929) loan the Seri a ramshackle fishing boat in need of serious repairs. Through Thomson, the Seri agreed to take out a loan of $1300 pesos to fix the boat (some of it fronted by Dworak) and then to use their catch to repay the loan. Given that General Topete was involved in the fishing industry, Dworak's suggestion that the Seri would now be able to avoid the middleman by bringing their fish directly to market probably meant that the Seri would be selling their fish to General Topete rather than to García and Ramírez.[51] In early 1929, the Seri ran the boat ashore, making it unserviceable and leaving the Seri with a large debt that they had no realistic chance to repay.[52]

It is hard to say just how effective these contracts and debts were in making the Seri dependent on Thomson. Even as Dworak reminded Thomson that since the Seri were "like children" and therefore should "never [be] left, for now, entirely alone," Thomson was complaining that he could not keep track of the Seri, let alone control them. They often moved more quickly on foot than Thomson could on horseback, and when they felt like it, they could purposely lose him. In addition, taking on debts that they, in the end, did not have to repay, did not necessarily put them into a dependent position. Nonetheless, the Seri did have troubling relationships with some outsiders. In the early 1930s, naturalists and writers Dane and Mary Coolidge noted that the Seri were still being fleeced on their fish catches in Kino Bay by "a piratical-looking Greek named Pedro" who bought fish from Mexican and American fisherman by the kilo at standard market prices but who used the lure of mescal to buy individual fish from the Seri at reduced rates.[53]

The Kino Bay–Costa de Hermosillo region continued to be contested territory. Thomson claimed that, with few exceptions, "Scientists . . . have been unable to make contact with [the Seri] owing to their undying hatred of all human beings except members of their own tribe" and that "at least fifty white men—Americans, Britons, Spaniards, Mexicans, and Frenchmen—have ventured into the land of the Seri and never returned."[54] These numbers are dubious; the Seri killed only four outsiders between 1844 and 1904, when overt hostilities ceased. That did not, however, change the perception of non-Seris about the region. When Thomson, his younger brother Luis, and Seri Chieftain Chico Romero escorted Dworak to the Seri's homeland in 1927, Thomson noted they were going to a land "that very few white people are familiar with due to fear of the Seri." Davis argued that the Seri's "gradual acquisition of modern implements and materials has gone along with centuries of warfare and bloodshed, and their submission to law entails a long story of violence."[55]

Claims about the impenetrable nature of the Seri's homeland were common. This is exactly what drew Charles Sheldon to the region: "And what is best," he exclaimed, "I am probably the first white man who ever made a hunting trip here."[56] The "savageness" of the Seri also served as a lure for Dane and Mary Coolidge, who noted that "the reports on the primitive Seris . . . drew us irresistibly to Kino Bay . . . we had gathered that the Seris were very fierce—the lowest savages in North America . . . But, after watching them a while, we decided there had been some mistake."[57] Sheldon also saw another side of the Seri. And although the claims made by Sheldon, the Coolidges, and others that they were the first white people to enter the region were false—for example, Sheldon was not the first Anglo hunter to enter the region; in the early 1920s Y. L. "Howdy" Holmes, another Anglo, "built a 'sportsmen's club' at Kino Bay, in hopes of attracting tourists"[58]—the number of outsiders who were actually able to enter the region and stay there long enough to see through the Seris's "savageness" was extremely limited. In the end, it is clear that the Seri, through their reputation, had a good amount of control over who could gain access to the region and on what terms.

Thomson and the Education Ministry wanted to overcome the Seri's reputation and gain some modicum of control over the region so that it could be better exploited, or as Thomson put it, they wanted "the creation within the Mexican economy of a meaningful niche for the Seri."[59] Dworak envisioned the government's involvement with the Seri as the "center of a peaceful conquest." Reminiscent of Encinas's desire to build a modern port, Dworak and Thomson convinced the Seri to begin construction of a road, suitable for automobile traffic, connecting the Seri's ancestral homeland with Hermosillo, a distance of more than 100 kilometers.[60] Their interest in the road coincided with the sudden expansion of the market for "the meat of the totoaba";[61] by 1930, Kino bay was the "last major camp on the gulf to be established for commercial totoaba fishing."[62] The road, when completed, would allow Thomson and other local businessmen to provide ice for commercial fishermen's catch.[63] Thomson and Davis also hoped that the Seri would join the ranks of commercial fishermen rather than continuing to feud with outsiders over access to the Seri's historical fishing grounds.[64] In sum, the transformation of the Seri and their homeland would integrate the Seri into the Mexican national economy and the Mexican nation even as it gave Mexico control over the region.

Dworak's "peaceful conquest" would need to wait at least another decade. It would be accomplished through the efforts of local fishermen, ranchers, and a slew of government agents in conjunction with "a succession of anthropologists, linguists, evangelists, school teachers, traders, and service groups."[65] In 1938, the Seri worked with the newly created Department of Indigenous Affairs to create a fishing cooperative in Kino Bay; the cooperative was relocated to El Desemboque in 1941, creating the "first permanent Seri community."[66] It also opened Kino Bay up to commercial fishermen and, over time, tourism.[67] By the mid-1940s, refrigerated trucks used the Kino Bay-Hermosillo road to haul off as much as 25 tons of commercially caught fish during the peak of the season.[68]

Anglo *Indigenismo* in "Seriland"

Not only did the absence of the Mexican state make the Seri's ancestral homeland physically a transnational space, it also provided the grounds for a transnational cultural space in unique and unexpected ways. Mexican elites deployed *indigenismo* as one tool among many to unify and consolidate power over a highly fragmented country.[69] *Indigenismo* entailed the "Indianization" of Mexico through embracing and esteeming "select aspects of indigenous culture" (and rejecting aspects of Asian and African culture) and extending education to "every little village" in the countryside.[70] Elites hoped that rural schools, coupled with community-wide education programs, would provide Indigenous people with the necessary tools to become fully functioning members of the Mexican polity. Until Indigenous people attained these tools (and used them to assimilate into mainstream Mexican culture), they would be treated as proto-citizens, in need of state tutelage.[71] Hence, from the point of view of Mexican elites, the social construction of a post-revolutionary Mexico would entail a state-led internal mixing—*mes-*

tizaje—of already existing cultural elements. In the case of the Seri, this process would entail converting them from hunter-gatherers, dressed in pelican skins and armed with bows and arrows, to modern sedentary farmers, equipped with plows and hoes, while still taking advantage of the "latent" positive physical and spiritual qualities inherent in their culture.[72] At one level, this was a mere continuation of the modernizing program promoted by Pascual Encinas and others during the Porfiriato. But this picture is incomplete. As historian Rick López notes, too many scholars "treat Mexican national culture as though it were created only by Mexican nationals within a context somehow cut off from international currents." In fact, "national identities are forged through intimate interactions that continually constitute (even as they confound) definitions of what is 'foreign' and what is 'national.'"[73] This was especially true of the post-revolutionary *indigenismo* deployed by the state through Thomson and Davis vis-à-vis the Seri.

Although Thomson and Davis did attempt to implement important parts of the SEP's standard formula for Indian assimilation, they—and the Sonoran officials with whom they worked—were heavily influenced by outdated pre-revolutionary borderlands and US policy approaches. Specifically, Thomson and Davis advanced three policies no longer acceptable in post-revolutionary Mexico: (1) Indian removal, (2) the payment of tribal members, and (3) the use of the Seri as "show Indians." All of these policies were strongly rooted in the borderlands and US policy approaches of the late nineteenth century and no longer reflected the newer approaches of the early twentieth century. Indian removal and the payment of tribal leaders were used in the nineteenth-century US-Mexico borderlands region as a means of responding to the Comanche and Apache threat,[74] but they were not tried elsewhere in post-revolutionary Mexico. Overall, this was a rather unique case in Mexico as it was shaped more by borderlands and US ideas than by post-revolutionary Mexican policy, leading local officials to implement an *indigenismo* not tried elsewhere in Mexico.

In 1925, the Seri agreed to leave their ancestral lands and relocate themselves onto a de facto reservation on Tiburón Island. As mentioned earlier, up until the 1880s both the United States and Mexico engaged in campaigns to resist and, when possible, remove *los indios bárbaros* (hostile Indian tribes) from the region.[75] These policies were continued in Sonora during the Porfiriato, freeing up land for modern agriculture and international investors.[76] Yet, the attempt by Thomson and the Sonoran officials to create a de facto Seri reservation on Tiburon Island had more in common with the creation of reservations in the United States than Indian policies in Mexico, which focused on integrating Indigenous people into the fabric of mainstream society. In fact, to my knowledge, there are no other contemporary cases in Mexico where the creation of a de facto reservation was attempted.

In August 1925, the Seri, with Thomson acting as liaison, signed an official accord with the State of Sonora creating a de facto reservation on Tiburon Island.[77] The accord was the result of two years of off and on negotiations relating to the Seri's practice of hunting on lands that were part of their ancestral homeland but that were also increasingly claimed by local ranchers as outer commons for pasturing their cattle.[78] A couple of things are worth pointing out here. First, Thomson claims that landowners, who wanted to further expand into the Seri's ancestral lands, went so far as to put a head price of $3 pesos on the Seri in an effort to exterminate them.[79] Sonoran officials did use the limited resources they had to back rancher claims to lands and access to commons for their cattle, but were no longer willing to expend the resources to engage in a campaign of extermination, the last of which occurred in 1904. Thus, the willingness of local landlords to take matters in their own hands in the absence of a full-fledged state campaign served as one impetus for the Seri to come to terms with Sonoran officials.

Second, the push by local landowners to intimidate and/or exterminate the Seri flew in the face of the on-again, off-again relationship that they had carved out with Thomson (though not that of Pascual Encinas, who had waged a war of extermination of his own a half century earlier). Even so, by the end of Encinas's War in 1865, he "allowed" the Seri free access to water sources on his hacienda and the right to hunt on "his" lands as long as they didn't poach his cattle. The poaching of his cattle by the Seri led to strained relations again in the late 1870s, but Encinas did claim that he forgave the Seri hunting of his cattle in times of dire need as long as they offered deference to him. The current problem, from the Seri point of view, was that the government was no longer willing to back the Seri's right to water sources and hunting grounds as it had done (through Encinas) in the past. Instead, local hacendados tried to harness the power of the state against the Seri by registering false complaints against them.[80]

The compact that the Seri signed with the government aimed at protecting the Seri from surrounding ranchers, limiting the Seri's ability to hunt on the mainland, and promoting Seri industriousness. Like reservations in the United States, no non-Indigenous people were allowed to enter the reservation without permission, and the Seri could not leave without a pass. Interestingly, the compact makes clear the government's modernizing ideology, claiming that a Seri reliance on hunting (and fishing) for subsistence was the result of backwardness and laziness, and demanded that Seri who robbed cattle or damaged fishermen's boats or ranchers' homesteads be sent to Hermosillo for punishment. Davis, based on his visits in the 1920s and 1930s—with the adjustment of an off-Tiburon Island addition for hunting, fishing, and gathering—viewed the "reservation" as a success:

> Within the last few years the Government has definitely set aside Tiburon as their exclusive home and sanctuary, with a strip along the mainland as their hunting and fishing ground, and where they can harvest the fruits of the giant cacti without fear of being killed. No person is allowed on this Island without special permission from the Governor of Sonora, or their Superintendent and devoted friend, Roberto Thomson. The Government has declared a permanent closed season on Seris.[81]

The use of reservations as a means of protecting Indigenous people from both extermination as well as the vices associated with modernity was also in keeping with the original intention of Indian removal and placement on reservations in the United States. William T. Hagan argued that when the United States adopted its reservation policy in the 1860s and 1870s, "[t]here was almost unanimous agreement among the whites that this was the [N]ative American's best hope of survival." Indian and non-Indian mixing was potentially more detrimental than helpful unless Indigenous people were exposed only to those people, like Thomson and Davis, approved by the government and thought to have their best interests at heart.[82] One example, noted by historian David A. Chang, is that the Round Valley Reservation in California was established to "create a hard-and-fast line separating Indians on the inside from whites and Indians on the outside . . . It would ideally appease white settlers who wanted off-reservation Indians . . . confined to reservations, but it also protected Indians from what agents considered to be the destructive actions and influences of whites."[83] Like their US counterparts, SEP officials were concerned about the possible negative impacts of contact between Indigenous and non-Indigenous people, but SEP officials were even more concerned about the isolation—geographic and cultural—of Indigenous people from Mexican society. Unlike in the United States, SEP officials proposed the immediate integration of Indigenous people into mainstream Mexican culture.[84] Hence, the willingness of the Sonoran government to separate and isolate the Seri flew in the face of standard post-revolutionary Mexican practices.

Like Indian removal, the payment of tribal members was a standard practice in the nineteenth-century US-Mexico borderlands region.[85] In fact, it was the breakdown of this system that led to an upsurge in cross border raiding by so-called *indios bárbaros*. Once cross-border cooperation had more or less eliminated the Apache threat, the United States moved to assimilate Native Americans. The United States focused on creating a cadre of Native American leaders who would serve to assimilate their brethren when they returned from boarding schools. Hence, the Office of Indian Affairs (OIA) prioritized the use of Native American boarding school graduates in the Indian School

Service between 1881 and 1908, and then continued to make use of Native Americans as OIA employees—especially as tribal policemen, teachers, and judges—thereafter.[86] Mexico did not begin to promote boarding schools until 1925 and even then only on a very restricted basis. Admittedly, some graduates of Mexico's *Casa del Estudiante Indígena*, an Indigenous boarding school located in Mexico City, also returned to their communities to teach in primary schools, but their numbers were very small.[87] For example, Ignacio León, a Tarahumara, returned from the Casa and helped establish a regional SEP boarding school for Indigenous people in Tónachich, Chihuahua, in 1933. By the early 1940s, he and his wife had trained an entire generation of Indigenous students who would go on to play pivotal roles in promoting Tarahumara governance and local democracy. But the SEP's hopes that Casa graduates would return to transform their local communities mostly failed. For instance, when SEP officials tracked down Francisco Domínguez, a Tohono O'odham Nation graduate of the Casa, in northern Sonora to see if he would teach in a local Tohono O'odham school, he repeatedly rebuffed them.[88] Although the Seri did not send anyone to the Casa, state officials did train one Seri, Kolusio, captured as a child prior to the revolution, to be a teacher. Kolusio occasionally went to visit the Seri, attempting to convince them to come to Hermosillo for schooling, but after a wave of smallpox decimated the majority of those who attended the school, the rest fled back to their ancestral homeland.[89] In any case, unlike in the United States, where certain job categories were set aside for Indigenous people, teaching (or other governmental) jobs in Mexico were not set aside for Indigenous people, even if officials did hope that some Indigenous people might eventually fill these positions.

Hence, the direct payment of Seri tribal authorities as a strategy for containing them as a threat is unique to post-revolutionary Mexico. Here is how it worked. Just as the Mexican Revolution was beginning to unfold in 1911, Sonoran officials signed an agreement with the Seri, recognizing their right to local self-rule in exchange for the Seri's agreement not to kill local ranchers' cattle and horses. Although it is not clear, it is likely that the Sonoran government began making payments to the Seri's chief, Juan Tomas, at that time. Whether they started in 1911 or not, there is evidence that $25 peso monthly payments to the Seri's leader was a standard practice as of 1923.[90] The Seri continued to report to state officials any changes in tribal leadership (and second-in-command) all the way up to their August 1925 accord and beyond.[91]

In November 1926, oversight of the Seri shifted from state to federal auspices as Thomson became a SEP employee and, in contravention to the accord that they had signed only a year earlier, established the aforementioned Seri primary school in Carrizal that was shortly thereafter relocated to Pozo Peña.[92] In 1927, the SEP agreed to pay the Seri's chief, Francisco "Chico" Romero, $25 pesos monthly as well as the "Indio" Herrera $15 pesos monthly to enforce school attendance (and later cleanliness). State officials also continued paying Romero his regular $25 pesos and also added Herrera to their payroll.[93] Not only did both the state and federal government pay tribal leaders, but the head of federal education in Sonora, Fernando F. Dworak, also asked his superiors to provide every Seri with $5 pesos monthly during their proposed transition period from semi-sedentary to sedentary living. Thomson echoed this, arguing that "it is not the work of the moment to remove them and change them . . . it will require patience and abnegation or a reserve where the government completely sustains them."[94] Thomson raised his request to $15 pesos monthly for every tribal member less than a month later.[95]

After the SEP refused to subsidize the Seri, Thomson and Davis proposed taking twenty-five Seri with them to "a special place near Hollywood" where the Seri—dressed in "dried pelican skins, painted . . . , and occupied with their habitual occupations"—would put on a six- to eight-week exhibition as "show Indians." The funds raised on the trip would be used to "buy abundant clothes, agricultural implements, axes, etc." necessary for the tribe's modernization and assimilation into mainstream Mexican culture.[96] As Rick López and Mauricio Tenorio-Trillo have shown, putting Indigenous people on display both inside and outside of Mexico was a regular practice. During the nineteenth century, Mexico participated in World's Fairs and put "pure" Indigenous people on display "in what amounted to a human zoo" to demonstrate, following the eugenics of the age, the ways in which each different race and nation had its unique place in the evolution and modernization of man. But in post-revolutionary Mexico, the focus shifted to that of demonstrating "the cosmic race" that José Vasconcelos, the celebrated leader of the SEP, embraced. This did not mean the Indigenous people did not have their place. Aztec hero and symbol of the nation Cuauhtémoc was still presented at the 1922 Rio de Janeiro Fair, but he no longer held center stage.[97] Furthermore, the ways in which Indigenous people were represented went through a wholesale change. For example, the India Bonita Contest staged by *El Universal* in 1921 sought to capture Indigenous women in their "authentic" and "natural" state. This "natural" state—which required some contestants to change their everyday look to qualify—incorporated "outward markers of how an indigenous woman was supposed to look," including the wearing of Indigenous clothes, the absence of makeup, and hair worn in braids.[98] However, the India Bonita Contest and Thomson and Davis's attempt to turn the Seri into "show Indians" had important differences. This is perhaps best demonstrated by the fact that the India Bonita Contest winner, María Bibiana Uribe, was incorporated into the state's official centennial program while the proposed Seri show was forcefully rejected. Here I would like to suggest that the US-Mexico border and the differing purposes of Indians on display played a central role in the SEP's rejection. In Mexico, the India Bonita Contest fit into a broader trend of "creating and valor-izing the Mexican Indian, ripe for redemption and incorporation into an ethnicized nation . . . intellectuals and state officials held that Mexico needed a collective personality rooted in the culture of the rural popular classes, and that it should include everyone living within the political boundaries."[99] Thomson's work, as captured in his 1931 *Popular Science* article about using glass beads to civilize the Seri, fits this theme.[100] Yet, Davis' vision of the Seri dressed in "dried pelican skins, painted . . . , and occupied with their habitual occupations" did not belong within the boundaries of a newly modernizing post-revolutionary Mexico; this, as Alexander Dawson has demonstrated, was reserved for Indigenous people who were already partly acculturated.[101] Instead, this proposed use of the Seri better fit into the pre-revolutionary eugenics-inspired practices of Mexico, where Aztecs "worked in Mexican brick, pottery, and copper" for live audiences and late nineteenth- and early twentieth-century US practices, where Buffalo Bill's Wild West Show ran until 1913.[102] In the United States, show Indians further reinforced the dominant society's racist and eugenics-influenced beliefs of its own superiority by tapping into "the public longing for noble savages as true, uncorrupted, honest primitives fading before the onslaught of modern, industrial commerce." Historian Louis S. Warren notes that there were ample reasons for Native Americans to want to participate in such displays, including the possibility of better pay and the ability to practice important aspects of their culture in a context in which outsiders might also come to appreciate and cherish them as well.[103]

Nonetheless, it is not clear that Davis took the Seri's desire to protect their cultural practices into consideration. In fact, Davis' writings and publications portrayed Native Americans, not just the Seri, as an agentless, backward, and vanishing race. An Indian elder's advice to an Indian youth, recorded by Davis, is but one of many examples:

> You have been to the white man's school, have learned the white man's ways, speak his tongue, eat his food and wear his clothes. Except your color you just like a white man. Times now are better for us. Our lands are set aside and guarded by the government. Our children are taught like the white children with whom they mingle. It is a losing fight. We can not stem the current. We must go under. Wherever the white man comes in contact with the red, the red goes down. The white race rules the world and their number is like the sands of the desert. When the strong wind comes out from the north and carries this sand in great clouds filling the sky, it smothers and covers everything in its trail.

> And so my son, will it be with us. A few years and our race will be done, our simple civilization smothered, buried, out of existence. Tis well—go![104]

Thus, putting the Seri on display as atavistic leftovers from a past age in such a highly visible location would have run against the post-revolutionary Mexican program of redeemable Indigenous people capable of being incorporated into the nation's fabric. In its place, it would have supported Davis' view of them as a people condemned to live in the past. The fact that they would be put on display in the United States, a country that in many ways served as a model of modernity for Mexican elites, would have been doubly damaging. Perhaps this is why the SEP not only rejected Davis' proposal but also demanded that Dwork, Sonora's education chief, do everything in his power to ensure that it did not come to pass.

Conclusion

In this chapter, I have tried to place the attempted assimilation of the Seri into mainstream Mexican society in a transnational perspective. It was transnational because the Sonoran state government and the Mexican federal government had yet to gain control over the Seri's ancestral homeland. In lieu of a state presence, local notable families, such as that of "Don" Pascual Encinas and his grand-nephew Roberto Thomas Encinas, attempted to use corporate patriarchy strategies to co-opt the Seri into mainstream society and gain access to their land and water resources. The Encinas's attempts at subordinating the Seri met with limited success, though they did serve to push the Seri off major chunks of their ancestral lands, as well as open their fishing grounds up to outsiders. In many ways, Thomson acted as much on behalf of his family as he did on behalf of the state. In the process, he continued using corporate patriarchy as a means of extending quasi-state influence over the Seri. The attempted assimilation of the Seri was not only transnational because the government had yet to gain control of a region over which it claimed sovereignty; it was also a transnational cultural space. As López has argued, the social construction and application of *indigenismo* was a transnational enterprise. This was nowhere more the case than in the state of Sonora, which long had economic, social, and cultural ties to the United States and which itself served as part of a borderlands region often disconnected from practices in south and central Mexico. State officials turned the assimilation project over to two Anglos—Thomson and Davis—who used their positions to implement policies, such as Indian removal, the payment of tribal members, and the use of the Seri as "show Indians," that were strongly rooted in pre-revolutionary borderlands and nineteenth-century US policy approaches. In fact, they used their positions to push policies, especially the teaching of the Catholic catechism, stringently opposed by Mexico's federal government. Although it would not be until the late 1930s, through the Department of Indigenous Affairs, that the state would acquire a permanent presence among the Seri in their ancestral homeland, Encinas, Thomson, and Davis paved the way for future state intervention in the Seri's affairs.

Notes

1. Pascual Encinas established the Rancho San Francisco de Costa Rica in 1844; 1904 marks the Mexican government's last formal campaign against the Seri. See Thomas Bowen, "Seri," in *Handbook of North American Indians, Vol. 10, Southwest*, ed. Alfonso Ortiz (Washington, D.C.: Smithsonian Institution, 1983), 233.

2. Neil B. Carmony and David E. Brown, eds., *The Wilderness of the Southwest: Charles Sheldon's Quest for Desert Bighorn Sheep and Adventures with the Havasupai and Seri Indians* (Salt Lake City: University of Utah Press, 1993), 121, 188.

3. Mexico struggled to control the borderlands not only with the Seri; the Comanche and the Apaches were more serious threats. See Pekka Hämäläinen, *The Comanche Empire* (New Haven: Yale University Press, 2008), especially Chapters 4, 5, and 6; Brian Delay, *War of a Thousand Deserts: Indian Raids and the U.S.-Mexican War* (New Haven, Conn.: Yale University Press, 2008), and José Angel Hernández, *Mexican American Colonization During the Nineteenth Century: A History of the U.S.-Mexico Borderlands* (Cambridge: Cambridge University Press, 2012), especially Chapter 1.

4. Laura Tuennerman and I have argued elsewhere that the modernizing project of the United States southwest and that of northwest Mexico had many similarities, but their differences still mattered in material ways. See Marak and Tuennerman, "Official Government Discourses about Vice and Deviance: The Early-Twentieth-Century Tohono O'odham," in *Smugglers, Brothels, and Twine: Historical Perspectives on Contraband and Vice in North America's Borderlands*, eds. Elaine Carey and Andrae Marak (Tucson: University of Arizona Press, 2011); and Marak and Tuennerman, *Gendering the Periphery of Empires: The Tohono O'odham, Gender, and Assimilation, 1880–1934* (Tucson: University of Arizona Press, 2013), Chapter 6.

5. Marak and Tuennerman, *Gendering the Periphery of Empires*.

6. Thomas Bowen and Mary B. Moser, "Seri," in *Encyclopedia of World Cultures*, editor-in-chief David Levinson, *Middle America and the Caribbean*, vol. 8, ed. James W. Dow and assoc. ed. Robert B. Kemper (Boston: G.K. Hall, 1995): p. 232–34.

7. Margarita Nolasco Armas argues that in the second half of the nineteenth century, the six bands of the Seri relocated to the area previously occupied by the Seris-Tiburones as a means of better responding to depredations committed by "los blancos." See Nolasco Armas, "Los seris, desierto y mar," *Anales del Museo Nacional de México*, 18 (1967): 133. For a much larger estimate of Seri territory based on Seri oral tradition, see Diana Luque Agraz and Antonio Robles Torres, *Naturaleza, sabers, y territories Comcáac (Seri): diversidad, cultural, y sustentabilidad* (Mexico: Secretaría de Medio Ambiente y Recursos Naturales, 2006), 25.

8. Luis Bourillón-Moreno, "Exclusive Fishing Zone as a Strategy for Managing Fishery Resources by the Seri Indians, Gulf of California, Mexico" (Ph.D. diss., University of Arizona, 2002), 19–21; and Edward W. Moser, "Seri Bands," *The Kiva* 28 (1963): 14–27.

9. W. J. McGee, "Expedition to Papagueria and Seriland: A Preliminary Note," *American Anthropologist* 9 (March 1896): 95–98; Robert Ascher, "Ethnography for Archeology: A Case from the Seri Indians," *Ethnology* 1 (July 1962): 361–62; Luis Arturo Gonzalez Bonilla, "Los Seris," *Revista Mexicana de Sociología* 3 (2nd quarter, 1941): 94–95; and Jack D. Forbes, "Historical Survey of the Indians of Sonora, 1821–1910," *Ethnohistory* 4 (Autumn 1957): 350.

10. Thomas E. Sheridan, *Empire of Sand: The Seri Indians and the Struggle for Spanish Sonora, 1645–1803* (Tucson: University of Arizona Press, 1999).

11. John Francis Bannon, "The Mission Frontier in Sonora, 1620–1687," in *The Jesuit Missions of Northern Mexico*, eds. Charles W. Polzer, Thomas H. Naylor, Thomas E. Sheridan, and Diana Hadley (New York: Routledge, 1991), 185, 188.

12. Gastón Cano Avila, "Semblanza de don Roberto Thomson," in *Pioneros de la Costa de Hermosillo (La Hacienda de Costa Rica 1844)*, ed. Roberto Thomson (Hermosillo, Sonora: Artes Gráficas y Editoriales Yescas, S.A., 1989), 17–18; and Manuel Robles Ortíz, "Pascual Encinas . . . Aquel que Conquisto el Desierto," in *Pioneros de la Costa de Hermosillo (La Hacienda de Costa Rica 1844)*, 87–90.

13. See Friedrich Katz, *The Secret War in Mexico: Europe, the United States, and the Mexican Revolution* (Chicago: University of Chicago Press, 1983), Chapter 1; Daniel Nugent, *Spent Cartridges of Revolution: An Anthropological History of Naimiquipa, Chihuahua* (Chicago: University of Chicago Press, 1993), Chapter 2; and Ana María Alonso, *Thread of Blood: Colonialism, Revolution, and Gender on Mexico's Northern Frontier* (Tucson: University of Arizona Press, 1995).

14. Katz, *The Secret War in Mexico*, 6. See also Eric R. Wolf, *Peasant Wars of the Twentieth Century* (Norman: University of Oklahoma Press, 1999), Chapter 1.

15. Mitchell Hudgins, "The White Chief: The Story of Edward H. Davis" (M.A. thesis, University of San Diego, 1987); Scott H. Ryerson, "'I Was the One to Make the Peace': Roberto Thomson and the Seri Indians," *Journal of the Southwest* 47 (2005): 121; and Edward H. Davis as told to John Edwin Hogg, "The Pursuits of a Museum Collector," *Touring Topics* 23 (October 1931), 18. Davis also claimed that the Mesa Grande Indians (Northern Dieguenos) made him a "ceremonial chief of the tribe" in 1907, which allowed him to take part in all of their ceremonies. See Charles Russell Quinn, "Life and Times," in *Edward H. Davis and the Indians of the Southwest United States and Northwest Mexico: A Harvest of Photographs, Sketches and Unpublished Manuscripts of the Indefatigable Collector of Artifacts of These Border Indians*, eds. Charles Russell Quinn and Elena Quinn (Downey, Calif.: Elena Quinn, 1965), 27.

16. Adrian A. Bantjes, *As If Jesus Walked on Earth: Cardenismo, Sonora, and the Mexican Revolution* (Wilmington, Del.: Scholarly Resources, 1998), 26, 46–48; Wilfrid Parsons, *Mexican Martyrdom* (New York: The Macmillan Co., 1936), 60–61; Lyle C. Brown, *Mexican Church-State Relations, 1933–1940* (Waco, Texas: 1964).

17. After crossing the border to seek his fortune, Roberto Thomson's father, Luis K. Thomson, married Concepción, the daughter of Ignacio María Encinas. His family may also have left the United States for Mexico because of the virulent anti-Catholic and anti-Irish sentiments related to white privilege and Manifest Destiny in the United States. See Horsman, *Race and Manifest Destiny: Origins of American Racial Anglo-Saxonism* (Cambridge: Harvard University Press, 1986), 208–28.

18. Gastón Cano Avila, "Semblanza de don Roberto Thomson," in *Pioneros de la Costa de Hermosillo (La Hacienda de Costa Rica 1844)*, 17–18; and Luis Encinas Johnson, "Presentacion," in *Pioneros de la Costa de Hermosillo (La Hacienda de Costa Rica 1844)*, 11. He was especially friendly with the Ciscomani, Clerici, Baranzini, Giotonini, Cecco, and Prandini families, all of whom were Italian and married into Mexican families.

19. Russell Quinn, "Life and Times," 21–23. Davis suffered from Bright's disease.

20. Ibid., 30.

21. Pekka Hämäläinen and Samuel Truett, "On Borderlands," *The Journal of American History*, 98 (September 2011): 355.

22. Rick A. López, *Crafting Mexico: Intellectuals, Artisans, and the State after the Revolution* (Durham, N.C.: Duke University Press, 2010), 49.

23. Karl Jacoby argues, "Once we begin to think of the West . . . as an extension of the Mexican north and as the homeland of a complex array of Indian communities, we allow far different narratives about this space to emerge." Jacoby, *Shadows at Dawn: An Apache Massacre and the Violence of History* (New York: Penguin Books, 2009), 6. See also Brian DeLay, "Independent Indians and the US-Mexican War," *American Historical Review* 112 (February 2007): 35–68; Rachel St. John, *Line in the Sand: A History of the Western US-Mexico Border* (Princeton: Princeton University Press, 2011), Chapter Two; Miguel Tinker Salas, *In the Shadow of the Eagle: Sonora and the Transformation of the Border during the Porfiriato* (Berkeley: University of California Press, 1997), 60–61; and Bowen, "Seri," 232–34. On US-launched filibuster attempts, see Robert E. May, *Manifest Destiny's Underworld: Filibustering in Antebellum America* (Chapel Hill: University of North Carolina Press, 2002); and Joseph A. Stout, *Schemers and Dreamers: Filibustering in Mexico, 1848–1921* (Fort Worth: Texas Christian University Press, 2002).

24. Edward H. Spicer, *Cycles of Conquest: The Impact of Spain, Mexico, and the United States on the Indians of the Southwest, 1533–1960* (Tucson: University of Arizona Press), 66–85; Sterling Evans, *Bound in Twine: The History and Ecology of the Henequen-Wheat Complex for Mexico and the American and*

Canadian Plains, 1880–1950 (College Station: Texas A&M University Press, 2007), 67–80. In fact, many fleeing Yaqui hid on Tiburon Island. Some Yaqui women eventually intermarried with the Seri. See Coolidge, *The Last of the Seris,* 137.

25. John J. Dwyer, *The Agrarian Dispute: The Expropriation of American-Owned Rural Land in Postrevolutionary Mexico* (Durham, N.C.: Duke University Press, 2008), 128. See also, Thomas E. Sheridan, "The Yoemem (Yaquis): An Enduring People," in *Paths of Life: American Indians in the Southwest and Northern Mexico,* eds. Thomas E. Sheridan and Nancy J. Parezo (Tucson: University of Arizona Press, 1996).

26. Elizabeth Dore, "One Step Forward, Two Steps Back: Gender and the State in the Long Nineteenth Century," *Hidden Histories of Gender and the State in Latin America,* eds. Elizabeth Dore and Maxine Molyneux (Durham, N.C.: Duke University Press, 2000), 10–11. See also John Tutino, *Making a New World: Founding Capitalism in the Bajío and Spanish North America* (Durham, N.C.: Duke University Press, 2011), 352–402. Hence, in the absence of the military, men became "arms-bearing" defenders of the weak. See Karen Hagemann, "A Valorous Folk Family: The Nation, the Military, and the Gender Order in Prussia in the Time of the Anti-Napoleonic Wars, 1806–1815," in *Gendered Nations: Nationalisms and Gender Order in the Long Nineteenth Century,* eds. Ida Blom, Karen Hagemann, and Catherine Hall (Oxford: Oxford University Press, 2000), 189.

27. Alonso, *Thread of Blood,* 90–91.

28. Sam R. Sweitz, *On the Periphery of the Periphery: Household Archaeology at Hacienda San Juan Bautista Tabi, Yucatan, Mexico* (London: Springer-Verlag, 2011); John Tutino, "The Revolution in Mexican Independence: Insurgency and the Renegotiation of Property, Production, and Patriarchy in the Bajío, 1800–1855," *Hispanic American Historical Review* 78 (August 1998), 377; Piedad Peniche Rivera, "Gender, Bridewealth, and Marriage: Social Reproduction of Peons on Henequen Haciendas in Yucatán, 1870–1901," *Women of the Mexican Countryside, 1850–1990: Creating Spaces, Shaping Transitions,* eds. Heather Fowler-Salamini and Mary Kay Vaughan (Tucson: University of Arizona Press, 1994).

29. Luis Encinas Johnson, "Presentación," in *Pioneros de la Costa de Hermosillo (La Hacienda de Costa Rica 1844),* 9–10.

30. Thomson, "La Hacienda de Costa Rica," 32.

31. William J. McGee, "Testimonios del Dr. William J. McGee," in *Pioneros de la Costa de Hermosillo (La Hacienda de Costa Rica 1844),* 69.

32. Thomson, "La Hacienda de Costa Rica," 35.

33. Ibid., 37; and Roberto Thomson, "La Sequia de 1877," *Pioneros de la Costa de Hermosillo (La Hacienda de Costa Rica 1844),* 43–47.

34. McGee, "Testimonios del Dr. William J. McGee," 69–71.

35. Thomas Bowen, "Seri," 233. McGee claims that the Seri started the war. McGee, Testimonios del Dr. William J. McGee," 72.

36. Ibid., 234.

37. Roberto Thomson as told to H. H. Dunn, "Sons of the Stone Age: The Seri—Modern Mexico's Most Savage Indians," *Travel* 56 (April 1931): 43.

38. McGee, "Testimonios del Dr. William J. McGee," 73.

39. Bowen, "Seri," 234.

40. Bourillón-Moreno, "Exclusive Fishing Zone as a Strategy for Managing Fishery Resources by the Seri Indians," 29.

41. Thomson, "Sons of the Stone Age," 73–74; and Bowen, "Seri," 233. Izábal's attempted extermination of the Seri was part of a larger extermination campaign against a range of Indigenous groups, including the Yaquis, Opatas, and Pimas, in Sonora. See Miquel Izard, "Del diezmo a la totalidad," in *Homogeneidad, diferencia y exclusión en América: X Encuentro-Debate América ayer y hoy,* eds. Gabriella Dalla Corte et al. (Barcelona: Universitat de Barcelona, 2005), 289–304.

42. McGee, "Testimonios del Dr. William J. McGee," 82–84.

43. Davis, "Unfinished Book Manuscript," 143.

44. Carmony and Brown, eds., *The Wilderness of the Southwest,* 121.

45. Roberto Thomson to Fernando F. Dworak, n.d.; and Roberto Thomson, "Los Indios Seris," 26 (July 1927), box 8415, Exp. 68, Sonora; Archivo Historico de la Secretaría de Educación Pública—

Escuelas Rurales (hereafter AHSEP-ER); Roberto Thomson to Governor, Aug. 31, 1923, Tomo 3611, Tribus/Seris, AHGES; and Ricardo Aragón Pérez, ed., *Historia de la Educación en Sonora*, Tomo 3 (Hermosillo: Gobierno del Estado de Sonora and Secretaría de Educación y Cultura, 2003), 82. Scott H. Ryerson claims that Thomson was named as an Indian agent between 1920 and 1922. Ryerson, "'I Was the One to Make the Peace,'" 130.

46. Fernando F. Dworak to SEP, Feb. 14, 1927, box 8446, Exp. IV/100(04)(II-5)(721.5), Sonora, AHSEP-ER. See also Andrae M. Marak, *From Many, One: Indians, Peasants, Borders, and Education in Callista Mexico, 1924–1935* (Calgary: University of Calgary Press, 2009), Chapter 4. According to Thomson, Davis was a strong supporter of Indigenous modernization through schooling. See, Roberto Thomson, "Reminiscences," in *Edward H. Davis and the Indians of the Southwest United States and Northwest Mexico*, 124, 128.

47. Convenio Celebrado entre el Gobierno del Estado y el Gobernador de los Seris, Aug. 4, 1925; Tomo 3814; Tribus/Seris; AHGES.

48. Thomson, "Semblanza de Don Roberto Thomson," 23.

49. Fernando F. Dworak to SEP, Nov. 10, 1926, box 8415, Exp. 68, Sonora, AHSEP-ER.

50. Contract, Dec. 13, 1926; and Fernando F. Dworak to SEP, Dec. 22, 1926, box 8415, Exp. 68, Sonora, AHSEP-ER.

51. Ryerson, "'I Was the One to Make the Peace,'" 143.

52. Fernando F. Dworak to SEP, Sept. 28, 1927, box 8446, Exp. IV/077.1(04)(721.5); Fernando F. Dworak to SEP, May 19, 1928; Fernando F. Dworak to SEP, July 21, 1928; Fernando F. Dworak to SEP, Jan. 9, 1929; and Fernando F. Dworak to SEP, Jan. 16, 1929, box 8415, Exp. 68, Sonora, AHSEP-ER.

53. Coolidge, *The Last of the Seris*, 75.

54. Thompson, "Sons of the Stone Age," 43.

55. Edward H. Davis and E. Yale Dawson, "The Savage Seris of Sonora—I," *The Scientific Monthly* 60 (March 1945): 193–202; quote, 193.

56. Sheldon, *The Wilderness of the Southwest*, 127.

57. Coolidge, *The Last of the Seris*, 12 and 21.

58. Ryerson, "'I Was the One to Make the Peace,'" 130, 143. Thomas Bowen suggests that the establishment date for the Kino Bay Club was closer to 1930; see Bowen, "The Seri," 234. According to Bourillón-Moreno, Holmes began construction in 1926 and made improvements in 1929. See Bourillón-Moreno, "Exclusive Fishing Zone as a Strategy for Managing Fishery Resources by the Seri Indians," 31.

59. Ryerson, "'I Was the One to Make the Peace," 131.

60. Fernando F. Dworak to SEP, Feb. 14, 1927, box 8446, Exp. IV/100(04)(II-5)(721.5); and Fernando F. Dworak to SEP, Nov. 10, 1926, box 8415, Exp. 68, Sonora, AHSEP-ER. For road distance, see the map on the inside cover of Bernice Johnston, *The Seri Indians of Sonora Mexico* (Tucson: University of Arizona Press, 1986).

61. Ryerson, "'I Was the One to Make the Peace,'" 140.

62. Conrad Bahre, Luis Bourillón, and Jorge Torre, "The Seri Commercial Totoaba Fishing (1930–1965)," *Journal of the Southwest* 42 (2000): 557.

63. Both Thomson and General Fausto Topete engaged in the business of providing ice and transportation for the export of totoaba. See Ryerson, "'I Was the One to Make the Peace,'" 143; and Fernando F. Dworak to SEP, Sept. 28, 1927, box 8446, Exp. IV/077.1(04)(721.5), Sonora, AHSEP-ER.

64. Davis and Hogg, "The Pursuits of a Museum Collector," 20.

65. Bowen, "The Seri," 234.

66. Bowen and Moser, "Seri," 233.

67. Spicer, *Cycles of Conquest*, 116.

68. Edward H. Davis and E. Yale Dawson, "The Savage Seris of Sonora—II," *The Scientific Monthly* 60 (April 1945): 261–268; quote, 268.

69. Alan Knight, "Popular Culture and the Revolutionary State in Mexico, 1910–1940," *Hispanic American Historical Review* 74:3 (1994): 393–444.

70. Educator Moisés Sáenz viewed indigenismo as the Indianization of Mexico, see Moisés Sáenz, *Mexico integro* (Mexico City: SEP/Fondo de Cultura Económica, 1982, [1939]), 155–56; Rick A. López, *Crafting Mexico*, 9; Ana María Alonso, "Conforming Disconformity: 'Mestizaje,' Hybridity, and the Aesthetics of Mexican Nationalism," *Cultural Anthropology* 19 (November 2004): 463.

71. Dawson, *Indian and Nation*, xix–xx; and Claudio Lomnitz, *Deep Mexico, Silent Mexico: An Anthropology of Nationalism* (Minneapolis: University of Minnesota Press, 2001), 73–78.

72. Boletín de la Secretaría de la Educación Pública 5:6 (1926), 5–8; and Vaughan, *Cultural Politics*, 28.

73. López, *Crafting Mexico*, 17.

74. As Karl Jacoby notes, the US policy of Indian removal continued even during Ulysses S. Grant's "Peace Policy" for those Indigenous groups who did not agree to settle permanently on reservations. In Mexico, the *establecimientos de paz*, which aimed to create "pacification by dependency" for the Apaches, Comanches, and Kiowas and other "uncivilized" Indigenous people during the Bourbon Reforms (after the 1780s), began to fall apart in post-independence Mexico as a result of the lack of resources. See Jacoby, *Shadows at Dawn*, 126–27; Hämäläinen, *The Comanche Empire*, 325–26; and Oscar J. Martínez, *Troublesome Border* (Tucson: University of Arizona Press, 1995), 56.

75. DeLay, "Independent Indians and the US-Mexican War"; Evelyn Hu-DeHart, *Yaqui Resistance and Survival: The Struggle for Land and Autonomy, 1821–1910* (Madison: University of Wisconsin Press, 1984); and Cynthia Radding, *Wandering Peoples: Colonialism, Ethnic Spaces, and Ecological Frontiers in Northwestern Mexico, 1700–1850* (Durham, N.C.: Duke University Press, 1997).

76. Sterling Evans, "Yaquis vs. Yanquis: An Environmental and Historical Comparison of Coping with Aridity in Southern Sonora," *Journal of the Southwest* 40 (Autumn 1998): 363–96.

77. Convenio Celebrado entre el Gobierno del Estado y el Governador de los Seris, Aug. 4, 1925, Tomo 3814, Tribus/Seris, *Archivo Historico General del Estado de Sonora* (hereafter AHGES).

78. Robert Thomson to the Governor [Alejo Bay], December 1923, Tomo 3611, Tribus/Seris, AHGES; Luis Thomson, Luis Felix, and Robert Thomson to Secretary of Government, Feb. 26, 1925; Governor to General Treasurer, Feb. 27, 1925; Governor to Robert Thomson, Feb. 12, 1925; Robert Thomson to Governor, Feb. 21, 1925; Robert Thomson to Governor, Feb. 25, 1925; Pascual Blanco to Alejo Bay, n.d.; Secretary of Government to Thomson, Feb. 28, 1925; Robert Thomson to Secretary of Government, Mar. 2, 1925; Secretary of Government to Robert Thomson, Mar. 7, 1925; Thomson to Secretary of Government, Mar. 24, 1925; Governor to Police Chief, April 17, 1925; Governor to Treasurer, April 17, 1925; Luis Felix to Governor, May 13, 1925; Chief of Purchasing Department to Secretary of State, May 9, 1925; Purchasing Department to Secretary of State, July 15, 1925; Tomo 2814, Tribus/Seris, AHGES. On the use of commons to dispossess Indigenous peoples of their lands, see Allan Greer, "Commons and Enclosure in the Colonization of North America," *American Historical Review* 117 (April 2012): 365–86.

79. Ryerson, "'I Was the One to Make the Peace,'" 132.

80. Thomson, "La Hacienda de Costa Rica," 32; and Coolidge, *The Last of the Seris*, 149–50. Thomson agreed that around 75 percent of the ranchers' claims of Seri cattle theft were bogus. "Los Indios Seris," Robert Thompson, July 26, 1927, box 8415, Exp. 68, Sonora, AHSEP-ER.

81. Edward H. Davis, "Unfinished Book Manuscript," in *Edward H. Davis and the Indians of the Southwest United States and Northwest Mexico*, 143.

82. William T. Hagan, "Kiowas, Comanches, and Cattlemen, 1867–1906: A Case Study of the Failure of U.S. Reservation Policy," *The Pacific Historical Review* 40 (August 1971): 333. This mirrored the arguments put forth by the Jesuits and Franciscans in favor of missions; they claimed that "if Spaniards or *castas* (individuals of mixed race) were allowed to settle among the Indians, the Native Americans would be exploited, corrupted, and destroyed." See Thomas E. Sheridan, *Where the Dove Calls: The Political Ecology of a Peasant Corporate Community in Northwestern Mexico* (Tucson: University of Arizona Press, 1988), 8.

83. David A. Chang, "Borderlands in a World at Sea: Concow Indians, Native Hawaiians, and South Chinese in Indigenous, Global, and National Spaces," *The Journal of American History* 98 (September 2011): 390. See also Philip J. Deloria, "From Nation to Neighborhood: Land, Policy, Culture, Colonialism, and Empire in U.S. Indian Relations," *The Cultural Turn in U.S. History: Past, Present, and Future*, eds. James W. Cook, Lawrence, B. Glickman, and Michael O'Malley (Chicago: University of Chicago Press, 2008): 358.

84. Prior to 1934, the Mexican government viewed the obstacles to educating rural peasants and Indigenous people as nearly identical. See, Rafael Ramirez, *La Escuela Rural Mexicana* (México: Secretaría de Eduación Pública, 1976); José Manuel Puig Casauranc, *La Cosecha y la Simbra* (México: Secretaría de Educación Pública, 1929); and *Boletín de la Secretaría de Educación Pública* 5 (1926): 8.

85. The Gálvez Peace Policy, begun in 1786, whereby colonial officials gave rations and gifts to Indigenous people who agreed to settle down, "eventually became the model on which our modern U.S. Indian reservation system was formed." Kieran McCarty, ed., *A Frontier Documentary: Sonora and Tucson, 1821–1848* (Tucson: University of Arizona Press, 1997), 32.

86. Wilbert H. Ahern, "An Experiment Aborted: Returned Indian Students in the Indian School Service, 1881–1908," *Ethnohistory* 44 (Spring 1997): 263–304; and Anne Ruggles Gere, "Indian Heart/White Man's Head: Native-American Teachers in Indian Schools, 1880–1930," *History of Education Quarterly* 45 (Spring 2005): 38–65.

87. Alexander Dawson, "'Wild Indians,' 'Mexican Gentlemen,' and the Lessons Learned in the Casa del Estudiante Indígena, 1926–1932," *The Americas* 57 (January 2001): 329–61.

88. Andrae Marak, *From Many, One*, Chapters 3 and 5.

89. Coolidge, *Last of the Seris*, 127–28.

90. Governor to State Treasurer, Dec. 11, 1923, Tomo 3611, Tribus/Seris, AHGES.

91. Coolidge, *Last of the Seris*, 157–58. Dane and Mary Coolidge argue that Thomson used his leverage with state officials to interfere in Seri elections, resulting in the election of Chico Romero rather than Juan Tomas. Luis Felix to Governor, May 13, 1925, Tomo 3814, Tribus/Seris, AHGES. See also, Ryerson, "'I Was the One to Make the Peace,'" 125.

92. It could also be that this was a different band of the Seri. Charles Sheldon notes that one band lived on Tiburon Island and another on the mainland. Neil B. Carmony and David E. Brown, eds., *The Wilderness of the Southwest: Charles Sheldon's Quest for Desert Bighorn Sheep and Adventures with the Havasupai and Seri Indians* (Salt Lake City: University of Utah Press, 1993), 177.

93. Governor to "Indio Herrera," Nov. 10, 1927, Tomo 82, Tribus/Seris, AHGES, Fernando F. Dworak to SEP, Nov. 10, 1926, Nov. 24, 1926, and Feb. 17, 1927; SEP to Fernando F. Dworak, Dec. 6, 1926, box 8415, Exp. 68, Sonora, AHSEP-ER; and Fernando F. Dworak to Thompson, March 22, 1927, box 8446, Exp. IV/100(04)(II-5)(721.5), Sonora, AHSEP-ER. The SEP paid Thomson and his brother Luis $150 and $75 pesos monthly to be teacher and teacher's assistant, respectively.

94. Fernando F. Dworak to SEP, Mar. 18, 1927; and Robert Thompson, "Los Indios Seris," July 26, 1927, box 8415, Exp. 68, Sonora, AHSEP-ER.

95. Fernando F. Dworak to SEP, Aug. 13, 1927, box 8556, Ex. IV/000(04)(721.5), Sonora, AHSEP-ER.

96. Cited in Fernando F. Dworak to SEP, May 15, 1928, box 8415, Exp. 68, Sonora, AHSEP-ER.

97. Mauricio Tenorio-Trillo, *Mexico at the World's Fairs: Crafting a Modern Nation* (Berkeley: University of California Press, 1996), 186–88, 202–04, (citation 186).

98. López, *Crafting Mexico*, 37–38; and Rick A. López, "The India Bonita Contest of 1921 and the Ethnicization of the Mexican National Culture," *Hispanic American Historical Review* 82 (May 2002): 291–328.

99. López, *Crafting Mexico*, 62.

100. Thompson, "Beads Tame Last Cannibal Tribe," 59.

101. Robert Thompson, "Los Indios Seris," July 26, 1927, box 8415, Exp. 68, Sonora, AHSEP-ER; and Alexander Dawson, "From Models for the Nation to Model Citizens: *Indigenismo* and the 'Revindication' of the Mexican Indian, 1920–1940," *Journal of Latin American Studies* 30 (1998): 279–308.

102. Teniorio-Trillo, *Mexico at the World's Fairs*, 188.

103. Louis S. Warren, *Buffalo Bill's America: William Cody and the Wild West Show* (New York: Vintage Books, 2005), 190–210.

104. "Secrets of the Desert," in *Edward H. Davis and the Indians of the Southwest United States and Northwest Mexico*, 61.

Chapter 7

"The Stubborn Disposition of These Indians"

Survival and Subsistence on the Upper Columbia River, 1820–1880*

Ian Stacy

For Indians living in the newly created Washington Territory, 1855 was a critical year. In less than ten months, most of the Indigenous peoples in the territory treated with the United States government, agreeing to remove to reservations and cede vast tracts of land in exchange for annuities, missions, and the other trappings of "civilized" American society. The treaties also offered to provide a measure of security from the relentless tide of American settlement. Northwestern Indians had, of course, coexisted with a handful of Euro-American explorers and fur traders for more than a century. By the mid-nineteenth century, Americans had become increasingly drawn to the seemingly boundless resources around Puget Sound and the dry but fertile soil east of the Cascade Mountains. So too came miners chasing gold dreams through the high country below the Canadian border. But despite the relentless efforts of the territory's first governor, Isaac I. Stevens, to extinguish the Indian title to vast swaths of the new territory, not all Indians agreed to cede their land or comply with the governor's master plan.

The Stevens treaties have proved to be a foundational set of documents in modern Pacific Northwest history. Native American communities, scholars, legal experts, and area residents began arguing over their meaning almost before the ink dried. The treaties were a major cause of the hostilities that rocked the region in the years up through the Nez Perce War of 1877 and continue to be important documents, cited by all sides,

* The author would like to thank Scott Manning, Dave Beck, Cary Miller, and fellow participants in the 2010 Newberry Consortium in American Indian Studies. The D'Arcy McNickle Center at the Newberry Library provided generous funding and resources during the early stages of this project. The Manuscripts and Special Collections staff at Washington State University also gave exceptional assistance.

in cases involving sovereignty, fishing rights, and territorial disputes. But despite their importance to the narrative of Pacific Northwest history, they do not tell the whole story of Indian-American relations in the nineteenth century. A collection of native groups on the Upper Columbia River—all of whom would fall under the jurisdiction of a single agency at Fort Colville—withstood Stevens's efforts and managed to dictate the pace of removal and their own absorption of American culture. Upper Columbia Indians were remarkably varied in their social arrangements and subsistence patterns, ranging from the pastoralist and militant Sanpoil to the independent, agricultural communities of Colville, to the highly diversified and (occasionally) urbanized Spokane. Other groups, including bands of Lakes, Southern Okanagan, and mid-Columbia Salish, maintained mixed-subsistence lifestyles incorporating hunting, fishing, and foraging. Each group adopted different strategies to deal with ever-shifting borders, but all shared similar trajectories. Their experience challenges easy assumptions about Indians' passive role in creating reservations; dependency; and how the ubiquitous but ill-defined group known as "white people" engaged in a deliberate plan to eliminate the native presence from their midst.[1]

The story of the Upper Columbia River Indians in the nineteenth century is not a tale of exploitation, broken promises, and dependence, but of neglect, promises never made, and a persistent refusal to accept government aid. Throughout the nineteenth century, Native Americans in the Columbia River Basin lived within an ever-changing kaleidoscope of transnational borders: fur company districts; territory, state, and international lines; mission territories; reservation boundaries; and a patchwork of ecoregions. Throughout, they faced recurrent disease epidemics, shrinking subsistence bases, and a paradoxical combination of local harassment and federal neglect. Having escaped the first round of restrictive treaties during the initial creation of Washington Territory in the mid-1850s, Upper Columbia River Indians spent the better part of the next three decades trying to accommodate their new neighbors and lobby for permanent reservations. These "party to no treaty" Indians found themselves largely forgotten by the US government and at times without even the nominal protection of an agent. They were forced to negotiate their own boundaries with each other and with encroaching American farmers and miners. Showing a remarkable understanding of the American political system—especially considering their isolation from traditional centers of power—they built relationships with farmers and influential citizens, met in council, and sent petitions to American presidents. To meet these challenges, they adapted older lifeways as they adopted new agricultural practices, political structures, and social arrangements. Not all their decisions resulted in success, and many had unforeseen negative consequences. But Upper Columbia River Indians had a meaningful role in defining the shape, structure, duration, and permeability of transnational borders in the greater Northwest.

Native peoples of the Upper Columbia River had maintained a durable presence in the region for centuries before contact with Europeans. Despite their cultural diversity, in the decades after 1855 all of these groups shared a single problem that cut to the heart of their very survival: their ambiguous status within a rapidly changing natural and social landscape. As Andrew H. Fisher has written of bands living further downstream, "Columbia River Indians are the product of social and political processes triggered by Euro-American colonization." Although Fisher is largely concerned with groups of Indians who actively resisted coming onto the Yakama reservation, Upper Columbia bands faced many of the same challenges to their own identity, both among themselves and in relation to American settler society. Yet this is not to suggest that Indian identity was subsumed or was determined from above by the US government. In the end, Fisher argues, "the U.S. government did not give Native Americans their identities any more than it gave them land or sovereignty."[2]

The frequently tense relationship between settlers and Upper Columbia Indians in Washington Territory was a sideshow to the much larger process of Euro-American expansion across the continent in the nineteenth century. Gray H. Whaley has examined the case of western Oregon Indians in the particular context of the American "empire republic." According to Whaley, the key elements of this peculiar brand of imperialism were "internationally contested territory, entrepreneurship, Christian proselytization, settler-colonialism, and national incorporation." To a certain extent, the situation east of the Cascades was similar, but with several important differences. The land in northeastern Washington Territory was generally less fertile than the Willamette Valley, and widespread land speculation and squatting were less common. In Oregon, Indian agitation mitigated somewhat the American settlers' encroachment onto Chinookan, Salishan, and other native lands. In northeastern Washington, cold winters and bare soils had the same effect. The small number of Hudson's Bay employees and their offspring (due largely to the native-only trapping policies in place north and east of the Columbia River) also meant that racial boundaries in the region were less ambiguous than those in other fur company areas of the greater Northwest.[3] But in one respect, the situation in western Oregon was identical to that in the Upper Columbia region: the inability of either colonized or colonizers to dictate fully the terms of settlement to leaders in Washington, D.C. "Unfortunately for the Oregon colonists," Whaley notes, "American empire was too complicated to be easily manipulated from the periphery, and the surviving Native population had several decades of experience dealing with competing empires and had no intention of surrendering the remaining core of their homelands." If the case of the Upper Columbia Indians is truly a core-periphery case of colonialism, as Whaley suggests about Oregon, it can best be analogized to the "salutary neglect" period of the British American colonies in the mid-eighteenth century.[4]

In *The Roots of Dependency*, Richard White sought to solve the seemingly simple question of how people that could once feed themselves became so detached from their familiar resource base that they had little choice but to resort to dependence on government largesse. The answer is not simple. White argues, "Dependency resulted not from a single material and economic process that obliterated or subordinated all else, but rather from a complex interchange of environmental, economic, political, and cultural influences understandable within specific histories."[5] White's three case studies, though distributed across space and time, all point to a common narrative: the Navajo, Choctaw, and Pawnee were unable to weather the transition from subsistence economies to the market. Anthropologist John A. Schultz has advanced a similar argument for natives in the Columbia Basin. "Basically," Schultz claims, "the fur trade led to severe economic exploitation, and dependency on Euroamerican material culture. In both cases, the results were deleterious to the Indian."[6] Ultimately, Schultz argues for a process of cultural disintegration. But these arguments do not fully account for the Indian role in shaping the fur trade, missionization, and the shift toward pastoralism and settled agriculture. They are thus reduced to passive recipients and helpless victims of Euro-American culture.

Isaac Stevens caught Upper Columbia River Indians in the middle of an abrupt ecological and social transition. By mid-century, populations were only just beginning to rebound from the effects of several major disease outbreaks. Indians probably encountered exotic diseases long before meeting Euro-Americans. The first to hit was smallpox around 1780, which spread out like a shockwave ahead of the first explorers, fur traders, and settlers. A decade later, the disease returned. All told, these two outbreaks might have killed half the region's Indigenous population. Measles struck in the winter of 1847–48, and influenza came two years later. Another smallpox outbreak occurred during the fishing runs in 1853.[7] Here, as elsewhere throughout the Americas, disease on this scale disrupted social organization and the ability to meet basic subsistence needs during periods of great crisis.

If Indians lacked control over disease, they had a stronger hand in two other concurrent areas of ecological change: equestrianism and the fur trade. Beyond immediate subsistence and economic impacts, horse culture created a new transnational boundary between plains and plateau, a broad, overlapping border that ebbed and flowed across the continental divide with the changing seasons. Oral histories indicate that the first horses may have appeared in the central Columbia Plateau as early as 1700, reaching the Upper

Columbia at the end of the eighteenth century.[8] Before the widespread adoption of the horse, plateau Indians probably made sporadic pedestrian journeys beyond the Rocky Mountains to hunt and trade. Horses replaced dogs for transporting bulky trade items like bison robes and hides, and "going to buffalo" on the plains became an increasingly important element of many plateau bands' lifestyles. But horses also increased the frequency of conflict. Their revolutionary impact on buffalo hunting and significance as a status symbol made them targets for raiders, both on the Plains and in the Columbia Basin. Blackfeet horse raids into the Columbia Plateau were common enough that some bands in the region maintained a network of spotter posts and fortifications to protect their homelands.[9]

Although proximity to the hunting grounds, politico-military events, and subsistence needs were factors in whether a band would go to buffalo, only personal status and access to horses allowed Columbia Plateau Indians to pursue this activity with regularity. Large horse and cattle populations were possible only because most basin bands occupied good grazing country. Ecologically, the Indians around Colville straddled two distinct ecosystems, the cold desert of the Columbia Basin and the grassy and forested foothills of the Cascade and Rocky Mountains. Each provided microhabitats well suited to grazing animals. A territorial survey of the eastern portion of the Columbia Basin in the 1850s found "immense plains or prairies admirably adapted for grazing, and where the horses and cattle of the savages find subsistence throughout the whole year."[10] Fertile bottomlands near most major streams and rivers provided protected habitat for horses. The region's overall carrying capacity was sufficient to support tens of thousands of horses for most of the nineteenth century. Only in the 1880s, long after the introduction of large-scale cattle operations, did the range show signs of overgrazing.[11]

Although the horse changed social structures, enlarged the diplomatic sphere between tribes, and bound Indians tightly to certain ecosystems, native participation in the fur trade had a more direct environmental impact. The Hudson's Bay Company (HBC), centered at York Factory in Manitoba, gained control of the Washington high country from their Northwest Company rivals in 1821. In the first decades of the nineteenth century, before the territorial issues between the United States and Britain had been resolved, and fearing competition from their American rivals, HBC factors aimed to make the region a "fur desert." Company administrator George Simpson outlined the plan during an inspection tour of the region in 1824. "If properly managed no question exists that it would yield handsome profits," he observed, "as we have convincing proof that the country is a rich preserve of Beaver and which for political reasons we should endeavour to destroy as fast as possible."[12] To this end, Simpson relocated the old Northwest Company post from Spokane House to a new post at Fort Colvile near the Indian fishing and trading hub at Kettle Falls.[13] Simpson recognized that the move would upset the Spokane, who had become attached to the fur traders, but noted that "the Indians in that neighbourhood [of Fort Colville] and towards the Lakes will exert themselves more than heretofore and in all probability make considerable Hunts as their Lands are tolerably Stocked with Beaver."[14] European fur companies moved the region toward a framework of trans-national borders recognizable in the modern sense. Significantly, local ecological and cultural concerns were no longer the sole consideration in defining the region's shape. Now the desires of outsiders wielding a new array of legal, political, and military tools entered into the negotiation process.

Unlike other geographical areas in their commercial empire, the HBC relied solely on native trappers to gather furs north of the Columbia River. Yet participation was not uniform across the northern tier and varied for several reasons. The traders' recurrent ethnocentric comments about lazy and indolent Indians who refused to trap to their full potential belie the statistics from Colvile's ledgers. Throughout the 1820s and 1830s, Colvile traders collected at least 7000 furs annually. Many years, the total approached 20,000.[15] This represents a significant number of animals in any case, but on the less well-stocked northern margins of the Columbia River Basin it was all the more remarkable. Elsewhere in North America, the HBC adopted a policy of "recruitment," a conservation measure allowing fur-bearing animal populations to recover. But Simpson's scorched-earth policy and fixed prices for pelts gave little incentive for either Indian or trader to recruit the land. Absent a full statistical analysis of contemporary animal populations, we can only guess at the effect of the fur trade on the region's ecology. But all the anecdotal evidence from fur traders, missionaries, and twentieth-century anthropologists indicates a significant impact.

The fur trade also brought a less direct but no less damaging impact on native subsistence through the hide and fresh meat trade. Although Simpson was adamant that trading posts become at least partially self-sufficient by limited agricultural pursuits, natives still supplied significant quantities of venison and other large game to the posts. Over time, this direct depletion of fur animals and game, as well as the indirect impact of steadily eliminating the region's keystone ecological species (beaver), clearly had an impact on native food resources. The cyclical nature of native diets meant that a reduction of a specific food item had a much greater effect on subsistence than we would find today in the case of someone who, for example, cuts red meat out of an otherwise varied diet. Traders and early travelers to the region often remarked about a persistent state of starvation or general wretchedness among native communities. We should, however, read these accounts of Indian food shortages with some skepticism, for as Elizabeth

Vibert reminds us, "Reports of starvation in the documentary record of the fur trade are frequently taken at face value, leading to potentially serious misunderstandings of Native American subsistence patterns."[16] The demasking of Eurocentric cultural beliefs has since challenged these early accounts, showing us the complicated nature of Indigenous subsistence practices.

Yet we should not be so sensitive to challenges of ethnocentrism that we dismiss out of hand actual privation and suffering. Vibert claims to have found only one documented account of death by starvation on the entirety of the Columbia Plateau during the fur trade era. However, death is only the end on the continuum of starvation and food deprivation. We might assume that native communities were not, in fact, starving at contact.[17] But by the early 1840s, a combination of factors had pushed native peoples to the limits of subsistence, at least in certain critical items. If missionary Elkanah Walker, who lived among the Spokane, is to be believed, these few years constituted a tipping point, at least in relation to large game. In the spring of 1843, Walker could remark, "The Indians get a [*sic*] plenty of deer & are as big & as confident as they need to be." Within two years, however, Walker noted that when the Spokane's normal regimen of game, fish, fruits, and roots failed, "they had & do to this day, recourse to the moss on the pine trees. At this moment it constitutes more than two thirds of their daily food." Whatever ethnocentric biases Walker held about the Indians, by this point he was well attuned to the nuances of local native subsistence patterns, remarking, "an Indian would live & do well where a white man would starve to death."[18] In noting the seeming dependence on moss, he was referring to the Indians' own self-identified food of last resort and not his perception of "good" or "bad" foods. In the 1850s, the problem of short-term gaps in the food supply deepened, as conflict throughout the region restricted movement from one seasonal ground to another.

Although the fur trade introduced natives to the market economy and commodified a subsistence resource, HBC policies intentionally buffered the natives from absolute dependence on the market. The HBC did adjust prices periodically, but with logic that defies easy generalizations. Posts like Colvile were too remote from overseas markets to adjust prices in real time. Traders always had an eye to their competition, real or perceived, and so did not want to risk their relationship with local Indians by being undersold. Moreover, they usually maintained high prices to encourage larger harvests.[19] Although the Indians had become accustomed to trading at the posts and had grown *attached* to many of the traders' goods, we should be careful not to assume this was a *dependent* relationship. After all, it was natives who supplied the traders with food, not the other way around.

Natives in the region certainly acquired a taste for HBC trade goods, especially blankets and tobacco. But traders did not supply alcohol, and although a few Indians engaged in wage labor for the post, this affected only a small segment of the total plateau population. Simpson claimed in 1837 that "many [Indians], formerly dependent on hunting and fishing, now maintain themselves by the produce of the soil."[20] Rather than force Indians into a dependent state, this early exposure to agriculture was a small but important step toward settled agriculture. Simpson either neglected or dismissed the simultaneous rise of equestrian culture. In fact, if Upper Columbia River Indians relied heavily on the posts for any imported goods, it was for the accoutrements of pastoralism like saddles and pack cord.[21]

The greatest impact of contact with HBC traders and the first generation of missionaries was less material than it was cultural and spiritual. Decades of contact with Franco-Indian Catholics and British Protestants had familiarized Upper Columbia Indians with the basic tenets of Christianity. Regional histories and ethnographies in the Pacific Northwest typically chart the diffusion of Christianity through the perspective of the missionaries themselves, leaving little room for native-driven acceptance of either Christianity or Judeo-Christian society. Under this framework, Christianity "officially" came to northeast Washington when the first Protestant missionaries arrived in the mid-1830s, followed shortly thereafter by Catholic Jesuits. After the murder of fellow missionaries at the Whitman mission at Walla Walla in 1847, the Congregationalist ministers Elkanah Walker and Cushing Eels departed the region and left the Jesuits without competition. The Walkers and Eels had some success in introducing Protestant Christianity to the Lower Spokanes, although they found fewer adherents beyond the horizon of Tshimakain Mission. The Jesuits, who had major missions among the Flathead and Coeur d'Alene to the east, established a permanent facility near Fort Colville. But missing from this narrative is the fact that the first proselytizer in the northern basin was not a Catholic priest or Protestant reverend, but rather "Spokane Garry" of the Upper Spokane. Throughout the critical decades after the 1855 treaties, Garry served as an important bridge between the region's native and American populations, working across the transnational boundary between Protestant and Catholic spheres in the Indian Northwest.

Both of Garry's biographers downplay his role as a central religious figure in light of his later importance as a diplomat. In April 1825, George Simpson selected Garry as one of "the Sons of the principal Spokan & Coutenais War Chiefs, Men of Great Weight and consequence in this part of the Country" to attend the Anglican mission school at Red River in Manitoba.[22] Life at the school could be difficult, and the Kootenai youth who accompanied Garry on his trip to Red River died there. Garry, however, seems to have taken to the program and returned to the Spokane years later fluent in French, English, and his local Salish dialect. The chiefs who gave their sons so freely to

Simpson also begged for formal missions in the region, although these would not appear for another decade or more. In the interim, Garry began preaching. Anthropologist Leslie Spier dated the spread of Christianity in the region to about 1830, consistent with Garry's return and years before the first missionaries arrived.[23]

Garry almost certainly carried back a considerable understanding of nineteenth-century Euro-American culture along with his newfound religious beliefs. Yet accepting the latter did not mean accepting the former. Despite the desire of many Spokane to have a permanent mission, Garry remained aloof from the Walkers after they arrived, and waited two years before calling on the mission. Even then he kept his distance. "Garry came up this morning quite early . . . and I had a long talk with him," Walker wrote of Garry's first social visit to the mission. But "[w]hen the time of worship came, he refused to rehearse & left me to my own resources." Walker's disappointment in Garry was a recurrent theme at Tshimakain. Throughout Walker's tenure, the missionary and Garry maintained a fragile relationship. Walker needed Garry's linguistic abilities. Garry's motivations are less clear, but his time in Red River seems to have instilled an intense anti-Catholicism. Garry would often refuse to work for the Protestant missionaries, but he did little to drive them from the region either. His visits to Tshimakain became regular only after 1842, when the Jesuits began to make headway in converting some of the Spokane.

Little information survives on the period in Garry's life between Red River and the Walkers' arrival at Tshimakain. Historians have given considerable weight to George Simpson's account of meeting Garry again in 1841. Simpson chanced upon a group of gambling Indians who, Simpson believed, were acting with Garry's tacit approval, if not his outright influence. "On his return to his countrymen, he had, for a time, endeavoured to teach them to read and write;" Simpson observed, "but he had gradually abandoned the attempt, assigning as his reason or pretext that the others 'jawed him so much about it.' He forthwith relapsed into his original barbarism . . . He was evidently ashamed of his proceedings, for he would not come out of his tent to shake hands even with an old friend."[24] But however much the Spokane may have "jawed him" for his beliefs, Garry maintained his status as an important figure throughout his life, indicating that his early, rigid approach to Christianity was not a serious cultural breach in the eyes of the community. His position within the Spokane social order, as well as his familiarity with Christian principles and Euro-American cosmology, complicates considerably the picture of Indians who did not understand American-style politics, treaty systems, or abstract Western concepts of land ownership. Garry put this knowledge to good use in the years to come as he became the principal diplomat and spokesman for his people once Isaac Stevens threw open the country for settlement.

The watershed year of Anglo-American diplomacy in the region came not with the creation of the border along the forty-ninth parallel in 1846, but rather in 1853. The border treaty did divide native family groups along this stretch of the Columbia River, and over time the boundary became less porous as Americans cracked down on the illegal import of Canadian liquor into northeastern Washington's native communities. But although the policy of policing the liquor trade established a rigid *international* border in a way federal survey markers could not, the major British interest in the region, the HBC, continued to operate as before and was the most important player in the relationship between Euro-Americans and Indians. Only in 1853, with the beginning of the Pacific Railroad Surveys and the formal creation of Washington Territory, did the Northwest come solidly into the American orbit. The central figure in this new drama was Isaac Stevens, territorial governor and civilian head of the military party surveying the northernmost of several potential transcontinental railroad routes.

As territorial governor, Stevens was also ex officio head of Indian affairs for the region. Long before he reached the territorial capital at Olympia, Stevens began laying the groundwork for future treaty negotiations. Chastened by the haphazard settlement of the Oregon country, Stevens and his superiors in Washington, D.C., were keen to avoid difficulties between settlers and Indians. Like most American politicians concerned with "the Indian problem" in the mid-nineteenth century, Stevens's ultimate vision was of a settled and pacified native population, diligently engaged in agriculture. But because this transition would take some time, Stevens understood the need to make temporary provisions for normal hunting and gathering cycles. This included access to traditional fishing or gathering sites and the elimination of a hostile atmosphere on the bison hunting grounds. Stevens hoped treaties with the Blackfeet and Indians on the Columbia River Plateau would limit the violence—an important consideration for both future settlers and the governor's political ambitions.[25]

In the late spring of 1855, after treating with Indian bands on the Puget Sound, Stevens headed east across the Cascades to begin negotiations with natives in the Columbia Basin. His aim was never in doubt. "In May, June and July I confidently expect to accomplish the whole business, extinguishing the Indian Title to every acre of land in this territory," Stevens informed his superior.[26] That summer, the governor's delegation and over 5000 Columbia Basin natives held a council in the Walla Walla Valley. Each of the three Walla Walla treaties followed the same generic pattern Stevens had developed with bands in western Washington. The treaties required Indians to cede to the US government "all their right, title, and claim to all and every part of the country claimed by them" except for well-defined reservations. In theory, Indians were to remain within the bounds of these reservations. However, the treaties' maddeningly imprecise language did permit them to hunt, fish, and gather roots and berries "at the usual and accustomed places" in addition to providing for annuities, a gristmill, a blacksmith shop, schools, and the personnel to operate them. Stevens and Joel Palmer, the superintendent for Indian Affairs in Oregon Territory, assured the assembled Indians they would still have access to the bison grounds on the far side of the Rocky Mountains.[27] The treaties thus had two sets of borders for Indians and settlers to negotiate. The first was an immediately recognizable physical boundary that sought to place Indians within well-defined geographical limits; this might properly be considered a national border, although modern concepts of Indian sovereignty were nowhere evident in Stevens's thinking. The second border was transnational and conceded the government's inability to feed the artificially constructed nation in its midst. The inherent tension between these mutually exclusive border systems has yet to be fully resolved to anyone's satisfaction. Although Garry is not listed as one of the speakers in the treaty proceedings, he was present at Walla Walla, no doubt observing Stevens and gauging his intentions.

After concluding the Walla Walla council, Stevens wasted no time moving to western Montana to treat with the Flathead. Stevens's attitude toward the Flathead bordered on contempt, and when Victor and his people proved to be less pliable than their plateau kin to the west, Stevens grew irate. As at Walla Walla, communications were a source of this difficulty. A Jesuit observer to the Flathead proceedings remarked, "'Not a tenth' of the council 'was actually understood by either party.'" Nevertheless, Stevens quickly concluded treaty negotiations and moved on to what he anticipated to be the biggest challenge of the summer: negotiations with the Blackfeet. Surprisingly, the Blackfeet gave Stevens the least resistance of any group.[28] Unaware that he had dealt primarily with Blackfeet living on the Canadian side of the international border, and thus unable to foresee that the treaty would do little to end violence in the region, Stevens came away emboldened. The encounter reaffirmed his self-confidence. He scarcely acknowledged Indian motivation or diplomatic tactics in any of the negotiations.[29]

Just how the messy reality of settlement and removal was to play out in Washington Territory as opposed to the sanitized version laid out in the treaties became clear shortly after Stevens concluded the Walla Walla council. On his return from the Blackfeet, Stevens received word that the Yakama had murdered their agent. Andrew Bolon had been investigating the murder of some miners when a Yakama holding a personal grudge waylaid and killed him. Historians have closely linked Bolon's death with the general conflict between the government and Columbia Basin Indians that followed. In truth, the relationship is tenuous at best. What is perhaps more striking (and less studied) is how the *spirit* behind Stevens's hasty treaties failed so quickly.

Army and militia reprisals quelled Indian agitation in the immediate aftermath of the murder, but the soldiers committed a number of outrages and summary executions, creating bad blood between the two sides. Garry urged his people to remain aloof from the hostilities, and was largely successful. But other Upper Columbia groups like the Sinkiuse-Columbia supported Yakama military efforts.[30]

Mindful that Garry's endorsement of the conflict could be the tipping point to a general Indian war in the Northwest, Stevens hastened to Spokane country. He had intended to treat with these Indians in any case, but the Yakama crisis added a new sense of urgency. Superficially, Stevens seemed less concerned with land cessions and removal than with keeping the peace and "setting the record straight" about rumors of his alleged underhandedness at Walla Walla. The assembled Indians challenged Stevens repeatedly and placed the blame for hostilities downriver squarely on the governor's shoulders. "I think Governor you have talked a little too hard," one Lower Spokane chief said. "It is as if you had thrown away all the Indians." Stellam, a Coeur d'Alene, criticized the paternalistic relationship Stevens and his contemporaries had come to depend upon. "Now if it is the truth you tell me, I will tell no lies," Stellam promised. "But we have not yet made friends—all the Indians are not yet your children. You have not yet made friendship." Several Indians warned Stevens not to send troops across the Columbia in pursuit of the Yakama. "We have not shaken hands yet," one said. "When we see the soldiers don't cross the Columbia we shall believe you will take us for your friends." Whether through humility, exhaustion, enlightenment, or some combination of the three, Stevens did not show the heavy hand he had with the Flathead, though the Indians' tone at the Spokane council was no less hostile than Victor's.[31]

Despite his assertions that the council's purpose was simply to clear the air, Stevens returned again and again to the question of land, always circling back to the topic of removal. He assured the chiefs that the decision to sell their land was entirely their own. But he left little doubt about the final outcome. Stevens "did not know where the Spokanes, Colvilles and Coeur d'Alenes would be moved to until I had consulted them, and they had given me their hearts about it."[32] In Stevens's mind, Indian consent was just a formality and a tactic of appeasement. Indians would move. The *how* and *where* of removal were mere details. Yet Stevens departed without a formal resolution or treaty. Perhaps trusting Garry's ability to keep the peace (Garry and the governor had met privately before the council), Stevens showed uncharacteristic restraint. With their steadfast refusal to cave to Stevens's cajoling, Garry and the other native leaders successfully rebuffed the governor's advance. For the time being, they had staved off the threat of a removal. This action would have profound consequences for the future.

In May 1858, contrary to the explicit warnings of the chiefs at the Spokane council, federal troops crossed into Spokane country in a show of force aimed at quelling rising Indian resistance. Historians Robert Ruby and John Brown have shown that by this point, "the Spokanes . . . were epicentral to disgruntled tribes—to the east, the Coeur d'Alenes; to the north, the Colvilles; to the south, the Palouses; and to the west, the Upper Yakimas and Columbias." The officer in charge of the expedition, Colonel E. J. Steptoe, aimed his force at Fort Colville, ostensibly with the purpose of establishing a garrison to protect an American survey party but also "to paw, but not maul, troublesome Indians there and along the way."[33] With confrontation inevitable, Big Star of the Lower Spokane withdrew his people from the general encampment at the camas gathering grounds. The Upper and Middle Spokane remained, although Garry did not, with factions from every major native group in the region. The first confrontation went badly for Steptoe and his troops. But within weeks, the army dispatched Colonel George Wright on a purely punitive raid. Wright's force soundly defeated the Indians at the battles of Four Lakes and Spokane Plains. Garry returned from Colville to help broker the peace between the government and the Indians. Wright warned Garry that if the Indians did not make peace, "war will be made on you this year and next, and until your nation shall be exterminated." As if to prove the seriousness of his intentions—and illustrating the increased importance of pastoralism and agriculture to the natives' subsistence economy—Wright slaughtered nine hundred Indian horses taken after the last battle. "Without horses," Lieutenant Lawrence Kip observed, "these Indians are powerless." Days later, on the shores of Coeur d'Alene lake, Wright's men discovered "four Indian lodges, full of wheat, which we burned."[34]

Although each band and family unit determined their own level of engagement with pastoralism and settled agriculture—and quite a few never made the transition at all—the overall subsistence patterns in the region had changed considerably since the beginning of the fur trade era. Losses of stock and crops were significant, and Kip's comment that "this outbreak will bring upon the Indians a winter of great suffering, from the destruction of their stores," was no doubt true.[35] But just as important was the general curtailment of regional travel brought on by suspicion of "wandering" Indians after the conflicts. The wars of the 1850s thus marked the beginning of a permanent northward shift from a seasonal cycle that straddled the boundary between the Columbia Plateau and Columbia Mountain ecosystems to a more fixed position in the highlands. By this point, extensive kinship networks and access to particular resource points had been a critical support structure for seasonal subsistence rounds for many generations. Prominent families, particularly among the Spokane, still went to buffalo, although the journey could be used as a diplomatic tool as well as for subsistence. As early as the troubles in

1855 and 1856, Garry assured Governor Stevens that he would take his people to buffalo as a sign of friendly intentions despite a particularly good salmon run that season.[36] Even without designated reservations and thus no "official" borders that could be found on a map, both Americans and Upper Columbia River Indians clearly recognized acceptable regions of Indian habitation as well as the appropriate reasons for leaving them.

Notwithstanding the recent conflicts and the frequent complaints of settlers, Washington Territory, in particular the lands between the Cascades and the Rockies, had always been something of a backwater in Indian affairs. The outbreak of the Civil War and a shift in national priorities did little to change this. Isaac Stevens, who had made many promises, ignored most of them, and reordered the lives of thousands of Native Americans, died at the battle of Chantilly, Virginia, in 1862. By then, the Oregon Superintendency had briefly absorbed Stevens's old post, only for the latter organization to be reestablished again. This bureaucratic shuffling did little to focus attention on the region east of the Cascades. Still, by the 1860s, the region had an agent, two physicians, and an interpreter operating out of Fort Colville. But what little funding the agency received came from the territory's surplus funds, under the catchall category of "for the removal and subsistence of Indians, parties to no treaty." This designation applied to native groups scattered across Washington, with the largest concentration residing around the Upper Columbia River.[37] Even two decades after Governor Stevens had begun his mission to confine the territory's Indigenous peoples, the Office of the Commissioner of Indian Affairs felt it necessary to remind Agent John Simms at Colville that his funding came from the department's "incidental expenses." Furthermore, although the commissioner's office sympathized with Simms's repeated requests to fund mission teachers, no additional monies could be expected. "While Education is one of the grand means of civilizing the Indians," Acting Commissioner H. R. Clum wrote in 1875, "there are prior claims resulting from their present necessities, and you can best judge how your funds can be best applied to meet the exigencies of the case."[38] The agent could distribute school primers or starvation rations, but not both.

This last exchange between Clum and Simms came after more than two decades of uncertainty about what to do with these "parties to no treaty." Without a formal treaty, Upper Columbia Indians occupied an ambiguous position, uncertain whether they would even remain in the territory at all. In September 1866, George Paige, the acting agent at Fort Colville, called together the local Indians to address rumors that Garry had offered to move his people to the Flathead Agency in Montana Territory. This sent up a cry among the crowd, and Garry flatly denied the accusation. On his return from buffalo, Garry had indeed met with Flathead agent Augustus Chapman, who told Garry the government would be coming to remove the Spokane, so Garry should pick a suitable place in Montana. But Garry did not accept Chapman's offer to "hunt a good place and reserve it for my tribe," insisting his people would stay in their traditional homelands. Garry explained his logic to Paige and the assembled Indians:

> My own country is "big," and if the government wants to make a treaty my own land is "big." I told Mr. Chapman that if any one wanted to buy *his* place, and the price did not suit him, he would say *no* but if the price suited him, he would say yes and go and get another place. If you had a good Horse and were offered a good price for him, you might sell him, and it is the same way with our country.

Whether the other participants at the September council understood the commercial value of land as Garry apparently did is unclear. But they too "expressed a willingness to treat with the government and cede their lands to it provided the terms were suitable and they be allowed a reservation in their own country." However, they strongly objected to removal from their traditional fishing grounds. Paige reckoned that the Indians received at least five-eighths of their sustenance from Columbia River salmon, a food source not available near the Flathead agency. "It is not the land I treat for," Garry argued, "but for my food the Salmon . . . My land is nothing but rocks." Recognizing that a reservation, however confining, might allow security, Garry's people accepted the inevitability of a treaty and reservation. But he warned Paige: "If a treaty is made with us, you will not do with us as has been done with the Indians Gov[ernor] Stevens treated with. When we make a treaty we will make it truly." More than a decade after Isaac Stevens reshaped the Indian Northwest, bitterness and distrust remained.[39]

Paige was sensitive to the Indians' desire to retain fisheries, but his overarching goal was to see the Indians under his charge settled into agriculture. Believing, as many of his peers did, that contact with American culture had turned the Indian from "an honorable Savage to a half civilized vagabond," Paige embarked on a plan to increase agricultural production. In the interim, he begged his superiors for additional funding. "We have deprived [the Indians] of their most valuable land and many of their accustomed means of support," he argued in his annual report for 1866, "and now that they are becoming helpless and dependent shall we no longer hesitate to provide for them?" Paige feared that the Indians would soon be destroyed, surrounded as they were by the "withering curses of civilization."[40] The territorial superintendent supported self-sufficiency in agriculture, although more for financial reasons than on humanitarian grounds. He explained to Paige that the price disparity between supplies around Fort Colville and the Puget Sound, "may be difficult to explain . . . to the satisfaction of the Department and as the responsibility of all your purchases rests on me I desire to have them as light as consistent with the necessary wants of Indians under your supervision." Creating dependent Indians was expensive so far removed from a major population center.[41] Throughout 1867, Paige fought to acquire agricultural tools for the agency and contracted with local American farmers to supply Indians with seed oats and seed potatoes. Families from all the region's bands received seed and simple tools like plows and hoes.[42]

Paige's bleak picture of helpless and dependent Indians did not square with the numbers. He would have been the first to admit that few, if any, rations made their way to Colville. Only the "sick and destitute" received rations and medical supplies in the winter, and Paige repeatedly had to justify even these minor expenditures. In fact, a survey of the agency's surviving ledger sheets for sick and destitute rations shows that only a handful of natives made the effort to receive rations from the agent, and then only through the harshest winter months. Moreover, the ledgers show that no single band or family monopolized this resource. Although a few individuals may have leaned heavily on federal resources during the winter, this was hardly a universal condition.[43]

Over the course of the 1860s and 1870s, native populations remained stable or increased across the region, despite greater encroachment from settlers and periodic disease outbreaks. With neither group powerful enough to remove the other by force, a tense degree of accommodation developed. With the agents' assistance, settled agriculture among the Indian population was becoming increasingly common around the agency. In 1870, Paige's successor, William Winans, completed a survey of Indian bands around Colville, showing a remarkable diversity of subsistence patterns.[44] Colville family groups who lived nearest the agency and in the richest bottomlands most closely resembled their American neighbors, with about one cultivated acre per person. Further out on the arid lands west of the Columbia River, families of Sanpoil had broken far less land but maintained a livestock-to-person ratio of nearly three to one. The Spokane also maintained high numbers of horse and cattle. But among the Spokane, farming and raising stock went hand in hand. With rare exception, only those Spokane with cultivated acres kept horses and cattle. The one constant across all groups was the presence of small potato patches grown from the agents' seed stock. Potatoes were popular even among Indian families without crop fields or livestock, perhaps because the tubers resembled familiar food sources and could be grown without special tools.[45]

But regardless of how much settled agriculture the Colville and others had incorporated into their subsistence base, the clock was running out on their most important food source. None of the principal players at the time foresaw how quickly commercial salmon fishing on the lower Columbia would reshape upriver societies. Just as some American policy makers and reformers argued for continued access to the buffalo hunting grounds as a way to cushion the hard landing onto the reservation for Plains peoples, so too did the advocates for northwestern Indians who tried to protect access to major Indian fishing sites. But as with bison, a combination of ecosystem alteration, market forces, and the actions of myriad American and Indian groups all but eliminated this important resource. The first cannery opened in 1866, and by 1883 Northwest canneries processed over 42 million pounds of fish per year.[46] As salmon populations dwindled, Indians in the vicinity of Fort Colville became more tightly bound to settled agriculture and wage labor.[47]

Creating a reservation or guaranteeing fishing rights to secure the lives of a few thousands Indians in a faraway territory was not a priority for American policy makers. Dismayed by this indifference, Indians and settlers advocated for more government involvement, treaties, and reservations. The surviving correspondence between commissioners, agents, Indians, settlers, and missionaries is difficult to decipher fully now because the personalities and motivations of the interested parties are largely lost to history. But by this time, Upper Columbia River Indians were clearly fluent in bureaucratic rhetoric and savvy to the system of petitions. One such exchange occurred in 1870 regarding the case of George Harvey, then the agency farmer at Colville. In a letter dictated through the local Jesuit missionary, the Sanpoil Kinkanagua implored E. S. Parker, Commissioner of Indian Affairs, to retain Harvey—"the White Indian Chief"—at Colville. Previous agents had been corrupt, Kinkanagua argued, and "instead of helping me to keep order they have grieved me & increased my troubles." He accused past agents of stealing women and goods, promoting illicit marriages, and supplying Indians with drink. "The Black Robe . . . who lives in our midst makes our heart good, & we are glad," Kinkanagua continued, "but I have always wished a good white Chief that should help him, and me, and all the Indians."[48] Both Kinkanagua and the priest wished to retain Harvey's services, although the individual motivations of each are unclear. The apparent intrigue between Protestant and Catholic settlers, clergy, and Indians is a persistent theme in agency records. Accusations of corruption and ecclesiastical scheming in the interior Northwest blend seamlessly into the narrative of corruption and religious favoritism during Ulysses S. Grant's administration.

Stevens County residents also urged Harvey's promotion to the vacant agent's position. The petitioners noted, "The Indians through their chiefs express the utmost satisfaction and unbounded confidence in Mr. Harvey both to the missionaries and to the citizens of Colville Valley." Interestingly, the settlers viewed themselves much as the Indians did, as increasingly isolated within a hostile territory over which they had little control. "Surrounded as your petitioners are," they wrote Parker, "and feeling sensibly the necessity of the proper wise and judicious management of the Indian tribes in this portion of the Indian Superintendency . . . we earnestly pray that he be appointed Special Indian Agent at Fort Colville." Absent a formal treaty, the best thing they could hope for was a stabilizing force in the community. But the most striking aspect of this otherwise routine petition—which could be dismissed as little more than local politicking—is signatures from twenty-two chiefs representing the Colville, Pend Oreille, Sanpoil, Coeur d'Alene, Spokane, and Okanogan. Two Jesuit priests are listed first among the citizen petitioners; the notoriously anti-Catholic Garry is listed first among the Spokane. Despite murmurings within the local Protestant community of collusion between missionaries and agents, something much more complex appears to have been at work here.[49]

The agency's personnel problem might have been settled with a letter-writing campaign, but the security and stability problem, as both Indians and settlers saw it, was not. Just a year before, William Winans had upbraided the territorial superintendent, General T. J. McKenny, after hearing of the army's decision to move Colville's garrison of troops to Fort Lapwai in Idaho. "I cannot for a moment think," Winans wrote, "if the General commanding this Department had a thorough knowledge of the country . . . and the interest this post has in keeping [the Indians] peaceable, that he would order the withdrawal of the troops at this time." Winans argued that he had spent the previous summer meeting with various bands of "haughty, arrogant, and insolent" Indians in the region (who, significantly, refused to accept gifts) and "ascertained their real feelings." Winans spoke of widespread anger toward settlers and warned that if troops were withdrawn before the reservation question was settled, "a general massacre will follow." Too many settler families had built a livelihood in the vicinity of the fort to be abandoned by "the troops who had promised them protection." Winans pleaded with the general to keep the troops in place until "this Indian question [is] settled" by treaties and reservations.[50] The settlers also wrote plaintive letters asking for more troops and expressing anxiety that the region's Indians were without a treaty.[51]

Although a treaty's ability to contain entire native populations within reservation boundaries was impracticable given the paucity of federal manpower and financial resources in the region, the transformation of ambiguous transnational borders into rigid national borders offered the settlers peace of mind. A legally defined national border identified a "right" side and a "wrong" side insofar as individual Indians were concerned, and transgressions could be enforced through the courts or with military or police action. But in the end, the Colville post was so far beyond the horizon of federal officials that even the Secretary of War was unsure of its status or existence. When Washington's territorial representative queried Secretary

William Belknap about the garrison, the secretary referred the question to the regional commander of the army's Department of the Columbia for "definitive information" because nothing was known in the War Department.[52]

When federal attention finally came, it did so swiftly and in a manner that displeased all involved. In April 1872, President Grant designated a new reservation via executive order. The reserve was bounded by Canada and Idaho to the north and east, the Columbia River to the west, and to the south by the Spokane River. Washington Territory's lone congressman, Selucius Garfielde, immediately protested to the Secretary of the Interior that over one thousand American farmers lived within the new reserve. Some had lived on and improved the land for decades. He urged the boundaries be shifted west of the Columbia River, which would provide "a more congenial home" for the Indians and include the important fishery at Kettle Falls.[53] Winans identified a smaller number of affected settlers but noted that they occupied nearly all the tillable land on the proposed reserve. "Will it not be much easier and more just," he asked Garfielde, "to change the lines of the Reservation than to compel the five or six hundred people to move[?]" Winans proposed shifting the reservation west of the Columbia, where there were no settlers; where adequate farmland (supposedly) still existed; and where the climate was more suitable for winter stock grazing. "And besides," he offered, "it is the country selected by the Indians themselves."[54] Colville Valley residents also petitioned Grant to shift the reservation. By July, a new executive order moved the reservation west of the Columbia River.

Garfielde and Winans had both argued that the region's natives would be happier living west of the Columbia. The Indians thought otherwise. An army inspection tour revealed intense unhappiness with the new reservation spelled out in the July order. The Colville, about a quarter of whom already lived within the new boundaries, were least upset, although this sentiment was hardly uniform. The Spokane and Coeur d'Alene, living entirely off the proposed reservation, were "greatly dissatisfied" with the specter of removal. The report noted "that the new reservation is not suitable to their wants, and that after attempting in good faith to carry out the instructions of the Indian Agent, and really making some progress in tilling the soil, it is unjust . . . to take their lands and drive them to a barren country." They were willing to take their chances among the American settlers, as they already were, and protested that they "had better be killed where they are than to starve on the reservation."[55]

All told, the 2300 Indians living outside the new reservation had cultivated at least 1000 acres. The Coeur d'Alene argued that General Wright had promised them the mild and fertile Hangman's Creek Valley after the 1858 hostilities and that the Indians had proved themselves good neighbors to the settlers nearby. Because the army was typically at loggerheads with the Department of the Interior over Indian affairs in the nineteenth century, the assistant inspector general's assessment of the situation at Colville might seem suspect. Yet the Indian voices that appear are consistent with early complaints. Regarding removal, the general believed "the Coeur d'Alene and Spokane Indians have been excited unnecessarily and without authority." According to the superintendent, no move was afoot to remove the Indians in the foreseeable future.[56] Any number of territorial citizens could have spread the rumor, although Winans is especially suspect. His word would have carried the weight of his official position at the agency.

Winans's successor, John Simms, repeatedly lobbied his superiors for an official treaty with the Indians near his agency and for an adjustment of the new reservation boundaries. His preference was to keep the Indians on their old homelands and, failing that, to extend the reservation boundaries 4 miles east of the Columbia to block the traffic in American liquor. On one occasion, Simms passed along the transcript of a council where Upper Columbia native leaders expressed complete and unambiguous dissatisfaction with the new reservation, debunking Winans's disingenuous claim that the Indians wanted removal nearly as much as the settlers wanted them removed. Garry was first to speak about the realities of the new reservation:

> The Indians all want to remain in this country. There is a little valley the "Ne-es-pellum" it is good land, and there is more good land just over the Columbia divide, but it is not large enough for all the Indians. When the President and the Queen of England made their line dividing this country they did not consult with us. They did us a great wrong and now it is not right for the President to make a reserve for us without our consent. I have been selected by the Indians to tell you that not one of them wants the reservation as it now stands. We have no objection to the Rail Road running through our country. I would sooner catch my fish, dig roots and hunt, than to give up my country.

The other leaders present expressed their feelings of betrayal, arguing that they had taken up farming just as the agents had asked, "and now you want to drive us from there." Two Colville men expressed their desire to retain their land, their church, *and* their agent.[57] In an accompanying letter to the superintendent, Simms noted the importance of agriculture to the Indians but acknowledged the Indians' opposition "to dissolving their tribal relations and assuming the duties of citizenship." He added, "I do not know of five out of the whole number who are willing to take upon themselves that responsibility."[58] Although the federal government viewed agriculture as a solid first step toward eventual citizenship, the natives of the Upper Columbia River emphatically did not.

The superintendent, Robert Milroy, sympathized with Simms's concerns but noted that the federal government no longer had a policy of treating with Indians as tribes. Individual citizenship was the order of the day. If Indians wanted to maintain their old relations with each other, keep chiefs, and have an agent, he suggested the following course of action:

> *Morally* and *socially* they can remain as Indian tribes, but not *legally*. They have everything to gain and nothing to lose by renouncing that worthless right. They simply cease in the eyes of the Gov't to be little Indian tribes of a few hundred each but at once become citizens of the great American citizen tribe of over forty millions, and every head of a family and unmarried adult, male or female, will acquire from the Gov't a title to his or her *reservation* by a deed that will be good against every white, black, red or any other man or devil, and has the protection of our laws, the rights to vote, & hold office and, in these, all the rights and privileges of white men.

Nor could Simms expect a revision of the reservation boundaries, even for the relatively insignificant buffer zone east of the Columbia, because "the policy of the Gov't is to have natural boundaries wherever they can be had." Federal bureaucrats simply redrew the map of North America along the most convenient lines and without acknowledging Indigenous social arrangements or subsistence needs.[59]

The breach between the War and Interior departments was not the only bureaucratic dysfunction plaguing the region. The government not only acted arbitrarily in many cases, but on occasion federal officials did not even inform the affected parties. For example, an 1867 executive order had set aside a reservation for the Coeur d'Alene, but no one informed the Indians or surveyed the reservation boundaries. When the Coeur d'Alene found out some four years later, they immediately protested that the reserve was too small. They were content to cede their land *without charge* if the government agreed to provide schools and sawmills and gristmills. But significantly, the Coeur d'Alene demanded to conduct negotiations with "a high officer, *direct* from the Great Father; the highest authority the Government can send; a man whose report will be respected at Washington, so that what he says will be law."[60] They rejected a suggestion that the Nez Perce agent solve the problem because the man was "not their friend or of sufficient official dignity." Clearly the Coeur d'Alene were tired of the parade of political hacks, opportunists, and parasites who cycled through the region's revolving door of Indian affairs.

Finding a solution for the Spokane would be more difficult because they unanimously refused to go onto the new reservation. They remained more or less in place until 1881, when President Rutherford B. Hayes finally created a reservation by executive order. Tucked into a pocket at the junction of the Spokane and Columbia Rivers, the reservation embraced much of the Lower Spokane homeland. The Upper and Middle bands were left outside the boundaries and maintained a tenuous coexistence with the rapidly growing American population around Spokane Falls. Some Spokane squatted and kept horses and small garden plots. Others filed on homesteads and became citizens. Many drifted into the city. Still others came onto the Colville or Coeur d'Alene reservation. Initially, the Coeur d'Alene were glad to receive the Spokane so long as they dispersed through the reservation and did not settle as a single block. Yet despite the formality of the reservations now in place, the region remained beyond the consciousness of most policy makers. The single agency at Colville maintained administrative control of the far-flung Colville, Spokane, and Coeur d'Alene reservations as well as individuals living off the reservation.

In assessing the status of the region's native inhabitants, agents, government inspectors, missionaries, and reformers were as quick to praise "industrious" farming Indians as they were to condemn the "indolent" Indians who ran afoul of American law in Spokane Falls. We should, of course, be as wary of the supposed completeness of "conversion" to agriculture as we are of claims of religious conversion. What is clear, however, is that many Indians in the region incorporated significant components of settled agriculture and ranching into their subsistence base despite the fact that agriculture on the new reservation was nearly impossible. In 1874, the agency farmer confirmed what the Indians already knew when he "made a thorough examination of the country . . . for the purpose of finding a suitable location for the government farm, but failed to find a sufficient quantity of good tillable soil in one body to justify the establishment of such a farm."[61] Yet even as the Colville and other Indian farmers found themselves crowded off their lands east of the Columbia, they continued to supplement their diet by passing through the fixed reservation boundaries to maintain their old fields. The curtailing of off-reservation travel and the loss of traditional resource areas through American settlement reduced access to traditional food sources, although as late as 1874 many native families still journeyed east to hunt bison on the Plains.[62] In the end, the reservation system did not entirely eliminate the traditional subsistence base. Upper Columbia River Indians managed to negotiate the ever-changing arrangement of transnational borders with a fair degree of success right up until the canneries and the big dams of the twentieth century eliminated their most important wild food source.

With fewer traditional subsistence opportunities available, many Indians gravitated toward wage labor, a circumstance that did not displease their agents. By the mid-1870s, the Office of Indian Affairs required Indians to perform labor in exchange for their annuities, although because none of the tribes around Colville were under treaty or receiving regular rations, most Indian laborers at the agency received cash payments.[63] As Americans slowly bought out Indian homesteads east of the Columbia River, the former occupants increasingly began to work as agricultural laborers for wages. A government inspection tour of the Colville Agency in 1873 found that "Many who had had farms before the recent influx of whites have sold their farms to whites and now work by the day for a living."[64]

Although the voices of individual Indians removed from their old farms east of the Columbia are impossible to recover, the agents' reports and the federal census give a rough picture. According to Agent Simms, the Colville and other farming families maintained about 1800 cultivated acres in their old lands despite living on the new reservation through the mid-1870s.[65] The 1880 census confirms the Indians' rapid displacement. Not a single independent Indian family seems to have remained east of the Columbia River by this date. The only "Indians" so classified in the census were the female spouses of American farmers, their children, and the odd hired man residing on an American farm.[66] Simms noted that about 180 Indians engaged in agricultural labor off the reservation, and another 225 worked off the reservation "in other civiliz[ed] occupations." Prostitution added another component to the informal economy. This practice ranged from the occasional exchange of favors around the fort to more sustained and regular practice in town. Prostitution's total economic contribution to the native economy is unknown, but the practice was widespread enough to draw the ire of the Jesuit fathers, government agents, and leaders within the Indian community.[67] Wage labor in the formal and informal economies of urban Spokane gave many Indians a legitimate reason to move fluidly across superficially inflexible reservation borders. It is perhaps the most durable evidence of the unsuccessful attempt to create a permanent border—physical, legal, or otherwise—between Indian and American societies in the Northwest.

Viewed from a distance, the story of the Upper Columbia River Indians seems inevitable and little different from most other interactions between Indigenous peoples and Euro-Americans throughout North America. Still, overt Indian actions contributed to the ultimate contours of native societies by the 1880s. This legacy began with participation in the fur and hide trades and ended with innumerable official and informal acts of protest in later years. In all probability, the Indians around Fort Colville might have ended up with a better reservation had they treated with Isaac Stevens in 1855. With only a handful of settlers in the region at the time—and thus fewer voices to complain to the president or influential friends back east—Stevens likely would have given the Indians a much larger parcel of land than the reservations they ultimately received. As it was, when the federal government began to pay more attention to the region, Spokane Falls was expanding rapidly, and many second- and third-generation American settlers were living on homesteads to the north. The purpose here is not to "blame the victim," but to show that Native Americans had an active, if often disadvantaged, hand in shaping their future. No doubt encroachment by farmers and miners would have whittled away the land base over time, although Upper Columbia Rivers Indians might have been able to maintain a core presence in the region's best agricultural land.

The new reservation boundaries were disruptive to social and subsistence networks and impacted the lives of every individual who crossed them to tend a field, work in the city, or visit family. As transnational boundaries in the greater Northwest became simplified and less ambiguous, they also became more rigid. A formerly overlapping collection of diverse Indian groups—Catholics and Protestants, fishers and farmers, buffalo hunters and horse raisers—was funneled first into a single Indian agency and then formal reservations. Yet the reservation system in northeastern Washington also lacked any coherent policy on the part of its creators. For several decades, Upper Columbia River natives negotiated a complex and fickle arrangement of outraged citizens, unscrupulous or well-meaning agents, ambitious politicians, and apathetic bureaucrats. At every step, the penurious Office of Indian Affairs often undercut its own mission of civilization and assimilation by refusing to fund even the most rudimentary items like a schoolhouse or garden tools. It is a credit to the Indian leaders in the region that they learned to navigate not only the region's ever-shifting transnational borders but also a bureaucratic structure that often confounded its own employees.

Whatever else was happening in the political process, both Native Americans and American settlers had to meet basic subsistence needs. Viewed at the tribal or band level, we can make some easy generalizations about this period. The Colville took extensively to farming and ranching, a fact still obvious today. The Upper and Middle Spokane settled into agriculture, both before and after removal—the Lower Spokane less so, as this group still clung to their fisheries and a limited fur trade until the late nineteenth century. The Sanpoil remained aloof from American culture except when absolutely necessary. With few exceptions, bands throughout the region refused to accept annuities or gifts, fearing it signaled tacit acceptance of payment for lands.

At the level of individuals and family groups, of course, the story is much more complicated. Upper Columbia River natives had maintained extensive kinship networks throughout the greater Northwest for centuries. Despite some difficulty with mobility in the immediate years after the creation of formal reservations, reservation Indians married extensively across former tribal lines and across transnational borders. To say that groups remained "intact" across these tumultuous decades would be an oversimplification, for native cultures had always been changing to one degree or another. In terms of self-identification and survival, however, people that had for so long lived beside one another and shared similar traits and affinities continued to do so at the end of the nineteenth century despite radical changes in the world around them.

Notes

1. Analyzing the experience of Upper Columbia River peoples as a singular block, as I often do here, is not meant to minimize their very important cultural differences, but to acknowledge that in this period they acted in common cause against federal neglect and settler encroachment. Moreover, in a world of constantly shifting boundaries, the old Hudson's Bay Post at Fort Colville was a stable feature.

2. Andrew H. Fisher, *Shadow Tribe: The Making of Columbia River Identity* (Seattle: University of Washington Press, 2010), 5, 11.

3. Gray H. Whaley, "Oregon, *Illahee*, and the Empire Republic: A Case Study of American Colonialism," *The Western Historical Quarterly* 36 (2005): 158.

4. Ibid., 168.

5. Richard White, The Roots of Dependency: Subsistence, Environment, and Social Change among the Choctaws, Pawnees, and Navajos (Lincoln: University of Nebraska Press, 1983), xix.

6. John Lawrence Schultz, *Acculturation and Religion on the Colville Indian Reservation* (Ph.D. diss., Washington State University, 1971), 26.

7. Verne F. Ray, *The Sanpoil and Nespelem: Salishan Peoples of Northeastern Washington* (Seattle: University of Washington Press, 1933), 21–22.

8. Francis Haines, "The Northward Spread of Horses Among the Plains Indians," *American Anthropologist* 40 (1938): 434–36. For some groups, like the Yakama, this may not have been until about 1750. See A. J. Splawn, *Ka-mi-akin: The Last Hero of the Yakimas* (Portland, Ore.: Kilham Stationary and Printing Co., 1917), 360.

9. Cleveland Kamiakin and Billy Curlew, interview with Cull White and Robert H. Ruby, October 7, 1956, Northwest Museum of Arts and Culture, Dr. Robert H. Ruby Collection, box 3, folder 112.

10. James Tilton in "Message of the President of the United States, to the two Houses of Congress at the commencement of the first session of the Thirty-fifth Congress, January 4, 1858," serial set vol. 919, sess. vol. 2, 35th Cong., 1st sess., S. Exec. Doc. 11, pt. 1, 248.

11. W. Matthew Vander Haegen et al., "Wildlife Communities of Eastside Shrubland and Grassland Habitats," in *Wildlife-Habitat Relationship in Oregon and Washington*, eds. D. H. Johnson and T. A. O'Neil (Corvallis: University of Oregon Press, 2001), 306–8.

12. George Simpson, *Fur Trade and Empire: George Simpson's Journal, 1824–25*, rev. ed., ed. Frederick Merk (Cambridge, Mass.: The Belknap Press, 1968), 46.

13. Fort Colvile bore the name of Hudson Bay Company's Andrew Colvile. Current spelling for the geographical area and the tribe is "Colville."

14. Simpson, *Fur Trade and Empire*, 134–35.

15. David H. Chance, "Influences of the Hudson's Bay Company on the Native Cultures of the Colvile District," *Northwest Anthropological Research Notes, Memoir Number Two* 7, no. 1, part 2 (1973): 46.

16. Elizabeth Vibert, *Traders' Tales: Narratives of Cultural Encounters in the Columbia Plateau, 1807–1846* (Norman: University of Oklahoma Press, 1997), 164.

17. This might not be a safe assumption given massive depopulation and attendant social disruption that occurred with the first smallpox outbreaks in the 1770s.

18. Elkanah Walker, *Nine Years with the Spokane Indians: The Diary, 1838–1848, of Elkanah Walker*, ed. Clifford M. Drury (Glendale, Calif.: The Arthur H. Clark Company, 1976), 232, 526.

19. Chance, "Influences of the Hudson's Bay Company on the Native Cultures of the Colvile District," 47–49.

20. Simpson in Chance, "Influences of the Hudson's Bay Company on the Native Cultures of the Colvile District," 31.

21. Ibid., 66.

22. Simpson, *Fur Trade and Empire*, 138.

23. Leslie Spier, ed., *Contributions From the Laboratory of Anthropology: The Sinkaietk or Southern Okanogan of Washington* (Menasha, Wisc.: George Banta Publishing, 1938), 38.

24. George Simpson, *Narrative of a Journey Round the World, during the Years 1841 and 1842*, vol. I (London: H. Coburn, 1847), 145.

25. Kent D. Richards, *Isaac I. Stevens: Young Man in a Hurry* (Pullman: Washington State University Press, 1993), 115, 223–34; and William E. Farr, "Lame Bull's Treaty," presented at the Fur Trade Symposium, Fort Benton, Mont., September 2003, 85–86, copy in author's possession.

26. Isaac I. Stevens to George W. Manypenny, May 1, 1855, Letters Received by the Office of Indian Affairs, Washington Superintendency, microfilm [hereafter referred to as "Wash. Sup."], roll 907.

27. This phrasing comes from the "Treaty with the Walla Walla, Cayuse, Etc., 1855," in *Indian Affairs: Laws and Treaties, Vol. II, Treaties*, ed. Charles J. Kappler (Washington, D.C.: Government Printing Office, 1904), 695. For an account of the treaty proceedings, see Isaac I. Stevens, *Official Proceedings: A true copy of the Record of the Official Proceedings at the Council in the Walla Walla Valley held jointly by Isaac I. Stevens Gov. & Supt. W. T. and Joel Palmer Supt. Ind. Affairs O. T. on the part of the United States with the Tribes named in the Treaties made at that Council, June 9th and 11th 1855*, ed. Darrell Scott (Fairfield, Wash.: Ye Galleon Press, 1982), 38–45.

28. Richards, *Isaac I. Stevens*, 226–30; Stevens, *A True copy . . .* 1855, 42–44; and Farr, "Lame Bull's Treaty." For the quote and a description of the proceedings with the Flathead, see R. Ignatius Burns, "A Jesuit at the Hell Gate Treaty of 1855," *Mid-America: An Historical Review* 34 (1952): 88, 96–102.

29. Richards, *Isaac I. Stevens*, 194.

30. Harold Weaver, "A Tour of the Old Indian Camp Grounds of Central Washington," typescript, Cull White Collection, Washington State University, Manuscripts and Special Collections, box 2, folder 84; and unknown editor, "Chief Moses Recalls Early Day When He Fought Whites," *Yakima* (WA) *Republic*, May 13, 1935.

31. James Doty, *Journal of Operations of Governor Isaac Ingalls Stevens of Washington Territory in 1855* (Fairfield, Wash.: Ye Galleon Press, 1978), 53–55 and 62–63.

32. Ibid., 62–63.

33. Robert H. Ruby and John A. Brown, *The Spokane Indians: Children of the Sun* (Norman: University of Oklahoma Press, 1970, 2006), 108–9.

34. Lawrence Kip, *Indian War in the Pacific Northwest: The Journal of Lieutenant Lawrence Kip*, introduction by Clifford E. Trafzer (Lincoln: University of Nebraska Press, 1999), 76.

35. Ibid., 76.

36. Isaac I. Stevens in *Reports of Explorations and Surveys, to ascertain the most practicable and economic route for a railroad from the Mississippi River to the Pacific Ocean* (Washington, D.C.: A.O.P. Nicholson, 1855–1860), vol. XII, 148; and Ruby and Brown, The Spokane Indians, 105.

37. On the use of surplus funds, see Samuel Ross to E. S. Parker, May 11, 1870, Wash. Sup., roll 911. The phrase "parties to no treaty" was a standard heading on the annual statement of funds.

38. Edward P. Smith to John Simms, July 2, 1875, and H. R. Clum to John Simms, July 6, 1875. Both letters in John A. Simms Papers, box 1, folder 8, Washington State University, Manuscripts and Special Collections.

39. "Report of George A. Paige, Special Agent at Fort Colville," September 19, 1866, Wash. Sup., roll 909. This source includes a statement from Garry refuting the specific accusations of collusion with Agent Chapman and Garry's speech before the council. Paige writes that all the Indian speeches were in accord, so he only included Garry's statement. See also Chapman's letter to the Commissioner of Indian Affairs of April 26, 1866, Wash. Sup., roll 909. Chapman's account shows Garry as the primary actor, with the agent merely acting as intermediary. Increased occupancy on the Flathead reservation would surely have boosted Chapman's funding and his political clout. Or perhaps Garry was intentionally playing the two agents off each other, knowing that his series of communications would have given him some attention, both in Washington Territory and in Washington, D.C.

40. George A. Paige, "Annual Report for Colville Agency," Sept. 30, 1866, Wash. Sup., roll 909.

41. T. J. McKenny to George A. Paige, Feb. 15, 1867, Wash. Sup., roll 909.

42. "Statement C: Account of seed issued to Indians at Fort Colville, W. T. during the quarter com-

mencing April 1st and ending June 30th, A. D. 1866, " in John A. Simms Papers, box 2, folder 20, Washington State University, Manuscripts and Special Collections.

43. "Statement 'B': 'Old,' Sick and Destitute," March 31, 1872, Fort Colville WT in William Parkhurst Winans Papers, box 5, folder 38B, Washington State University, Manuscripts and Special Collections.

44. Winans was technically the agency's demonstration farmer and industrial instructor, but in the absence of a formally designated agent he also acted in that capacity.

45. William P. Winans, "Census of the Sui-el-pee or Colville Indians, June 1870," "Census of the Sanpoil and Nespeleum Indians, July 1870," and "Census of Spokane Indians, August 1870," in William Parkhurst Winans Papers, box 6, folder 44, Washington State University, Manuscripts and Special Collections.

46. Joseph E. Taylor III, *Making Salmon: An Environmental History of the Northwest Fisheries Crisis* (Seattle: University of Washington Press, 1999), 122. See also Lissa K. Wadewidtz, The Nature of Borders: Salmon, Boundaries, and Bandits on the Salish Sea (Seattle: University of Washington Press, 2012) for insight into the fluid political and social borders of the Puget Sound's multicultural, transnational salmon fisheries in the late-nineteenth and early-twentieth centuries.

47. Paige, "Annual Report for Colville Agency," 1866.

48. U. Grassi to E. S. Parker, May 27, 1870, Wash. Sup., roll 911.

49. Petition to Mr. E. S. Parker from the Citizens of Stevens County, W. T., June 16, 1870, Wash. Sup. roll 911. In this document, Kinkanagua is listed among the Colville, not the Sanpoil as in Fr. Grassi's letter.

50. W. P. Winans to T. J. McKenny, Feb. 5, 1871, Wash. Sup., roll 911.

51. James K. Kennedy to Selucius Garfielde with attached petition, June 13, 1871, in William Parkhurst Winans Papers, box 5, folder 38A, Washington State University, Manuscripts and Special Collections.

52. William W. Belknap to Selucius Garfielde, August 17, 1872, in William Parkhurst Papers, box 5, folder 38A, Washington State University, Manuscripts and Special Collections.

53. Selucius Garfielde to Columbus Delano, May 31, 1872, Wash. Sup., roll 912.

54. William P. Winans to Selucius Garfield, May 27, 1872, Wash. Sup., roll 912.

55. The 1100 Indians already living on the reservation tilled 180 acres. E. H. Ludington and others, Inspection Report for Fort Colville, Aug. 11, 1872, Wash. Sup., roll 912. This consolidated report contains contributions from several members of Ludington's staff.

56. Ibid.

57. John Simms, transcript of council, Nov. 6, 1872, Wash. Sup., roll 912.

58. John Simms to Robert H. Milroy, Nov. 20, 1872, Wash Sup., roll 912.

59. Robert H. Milroy to John Simms, Dec. 14, 1872, Wash. Sup., roll 912. Emphasis in original.

60. Charles Ewing to Columbus Delano, June 5, 1873, Wash. Sup., roll 912.

61. George W. Harvey to John Simms, Oct. 31, 1874, Wash. Sup., roll 913.

62. John Simms to E. P. Smith, Oct. 31, 1874, Wash. Sup., roll 913.

63. Department of the Interior, Office of Indian Affairs, "Circular," April 1, 1875, in John A. Simms Papers, box 1, folder 8, Washington State University, Manuscripts and Special Collections.

64. John P. C. Shanks in US House of Representatives, "Proposed Indian Reservations in Idaho and Washington Territories," 43rd Congress, 2nd session, executive document 102, Feb. 2, 1874, 3.

65. John Simms, undated survey of the Colville Indian Reservation (probably September 1874), Wash Sup., roll 913.

66. US Bureau of the Census, Population Schedules of the Tenth Census of the United States, 1880, Washington, Bureau of the Census, Washington, D.C.

67. Shanks in US House of Representatives, "Proposed Indian Reservations in Idaho and Washington Territories," 5.

Chapter 8

Shifting Borders

Indian Territory in Crisis

Clarissa W. Confer

Conflict can call into question long-held beliefs, challenge traditional practices, and upset patterns of behavior. Military conflict often exhibits all these aspects. It tends to stretch and distort common assumptions and practices. By nature, war involves borders. Borders define enemy and ally. They delineate achievement and loss and offer tangible proof of progress or success. In other ways, borders force an evaluation of identity, of membership, of belonging.

The American Civil War can certainly be characterized as a war of borders. The act of declaring the Confederate States of America, of withdrawing parts of the American Union into a separate political entity, created both tangible and intangible borders. It divided Americans into Confederates or Unionists, loyalists or secessionists, blue or gray. Of course, it was not nearly that neat or that clear. The division and the subsequent upheaval shattered lives and forced tens of thousands of people to make difficult choices, to choose their "side" of the new border, to define themselves as one or the other of two choices.

Some groups did not fit well into a clearly defined division. They had not previously identified themselves in that way, had sympathies with both sides, or hoped to avoid externally imposed choices. The natives of Indian Territory exemplify this position.

Indian Territory was a borderland. For much of its existence it remained so. It was conceived as a border between east and west, frontier and settlement, civilized and uncivilized, assimilated and wild native peoples. Cultural geography also made it a border between the American South and the American West. Then, in the mid-nineteenth century, soon after its creation, Indian Territory became the border region between two clashing views of the US future. Residents of the region had to identify themselves and choose sides. Outside, non-native policies forced a cultural evaluation of the meaning of identity and loyalty among native residents. The Cherokee, Creek,

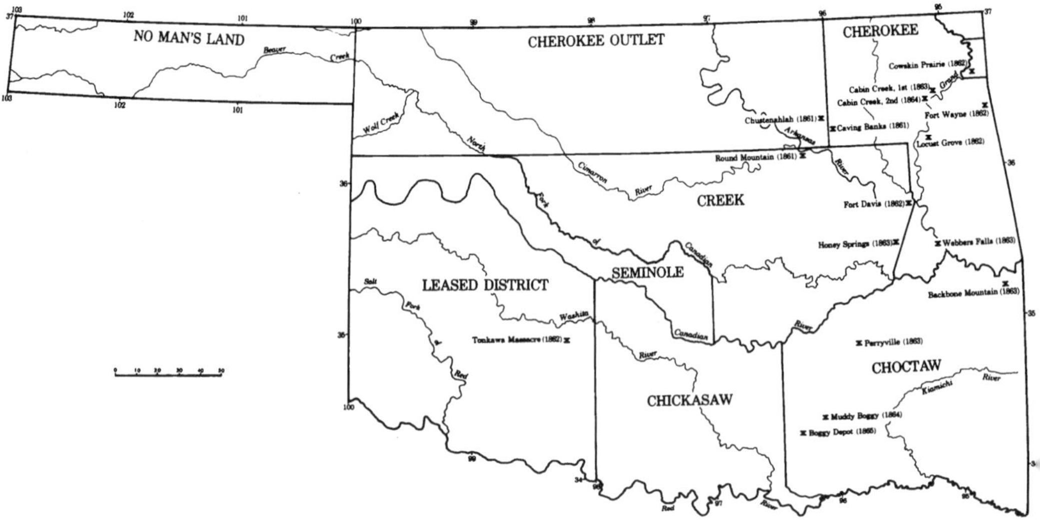

Indian Territory 1861. Courtesy of Historical Atlas of Oklahoma, by John W. Morrie, Charles R. Goins, and Edwin C. McReynolds. Copyright 1965, 1976, 1986 by the University of Oklahoma Press, Norman, Publishing Division of the University. Reproduced with Permission. All Rights reserved.

Choctaw, Chickasaw, and Seminole nations that had been forcibly removed to the region in the late 1830s now faced difficult choices as the border threatened to split their new homeland.

In 1861, with talk of war all around, the natives of Indian Territory faced difficult choices. The larger nation had divided itself into warring camps. Inherent in that division was the identification of each individual with some set of standards, symbols, and principles of membership. For many outside the Indian nations, the choice could be remarkably easy. Geographic location, heredity, friendships, and political beliefs all pointed people toward Union or Confederacy. Others struggled to reconcile divided families, disparate beliefs, or clashing ideologies. But which identities would natives use to choose their side of the border? National or tribal membership, kin group, religious affiliation, economic interests, or political leanings might all factor into the decision. The natives of Indian Territory did not hold United States citizenship so did not give up one political membership in exchange for another. Ties, mostly political and economic, bound them to the Union, while other affiliations such as religion, business, and kinship drew them to their southern neighbors. Given the difficult nature of the period, it is easy to assume that natives really did not want to make a choice, did not want to deal with the problems of a larger nation. But neither did they want to live in an isolated or static society. They held strong opinions on the topics of the day and were motivated by some of the same reasons as whites in ultimately choosing sides. People committed their allegiance due to loyalties to clan and family, views on slavery, and belief in the obligations of treaty terms, as well as perceived opportunity for power and money. Above all, however, natives made their choices as Cherokee, Creek, Choctaw, Chickasaw, or Seminole in that unique position of noncitizen residents of the United States. Their identity as natives could never be separated from their outlook, and most viewed choosing a side in the impending conflict as imperative for their own and their tribe's survival.

As with any large and disparate group, crisis precipitated different reactions. Some individuals welcomed the opportunity to settle on a side of the new border, whereas others resisted pressure to choose. Three choices presented themselves: Union, Confederacy, and neutrality, or a type of no man's land in between starkly drawn divisions. And clearly there would be a limited time available to make the choice.

As the conflict neared, the pressure from outside the territory increased. The pressure seemed most intense from the surrounding region. Politicians, neighbors, and ardent secessionists scrambled to ensure that the Five Nations sided with the South in the looming war. Although communication on the border of the Confederacy could be slow and inefficient, native leaders kept abreast of the news from the secessionist South.[1] The pressure placed on the Indian nations was intense and continued to escalate as the outbreak of war drew nearer. From the governor to citizen groups, Arkansans pushed their native neighbors to side with them. Arkansas also sent emissaries to the chiefs. In fact, Arkansas was so concerned with the allegiance of the Indian nations that its western counties hesitated to declare secession without them. Texans journeyed through Indian Territory, attending councils, where they strongly stated the case for disunion.[2] The national Confederate government recognized the advantages of an alliance with the natives of Indian Territory and quickly organized to engage them. In March 1861, Richmond organized a Bureau of Indian Affairs and appointed David Hubbard as commissioner. Confederate intervention in the affairs of the Indian nations increased dramatically from that point. Within a few months, three men—Hubbard, Albert Pike, and Brigadier General Ben McCulloch—all had official missions to Indian Territory. Pike and McCulloch achieved the most, the former negotiating treaties of alliance and the latter recruiting military units.[3]

The response of the United States government aided Southerners' efforts to secure the loyalty of the Indian nations. The Lincoln administration often is accused of being idle in Indian affairs in 1861; however, it actually took steps that damaged its relationship with the tribes. For example, the Interior Department did nothing to rectify the deteriorating situation in the Office of Indian Affairs. The superintendent of the region openly supported an Indian alliance with the South, and the agents under his supervision also expressed southern sympathies. The influence of white officials among the Indians would not alone have been that harmful, but Confederate emissaries could point to alarming examples of current federal policy. Any diplomat willing to resort to scare tactics to win Indian alliance had ample ammunition. Confederate Indian Commissioner Hubbard laid out all the impending evils of northern victory in the conflict in a letter to Cherokee Chief Ross. One of the most serious threats was the loss of revenue. Tribal trust funds were heavily invested in southern state bonds that were forfeited by the impending war. In a poorly conceived decision, the United States government stopped the payment of tribal annuities in 1861, citing security concerns in transferring money to Indian Territory. Although the goal of keeping the money from falling into enemy hands was understandable, the tribes suffered severely. The governments of the Five Nations relied heavily on these payments to fund all aspects of the bureaucracy, including schools and police forces. The specter of bankruptcy was daunting.[4] Tribal leaders had little reason to trust a government that had suspended payments guaranteed by treaty.

Native leaders, although not immune to the pressures of persuasion thrown at them, maintained a sense of native identity and native destiny. They needed to navigate this perilous period with native interests at the forefront. The stakes could be high. "We do not wish our soil to become the battleground between the states and our homes to be rendered desolate and miserable by the horrors of civil war," Chief John Ross of the Cherokees, pictured on the next page, wrote to one Confederate officer what proved to be sadly prophetic words.[5]

One major obstacle to a positive outcome in Indian Territory loomed large—the age-old problem of unity. White observers have long bemoaned the "lack of unity" among "Indians." This outlook of course ignores the diversity, autonomy, and identity of Indigenous peoples. A united approach to the challenges facing native peoples in 1861 might have prevented suffering, but it would not have been realistic. Indian leaders did attempt a unified reaction to outside pressures, but it gained little traction. The Indian nations were already on their way toward the disunity that would prove a serious liability; a facade of unity did not even last through one intertribal council. The Chickasaws called for such a meeting on January 5, 1861, citing the need to renew harmony and good feeling among the Five Nations. By the time the council assembled in the Creek Nation in mid-February, the Chickasaws did not even bother to send delegates. William Ross, sent reluctantly by his uncle Chief John Ross to represent the Cherokees, found himself meeting only with Creeks and Seminoles. The meeting accomplished little, and the absentee Chickasaws and Choctaws continued to pursue their own course in regard to the war.[6]

The disorganized situation in Indian Territory proved favorable to Con-

John Ross, Cherokee chief. Courtesy of the Library of Congress.

federate overtures, and the new government had chosen its emissaries well. Albert Pike, a colorful, wealthy, Arkansas poet and lawyer knew Indians better than many whites in the region. His reputation in gaining a $140,000 settlement for the Creeks ensured he would at least be granted a hearing by the tribes. Pike met with representatives of the Five Nations and offered attractive terms for an alliance. The Confederacy understood the importance of securing its western border and was willing to promise money, political participation, and sovereignty to the Indian nations to get it. Sovereignty included the right to determine citizenship, restrict residency within the nations, reject allotment and statehood, and control trade. The Confederacy also offered to put Indian delegates in the national legislature, a privilege the United States had never conferred. Financial concerns were extremely important to the Indians, and they received protection of existing trust funds and guarantees of future annuity payments. The Confederate provisions incorporated many rights that the tribes had tried unsuccessfully to obtain from the federal government, which if faithfully adhered to would have empowered the nations of Indian Territory. Four nations agreed to a Confederate alliance under these terms, leaving only the Cherokee outside the Confederate mantle.[7]

The Choctaw and Chickasaw were the first Indian nations to declare for the Confederacy. The Choctaw council issued a resolution on February 7, 1861, asserting that the "natural affections, education, institutions, and interests" of the people bound them to the destiny of the South. The Choctaws' and Chickasaws' geographic location and rich cotton-growing lands made them a likely target for overzealous secessionists. Two paragraphs of the Choctaw resolution emphasized their decision to the neighboring states. They asserted a "firm reliance" that their neighbors would "respect and protect" the "rights and feelings so sacred" to the Choctaw.[8] This points to a strong sense of coercion by neighbors. However, Choctaw delegates in Washington, removed from the reach of vigilante committees, expressed apprehension of attack by Texas and Arkansas while asserting the Choctaw Nation's intention to remain neutral. The discrepancy in official policy reveals divisions within the supposedly unified Choctaw Nation. Because the Choctaws and Chickasaws declared for the Confederacy early and never renounced their decision, historians often have credited them with avoiding the internal divisions that plagued other nations. But contemporaries repeatedly asserted that average citizens in the nations preferred neutrality to entering the war on either side. Under the leadership of Chief George Hudson, the Choctaw council may have acted under pressure from a vocal minority of southern sympathizing slaveholders, such as the wealthy and influential Robert Jones. Indeed, a letter from missionary S. Orlando Lee charged the legislative body with reversing its neutral stance due to such pressure. The borders between the many identities that coordinated in the person of a Choctaw citizen could be convoluted.

Once decided for the Confederacy, the Choctaws and Chickasaws did unite and maintain their national harmony throughout the war, which in the long run may have been more important to their future than which side they chose.[9] The Nations maintained autonomy in the process of supplying troops for the Confederacy. Understanding the import of this action, the leaders of both nations justified and defended their decisions in eloquent prose. Governor Cyrus Harris gave his Chickasaw troops the broad and noble objective: "to resist by all means and to the death any such invasion . . . by the Lincoln hordes and Kansas robbers, who have plundered and oppressed our red brethren among them, and who doubtless would extend towards us the protection which the wolf gives to the lamb should they succeed in overrunning our country."[10]

Within the proclamations of adherence to the Confederacy was the unmistakable message that the Chickasaws intended to remain in control. They had not just been subsumed into the South, but rather drew a strong border around their part of the Confederacy. They did not mean to provide soldiers without retaining power over the spoils of war. Governor Harris defined the Chickasaw goal of self-governance by claiming the right to hold "undisputed possessions of land and forts lately occupied by federal forces and have the same garrisoned, if possible, by Chickasaw troops, or else by troops acting expressly under and by virtue of the authority of the Chickasaw or Choctaw nations." The Texans who marched in to seize the abandoned forts were reminded that the land belonged to the Indians. The Chickasaw's former protectors, the United States military, censured Harris's independence in trying to "disarm and disgrace" their soldiers leaving Fort Washita.[11]

Both Chickasaws and Choctaw leaders encouraged men to enlist to defend their nations. The Chickasaws called for volunteer companies under their own officers, modeled on American minutemen, to be ready at a moment's notice for defense of country. Chief George Hudson decreed compulsory service for all Choctaws subject to military duty. This order outlined how many men each district had to provide to reach the total of seven hundred men to be sent to the Chickasaw and Choctaw regiment. Those not included in these conscription laws were to form squads under local headmen to serve as home guards "for the protection of the country and preservation of order."[12]

The Confederacy soon placed these early recruits into their military structure. The 1st Chickasaw and Choctaw Mounted Rifles was formed by July 31, 1861, a speedy response for two small nations. The unit was led by a white man, but the lower officers were Indians, and the rank and file mostly full-bloods. The Choctaws and Chickasaws chose their former agent, Douglas Cooper, as colonel. These tribes continued to express the utmost faith in Cooper's leadership throughout the war, often requesting that he be given a higher rank and greater authority over Indian Territory. The Chickasaw Infantry Regiment, Secoe's Chickasaw battalion, and the 1st Battalion of Chickasaw Cavalry also enlisted in the first rush of enthusiasm for the Confederate cause. Flushed with the ease of filling the first regiment, Cooper bragged to Jefferson Davis that the Chickasaws and Choctaws were "extremely anxious to form another regiment" and could furnish ten thousand warriors if needed. Choctaw officer Tandy Walker nearly begged Davis to allow the formation of at least another battalion, partially to enable the Chickasaws to enlist more men. Apparently the Chickasaws felt some resentment against the Choctaws, who had filled all but about twenty of the spots in the poorly named Choctaw *and Chickasaw* regiment. These Choctaw and Chickasaw troops would be the most constant allies the Confederacy had in Indian Territory.[13]

The Creek Nation technically allied with the Confederacy when Chief Moty Kennard and others signed a treaty in July 1861.[14] As with so many treaties between governments and Indian tribes, the validity of the document lay in the signatures. Who had the authority to bind the Creek people to a military alliance? The treaty negotiations included only pro-southern Lower Creek leaders because meetings were intentionally held while opposition leaders visited Plains tribes to the west. Upon returning, the absent leaders found the treaty signed and some of their forged signatures attached. Unaccustomed to coercive rule, dissenters immediately chose Sands as the new chief to represent them and disassociated themselves from the treaty signers.[15] The divisions—indeed, the borders between different groupings and different identities of the Creek people—gained more ascendancy as the non-native society pressed in on them. The insistence of the national dialogue on drawing strictly defined borders and on choosing sides forced the Creeks, traditionally a loose alliance of people, into drawing borders of their own, soon to be to their detriment. Unfortunately, the Creek people were not alone in their struggles to negotiate in this newly divided society.

The Cherokee situation offers an opportunity to examine the concepts of identity, belonging, and loyalty among native nations. The Cherokee nation remained seriously divided over the quarter century since removal. The debate over removal had split the Cherokees violently, and the rift had barely healed by the time they faced another crisis, demanding them to define borders and choose sides. When John Ridge; his father, Major Ridge; and his cousin Elias Boudinot had signed the *Treaty of New Echota* in 1835, they had become enemies of the state as represented by Chief John Ross. It was easy to use their persons as symbols of blame for the tremendous hardships of the Trail of Tears. Their murders in 1839, probably by Ross supporters, nearly destroyed the nation. The animosity engendered by the blame for removal and the murders festered in Cherokee society and politics so that, despite a government-brokered settlement between the groups in 1846, in 1861 Ross faced considerable hostility from the "Treaty Party" adherents. The opposition had coalesced around Stand Watie, the brother of murdered Elias Boudinot. Stand Watie had escaped planned assassination, seen relatives and friends murdered, and killed a man blamed for the death of his brother.[16] He was a strong leader and a committed adversary. His group appeared ready to challenge and defy every position taken by the Ross government. So now the Cherokees had two choices, two paths, both led by their own people.[17]

The traditional members of each tribe, often described by witnesses as "full bloods," appeared opposed to breaking US treaty obligations and entering a war; however, only in the Cherokee Nation did this group have access to power. The Keetoowah society provided them with organization and a vehicle for expression. Cherokee Chief Ross always had respected the will of the majority. By the 1860s, he had established a long history of defending its rights against the vocal minority, now led by Stand Watie and loosely defined as the Treaty Party. An intense rivalry between these factions, which stretched back many years, clearly continued at the start of the Civil War.

So in 1861, the concept of borders, identity, and loyalty existed within a tangled web of past grievances, grudges, and revenge. The Treaty Party/Stand Watie/Pro-South contingent viewed the offer of Confederate alliance as an opportunity to gain power and prestige at the expense of their rivals. The Confederacy was offering recognition, political autonomy, and military standing. The group had already organized into an armed company created to defend themselves from Ross party aggression. Joining the CSA would secure legitimacy as well as military supplies. Stand Watie quickly offered his military group for Confederate service. His supporters expressed this decision more in terms of what it would do for them as Cherokees than any connection to the southern cause. "Our party . . . want[s] . . . our rights provided for[,] and place us if possible at least on an honorable equity with this old Dominant party that has for years had its foot on our neck."[18]

The rush of his political enemies to take a strong stand seemed to influence Ross's inclination to maintain neutrality and avoid entangling alliances with unproved governments. He spent much of the spring and summer of 1861 asserting the neutral position of his nation and waging an increasingly difficult battle to keep the Cherokee Nation unified.[19] This might seem to be the prudent course when analyzing the relative strength of the Cherokee nation against the national powers. However, Ross paid more attention to internal native politics and power struggles. He could not allow Watie's adherents to gain any type of advantage in the ongoing struggle within the nation. Chief Ross ordered the creation of a regiment of twelve hundred men, led by his relatives and close associates John Drew, Tom Pegg, and William P. Ross.[20] Although this unit soon accepted Confederate enlistment, Watie followers described it in terms of the internal politics of the Cherokees—*Ross's tyranny*.[21]

Those familiar with the tensions in the territory, like Albert Pike, also understood how to use them. His correspondence with Secretary of State Robert Toombs explained the rivalries in the Cherokee Nation and declared Pike's intention to deal with the "half-breeds" (Watie Party) if Ross would not cooperate. Pike preferred to have the recognized government of the Cherokees as allies with the Confederacy, but described Chief Ross as "very shrewd."[22] Eventually the internal dynamics of the Cherokee Nation swung Ross over to the CSA, at least for the beginning of the war. Ross committed his nation to an official alliance with the Confederacy in October 1861. His speech to four thousand male citizens conveyed his desire to ensure harmony, prosperity, and autonomy for Cherokees.[23]

> The great object with me has been to have the Cherokee people harmonious and united in the full and free exercise and enjoyment of all their rights of person and property. Union is strength; dissension is weakness, misery, ruin. In time of peace, enjoy peace together; in time of war, if war must come, fight together. As brothers live, as brothers die. . . . When your nationality ceases here, it will live nowhere else.[24]

By 1861, the drawing of new borders and the insistence on identification with one group or the other brought the natives of Indian Territory to a crisis. There was no way to continue being Cherokees or Creek or Seminoles without a larger identification as Union or Confederate adherents. By the fall of the first year of war, the Confederacy claimed the allegiance of all five of the Southeastern nations in Indian Territory. *Claimed* is an apt word here because the Confederacy's understanding of allies relied on non-native concepts. Written documents signed by designated officials proved the will of the people to white-dominated governments. Native groups harbored few such illusions that paper, signatures, or individuals could determine or coerce the loyalties of independent people. So, the Creek crisis should not have come as a surprise.

In the fall of 1861, the perceived threat to the newly organized Confederate forces came from the Creeks organizing under Opothleyahola, an elderly Upper Creek spokesman. Anti-removal Creeks respected his role as opposition leader during the removal crisis and trusted his judgment. Opothleyahola did not favor the South despite his position as a large slave owner. He trusted the power of the United States government more than the newly formed Confederacy and held firm to that existing alliance. Individuals and families dissatisfied with the nation's adherence to the South rallied around this traditional leader, who refused to abide by the treaty signed by Lower Creek Chief Moty Kennard and others in July 1861.[25] The dissenters later chose Sands as the new chief to represent them and disassociated themselves from the treaty signers.[26]

In 1861, southern sympathizers empowered by Confederate promises of support dominated the Creek Nation. Pro-Union Creeks, or loyal Creeks as they called themselves, sought reassurance that the United States government remained committed to their protection. Government representatives became increasingly hard to find after the military abandoned Indian Territory, however, and Indian agents hastily chosen to replace defectors dared not venture into the region. The chiefs wrote to their "father in Washington," asking for his assistance. They reminded President Abraham Lincoln of treaty obligations of protection and explained that "now the wolf has come, men who are strangers tread our soil, our children are frightened and the mothers cannot sleep for fear."[27] Confederate forces later found the reply from agent E. H. Carruth in the abandoned Creek camp. Carruth promised the Creek leaders that the president was not dead and that his soldiers would soon come and redeem Indian country from the rebels. The rhetoric was impressive, but the reality was not. The fact that Carruth had to assure the Indians that Lincoln was alive reveals the administration's lack of involvement in native affairs during the preceding year. Indifference, distance, and unreliability of former Indian agents combined to alienate the federal government from Indian Territory. Although the letter announced that the Union army would soon go south to aid the Indians, in the following two months no army arrived. Loyal Creeks could not wait that long for assistance. Increasingly threatened by secessionist activities in their own nation, they gathered for mutual protection.[28] The Creeks now moved from rhetorical or political borders to actual physical borders.

The formation of a large group opposed to the Confederate treaty worried southern Creeks, who set out to separate and disempower the dissenters. Confederate Colonel Douglas Cooper, a former Indian agent, also viewed the gathering of "dissident" Creeks with growing alarm. He attempted to contact Opothleyahola and "exhausted every means possible" in his opinion, but to no avail. Opothleyahola no longer trusted even Chief John Ross, a former Indian ally in the fight against removal, so he certainly would not deal with a white Confederate agent. Opothleyahola had counted on the support of the Cherokees under John Ross, believing that he would hold true to his initial refusal to sign with the Confederacy. A report from Ross that he had altered his course and declared for the South was a major blow. Opposition leaders at first did not believe the news. Ross attempted to win the Creeks over to his change of heart, and Lower Creek Chief Moty Kennard asked him to intervene to relieve the growing tension. Kennard and Ross both feared an internal conflict.[29]

This dreaded civil conflict, this momentous crossing of borders, occurred in November 1861, when Confederate forces under the command of Douglas Cooper, including Creeks led by Chilly and Daniel McIntosh, converged on Opothleyahola's group, whom they referred to as hostiles. Opothleyahola had anticipated this action by seeking the protection of national borders. The old chief moved his people north toward the perceived safety of Union lines. In a series of three engagements—Round Mountain, Chusto-talasah, and Chustenahlah—Confederate Indian forces aided by Texans drove several thousand pro-Union Creeks and Seminoles from the Creek Nation and into a desperate trek to Kansas to cross the starkly drawn border between North and South.

Short, swift skirmishes, these engagements had a profound impact on the perceived identities of the Indians and their wartime experience. Cooper instigated the attacks on the loyal Indians camped in the Cherokee Nation and took full credit for the aggression in his report to Confederate Secretary of War Judah P. Benjamin. He claimed knowledge of correspondence between Creek chiefs and the federal government, which he misrepresented as an alliance in order to justify his military actions against civilians. Acting on his assertion of an impending Creek–Union alliance, Cooper went on the offensive against the loyal Creeks. He was in charge of the region for the Confederacy because appointed leader Albert Pike had not yet arrived. Perhaps a desire to act under his own authority before becoming second-in-command motivated Cooper's impulsive action. In addition, Cooper did not want his power usurped by his Indian allies. Even allies drew borders and protected territory within their authority. Lower Creek chiefs Moty

Kennard and Echo Harjo informed Cooper, at the end of October, that they intended to march on Opothleyahola. They told him that the captured free blacks, slaves, ponies, and property would become the property of the Creeks.[30] Cooper immediately replied that all captured property belonged to the Confederate government, and may have moved to protect his authority. Additionally, the presence of a respected native leader who opposed the southern cause annoyed Cooper. Opothleyahola represented a challenge to the carefully constructed sense of authority that whites gained from government and military positions. There is no evidence that Opothleyahola posed a serious military threat; he merely represented an alternative for Indian Territory residents. The traditional Creek leader served as a focal point for all those uncomfortable with either Confederate alliance or the associated resurgence of McIntosh family power.[31]

Cooper commanded the 1st Choctaw and Chickasaw Mounted Rifles, the 1st Creek Regiment, the Creek and Seminole Battalion, and a detachment of Texas troops. He had gained strength from the 9th Texas Cavalry when it marched through Indian Territory en route to Arkansas in November 1861. When the Texans paused at Boggy Depot, they learned of Cooper's request for additional forces, and the officers detached five hundred men under Lt. Col. William Quayle for service in Indian Territory.[32]

The fourteen hundred white and Indian soldiers took up pursuit of Opothleyahola's group of families. Proceeding up the Deep Fork of the Canadian River, the Confederates found the loyal Indians' camp deserted and helped themselves to abandoned cattle and corn. It took Cooper four days to catch up to the civilian Creek entourage, after which he relied on captured prisoners for information. On November 19, 1861, the Confederates believed they had overtaken Opothleyahola's party when they saw smoke from fires, clearly indicating a camp. The Confederates charged the supposed camp, only to find it recently vacated. The Texans under Quayle, eager for their first military encounter, impetuously rushed forward, following a few scouts. The scouts led the cavalry directly to an ambush by concealed Creek and Seminole warriors. The result was chaos. Cooper formed the Choctaw and Chickasaw regiment for an attack, but the Texans were so far forward that no one could safely fire. The officers hesitated and called out to ascertain the location of their troops. Darkness hampered the efforts of both sides, and even fires lighted on the prairie did little to alleviate the confusion. The skirmish ended after a mere fifteen minutes, and the causalities were correspondingly light.[33]

The effect of the contest was evident the next day. This brief encounter had forced the loyal Creeks and Seminoles to flee in haste, leaving much of their wealth behind. Cooper's men rode into the abandoned camp and enumerated their booty: Opothleyahola's buggy, twelve wagons, flour, sugar, coffee, salt, cattle, and ponies. These captured supplies—a nice benefit for the Confederate forces on the march—represented a serious blow to their owners. Because Opothleyahola's people were civilians, no government supported the group, and no army commissary supplied them. They subsisted on what they could carry and forage. Cooper's forces denied them all means of subsistence by capturing supplies and keeping them on the run. This situation underscores the reality that the Confederate troops attacked civilians. Warriors did not take women and children into battle, yet these groups constituted the majority of Opothleyahola's band. Loyal Creek and Seminole men could not fight a conventional battle because they had to protect their families. At best, they waged delaying actions to allow the women time to move again. These were Indian men protecting their kin groups in a traditional manner, not an offensive army.[34] Another border had been crossed. Most conventional military leaders of the time prided themselves on conducting a "civilized" conflict that did not involve civilians. Native people apparently occupied a quite different category in which such conventions did not apply.

The pursuit of the loyal Indians continued into December 1861, with weather and attrition adding to the hardship on both sides. When Cooper resumed the chase after a short interval, he caught up with the travelers. They had crossed the federally drawn border between their own nation and that of the Cherokees. This development proved alarming because many Cherokees were known to be lukewarm Confederates, and the presence of dissidents might spark a defection. Reports of an impending attack by Opothleyahola magnified the sense of urgency, although it is unlikely that this band of fleeing families intended to deliver an offensive blow against mounted soldiers. Cooper believed this news elicited from a prisoner, however, and added Colonel John Drew's Cherokees to the Confederate effort.

Drew commanded traditionalists who had enlisted to defend their nation and who were loyal to John Ross rather than Jefferson Davis. The 1st Cherokee did not embrace the Confederate cause with the dedication of their southern allies and probably were considered a supporting force to the main thrust. Unfortunately for Cooper, Drew's men made first contact with Opothleyahola's people at Bird Creek. When this happened, several types of borders collided. The borders between Union and Confederate, between white and Indian, and between Creek and Cherokee converged. Each man had to determine which identity would guide his actions. Ross's Cherokees remained anxious to settle the Creek matter by diplomacy instead of conflict, and with Cooper's approval, Major Thomas Pegg, of Drew's regiment, tried to meet with Opothleyahola. The situation quickly degenerated into confusion. Pegg returned empty-handed from his diplomatic mission, and his report of Creeks painted for war alarmed Cooper. The Confederate effort suffered a further setback when Drew discovered that most of his men had abandoned his camp and apparently the Confederate cause.[35]

The defection of Drew's men should not have come as a surprise. The rank-and-file soldiers had enlisted out of loyalty to their chief and a belief in his assertion that the borders of their beloved nation must be protected. Drew's regiment had been raised to combat enemies of the Cherokee Nation, not of the Confederacy. The Creeks posed no immediate threat to the Cherokees and thus did not fall under a strict definition of enemy. Many Cherokees had personal relationships with Creeks who had been neighbors across artificial borders in Indian Territory for over two decades. Furthermore, their chief had often expressed his desire to talk to Opothleyahola and other Creek leaders, not to shoot them. Ross even tried to keep Drew out of the impending confrontation by insisting he was needed in his "own country."

James McDaniel was among the men who Cooper believed went over to the Union side. Chief Ross had sent McDaniel to contact Opothleyahola and to escort the Creek chief to Drew's headquarters or Lewis Ross's house for a discussion of his grievances. It would have been an act of deception for McDaniel to have fired on the fleeing Creeks. Hundreds of other Cherokee soldiers also chose not to fight the "hostile" Creeks and Seminoles. Drew's men deserted the Confederate side with alacrity, leaving behind tents, horses, and guns. The teamsters freighted the supplies out of the empty camp while a chagrined Colonel Drew rode to Cooper's headquarters to report on the debacle. Cooper sent the Texans to evaluate the situation; Drew gamely pledged his remaining twenty-eight men for service.[36]

The battle of Chusto-talasah (Caving Banks) went on despite the defection of the 1st Cherokee Mounted Rifles. The site was well chosen for defense. Opothleyahola sheltered his warriors along the high banks (30 feet in places) of Bird Creek. Cooper's men found it difficult to attack this natural stronghold, but they kept up the effort throughout the afternoon of December 9, 1861. After four hours of fighting, the loyal Creeks withdrew at dusk, and the Confederates regrouped in camp. That night they experienced the hardships of winter campaigning as three inches of snow fell. Cooper exaggerated enemy losses and claimed a victory at Chusto-talasah—despite the fact that the dissident Creeks and Seminoles remained on the loose.[37]

After two engagements, Cooper was not confident in his ability to drive Opothleyahola from Confederate soil. The renegade band of families had proved difficult to overcome, and it appeared that more Cherokees were joining them. Cooper requested that white troops be stationed in the Cherokee Nation for their "moral effect," yet he was surprised when Colonel James McIntosh arrived with two thousand troops of the 2nd Arkansas Mounted Rifles. The surprise really resulted from McIntosh's bold assertion of command and immediate movement into the field. Cooper had been planning to spend December at Fort Gibson rather than in an arduous winter campaign on the prairie. He did not manage to join McIntosh for the impending battle against the warriors, contenting himself with chasing a few civilians around the northern part of the territory and grumbling that much more would have been accomplished if McIntosh had waited for him.[38]

McIntosh's pursuit of the loyal Creeks resulted in the battle of Chustenahlah on December 26, 1861. After four days in the field, he cut free from his baggage train. His men became aware of the presence of the enemy as they moved across the country. Opothleyahola also knew of his pursuers and prepared to meet them yet again. The Creek leader always chose his ground carefully, with an eye to natural protection, and the site along Shoal Creek met his requirements. The women, children, and supplies remained sheltered while warriors took up a fine defensive position half a mile to the south. Although McIntosh impetuously charged an enemy well ensconced in a defensive position, his assault was successful. The Confederates dislodged the Creeks and Seminoles with a rapid onslaught. Many defenders fought fiercely, but the majority were routed and fled to the north. McIntosh's men continued the chase, cutting down pro-Union Indians wherever they scattered.[39]

The battle of Chustenahlah doomed the unfortunate loyal Indians. Colonel McIntosh reported that the enemy was completely broken up and his force scattered. The military defeat of the warriors, represented by retreat from the field, was less critical than the material losses the civilians sustained. The Confederates pushed north to the Creek encampment, "shooting and cutting down the enemy" along the way, and wreaked havoc there. They captured 180 people and quantities of property including wagons, horses, cattle, and sheep. These losses deprived the Creeks and Seminoles of the means to continue their journey. Both food and transportation were severely reduced, and the women and children who escaped had to flee on foot. Stand Watie's 2nd Cherokee Mounted Rifles arrived after the battle and inflicted further misfortune by seizing nearly a thousand head of livestock and hundreds of ponies. Colonel Cooper's men also chased the dislocated Creeks and Seminoles toward the Kansas border until forced back due to the bitter winter weather.[40] The first military campaign in Indian Territory had come to an end.[41]

The ramifications of the fall 1861 campaign lasted throughout the war, as Creeks and Seminoles who fled Confederate jurisdiction became refugees in Kansas, where their warriors joined the Union army. In a few short months they had crossed both physical and political borders. The battles drove them northward across the border between Indian Territory and Kansas, between the Union and Confederacy, between slavery and free labor. Most problematic for the natives, the war had reignited deep divisions and created borders among their own people. The distrust between Creek factions that sparked the military encounters only increased. For example, Colonel Daniel McIntosh dismissed his fellow Creeks as "the enemy" in his reports, revealing no recognition of their kinship. Texas troops reported that the Creeks fought their relatives with ferocity and even scalped the dead. John Drew's men had refused to fight fellow Indians, but other Cherokees willingly had followed their white commander into battle against their neighbors. Choctaws and Chickasaws, Cherokees, and Seminoles had all spilled the blood of Indians. There could be no pan-Indian unity, no cooperation of the minority against the white majority. Not only each Indian nation, but also groups within three divided nations defined their own borders and followed their own courses through the war.[42]

The unsteady relationship between the nations of Indian Territory and the Confederacy continued into 1862. With the dissident Creeks and Seminoles removed to Kansas, the Cherokees remained the only questionable facet of the Confederate alliance. Albert Pike received command of the Confederate Army forces in the territory in appreciation for his work in negotiating the Indian treaties. He spent much of his brief military career justifying his actions and complaining of mistreatment at the hands of others, but he did manage to engage his native troops in a sizable battle outside their homeland. Pike responded to a call for reinforcements from McCulloch and marched his men to Arkansas to participate in the Battle of Pea Ridge, Arkansas, on March 7–8, 1862, despite treaty assurances that Indian forces would not leave their nations without their consent.[43]

The issue of borders loomed large in this event. The concepts of identity, borders, and allegiance swirled through this battle that most historians view as a simple military engagement. In the haste to concentrate men against a Union invasion that threatened Confederate control of the trans-Mississippi West, no one had officially consulted the tribes about fighting outside their territory as required by the 1861 treaties. This march to Arkansas required a clear crossing of borders from "Indian country" to Confederate territory. The Confederacy was asking—actually, expecting—native soldiers to view the cause as one that encompassed the entire South, or all of the CSA's war strategy. Native soldiers should view themselves as part of a larger entity that could command participation in actions that had little relevance to native issues. Indian soldiers had become Confederate soldiers, had crossed a border that subsumed their identity into a larger association. Or had they? The Indian troops did not go willingly to this battle.

The orders to march to Bentonville, Arkansas, clearly did not involve a direct threat to Indian homes or families. This was not a matter of self-defense. Not only were the native soldiers crossing a physical border but also a psychological border. By fighting away from home at Pea Ridge they entered into a conflict fought for larger causes that may not have fit their concepts of identity, homeland, and allegiance. All this contributed to their reluctance to march to Arkansas. Pragmatic reasons also fed their reluctance. Confederate Indian regiments had good reason to be disgruntled with the southern military administration. They had not been paid. Families relied on the military wages, and soldiers were determined to get what was due them. The Choctaw and Chickasaw regiment saw no reason to participate without compensation and refused to march. Pike paid out the funds he had on hand for other purposes in an effort to induce loyalty to the cause, but bemoaned the delay of several days. Even after the payment, the Choctaws and Chickasaws participated unwillingly, following slowly on the march. Drew's Cherokees also moved out reluctantly. Most Indians could show little enthusiasm for this trek across their border into Arkansas, and only Watie's regiment went with alacrity.[44]

Unfortunately, after all the tumult, the battle resulted in a negative experience for native participants. These Indian soldiers marched toward an experience they knew little about. They could be classified as the greenest of troops due to their unfamiliarity with conventional military training. Native enlistees showed little tolerance for drill or military discipline and rarely received much of it. Scant attention had been paid to their preparation, either outfitting or training. They had spent little time in practicing battlefield maneuvers, and generally disdained the infantry, preferring to be mounted. In addition, the troops had not trained with artillery, an oversight that would come to haunt the Confederacy.

This was to be a major battle in the competition for dominance in the West. Twenty-six thousand troops fought for two days in a struggle that cost nearly six thousand casualties. The native troops served in the army of Confederate General Van Dorn, who had his men complete an exhausting march around the Union rear in cold weather and then attack on March 7. The Union countered a series of uncoordinated assaults as the day passed in heavy fighting. Soldiers on the Confederate right, where Indian troops were positioned, fled the field after the death of both General McCulloch and his second-in-command, General McIntosh, within fifteen minutes of each other. Curtis then counterattacked on March 8, forcing Van Dorn to withdraw from the field in defeat.[45]

The battle of Pea Ridge was not a success for either the Confederacy or the thousand Indian troops. The lagging units of Choctaw, Chickasaw, and Creek missed the battle while the Cherokees faltered after charging an artillery position. Another border, or division, came into play on the battlefield. Native troops who showed little interest in or patience for white-style military training and drill and had never been trained in the use of artillery. Artillery had never figured into their traditional conflicts. So the Union cannons they captured remained useless.[46] Worse yet, the lack of training and experience meant that subsequent Union artillery barrages wreaked havoc among Indian troops. Terrified by the heavy fire, the Cherokees sought shelter in the woods and lost the advantage. The confusion worsened as the Indian troops remained pinned down by heavy fire, and the generals commanding their section of the line died.

The general disintegration of the Confederate line caught up the already disorganized Indian troops, most of whom fled the field. The sweep of prisoners after the Confederate defeat caught up at least eleven Indians, all of whom were shot down by their guards as they tried to escape during the transfer to Springfield.[47] This was not the type of fighting that the Cherokee soldiers had expected, and many simply threw down their arms and went home.[48] Cherokee soldiers headed back to Indian Territory and their nation, which they had been reluctant to leave in the first place and where General Pike would have to travel to find them.[49] Pike realized that Confederate strategy had little relevance to Indian troops, so with his remaining men he ventured far into the heart of Indian Territory rather than patrolling its borders.

The Cherokees had suffered in Arkansas and would be even more reluctant to leave their nation again. A young Cherokee girl in school at Van Buren witnessed the return of troops whom she described as "a terrible looking crowd, bringing their wounded with them." Their arrival upset the routine of the town as schools, churches, and stores filled with wounded.[50]

If the physical losses were not enough, native participation in battles across their borders would ignite a firestorm of accusations and stereotypes. Cultural borders clashed, and old impressions reverberated in the popular press.

The battle of Pea Ridge prompted public debate over the supposed propensity of Indian troops to act in an uncivilized manner. When the Union victors collected their dead and wounded at Pea Ridge, they claimed to find evidence of "barbarity."[51] Witnesses attested that Iowa soldiers were scalped and their necks pierced with long knives. The Iowans' strongly held opinions that this was the work of Indians quickly fanned public indignation. The *New York Tribune* accused Albert Pike of leading an "Aboriginal Corps of Tomahawkers and Scalpers" at Pea Ridge. The behavior of Cherokees accused of scalping and mutilating the federal dead even came before the Joint Committee on the Conduct of the War. The Confederacy showed little inclination to stand behind its allies in putting down this talk of barbarism.[52] General Van Dorn declined to comment officially about any Indian participation in the battle. He did however respond to the Union's claim by stating that he hoped the reports were erroneous because of "the Indians who formed part of his forces having for many years been regarded as civilized people" and then ended the exchange with the counterclaim that alleged Germans had murdered Confederate prisoners in cold blood.[53] The Confederate command did not try to understand the cultural border that separated them from their allies and preferred to simply forget the accusations as quickly as possible.

Scalping appeared to appall white sensibilities. Army officers whose daily duties demanded inflicting death and suffering on the enemy purported to be outraged by this behavior. The fact that whites had long paid a bounty for Indian scalps during warfare, dating at least back to the French efforts against the Chickasaws, never entered the discussion.[54] Cultural borders loomed large. It is obvious to modern scholars that such pronouncements of barbarism are based in cultural norms. Native troops merely acted according to their own traditions. They were, however, aware of white officials' distaste for such activity and occasionally promised to desist. The Cherokee National Council sought to ward off accusations of cruelty and scalping with a plea to its members to conduct war on the basis of "humane principles." It should be noted, however, that native troops were not the only combatants practicing barbarism in the Civil War. Warfare in the trans-Mississippi West has been described as "war to the knife and the knife to the hilt." Numerous accounts of inhumane behavior, including scalping, characterize white men in the West. Most tales of Indian atrocities seem minor in comparison to the conduct of Jayhawkers and guerrillas such as Quantrill and Anderson.[55]

All non-white troops in the war encountered a chasm between them and the dominant white army in which they served. The charges of barbarism stemmed from the belief that Indians were uncivilized and inferior. Indian soldiers faced an incredible amount of racism from white officers. On the other hand, Indians also exhibited racism in their encounters with black troops.[56] Colonel Charles DeMorse unapologetically stated his firmly held opinion that "[t]he Indian is physiologically recognized as an inferior race." He added, "[N]o Indian is qualified by attainments for such duty as regulations of the army call for" because of the "well-known incapacity of that people to direct operations which require promptness and concentration of mind." DeMorse's attitude reflects the stereotype of the perpetually late, inherently lazy, dull-witted native person. Unfortunately, his views were probably not remarkable among white officers.[57] Many white officers had no intention of serving under native officers.[58] DeMorse couched his refusal to enter into such a situation in what he surely believed was a rational explanation: "It is an obvious trait of the Indian's character that those people are naturally indisposed, as well as unfitted, to lead and of their own impulses always prefer to be led and to repose upon the judgment and superior mental acuteness of the white man."[59] Stand Watie and many other native leaders surely would have disagreed.

Many white officers and enlisted men believed that innate inferiority rendered Indians poor soldiers. General William Steele represented the feelings of many white commanders of native troops when he described Indians as "wholly unreliable as troops of the line." The main complaint seemed to be that Indians did not follow orders and generally disregarded military procedure. Even their primary champion, Albert Pike, announced, "Indian troops are of course entirely undisciplined."[60] Not surprisingly, the issue of discipline caused the most friction between Indian troops and white officials, as even Indian officers were regarded as "indisposed to enforce discipline." One evaluation charged Indian troops with being "almost as destitute of every attribute of a soldier as if they were raw recruits." The same charges could be leveled at any green recruits in either army, and Indian troops never received extensive training to alter their concepts of proper military behavior.

Much of the antipathy toward Indian soldiers came from both sides' inability to cross cultural borders. There is no doubt that rank-and-file native troops rarely performed drill or fought as units in the manner of white and black soldiers.[61] However, there is no reason to assume that they would. These troops were poorly armed and thrown into regiments without military training. Despite considerable assimilation, the men from the Five Nations came from a much different background than the average Union or Confederate soldier. In their culture's historic past, glory and honor accrued to native leaders through quick, decisive raids that accomplished their objective and returned as many unscathed men as possible to their families. Thus it made little sense to Indians to sit in winter quarters with the knowledge that there likely would be no fighting until spring, or to line up and march across a field toward the enemy when nearby trees provided life-saving cover. Indian troops had signed up to defend their homes, not to build huts and wait out the winter without their families. Consequently, orders to assemble in camps had little effect except to frustrate white officers.[62] Another major complaint about Native commands focused on deficient paperwork. The military functioned on endless inspections, rosters, and reports, but it proved amazingly difficult to get such communication from the commands in Indian Territory. Indian officers ignored this duty for a variety of reasons that probably included the tedium of paperwork, illiteracy, lack of supplies, and a general disregard for the importance of records in a traditionally oral culture.[63] Not all white officers had negative impressions of their Indian soldiers. Albert Pike and Douglas Cooper, who had experience with native culture and allowed the men to fight as they wished, fared much better in their relations with the troops than outsiders.[64]

Indian troops left observers with definite impressions of a difference. Many whites commented on the unique whooping sounds made by Native troops in battle. Union officers at Neosho, Missouri, blamed the screaming and whooping of the Indians for rendering their horses nearly unmanageable. Wiley Britton, who often fought with Union Indian troops, recalled the war whoop that resonated through the woods when the Indian units got underway. Indian soldiers often added traditional warpaint to these characteristic noises. This traditional behavior was meant to both embolden the Indians and terrorize the enemy.[65] Britton noticed that whites were afraid of the Indian soldiers, but noted it was due to their strange appearance, not their behavior. He reported that Indian troops marching and camping in Arkansas did not molest any one in their homes. In fact, native soldiers were rarely charged with pillaging or similar activities.[66] Many whites would be surprised to learn that men they regarded as "savages" often behaved better than white soldiers.

The ill-fated excursion to Arkansas marked the last time native troops crossed their geographic borders to fight in a major Civil War battle. As the war dragged on, the fighting in Indian Territory devolved into raids, guerrilla-style engagements, and retributive actions. Essentially off the radar of the major combatants, Indians became mired in their own challenges brought on by stresses of war and the deep-seated disunity of several tribes.

The experience of war—not just combat, but an internal conflict within the larger national Civil War—challenged the very meaning and existence of the Five Nations. One idea of an autonomous people is that they control their identity and actions. They maintain the borders that define polity and culture. The 1860s stretched and broke the borders of the Five Nations, causing them to reinvent what it meant to be native in the nineteenth-century West.

Notes

1. Elias C. Boudinot to Stand Watie, Feb. 12, 1861, in *Cherokee Cavaliers: Forty years of Cherokee History as Told in the Correspondence of the Ridge-Watie-Boudinot Family*, eds. Edward Everett Dale and Gaston Litton (Norman: University of Oklahoma Press, 1939), 103.

2. The Texas secession convention appointed commissioners to the Choctaw, Cherokee, Chickasaw, Creek, and Seminole nations to "invite their prompt co-operation in the formation of a Southern Confederacy." US War Department, *The War of the Rebellion: A Compilation of the Official Records of the Union and Confederate Armies*, 127 vols., index, and atlas (Washington, D.C.: Government Printing Office, 1880–1901), ser. 4, 1: 322 [hereafter cited as *OR*; all references to series 1 unless otherwise noted].

3. James Harrison to Edward Clark, April 23, 1861, *OR*, ser. 4, 1: 322–25; David Hubbard to Andrew Moore, Jan. 3, 1861, reprinted in Annie Heloise Abel, *The American Indian as Slaveholder and Secessionist*, 1915 (reprint, Lincoln: University of Nebraska Press, 1992), 109–10; and L. P. Walker to President Davis, April 27, 1861, *OR*, ser. 4, 1: 248.

4. David A. Nichols, *Lincoln and the Indians: Civil War Policy and Politics* (Columbia: University of Missouri Press, 1978), 27; Edmund J. Danziger, *Indians and Bureaucrats: Administering the Reservation Policy During the Civil War* (Urbana: University of Illinois Press, 1974), 168; Elias Rector to John Ross, Feb. 14, 1861, frame 380, reel 100, M234, RG 75, National Archives; Abel, *American Indian as Slaveholder*, 83; and David Hubbard to John Ross and Ben McCulloch, June 12, 1861, *OR* 13: 497–98.

5. Henry Rector to John Ross, Jan. 29, 1861, *OR* 1: 683; Mark Bean et al. to John Ross, May 9, 1861, frames 397–98, J. R. Kannady to John Ross, May 15, 1861, frame 388; and John Ross to J. R. Kannady, May 17, 1861, frame 392, reel 100, M234, RG75, NA.

6. Cyrus Harris to John Ross, Jan. 5, 1861, *OR* 1: 691; and William Ross to John Ross, frame 374, reel 100, M234, RG75, NA.

7. T. Paul Wilson, "Delegates of the Five Civilized Tribes to the Confederate Congress," *Chronicles*

of Oklahoma 53 (Fall 1975): 353–66; Walter Lee Brown, *A Life of Albert Pike* (Fayetteville: University of Arkansas Press, 1997), 353–81; and Abel, *American Indian as Slaveholder*, 160–77.

8. Resolution of the General Council of the Choctaw Nation, Feb. 7, 1861, *OR* 1: 682. A small group of Choctaws did renounce the Confederacy and elect an opposition government in March 1864. See Abel, *The American Indian and the End of the Confederacy, 1863–1866* (1925; reprint, Lincoln: University of Nebraska Press, 1993), 18–19.

9. Harvey Chaplain, 17: 107, *Indian Pioneer Papers* [hereafter cited as *IPP*, all material from this collection is personal narrative], Western History Collection, University of Oklahoma, Norman [repository hereafter cited as WHC]; Jonathan Copeland, May 5, 1861, no. 276, box 10, reel 1, American Indian Correspondence, WHC; S. Orlando Lee to Commissioner William Dole, March 15, 1862, reprinted in Abel, *Indian as Slaveholder*, 75–79.

10. Chickasaw Resolution, *OR* 3: 585; *OR* 1: 648

11. Ibid.

12. *OR* 3: 593

13. *OR* 3: 625; Petition of officers to Jefferson Davis, June 6, 1863, and Tandy Walker to Davis, June 24, 1863, reel 77, M258, RG 190, NA; and *OR* 3: 614, 625.

14. For text of treaty see *OR*, ser. 4, 1: 426–43.

15. Carter Blue Clark, "Opothleyahola and the Creeks during the Civil War," in *Indian Leaders: Oklahoma's First Statesmen*, eds. H. Glenn Jordan and Thomas M. Holm (Oklahoma City: Oklahoma Historical Society, 1979), 50, 53; Charles Mix's report, *ARCIA 1865*, 328–30; and Abel, *American Indian as Slaveholder*, 244.

16. Morris Wardell, A *Political History of the Cherokee Nation, 1838–1907* (Norman: University of Oklahoma Press, 1938), 53.

17. Mary Jane Warde, *When the Wolf Came: The Civil War and the Indian Territory* (University of Arkansas Press, 2013), 19.

18. W. P. Adair James Bell to Stand Watie, Aug. 29, 1861, in Dale and Litton, *Cherokee Cavaliers*, 109.

19. Elias Boudinot to Stand Watie, Oct. 5, 1861, file 8, box 149, Cherokee Nation Papers, [collection hereafter cited as CNP, WHC].

20. James Bell to Stand Watie, Aug. 29, 1861, in Dale and Litton, *Cherokee Cavaliers*, 109.

21. Ibid.

22. *OR*, series 4, 1: 359–61.

23. Charles Lee Bahos, "John Ross: Unionist or Secessionist in 1861?" (M.A. thesis, University of Tulsa, 1968), 167; and Moulton, *John Ross*, 172.

24. *OR* 3: 675.

25. For text of treaty, see *OR*, ser. 4, 1: 426–43.

26. Clark, 50, 53; Charles Mix's report, *ARCIA 1865*, 328–30; and Abel, *American Indian as Slaveholder*, 244.

27. Opothleyahola and Ouktahnaserharjo to Abraham Lincoln, August 15, 1861, reprinted in Abel, *American Indian as Slaveholder*, 245–46, 248.

28. *OR* 8: 25.

29. *OR* 8: 5; and John Ross to Opothleyahola and other chiefs and headmen of the Creek Nation, Sept. 19, 1861, and Moty Kennard and Echo Harjo to John Ross, Oct. 18, 1861, in *The Papers of John Ross, 1840–1866*, 2 vols., ed. Gary Moulton (Norman: University of Oklahoma Press, 1985), vol. 2: 487–88, 496–97.

30. *OR* 8: 5–14; and Moty Kennard, Echo Harjo to Cooper, Oct. 31, 1861, Creek National Records, Oklahoma Historical Society, Oklahoma City [repository hereafter cited as OHS].

31. Chilly McIntosh and Daniel N. McIntosh were half-brothers and sons of Creek chief William McIntosh, the architect of Creek removal.

32. Douglas Hale, "Rehearsal for Civil War: The Texas Cavalry in the Indian Territory, 1861," *Chronicles of Oklahoma* 68 (1990): 235.

33. Robert Mayberry, "Texans and Defense of the Confederate Northwest, April 1861–April 1862: A Social and Military History" (Ph.D. diss., Texas Christian University, 1992), 215; and *OR* 8: 15.

34. *OR* 8: 6; and Pascofar to President Lincoln, March 10, 1864, frame 154, reel 803, M234, RG75, NA.

35. *OR* 8: 7; and W. Craig Gaines, *The Confederate Cherokees: John Drew's Regiment of Mounted Rifles* (Baton Rouge: Louisiana State University Press, 1989), 45–47. John Ross later pardoned these deserters, and many returned to Confederate service for a short time.

36. *OR*, 8: 8.

37. Hale, *Rehearsal for Civil War*, 244; Cooper estimated five hundred dead, whereas Col. D. N. McIntosh counted only twenty-seven bodies.

38. *OR* 8: 11, 13.

39. *OR* 8: 23.

40. The weather was so bad that one of Cooper's men froze to death, a light loss compared to the sufferings of the ill-supplied Creeks.

41. *OR* 8: 24, 31.

42. Hale, *Rehearsal for Civil War*, 243. Drew's regiment had been reorganized shortly after their desertion. Chief Ross spoke to the men to rally them to the Confederate cause. He turned against Opothleyahola, blaming him for the problems in the Cherokee Nation, in order to retain Cherokee unity. *ARCIA 1865*, 355–57.

43. Brown, *A Life of Albert Pike* (Fayetteville: University of Arkansas Press, 1997), 375.

44. John Ross to Albert Pike, Feb. 25, 1862, Moulton, *Papers of Chief John Ross*, 2: 509; and *OR* 8: 287.

45. James McPherson, ed., *The Atlas of the Civil War* (New York: MacMillan, 1994), 48–49.

46. Hess and Shea claim that Indians were not involved in the attack on the Union artillery in Earl J. Hess and William L. Shea, *Pea Ridge, Civil War Campaign in the West* (Chapel Hill: University of North Carolina Press, 1992), 101. However, this seems to contradict the report of Union Colonel Peter J. Osterhaus, who noted "a great many Indians" among the cavalry who overwhelmed him. *OR* 8: 217. See also Wiley Britton, *The Civil War on the Border* (New York: Putnam, 1890), 247.

47. Ibid., 249.

48. Britton, Wiley, *The Union Indian Brigade in the Civil War* (Ottowa: Kansas Heritage Press, 1922), 55.

49. Jay Monaghan, *Civil War on the Western Border, 1854–1865* (Lincoln: University of Nebraska Press, 1955), 246.

50. Ella Coody Robinson, 107: 466, *IPP*, OHS.

51. The alleged "barbarities" took place away from the center of the fighting, in an area where officers exercised little control during the battle. Hess and Shea, *Pea Ridge*, 357, n. 32.

52. Hale, *Rehearsal for Civil War*, 228–265; Britton, *Civil War on the Border*, 275; Abel, *American Indian in the Civil War* 31: 33; and *OR* 8: 194, 207, 288, 820.

53. *OR* 8: 195.

54. Arrell M. Gibson, *The Chickasaws* (Norman: University of Oklahoma, 1971), 43.

55. *OR* 3: 625; *OR* 13: 826; and William C. Davis, *The Cause Lost: Myths and Realities of the Confederacy* (Lawrence: University of Kansas Press, 1996), 90–91.

56. Watie's men slaughtered members of the 1st Kansas Colored Infantry at Prairie Springs. Davis, 71, 85–86.

57. *OR* 34: 699–700.

58. *OR* 22: 35; Captain B. W. Marston report, December 1864, Ashcraft, "Confederate Indian Troop Conditions," 446; and *OR* 34: 699.

59. *OR* 34: 701.

60. *OR* 13: 819.

61. Some white men tried to join Indian regiments in order to avoid discipline. See *OR* 22: 1104.

62. Captain B. W. Marston report, Dec. 1864, Ashcraft, "Confederate Indian Troop Conditions," 445.

63. *OR* 22: 28–29.

64. Pike was the Indian soldiers' greatest supporter, and Choctaws and Chickasaws petitioned Richmond to give D. H. Cooper command of Indian Territory.

65. *OR* 13: 93; Wiley Britton, *Memoirs of the Rebellion on the Border, 1863* (1882; reprint, Lincoln: University of Nebraska Press, 1993), 201; and Mary Jane Warde, *George Washington Grayson and the Creek Nation, 1843–1920* (Norman: University of Oklahoma Press, 1999), 93–94.

66. Britton, *Union Indian Brigade*, 188.

Chapter 9

Struggles for Place and Space

Kickapoo Traces from the Midwest to Mexico*

Kristin Hoganson

In 1982, some members of the Kickapoo nation gathered in a Congressional committee room in Washington, D.C., to make a case for US citizenship. This band had lived for many years next to the northern side of the International Bridge connecting Eagle Pass, Texas, to Mexico. After their camp had been bulldozed and turned into a parking lot, the Eagle Pass Kickapoos rebuilt their homes *under* the bridge, literally on the US-Mexican border. Life in this liminal zone was marked by daily tribulations. Commuters tossed their garbage down upon the cane and cardboard houses. The area was too small to perform important ceremonies. Given their uncertain citizenship status—some having been born in Mexico, some in the United States, with no documentation in many cases—the Eagle Pass Kickapoos did not qualify for US public health services and could not enroll their children in public schools.[1]

Things had only gotten worse. Local officials had recently forced them to relocate to city land. As Wipecuinacudita (also known as Jose Naco Jiminez) put it: "We have no outhouses and sometimes no water. We have many mosquitoes . . . My biggest fear is that we could be thrown out at any moment." In introducing the citizenship bill, Texas congressman Abraham Kazan played up this theme of dispossession, claiming, "They just want a place they can call home." Kickapoo representative Makateonenodua (also known as Raul Garza) underscored this desire in his plea for "a permanent land base where we can worship in peace and privacy."[2] This logic seemed compelling to the

* Many thanks to Howard Allen, Brian DeLay, Dave Edmunds, Andy Fisher, Amy Greenberg, Peter Guardino, José Angel Hernández, Joseph Herring, Fred Hoxie, Bill Kemp, Greg Koos, Jenny Marie Johnson, Andrae Marak, Karen Marrero, George F. Perkins, Cynthia Radding, Andrés Reséndez, Michael J. Sherfy, Andy Siebert, Tracy Smith, and Pamela Voekel for their advice and help. Note: All nineteenth-century newspapers cited were accessed through the Nineteenth-Century U.S. Newspapers database, Gale Publishers, unless noted otherwise.

committee and later to Congress and the president. In 1983, the Eagle Pass Kickapoos obtained US citizenship and tribal recognition.[3]

But the Kickapoos wanted more than a home. Those who spoke at the hearing also made it clear that they wanted the right to cross the border—into the United States and back to Mexico again.[4] They did not want to be localized any more than they wanted to be dislocated. They wanted what their people had been struggling for since their first encounters with US colonialism: rights not only to place but also to free movement through space.

It may seem that the greatest costs of US colonialism for the Kickapoos stemmed from being forcibly uprooted and stripped of land. But significant though these changed relations to place were, they were not the only upshots of colonialism with geographic dimensions. Colonialism also changed the Kickapoos' relations to space by constricting their ability to go wherever they pleased whenever they chose to do so. Although the Kickapoos strenuously opposed the coercive nature of the nineteenth-century removals that had dislodged them from their lands in Illinois, they did not object to all forms of mobility. To the contrary, they considered the ability to move freely through space to be a fundamental aspect of being Kickapoo. The very name *Kickapoo* alludes to their freedom of movement, for it translates roughly as "he moves about, standing now here, now there."[5]

The Kickapoos had a long history of mobility. In the early seventeenth century, most Kickapoos were located in what is now the Detroit and Windsor, Ontario, area. As the Iroquois strove to increase their power in the fur trade, the Kickapoos moved to southwestern Michigan, southern Wisconsin, and northern Indiana and Illinois.[6] By 1712, some had migrated south to central Illinois.[7]

In addition to moving vast distances over time, the Kickapoos were seasonally mobile. From spring to fall, they gathered in villages to plant. In the winter, they traveled to hunt—including from Illinois to Iowa and Missouri. Given that the Kickapoos did not all live in close proximity, they traveled to sustain community ties.[8] They also traveled to trade and for diplomacy and warfare. Documents from the early nineteenth century mention Kickapoos in Tennessee, Mississippi, Canada, the Floridas, Northern Michigan, Oklahoma, Texas, Arkansas, and Minnesota.[9] Yet just as the Kickapoos' ability to claim place came under increasing attack in the nineteenth century, so did their ability to move freely through space. For the Kickapoos, the nineteenth century was not only a period of forced mobility and land loss but also a terrible time of sedentarization.

The more that land became privatized, the harder it was for the Kickapoos to move through it, because of fencing, hedgerows, and hostility to trespassers.[10] As the inrush of white settlers depleted game, it became more difficult

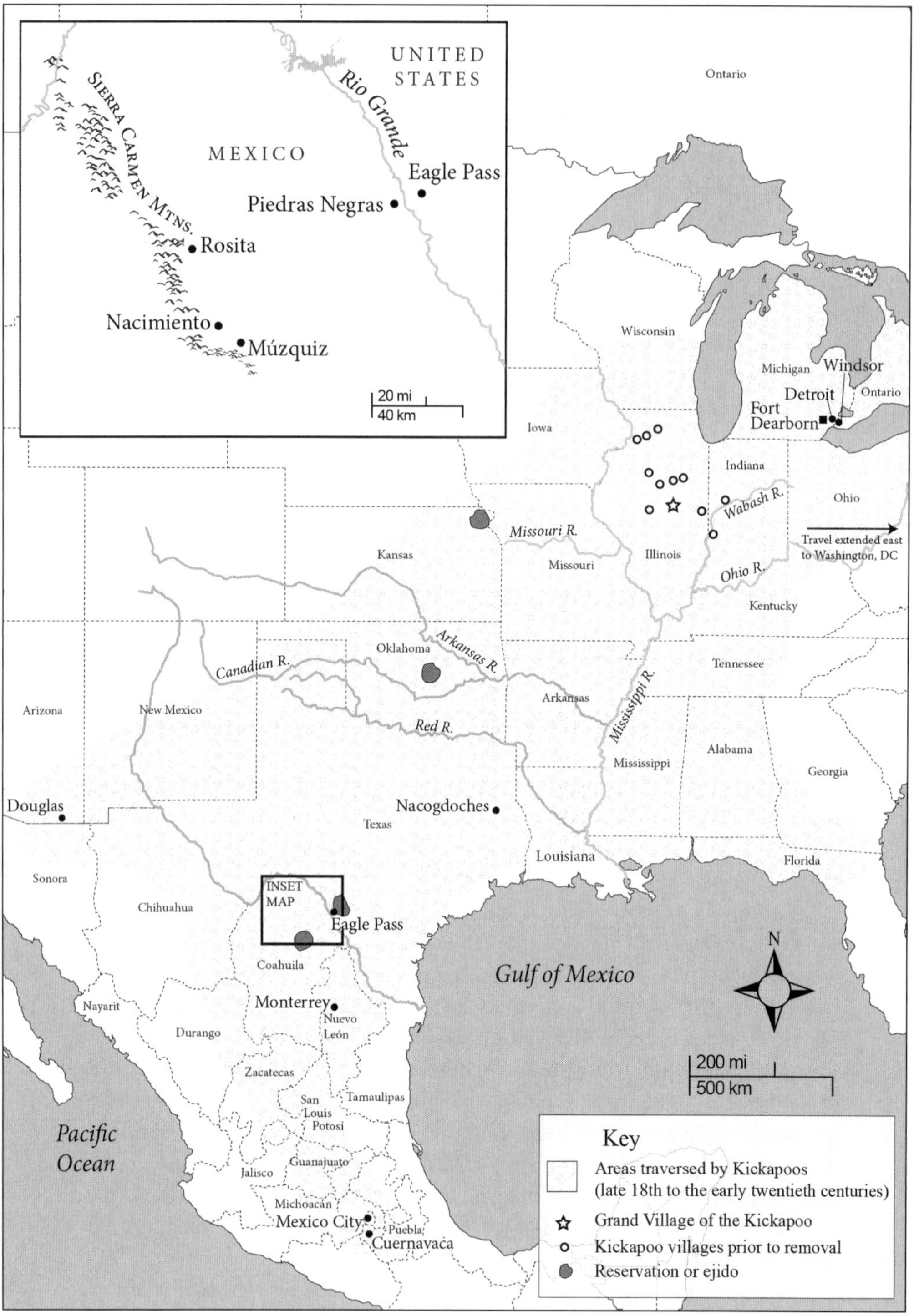

Documented Kickapoo mobility in the long nineteenth century. An approximation of Kickapoo geographies based on textual records. Map by Tracy Ellen Smith and Ted Avila.

for the Kickapoos to live off the land. Their changing visibility in ever-whiter ethnoscapes also had implications for the Kickapoos' relations to space. The scrutiny to which off-reservation Kickapoos were subjected can be gleaned from newspaper reports, which mentioned crowds that gathered to watch them "in open-mouthed wonder."[11] This kind of visibility made it more difficult to travel without altercations or assault.[12]

Indian policy also played a major role in sedentarizing the Kickapoos. Even as they uprooted the Kickapoos, one of the main stated goals of US agents was to turn them into settled farmers. As the head of the Kickapoo Indian School in Kansas told his students: "Farm your own land and as much of the other fellow's as you can get, do your own work, stay at home."[13] To this end, Indian agents located the Kickapoos on reservations in Kansas and Oklahoma, from which they could not leave without passes, and typically without an accompanying agent.[14] They forced children to attend boarding schools, sometimes using reservation police to "seize and convey" them to their classes.[15] When smallpox hit the Oklahoma Kickapoos, a company of armed soldiers enforced the quarantine placed upon them.[16] The most extreme form of sedentarization was imprisonment, a practice alien to the Kickapoos prior to colonization.[17]

For a people who called migratory birds "Indian birds" because of their travels to distant reaches, to be penned in meant to lose an important part of what it meant to be Kickapoo.[18] In contrast to the pioneers, the Kickapoos did not consider locality to be a hard-won achievement. Instead, they saw it as a form of colonial oppression. The Kickapoos experienced localization as a matter of surveillance, control, material deprivation, attenuated social ties, and an existential threat to their existence as a people. So how did the Kickapoos resist? Through ongoing mobility, most notably to Mexico.

The Kickapoos who headed south in the nineteenth century followed earlier footsteps. In 1763, a Kickapoo band accepted a Spanish invitation to build a village on the Missouri River.[19] Building on that earlier relationship, the Spanish persuaded some Kickapoos to move to Texas in 1805, as a bulwark against Americans in Louisiana and Kiowas and Comanches on the plains. Another band of Kickapoos relocated to the Nacogdoches area (then part of the Lone Star Republic) in 1838. Yet another group crossed the Rio Grande in 1850, in company with a band of Seminoles and their slaves.[20]

Like the Spanish before them, the Mexican government welcomed the newcomers as allies against the Comanches, Kiowas, and Apaches who had been devastating their northern settlements. When the Kickapoos sent delegates to Mexico City in the 1850s to ask for land, they received grants in Coahuila. This fostered further settlement, for in 1862, about six hundred Kickapoos went from Kansas to Mexico.[21]

Wherever the destination, the choice to move came with considerable costs. First, it meant greater distances from other Kickapoos. The pain of diaspora can be glimpsed in an appeal to the Office of Indian Affairs, which lamented how the tribe had been "broken up and scattered."[22] Second, rather than ending the violence that the Kickapoos had known in Illinois, relocation produced new conflicts, including with other native nations, who had reason to see groups such as the Kickapoos as encroachers who exacerbated the threat posed by Anglo pioneers.[23] White settlers were no more welcoming. Texas Rangers and Confederate Texans launched particularly brutal attacks against the Kickapoos.[24]

In addition to stretching group ties and embroiling the Kickapoos in new cycles of violence, moving distanced the Kickapoos from places that were meaningful to them, and it took them farther from the ecosystems that had sustained their ancestors in the Great Lakes area. As one group of Kickapoos that decided not to relocate said of northern Mexico: "There was no grass and the land was no good, and the weather was too hot."[25] The decision to move also had implications for place claims. Although the Kickapoos who chose to move did so in part to secure such claims, the more they moved, the more tenuous their claims became. "All were intruders," said an 1841 history of Texas in reference to the Kickapoos and other native newcomers, "who took advantage of the weakness of the authorities, and the confusion which reigned in Mexico, to 'squat' upon a fertile soil."[26]

Given the costs of moving, why did some Kickapoos choose to resettle far from their kinspeople, in the dry reaches of northern Mexico? Some of the things that might seem to have made Mexico unattractive—such as its aridity and history of intergroup violence—actually added to its appeal. The terrain might have been forbidding, but that meant a thinner population. The region might have been scarred by violence, but for that reason the Mexicans welcomed the Kickapoos, hoping to use them as buffers like the Spanish had. In sum, the wildness of northern Mexico offered the Kickapoos a chance to live their lives without so much meddling from US Indian agents. Their success in this respect can be seen in the assertions by US anthropologists in the 1950s that the best place to learn about Algonquian customs from the Great Lakes region was Mexico, because the Kickapoos there "comprise without doubt the best preserved island of Woodland culture extant."[27]

In addition to seeing Mexico as offering more control over their own places, the Kickapoos who went to Mexico had grounds to see their move as offering them a more open relation to space. The Kickapoos did not need passes to leave their communal lands in Mexico. They could hunt more widely in the surrounding hills. And they could raid Texan ranches with less danger of pursuit.

Texans living along the border complained that the Kickapoos frequently crossed the Rio Grande to "pounce upon the frontier." They would then drive their booty of horses and cattle back to their refuge in Mexico.[28] According to an 1871 report, their raids were so frequent "that stock raisers in many instances have been compelled to abandon their ranches and drive their cattle into the interior for safety."[29] What particularly enraged the Texan ranchers was the Kickapoos' impunity. There was much truth to their critics' livid claims that the Kickapoos "care little for boundary lines."[30] But when it came to raiding, the Kickapoos cared a lot about boundary lines, because the international border protected them from retaliation. Rather than restraining them, the border opened up new spatial possibilities—until the US cavalry went after them, that is.

Sending in the cavalry was a last-ditch option that followed a number of other attempts to control the Mexican Kickapoos. In 1868, the Committee on Indian Affairs commissioned Stephen S. Brown to meet with the Kickapoos living near Santa Rosa, in hopes of persuading them to "consent to their removal to some portion of the United States." Upon arrival, he found that many of the Kickapoos were out "on the war path." Despite this inauspicious start, Brown managed to meet with some Kickapoo men. In the course of these meetings, he discovered that the Kickapoos had divided up their camps, to avoid being "gobbled up" by invading US forces or extradited to the United States by the Mexicans. These camps, Brown reported, were so isolated that their locality was "unknown." Brown castigated the Mexicans for having "neither the material means the physical nor the moral power to control—to civilize—to support and keep these people in subjection." Instead of tracking them down in their wilderness haunts, the Mexicans seemed to regard the Kickapoos with favor. To Brown's horror, when the warriors returned "flushed with triumph" from their raid, the townspeople of Múzquiz greeted them with "the ringing of Bells." (Such local support may explain why Texas vigilante groups did not go after the Kickapoos.) The gap between Brown's desire for subjection and the Kickapoos' desire to avoid being gobbled up did not augur well for the talks. When pressed to go "back to your own lands," one old man told Brown that "god is my Captain, the world my camping ground, and I am at liberty to go where I choose."[31]

Brown returned to the United States. The Kickapoos continued to raid. The US government did not give up. In 1870, it sent John D. Miles, the agent for the Kansas Kickapoos, to Mexico in hopes of persuading the Mexican Kickapoos to "return to their reservation in Kansas, and again become wards of our government."[32] Miles failed to persuade the men he met to "return" to a place where many had never lived.[33]

When appeals to the Mexican Minister of Foreign Affairs proved no more effective than appeals to the Kickapoos, the US military took action in 1873.[34] Guided by Seminole Negro Indian Scouts, a cavalry company led by Colonel Ranald S. Mackenzie marched 80 miles into Coahuila in search of

Kickapoos, Lipans, Potawottamies, and Mescalero Apaches. After traveling all night, they reached the Kickapoo settlement at dawn.[35] They burned it to the ground and then proceeded about a quarter of a mile to a Lipan village, which they also destroyed. Mackenzie reported killing nineteen people and wounding two more, but these were just the casualties his men were able to count before beating it hastily back to Texas. They brought with them their prisoners: a Lipan man and forty-one women and children, mostly Kickapoos.[36] Using these captives as hostages to force their family members to move to the United States, the US government relocated about five hundred Mexican Kickapoos to Oklahoma (after some back and forth with the Mexican government over whether the Kickapoos' belongings could enter duty-free).[37] The resettled Kickapoos planted corn and vegetables. But their agent seems to have questioned their intention to stay, for when some asked to go out on the plains, he said no.[38]

The Mackenzie raid showed that even an international border did not protect the Kickapoos' place and space claims from the US government. True, when Mackenzie went after the Mexican Kickapoos, he feared that he might face the gibbet for his cross-border incursion, having been issued only oral orders to do whatever necessary to "clean up this situation." Knowing he was on dicey diplomatic ground, Mackenzie had to exercise restraint. It was a quick in and out operation. No US forces followed the Kickapoos who had avoided capture when they fled the area to the Santa Rosa Mountains and later to Monterey, about 500 miles into the interior of Mexico.[39] There were no subsequent incursions, despite the urgings of Texan ranchers who suffered further depredations.

Yet Mexican sovereignty had its limits. Rather than follow an 1862 extradition treaty, the United States had taken matters into its own hands.[40] Mackenzie's commanding officer summed up the matter by saying: "There can not be any valid boundary line when we pursue Indians who murder our people and carry away our property."[41] Mexico protested the raid, but it did not become a full-blown diplomatic incident, in part because Mexican troops had their own history of border crossings in pursuit of Indians.[42] When the raiding into the United States continued, US Secretary of State William M. Evarts reaffirmed his nation's right to send forces into Mexico in pursuit of marauders: "Undoubtedly it would be preferable to enter Mexican territory for the purpose indicated with the consent or with the acquiescence of the government of that republic. If, however, these should be refused and the outrages persisted in, this government may deem itself warranted in punishing the wrong-doers wherever they may be found."[43]

Nine years after the Mackenzie raid, the United States and Mexico signed a reciprocal agreement authorizing troops from both nations to cross into the other to pursue Indians. This treaty lasted until Geronimo's surrender in

1886.[44] In authorizing cross-border raids against Indians, and Indians only, the two governments agreed that place claims meant different things to Indians than to other people. They also revealed that the Kickapoos were not the only ones who associated security with an ability to move unfettered through space.

Following the Mackenzie raid, the Mexican government worked harder to monitor the remaining Kickapoos so as to avoid a repeat incident. Yet cross-border raiding continued, with the blame falling on Kickapoos even in cases when they were not at fault.[45] The Mexican government allowed the United States to send a special commissioner to try to remove the Kickapoos who were not captured by Mackenzie.[46] When it became clear that the commissioner would not be able to entice the Kickapoos to Oklahoma, Mexican officials prodded them to move farther from the border. They moved about two hundred Kickapoos to Durango, several hundred miles to the southwest.[47] Yet by 1876, there were enough Kickapoos back in Santa Rosa to merit another visit from a US Indian agent. This one, too, failed to persuade the Kickapoos to move to the United States, but the visit did prompt about sixty families to move to Chihuahua, farther from the threat of US forces.[48]

Fearful that the United States would again go after the Santa Rosa Kickapoos, the Mexican government intervened. It moved one group of Kickapoos to Mexico City, where they subsisted for a while as street beggars, and from there to Querétaro. It moved others to Guerrero, in hopes that the German colony there would transform them. It set others to work on the railroad line between Mexico City and Cuernavaca. Resisters went to prison.[49] The US military did not intervene because it did not have to; the Mexican government having done the dirty work for them.

Just as the Mexican Kickapoos could not escape the long arm of the US government, if only by proxy, neither could they escape the reach of US border crossers. By the 1880s, the Santa Rosa Kickapoos had to compete for game with wealthy US hunters who went down to the Sierra del Carmen Mountains to bag trophies.[50] Soon the competition for resources came to involve land. During the regime of Porfirio Díaz, the Mexican government gave collectively owned Indian lands to railroad builders and hacienda owners. Among the expropriated were the Kickapoos, who lost about 60,000 acres in Nacimiento to some Texas cattlemen in 1883.[51] When the Kickapoos refused to vacate the property, the Mexican government removed them in hopes of assuring investors "that property rights of strangers will meet with full protection."[52]

Things got worse in 1898, when three US investors purchased the first chunk of what eventually became a 1.2 million–acre hacienda, Piedra Blanca. The Kickapoos charged them with "usurpation," to no avail. Although the Kickapoos had been living in Mexico for years, the US *hacendados* who ended up with parcels of their land benefitted from closer ties to the Mexican political elite and a greater ability to negotiate the Mexican court system. In pressing their claims, the investors dismissed the Mexican Kickapoos as Oklahomans, the implication being they had no rights to place in Mexico. The Kickapoos cut down the ranchers' pecan trees in protest, but they could not recover the disputed land titles.[53] The ranchers proceeded to string up fences that impaired the Kickapoos' ability to hunt.[54] By 1903, papers in Mexico City were reporting on "Kickapoo Indian Chieftain," Wapichi Cucha, seen wandering the streets of the capital, as he sought a government grant of land.[55]

In addition to reducing the Kickapoos' access to land and game, US border crossers threatened another resource fundamental to the Kickapoos' survival: their water. In 1919, the American Smelting and Refining Company (ASARCO) purchased a coal operation in Rosita. A corporate history of the 1940s praised ASARCO for providing water to its workers and their families, and not just any water either, but water "treated in a modern treatment plant, which includes chlorination, filtration, and sedimentation." What this account did not say was that the company had polluted the Kickapoos' water supply, and making matters worse, it had in a time of drought further drained their depleted water table.[56] Already suffering from restricted hunting possibilities, the Kickapoos had to contend with withered fields and decimated herds.[57]

Rather than being a refuge, by the turn of the twentieth century, Mexico had become like the United States, with its forced removals and land grabs. Instead of standing up for the Kickapoos, Mexican officials collaborated with US opportunists, including those who sought Kickapoo holdings *north* of the border. In the spring of 1907, a partnership of US deed seekers—referred to in the subsequent hearings as "the Chapman, Grimes and Conine people" but known more widely as the "Shawnee wolves"—traveled to Coahuila to defraud some visiting Kickapoos of their increasingly valuable lands in Oklahoma. The conspirators paid the Múzquiz police to have all the leading members of the tribe arrested and thrown into jail. Having intimidated their intended victims, they then took "a large number of Indians by force and under guard of policemen" to the house of the "jefe politico of that district." There they urged the Kickapoos to sell their lands in the United States. The captive men declined.

Undeterred, the conspirators faked the papers, putting down the names of men who were not in the area at the time. They also claimed to have a deed executed at the *jefe politico*'s house by a Kickapoo woman named Pah-na-tho, who had died more than five years earlier. Another deed bore the name of Paw-kaw-kah, "a known imbecile . . . to whom no member of the tribe could talk nor make himself understood." Minors too supposedly signed their names to deeds. From Múzquiz, the schemers headed north, to the border town of Eagle Pass. After supplying the Kickapoos there with liberal amounts of whiskey and mescal, they "herded" them into a wagon yard where they kept them interred until they signed away their Oklahoma land. Resisters were arrested and sent across the border to Múzquiz to work on the streets in chains.[58]

Fortunately for the defrauded Kickapoos—or at least it seemed at the time—their agent from Oklahoma, Martin Bentley, took the conspirators to court. But Bentley had his own ambitions involving Kickapoo land. Bentley's scheme was to buy deeds from the Kickapoos near Shawnee, Oklahoma, and resell them for much higher amounts. He planned to pocket most of the difference, avoiding detection by using the proceeds to buy cheaper land in Mexico. After one of his victims, Thapathethea, complained that she had never meant to sell her land, investigators found Bentley guilty of fraud. But Congress ignored their findings, leaving Bentley free to machinate.[59]

Promising his followers that in Mexico they would find "room to roam once more limitless prairie," Bentley persuaded over one hundred Oklahoma Kickapoos to go from Coahuila to Sonora with him in the latter part of 1907. Cashing in some of the titles that had been signed over to him in trust, Bentley bought an abandoned ranch. It was a disappointment, a tract of "mountain breaks and crags, through which is the channel of an intermittent stream, at times so violent with the water rush from the mountains as to tear out the surface of the only little valley they have." If this were not bad enough, the title to all this was of doubtful legitimacy. Left in straitened circumstances, the Sonoran Kickapoos were taken in by Yaqui Indians, who had long been fighting their own cross-border struggles against exploitation and dispossession.[60] Upon realizing that Mexico was not the answer to their dreams, some of Bentley's former followers sued him for defrauding them of their land in Oklahoma.

The brief filed on their behalf by their new agent suggested that Bentley's motives had been more sinister than his followers had realized. As long as the Kickapoos lived in the United States, they could not alienate their land without consent of the US government. But if they became "resident citizens of some foreign country," such consent was no longer necessary. From Bentley's perspective, expatriation was not so much the pathway to self-determination as the pathway to expropriation. The court sided with the plaintiffs. When their allotments were restored, some of the emigrants returned straightaway to their former homes.[61] Others did not. In 1912, the Secretary of the Interior authorized the First National Bank of Douglas, Arizona, to cut checks payable to fifty-two Mexican Kickapoo Indians, ranging in age from about seventy-one (Ah che che), to a ten-year-old youth (Thy ka toke).[62] Some of these so-called Mexican Kickapoos circled for years between Sonora, Coahuila, and Oklahoma, preferring the freedom of movement, however hard, to fixed residence in one place.[63] Even as cross-border incursions and Mexican policies infringed on the place and space claims of the Coahuila Kickapoos, the Sonoran Kickapoos continued to seek a way to avoid the power of imperial states.

Recognizing that the history of the Kickapoos stretched from Ontario to Guerrero in the nineteenth century reminds us that for the Kickapoos of that time, foreign relations implied far more than resisting US colonialism; it also meant dealing with different native nations, the Spanish and British empires, Mexico, the Lone Star Republic, the Confederacy, various states in the US and Mexican federal systems, and local officials in places like Coahuila and Eagle Pass. In addition to negotiating relations with a number of other groups as boundaries and spheres of influence shifted around them, the Kickapoos resorted to strategic mobility (including across the US-Mexican border) to try to elude the expanding power of the United States during the removal era. Histories of this period have often emphasized the violence of forced relocation and the accompanying loss of place, but the Kickapoos also experienced removal as a localization process that took a great personal toll and posed an existential threat to their culture and survival as a people. Hence some Kickapoos' decision to go to Mexico, which seemed for a while more likely to offer both secure place claims and the ability to move freely through space.

It was this desire for free movement, as much as the desire for a secure home, that explains the Eagle Pass Kickapoos' claims to US citizenship in the 1980s. For most of the twentieth century, the Mexican Kickapoos had crossed the border at Eagle Pass with notarized photocopies of a pass written for them at Fort Dearborn, Michigan, on September 28, 1832. This document, signed by a US Army major, certified that the Kickapoos were "to be protected by all persons from any injury whatever, as they are under the protection of the U.S. and any person so violating shall be punished accordingly."[64] Even when border crossing became more tightly enforced in the early twentieth century, this document enabled the Coahuila Kickapoos to visit friends and relatives in the United States and, increasingly, to work.

As their water dried up, their hunting options shrank, and their land began to suffer from overgrazing, the Coahuila Kickapoos sought work as migrant laborers in the United States. Starting in the drought years of the 1940s, they sought seasonal agricultural work in Texas, Arizona, Oklahoma, Colorado, Idaho, Montana, Nebraska, Wisconsin, Michigan, Illinois, Ohio, California, and New York. With the end of the Mexican *bracero* (guest worker) program in 1964, the demand for Kickapoo workers increased.[65] Unlike most Mexican farm workers, the Kickapoos were still allowed to enter the United States from the Eagle Pass area thanks to their notarized documents, allowing them to move around the Detroit area without injury.

However, as border enforcement grew tighter, the photocopies no longer sufficed, even among Eagle Pass agents. By the 1970s, the Coahuila Kickapoos had to obtain "parole papers" from the immigration officers at Eagle Pass. These papers identified the bearers as: "Parolee, Kickapoo Indian, pending clarification of status by Congress."[66] Although the agents insisted that "it's not a criminal thing," the affected Kickapoos objected to the language of "parolee," understanding this all too keenly as the status of being outside a penitentiary on condition. Officials considered them to be US citizens when in the United States and Mexican citizens when in Mexico, pending a determination of their status by Congress.[67]

Taking advantage of their ability to cross the border, a number of Mexican Kickapoos continued to travel to the United States. Despite the local histories that proclaimed the Kickapoos long gone from the places where their ancestors had once lived, they labored as Mexicans in the cucumber and tomato fields of the Midwest.[68] In a reversal of longstanding seasonal patterns, summer mobility enabled settled winters in their Nacimiento village. Yet in the 1980s, all this was imperiled by even tighter border controls, which made it ever more difficult for Chicapoos (a term some Kickapoos adopted in jest to mean Chicano and Kickapoo mixed together) to circulate between the United States and Mexico.[69] The Eagle Pass Kickapoos wanted dual citizenship so they could go back and forth across the border. Like their ancestors before them, they sought both place (a home) and space (the ability to move freely, including across borders). The great irony of the hearings—one that went unremarked at the time—was that one of the Kickapoos' witnesses cited the Mackenzie raid on behalf of their claims. The violent incursion that had quashed the aspirations of Mexican Kickapoos in the nineteenth century had become proof in the twentieth that the border-dwelling Eagle Pass Kickapoos were indeed US citizens and should be able to cross into the United States if they pleased.[70]

Notes

1. *Confirming the Citizenship Status of the Texas Band of Kickapoo Indians*, Hearings before the Committee on Interior and Insular Affairs, House of Representatives, 97th Congress, on H.R. 4496, Washington, D.C.: US Government Printing Office, 1983; on location of homes, 7, 96; on garbage, 98; on ceremonies, 12; on citizenship status and services, 68, 74. On cane and cardboard, see Donald D. Stull, *Kiikaapoa: The Kansas Kickapoo* (Horton, Kan.: Kickapoo Tribal Press, 1984), 83.

2. Confirming the Citizenship Status of the Texas Band of Kickapoo Indians, living conditions, 74; Kazan's claim, 12; peace and privacy, 13.

3. Richard A. Thompson, *Crossing the Border with the 4th Cavalry: Mackenzie's Raid into Mexico—1873* (Waco: Texian Press, 1986), 77. The legislation created a fourth tribe of Kickapoo, the Kickapoo Traditional Tribe of Texas, the same as the Mexican Kickapoo, just under US jurisdiction. Mary Christopher Nunley, "Foreword," in Bill Wright and E. John Gesick Jr., *The Texas Kickapoo: Keepers of Tradition* (El Paso: Texas Western Press, 1996), xiii–xvi, xiv; Stull, *Kiikaapoa*, 85.

4. *Confirming the Citizenship Status of the Texas Band of Kickapoo Indians*, 13.

5. George R. Nielsen, *The Kickapoo People* (Phoenix: Indian Tribal Series, 1975), 2.

6. Father Julien Binneteau, letter, in *Travel and Explorations of the Jesuit Missionaries in New France, 1610–1791, Vol. 65, Lower Canada, Mississippi Valley, 1696–1702*, ed. Reuben G. Thwaites, (Cleveland: The Burrows Brothers, 1900), 65–77, 73. Susan Sleeper-Smith, *Indian Women and French Men: Rethinking Cultural Encounter in the Western Great Lakes* (Amherst: University of Massachusetts Press, 2001), 15.

7. Nielsen, *The Kickapoo People*, 12. On Kickapoo migrations from Wisconsin to Illinois and Indiana by 1700, see David Edmunds, "A History of the Kickapoo Indians in Illinois from 1750–1834" (M.A. thesis, Illinois State University, 1966).

8. Edmunds, "A History of the Kickapoo Indians in Illinois from 1750–1834," 50. On Lewis and Clark's encounters with Kickapoo in Missouri, see Meriwether Lewis, *History of the Expedition under the Command of Captains Lewis and Clarke*, vol. 1 (New York: Allerton Book Co., 1922). Nielsen, *The Kickapoo People*, 10–11; on visits between the Pottawattomie and Kickapoos, see "An Indian Pow-wow," *Inter Ocean* (Chicago), August 30, 1874.

9. On trading, see "Kickapoo Braves," *The Atchison Daily Globe* (Atchison, Kan.) July 11, 1887; on finding salt, see Louise Green Hoad, *Kickapoo Indian Trails* (Caldwell, Idaho: Caxton Printers, 1946), 86. *An Affecting Narrative of the Captivity and Sufferings of Mrs. Mary Smith* (Williamsburgh, Mass.: Ephraim Whitman, 1818) [Early American Imprints], 3, 7. On Fort Towson, see Alexander Cummings to the Adjutant General, Fort Towson, Jan. 18, 1826, 184–85; on Texas, see Benjamin W. Edwards to George Gray, Natchitoches, May 28, 1827, 482–83; on Arkansas, see Peter B. Porter to Governor George Izard, June 11, 1828, 697, all in *The Territorial Papers of the United States, Vol. 20, The Territory of Arkansas, 1825–1829*, ed. Clarence Edward Carter (Washington, D.C.: Government Printing Office, 1954). On Michilimackinac, see Stull, Kiikaapoa, 44. On other examples of Native American mobility in this period, see Helen Hornbeck Tanner, ed., *Atlas of Great Lakes Indian History* (Norman: University of Oklahoma Press, 1987), 12. On Florida, see Grant Foreman, *Indian Removal: The Emigration of the Five Civilized Tribes of Indians* (Norman: University of Oklahoma Press, 1932), 348.

10. Felipe A. Latorre and Dolores L. Latorre, *The Mexican Kickapoo Indians* (Austin: University of Texas Press, 1976), 52–54.

11. "Will Migrate to Mexico," *The Dallas Morning News*, 12 May 1904, accessed via America's Historical Newspapers database, Readex publishers.

12. On 1862 and 1865 attacks by Texans, for example, see Shelley Bowen Hatfield, *Chasing Shadows: Indians Along the United States-Mexico Border, 1876–1911* (Albuquerque: University of New Mexico Press, 1998), 18.

13. Edwin Minor, "Annual Report Kickapoo Indian School," 1914, Superintendents' Annual Narrative and Statistical Reports from Field Jurisdictions of the Bureau of Indian Affairs, 1907–1938, roll 70, National Archives Microfilm Publications, Washington, 1975.

14. On pass laws, see Louis S. Warren, *Buffalo Bill's America: William Cody and the Wild West Show* (New York: Alfred A. Knopf, 2005), 361; "Lost——One Hundred and Fifty Kickapoos," *The Atchison Daily Globe* (Atchison, Kan.), Jan. 2, 1897; "Street Fair Notes," *The Emporia Weekly Gazette* (Emporia, Kan.), Oct. 5, 1899.

15. J. A. Scott to Dan Kan-ke-ka and Jno Mas-que-qua, Policemen, Oct. 20 1892, in folder 6: Arrest Warrant, box 6, Kickapoo, Milo Custer Collection, McLean County Historical Society.

16. "All Have Smallpox," *The Milwaukee Journal*, Jan. 19, 1899.

17. Brig. Gen. Henry Atkinson to Edmund P. Gaines, St. Louis, Oct. 7, 1826, in *The Territorial Papers of the United States, Vol. 20, The Territory of Arkansas, 1825–1829*, ed. Clarence Edwin Carter (Washington, D.C.: Government Printing Office, 1954), 294. On jail, see John W. Spencer, *Reminiscences of Pioneer Life in the Mississippi Valley* (Davenport, Iowa: Griggs, Watson & Day, 1872), 31; "Kickapoos Shot," *Daily Evening Bulletin* (San Francisco), July 11, 1887, accessed via America's Historical Newspapers database, Readex publishers; "To Recover Lands," *The Dallas Morning News*, Nov. 30, 1907.

18. Latorre and Latorre, *The Mexican Kickapoo Indians*, 348.

19. Nielsen, *The Kickapoo People*, 21, 33.

20. Nielsen, *The Kickapoo People*, 41, 50–51. On settlement in Texas, see Gary Clayton Anderson, *The Conquest of Texas: Ethnic Cleansing in the Promised Land, 1820–1875* (Norman: University of Oklahoma Press, 2005), 164–69; "Mexican Intelligence," *The Boston Daily Atlas*, June 4, 1852.

21. On land in Coahuila, see Hatfield, *Chasing Shadows*, 18. On trips to Mexico City, see *Reports of the Committee of Investigation Sent in 1873 by the Mexican Government to the Frontier of Texas*, trans-

lated from the official edition made in Mexico (New York: Baker and Godwin, 1875), 409; "Mexican Intelligence," *The Boston Daily Atlas*, June 4, 1852; José Guadalupe Ovalle Castillo and Ana Bella Pérez Castro, *Kikapúes: Los Que Andan Por la Tierra: El Proceso de Proletarización y la Migración Laboral del Grupo de Coahuila* (México: Consejo Nacional para la Cultura y las Artes, 1999), 22–23.

22. Na she nan et al. to Col. Cumming, Nov. 21, 1855, Letters Received by the Office of Indian Affairs, 1824–81, roll 371, Kickapoo Agency, 1855–1876, National Archives.

23. On Comanches, "Affairs in Texas," *North American and United States Gazette* (Philadelphia), Jan. 17, 1852. On Osages, "Treaty with the Kickapoo Indians," *St. Louis Enquirer*, Dec. 8, 1819. On Wichitas and Caddos, see Anderson, *The Conquest of Texas*, 6. On eastern Indians as pioneers in the trans-Mississippi west, see John P. Bowes, *Exiles and Pioneers: Eastern Indians in the Trans-Mississippi West* (New York: Cambridge University Press, 2007), 4.

24. Anderson, *The Conquest of Texas*, 8, 169, 174, 342.

25. "Kickapoo Indians Not Satisfied," *The Dallas Morning News*, Feb. 10, 1899.

26. William Kennedy, *Texas: The Rise, Progress, and Prospects of the Republic of Texas*, vol. 1 (London: R. Hastings, 1841), 349–50.

27. Robert E. Ritzenthaler and Frederick A. Peterson, *The Mexican Kickapoo Indians* (Milwaukee, Wis.: Milwaukee Public Museum, 1956), 11.

28. On pouncing and booty, see "Indian Atrocities in Texas," *Little Rock Daily Gazette*, May 28, 1866. On horse and cattle theft, see "The Kickapoos and Mexican Annexation," *Daily Evening Bulletin* (San Francisco), June 17, 1873, accessed via America's Historical Newspapers database, Readex publishers; "Washington Letter," *The Galveston Daily News*, June 23, 1874; "Ghastly Trophies," *St. Louis Globe-Democrat*, Sept. 24, 1877.

29. On the Kickapoo as agriculturalists, see "In General," *Boston Daily Advertiser*, April 9, 1864; "Mexicans and Indians on the Rio Grande," *The Weekly Arizona Miner*, Nov. 25, 1871.

30. "Will there be War with Mexico?" *The Cleveland Morning Daily Herald*, May 27, 1873. On Anglo robbers dressing like Indians and claiming to be Kickapoos, see Anderson, *The Conquest of Texas*, 302, 307.

31. On removal, see E. Degener to S. S. Brown, April 9, 1868; on the meeting, see S. S. Brown to Brevet Major General J. J. Reynolds, Sept. 1, 1868; on absence and return, isolated camps, world as camping ground, and Mexican incapacity, see S. S. Brown, "Explanatory Letter A"; on Kickapoo as foreign to Mexico, see S. S. Brown to His Excellency Victoriano Cepada, June 7, 1868; on thousands of Indians seeking refuge, see S. B. B., "Statement C," Sept. 1, 1868. All in Letters Received by the Office of the Adjutant General (Main Series) 1861–1870, roll 642, National Archives Microfilm Publications, Microcopy no. 619, Washington, D.C.: National Archives, 1965.

32. Testimony of Lt. Major A. McD. McCook, Brownsville, Texas, July 30, 1872, in *United States Commission to Texas, Vol. 9, Proceedings July 4–Oct. 3, 1872, Depositions 1–364*, record group 76, International Claims Commissions, US and Mexico Claims Commissions, National Archives, College Park, Maryland, 32; and A. M. Gibson, *The Kickapoos: Lords of the Middle Border* (Norman: University of Oklahoma Press, 1963), 228.

33. Buntin, "The Mexican Kickapoos," 698. Wah-pah-ka quotation and offer to return without an escort in John D. Miles, report of July 7, 1871, in Letters Received by the Office of the Adjutant General (Main Series), 1861–1870, roll 799, National Archives Microfilm Publications, Washington, D.C., 1965.

34. On the appeal to the Minister, see Thomas H. Nelson to Secretary of State Hamilton Fish, Aug. 30, 1871, Letters Received by the Office of the Adjutant General (Main Series), 1861–1870, roll 799, National Archives Microfilm Publications, Washington, D.C., 1965.

35. "The Texas Raids," *Daily Rocky Mountain News* (Denver), May 30, 1873.

36. P. Sheridan to General W. W. Belknap, May 22, 1873, Letters Received by the Office of the Adjutant General (Main Series), 1861–1870, roll 799, National Archives Microfilm Publications, Washington, D.C., 1965; [Mackenzie] to Col. Williams, May 22, 1873, US Army Continental Commands, Department of Texas, box 18, 1873, record group 393, National Archives; and "Will there be War with Mexico?" *The Cleveland Morning Daily Herald*, May 27, 1873. Two accounts that lionize Mackenzie are R. G. Carter, *On the Border with Mackenzie or Winning West Texas from the Comanches* (1935; reprint New York: Antiquarian Press, 1961), 422–66; and Richard A. Thompson, *Crossing the Border with the 4th Cavalry: Mackenzie's Raid into Mexico—1873* (Waco: Texian Press, 1986).

37. "The Mexican Kickapoos," *Atchison Daily Globe*, Sept. 30, 1873.

38. Buntin, "The Mexican Kickapoos," 704–6.

39. "H. M. Atkinson . . . ," *The Galveston Daily News*, Nov. 3, 1874. On Mackenzie's orders and fears, see Carter, *On the Border with Mackenzie*, 422, 431.

40. On the treaty, see *Mexican Border Troubles: Message of the President of the United States in Answer to the Resolution of the House of Representatives of Nov. 1, 1877* (Washington, D.C.: Government Printing Office, 1877), 19.

41. Lieutenant-General P. Sheridan to Secretary of War W. W. Belknap, May 28, 1873, Letters Received by the Office of the Adjutant General (Main Series), 1861–1870, roll 799, National Archives Microfilm Publications, Washington, D.C., 1965.

42. Hatfield, *Chasing Shadows*, 19; [Mackenzie] to Mr. Schuhardt [illeg.], May 22, 1873, US Army Continental Commands, Department of Texas, box 18, 1873, record group 393, National Archives.

43. William M. Evarts to Mr. Foster, March 31, 1877, in *Mexican Border Troubles*, 4.

44. Hatfield, *Chasing Shadows*, 53.

45. On unjustified accusations, see *Reports of the Committee of Investigation Sent in 1873 by the Mexican Government to the Frontier of Texas*, translated from the official edition made in Mexico (New York: Baker and Godwin, 1875), 414.

46. "H. M. Atkinson . . . ," *The Galveston Daily News*, Nov. 3, 1874.

47. On returning under Mesque and Tapicua, see "Texas Press," *The Galveston Daily News*, March 12, 1874; "Interesting Letter from Durango," *The Galveston Daily News*, June 3, 1874.

48. On the agent and President Lerdo de Tejada's promises to remove the Kickapoo to the interior, see "Our San Antonio Letters," *The Galveston Daily News*, March 8, 1876. On returning under Mesque and Tapicua, see "Texas Press," *The Galveston Daily News*, March 12, 1874; and "Interesting Letter from Durango," *The Galveston Daily News*, June 3, 1874. On Chihuahua, see *Mexican Border Troubles*, 241; and "The Indians and Texas," *Bangor Daily Whig & Courier*, May 25, 1869.

49. On relocation, see Castillo and Castro, *Kikapúes*, 28.

50. "A Hunter's Paradise," *St. Louis Globe-Democrat*, Dec. 31, 1887.

51. Hatfield, *Chasing Shadows*, 5. On the 60,000 acres in 1883, see "Texans Claim Mexican Land," *The Dallas Morning News*, Feb. 25, 1909.

52. "Grazing and Farming Lands on the Mexican Frontier," *The Galveston Daily News*, Feb. 27, 1883.

53. John Mason Hart, *Empire and Revolution: The Americans in Mexico since the Civil War* (Berkeley: University of California Press, 2002), 244–16.

54. Nunley, "The Mexican Kickapoo Indians," 45.

55. "Kickapoo Indian Chieftain," *Mexican Herald*, Sept. 11, 1903, accessed through World Newspaper Archive, NewsBank database.

56. Latorre and Latorre, *The Mexican Kickapoo Indians*, 90. On the contamination, see Castillo and Castro, *Kikapúes*, xii.

57. Isaac F. Marcosson, *Metal Magic: The Story of the American Smelting and Refining Company* (New York: Farrar, Straus and Co., 1949), 215, 219–20, 223, 280.

58. H. M. Teller, Chairman of the Committee on Indian Affairs, "Affairs of Mexican Kicking Kickapoo Indians," Senate Report no. 5, 60th Congress, 1st session, 1–12; and Gibson, *The Kickapoos*, 340.

59. "Kickapoos Here," *Mexican Herald*, Jan. 25, 1901, accessed through NewsBank World Newspaper Archive. On Thapathethea, see Gibson, *The Kickapoos*, 329.

60. On conditions in Sonora, see John Embry to S. W. Brosiuis, Agent Indian Rights Association, July 18, 1912, folder 4; on Bentley's acquisition of land titles in 1905 and 1906, see "Abstract of Testimony, Bentley and the Seven," in folder 3, both in box 1, Records Concerning Affairs of the Mexican Kickapoo, 1895–1914, record group 75, Records of the Bureau of Indian Affairs, National Archives. On a Kickapoo residing in Sonora, see "Extradition Application," *The Dallas Morning News*, Oct. 28, 1910; and "Yaquis Prove they are Worthy Foemen," *The Dallas Morning News*, May 30, 1915. On the Yaquis, see Claudia B. Haake, *The State, Removal and Indigenous Peoples in the United States and Mexico, 1620–2000* (New York: Routledge, 2007), 95–96, 121–34; and Eric V. Meeks, *Border Citizens: The Making of Indians, Mexicans, and Anglos in Arizona* (Austin: University of Texas Press), 2, 28–31, 72.

61. "Discuss Move to Mexico," *The Dallas Morning News*, April 24, 1904; Frank A. Thackery, Plaintiff vs. R. C. Conine, L .C. Grimes, M. J. Bentley, and W. W. Ives, Defendants, Territory of Oklahoma,

Pottawatomie County, Dec. 15, 1906, folder 3, box 1, Records Concerning the Affairs of the Mexican Kickapoo.

62. John A. Buntin to The First National Bank, Sept. 11, 1912, folder 2, box 1, Finance Division, Records Concerning the Affairs of the Mexican Kickapoo, 1895–1914, record group 75, National Archives.

63. Gibson, *The Kickapoos*, 359.

64. Ritzenthaler and Peterson, *The Mexican Kickapoo Indians*, 21.

65. Latorre and Latorre, *The Mexican Kickapoo Indians*, 90–91.

66. *Confirming the Citizenship Status of the Texas Band of Kickapoo Indians*, 8.

67. Ibid.; "The Kickapoos Who Have Citizenship in two Countries," *Wassaja* 3 (September 1975): 5, in the Princeton University Rare Books Collection.

68. Latorre and Latorre, *The Mexican Kickapoo Indians*, 90–93.

69. On "Chicapoos," see "Testimony of Ekoneskaka (Aurelio Valdez Garcia) as reported by Jim Salvator, in "An Oral History," *Parnassus: Poetry in Review* 17 (1992), 170–83, 173, 174–75.

70. *Confirming the Citizenship Status of the Texas Band of Kickapoo Indians*, 24.

Chapter 10

Finding Transnationalism in the American Interior

A Shared Past: Washoe Indians and the Dawes Act of 1887

Matthew Stephen Makley

About 60 miles south of Reno, Nevada, highway 395 rises to a summit identified by a road sign as "Simee Dimeh." The name comes from a Washoe Indian phrase meaning "double water," and the area it signifies is known as Double Springs. Many Washoes today use the lands adjacent to the summit for their fall pinion pine nut harvests. Some remember a different name for the place: "Tzimél Dimé," which translates as "whisker water." This name refers to a grisly encounter between newcomers and Washoes in the nineteenth century. Foreigners from nations around the world rushed through Washoe lands to get to California gold, and the water of the natural springs became contested space. A skirmish near the springs led to Washoe individuals killing a Euro-American who had a long beard. They cut off his head and placed it on a rock above the springs as a warning.[1]

Non-Washoe passersby likely have no idea that the words on the sign are Washoe and that the thousands of acres of pinion pine forests surrounding it form a cultural center for people who have been in the area thousands of years. Most do not know that one of the region's largest tourist attractions, Lake Tahoe, derives its name from the Washoe phrase *da ow a ga*, meaning "edge of the lake." Nor do many consumers of the protein-rich pinion pine nut realize its deep historical significance to Washoes and many Western Native communities.

The sign on Simee Dimeh pass signifies a shared past. It is not the only signifier. Every night in the towns of Minden and Gardnerville, Nevada, slightly north of Simee Dimeh, a siren marks the six o'clock hour. Many Washoes in the area remember a time when the siren did more than signal the hour: it sounded a warning for Washoes to leave. During World War I the Douglas County Board of Commissioners passed Ordinance No. 6, proclaiming all Indians had to be out of town daily by 6:30 p.m. Those in violation of the ordinance faced misdemeanor charges, which could include a twenty-five-dollar fine, imprisonment, or both. The origins of the siren and its link to the curfew are unclear, but many Washoes in the twentieth century believed the nightly wail served to remind them it was time to leave. The sign and the siren represent elements of a past largely overlooked—one not taught regularly in schools, one not presented thoroughly in history texts dealing with the region.[2]

The history of the American West is a complicated tangle of diverse peoples, experiences, customs, and beliefs. Long before European colonists reached the region, civilizations rose and fell. Indigenous communities fought wars and forged peace; they built cities, dams, irrigation works, and technologically sophisticated astronomical calendars. The arrival of Europeans in the sixteenth century added to the already knotty calculus of human relationships. The history of nations that emerged from these complex encounters needs to include Native pasts.[3]

Over one hundred years ago, the American historian Frederick Jackson Turner established a historical model that shaped the American understanding of western conquest. His thesis described Native people as significant only in the sense that they helped to define Americaness. Americans redefined themselves through continual interaction with "savage" Indians. The westward advance of the frontier meant "a steady movement away from the influence of Europe, a steady growth of independence." Here, on the frontier, Americans gained their "uniqueness."[4]

By the late twentieth century, a growing number of western historians and Native scholars began challenging Turner's thesis. They realized that Indigenous peoples' experiences were distinctly different from Turner's perception and that Indians helped shape the West just as much as Turner's frontiersmen did. Alfonso Ortiz (San Juan Tewa) described one community's frontier as another's "backyard."[5]

To start telling a transnational history, the story must begin with the Native inhabitants of the West. They cannot be confined to the first chapters of regional history texts or treated as a stone-age preface for a more significant national American history. Most historians of the American West are aware of this, and the field is moving quickly to address this historical blind spot. But that process must ultimately include histories of *all* communities who lived and shaped their lands for thousands of years before Americans would deem their ancient lands part of the "West."[6]

Many small, non-equestrian western tribes had colonial experiences distinctly different from larger, well-established equestrian peoples. Small Sierra communities lived in relative isolation from European, Mexican, and early American colonization. By the time Americans reached their lands in

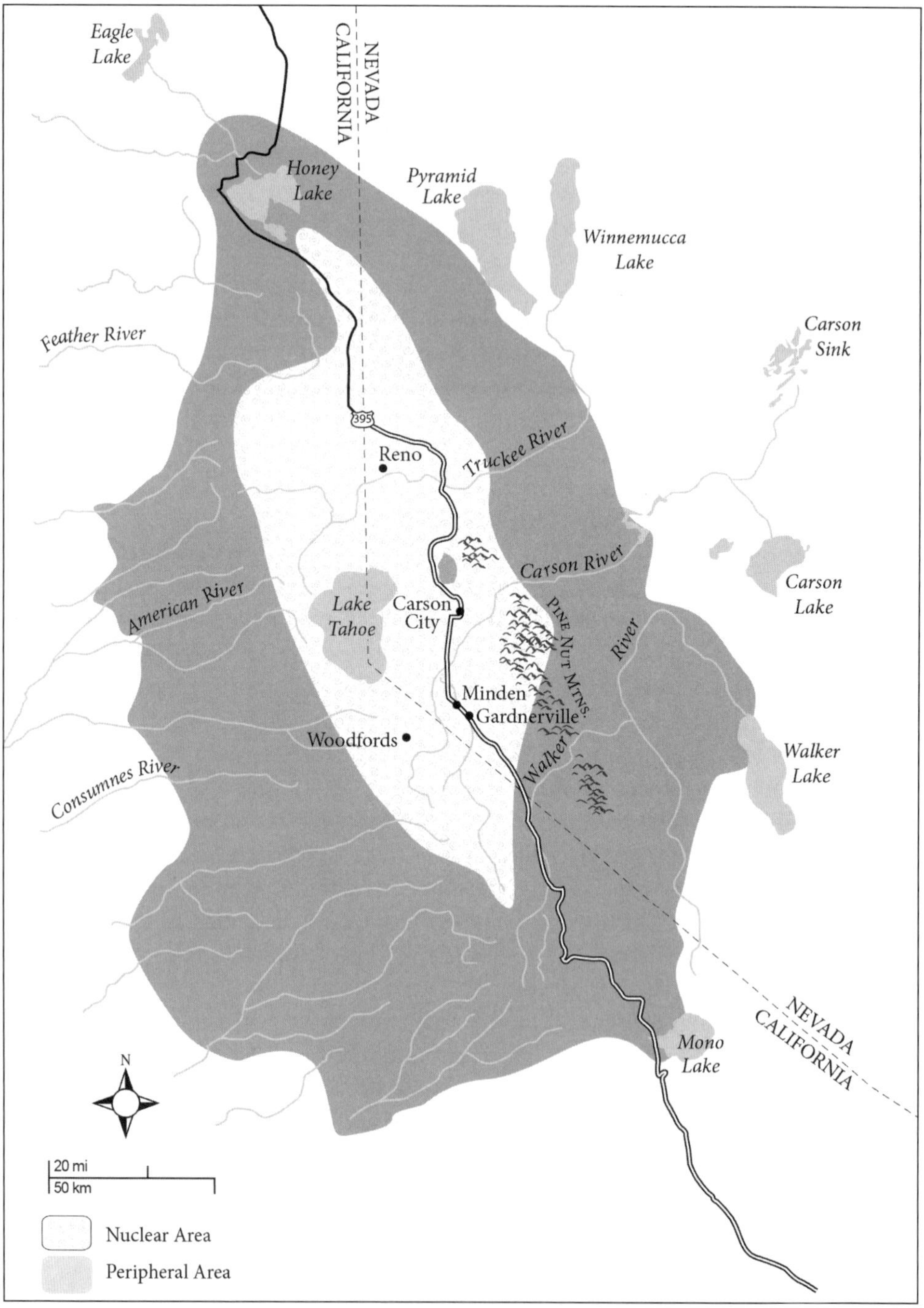

The traditional Washoe homelands. Today, Simee Dimeh or "double water" pass sits just south of Gardnerville, Nevada, on highway 395. Washoe families own thousands of acres of pinion groves in the adjacent Pine Nut Mountains. Notice also Lake Tahoe at the center of Washoe nuclear territory. Map by Tracy Ellen Smith and Ted Avila.

the 1850s, mechanisms of colonialism were fully in place. America had been entering into treaty negotiations with Indians regularly since the Revolutionary War. Even if the treaties operated from a belief in American hegemony, the young United States at least recognized on paper some level of sovereignty among Native people. But by the 1850s, the United States believed they had rendered Indian societies fully "legible and hence more understandable." Small western peoples "in the way" of the American colonial march were, by this time, pushed aside, ignored, dispossessed, and, in the case of some like the Washoes, identified as nearing extinction. Larger, more "threatening" tribes continued to earn American attention; in many of those cases, American officials invoked the treaty system, giving them land. The small "harmless" communities were most often left landless.[7]

In the chapter that follows, *transnational* refers to a history that is not rooted in the narrative of one conquering nation or one group of people. A reader might wonder how the western Great Basin can be considered "transnational," or how the period under consideration can be anything other than the story of one nation: the United States. In keeping with a central premise of this collection, I argue that any history of relations between a colonizing nation and Native groups is, at its root, transnational. The points of intersection and interaction between colliding peoples, in this case the United States and western Indigenous peoples, are the places, as Andrae Marak suggests, "where cultural negotiations, cultural cooperation and sharing, and the social construction of identities and difference" occurred. These negotiations are best understood when they are grounded in an understanding of the distinct cultural practices and worldviews of the respective participants. It is important to acknowledge that the process of negotiation continues to the present day. While Washoes initially had very little power to shape their existence, over the past century they have established a presence in regional politics and economic development. Although it is circumscribed, Washoe sovereignty today reflects the priorities and practices of a distinct people, just as their efforts in the late 1800s did.

A case study of the Dawes Severalty Act (1887), also called the Allotment Act, provides an opportunity to demonstrate the unique way Washoes used the act to acquire their culturally significant pine nut lands. The act is one of the most significant in American Indian history. The American legislators and progressive-minded lobbyists who pushed for the act believed it would be a major step toward Americanizing Indigenous people, by carving up reservation lands into distinct farming parcels for Indians. A byproduct of the act would be the opening up of "surplus" lands for American "settlement." This byproduct resulted in the loss of over 150 million acres of Native lands.

The history of Allotment has been told in many places. However, when viewed through a transnational lens, the Washoe use of the act contradicts much of what historians formerly thought about it. This chapter will join the work of others, like Elizabeth James-Stern and Emily Greenwald, who have reinterpreted the Dawes Act and the role of Native communities in shaping its implementation. A primary thrust of Greenwald's work, *Reconfiguring the Reservation: The Nez Perces, Jicarilla Apaches, and the Dawes Act*, pivots on the idea that both American federal administrators and Native participants shaped the actual process as well as the final outcome of allotting. The creation of surveyed pieces of land clearly reflected an American desire to promote land privatization and the ethic of individuality. The land *selections* made by Nez Perces and Apaches often reflected cultural values grounded in their particular community's priorities. Told exclusively from the American or Nez Perce or Apache perspective, the history, and our understanding of it, changes considerably, just as weaving the perspectives together alters our perception.[8]

The Washoe case is distinct because they did not own reservation lands for allotting. Under a little-studied provision, Article 4 of the act, landless communities could apply to receive allotments. Federal legislators hoped landless communities would acquire farmlands to help encourage their transition into the American capitalist economy. Instead, Washoes claimed non-irrigable pinion pine nut stands.

In telling the history of the Washoe and their use of the Dawes Act, the historical point of view shifts from the idea that Native people passively accepted the act and all it entailed. Washoe people did suffer terribly in their confrontations with the Americans. Their homeland and way of life were destroyed; but through it, they protected and maintained an important part of their ancestral lands. Studying how they did not only brings to light their unique experience but also sheds light on the present. It reminds residents of the Double Springs area, Minden, Gardnerville, and the American West that they are a constituent part of a much longer human experience. It also reveals how a transnational perspective can lead to new interpretations of pivotal historical eras, events, and policies.

Prior to the arrival of Euro-Americans, Washoes used a wide swath of land, stretching from Susanville, California, in the north to Sonora Pass, California, in the south. The Sierra provided a fluid western boundary, as did the pine nut range in the east. Across this land, families cycled annually, using the Lake Tahoe area for homes in the snowless seasons while maintaining sites in the fertile river valleys east of the Sierra in winter. Extended kinship groups, made up of several families, formed regional groups. The southern Washoe, or Hangalelti, occupied the canyons, brush lands, and valleys surrounding the west fork of what is today called the Carson River. The central Washoe, Pawalti, made homes near the east fork of the Carson, today the Carson Valley; northerners, Welmelti, occupied lands in Washoe Valley up to Susanville, California.[9]

A worldview developed over thousands of years layered the landscape with meaning. The ever-present, universal force of *wegeléyu*, translated as "power," animated the region. The land, animals, and humans maintained various amounts of wegeléyu. Some places, people, and animals held extraordinary power. The places came to be considered sacred and demanded special attention from humans. Failure to respect and minister to these places could bring about dire consequences for the area and people living there. One such area sits on the eastern shore of Tahoe; it is De-ek Wadapush, "Rock Standing Grey," today "Cave Rock." Cave Rock is a center of power that shamans have ministered to for hundreds of years.

Dreams were the primary vehicle for the acquisition of power, and they came unbidden. Once touched by wegeléyu, a person had to seek the mentorship of a shaman, or the power could sicken and kill the neophyte. Wegeléyu was a neutral force, neither good nor bad. Some used their power for good and became shamans or doctors. Those who used power maliciously earned the designation of "witch." Washoe tradition is rich with stories of power. One tells of a witch who cast a spell over a large distance, killing many people. A scarred swath of land is pointed out to this day as the path the spell traveled.[10]

Snowless months brought members of the regional groups together on the shores of their ancestral lake: Lake Tahoe. Washoes have long described the lake as the center of their lands. Once they reached their homes on the lake's shore, individuals "blessed the water and themselves because they had come to a sacred place. Da ow [Lake Tahoe] was the giver of life; it fed fish, animals, and humans."[11]

In the summer, from their homes at Tahoe, families could use the high Sierra. Some made treks to acorn lands, where they traded with California communities in the western Sierra. And they could fish the countless mountain streams, rivers, and lakes. Washoe fishers, both male and female, used nets woven from plant fibers supported by willow frames to trap fish in rivers and streams. They also employed weirs, dams, and diversion ponds, and used spears and poles in deeper bodies of water. Custom dictated that fish could not be taken wantonly or excessively. During spring runs, fishers protected female fish while removing those that were parasitic.[12]

Women used the summer and fall seasons to collect foods that grew in higher elevations. Girls began training early in life in order to gain command of the eastern Sierra flora. By adulthood, many women had encyclopedic knowledge that allowed them to tend and harvest up to 250 edible and medicinal plants. Part of a girl's training included lessons in conservation and plant management.[13]

Hunters, mostly male, acquired and exercised a similarly vast knowledge. They monitored animal populations regularly and hunted year round. But the high hunting days arrived in the fall, when animals would be fat from a summer of grazing. Fall also signified the time for a gathering of families in the pine nut hills for the first pine nut festival. Pine nut ceremonies likely took place in different regions of the Pine Nut Mountains, but elders in the twentieth century remembered an annual large celebration, held near Simee Dimeh, that brought together people from across Washoe country. The ceremony lasted for up to four days and included game playing, gambling, and other light-hearted activities. But each night, ceremonial dancing and prayers were performed from dusk until dawn to give thanks for the sustenance. On the final day of the ceremony, an elder or spiritual leader offered a prayer before families set to work harvesting the nuts.[14]

A harbinger of how things were to change came to Washoe country in the last week of May 1827. A small party of American fur trappers, led by Jedediah Smith, was fighting their way through a Sierra storm. Washoes who encountered the party likely referred to them as *da ba ah* ("dangerous men") and *mushege* ("wild due to madness"). A small group tried to chase the foreigners away. Poised upon a hill above the American's camp, Washoes sent large boulders hurling down. When that did not work, the Washoes disappeared. The next day, May 28, 1827, Smith and his men encountered two Washoe women. Upon seeing the dab ba ah, the women began wielding their harvesting sticks as weapons. Smith described them as looking like mothers trying to "scare away some beast that would devour her child." Smith's words provide an eerie foreshadowing: the nation Smith represented would devour Washoe lands, plants, and animals, rendering the pre-contact Washoe lifestyle impossible.[15]

By 1844, Americans had become increasingly interested in western lands owned by Mexico. Specifically, California with its ecological diversity and Pacific access to eastern markets captured American attention. In that year, the federal government sent John C. Frémont on a reconnaissance mission that led him through Northern Paiute and Washoe lands. His journal of the expedition represents the first extensive American description of Washoe people. Upon his arrival, individuals extended handfuls of pinion pine nuts to the travel-weary and hungry Americans. Frémont described the nuts as delicious when roasted and appreciated their contribution to his depleted food store. By the end of his stay in the eastern Sierra, Frémont was convinced that Washoes had never before encountered light-skinned foreigners. He described their ignorance of firearms and colonial desires.[16]

Five years after Frémont's appearance, thousands of people passed through Washoe lands on their way to the gold fields in California. But it would be the discovery of the Comstock Lode, in what became Virginia City, Nevada, in 1858 that doomed the Washoe way of life.

Washoes reeled in the wake of two of the most significant mineral rushes the world has known. The son of a mine superintendent on the Comstock Lode recalled: "All of California rang with the call . . . It was a universal summons! A call to all creeds, to all manner and condition of men! A call as peremptory as the summons of a bugle! 'To Washoe!' it ordered. 'To Washoe, charge!'" The people who had populated the eastern Sierra lands for thousands of years now had their name appropriated to signify lands that included one of the richest silver discoveries ever unearthed. Environmental destruction along with innumerable and well-armed settlers forced them to the peripheries of their once vast territory.[17]

In 1862, an agent for the federal government described the devastation. He noted that American axes had decimated ancient forests, and whites were killing the once vast herds of deer, antelope, and mountain sheep. Another contemporary observer described what he saw: "Myriads of swarthy, bearded, dust-covered men [piercing] into the grim old mountains [cutting] murderous holes [in the earth] and cut[ting] out their (the mountains') vital arteries." Mechanized mining tools carried out the "stamping and crushing" of Washoe lands and resources, while the newcomers held "fiendish revel amid the chaos of destruction."[18]

By 1866, one federal official deemed the Washoe people near the brink of extinction. In a letter dated September 10, the Superintendent for Indian Affairs in Nevada, Hubbard G. Parker, informed superiors in Washington, D.C., that no reservations would be needed for Washoe people due to their "rapidly diminishing numbers." Federal records for the years between 1866 and 1887, the year the Dawes Act was passed, make for grim reading. Disease, dislocation, and death held sway. But the records also contain kernels of information that reveal Washoe determination.[19]

Washoe individuals, like many Native people in the American West, demonstrated great ingenuity as they adapted to American capitalism. Some began working for resorts at Lake Tahoe as hunting or fishing guides. Others took to selling fish, game, and pine nuts. Women began marketing their intricately crafted basketry. A vigorous demand for Washoe curio baskets quickly developed. The most famous of the Washoe weavers, Louisa Keyser, "Datsolalee," earned the patronage of a storeowner, allowing her to spend all her days pursuing her craft.[20]

By the end of the nineteenth century, Washoes had managed to reach a precarious balance. From small communities, families reconstructed their seasonal cycle to fit the new colonial world. Many worked close to the shores of Tahoe as hired hands or domestics during the summer and returned to the eastern valleys in fall and winter to work on American ranches and farms.

From these centers, Washoes initiated the difficult process of attempting to recover ancestral lands.

Meanwhile, the federal government had plans of its own for Western Indian communities. Tired of the costly wars on the plains and sensing an easier, perhaps more cost-effective way of consolidating Indian peoples, federal officials turned their full attention to assimilation. The idea of Americanizing Indian people had been circulating in American intellectual currency since the earliest days of the republic. Thomas Jefferson, in a letter to William Henry Harrison dated 1802, had suggested drawing Natives to the American agricultural way of life. He hoped that once Indian families had run into debt buying their tools, they would be willing to lop off lands in order to meet their financial obligations.[21]

The vigorous agenda of those seeking Indian assimilation reveals both the interests of a land-hungry government and the belief of altruistic easterners that Americanizing and Christianizing Indian people was the only hope for their survival. Whatever the intentions, the policies crafted during this time stripped Natives of their land.

The Dawes Act served as the nucleus for the assimilative-minded federal policy. The act promised to create individually held properties out of large, communally owned reservations. The creation of private parcels of land would theoretically break the long-standing economic and social bases of Native communities. Male heads of households received a quarter section of land, 160 acres; single individuals, including women, received 80 acres, while orphans under age eighteen could claim 40 acres. "Leftover" lands after the allotments could be purchased and resold. Some of the profit from land sales would be put toward Indian education, working to erode Native languages, cultures, and customs, thus further hastening the assimilative agenda.[22]

Army Captain Richard Pratt established Carlisle Indian School in the late 1870s to "kill the Indian and save the man." The success of Carlisle encouraged the spread of Indian schools across the American West. The Stewart Indian School, on what had been Washoe Indian land near Carson City, opened its doors in 1890. Teachers and administrators trained the Native students in the vocational arts. Girls learned domestic skills while boys studied blue-collar trades like blacksmithing, carpentry, and typesetting.[23]

As the government worked to assimilate students, Washoe leaders were poised to try to protect their pine nut lands. On April 15, 1892, a two-man Washoe delegation began the long journey to Washington, D.C., to meet the "Great Father." The leader of the delegation came from Simee Dimeh. He was known as Gumalanga, although Americans called him Captain Jim. He characterized the traditional Washoe virtues of modesty, generosity, and kindness. He did not wield authority; his years of experience and gentle nature drew people to him.

Like many Native delegates who visited the nation's capital, Gumalanga encountered a wide range of political figures. He managed to get an audience with Nevada's congressional members, where he lobbied through the other delegate, interpreter Dick Bender.

Nevada Senator William Stewart tried to convince Gumalanga to apply for farming allotments in the Humboldt River Valley, beyond the boundaries of their traditional territory. But the Washoe delegates remained steadfast in their insistence that they wanted their pine nut lands. Washoe tradition holds that at some point during their thirteen-day stay, the delegates met with President Benjamin Harrison. On meeting the president, the Washoe account reports, Gumalanga extended a handful of pine nut flour and said, "My brother . . . this food from the pine nut trees is what my people eat . . . it is the same as our mother's milk when it is made into soup . . . your people are destroying our trees and our food . . . we ask you to help us so we can live."[24]

If Gumalanga and Bender met President Harrison, it is unlikely he was a sympathetic listener. He ran one of the most notoriously corrupt administrations in the nineteenth century, and his Indian policies were decidedly unfriendly to Native peoples. Critics labeled him a "tool of industrialists," and a "party hack." Harrison had spent the months leading up to the midterm elections of 1890 handing out federal offices in the Indian service to people whose only prerequisite was that they were likely to promote Republican voting. Set against the backdrop of Harrison's administration, Gumalanga's return home with assurances from federal officials that they would be able to retain their pine nut lands becomes all the more remarkable.[25]

Nevada's lone house representative at the time, Richard Bartine, addressed a letter "To the Washoes," following Gumalanga's visit. The letter stated that the Commissioner of Indian Affairs understood their claims and that the federal government would help them. The following year, 1893, special allotting agent Michael Piggot arrived in Carson City, Nevada, and began receiving groups of Washoe to allot land. In the end, the Washoe acquired over 87,000 acres of their pine nut lands. It all happened so fast that it is likely no federal officials realized that the Washoes had turned the assimilative intentions of the Dawes Act on its head.[26]

Although securing the pine nut lands represented a significant victory for Washoes, the arid acres would not sustain families year round. It was only a matter of time before federal administrators realized a mistake had been made. Directives coming from the Commissioner of Indian Affairs, Robert Valentine, in the first decade of the twentieth century, informed agents and superintendents that Indians should not be allowed to hold unused allotment lands. He suggested non-irrigable allotments be disposed of and imagined that the "habits of thrift and industry" would follow.

Valentine's directive promoted a process by which individual Indians could start living without "departmental control" and become American.[27]

Washoes realized quickly that allotment boundaries created by a distant bureaucracy would not be respected. On a spring day in 1905, Hangalelti community members traveled from their homes near Woodfords Canyon, California, to the office of Calvin H. Asbury, superintendent of the Carson Indian School, in Carson City, Nevada. The group lodged an official complaint about trespassers on their allotted lands. One non-Native man in particular, they explained, regularly cut timber on their property, "claiming that it was his right in payment for water" Washoe families used. The man, who goes unnamed in the documents, owned land up river from the allotments. Asbury noted that he would have suggested the families take the matter up in court, but he doubted they "would get justice." The superintendent concluded a letter to the Commissioner of Indian Affairs by stating that he did not have "time to go into the details" of the situation; consequently he took no action.[28]

Five years later, in 1910, representatives from Hangalelti country again informed Asbury about the trespassing. In the years since the first report, the newcomer had enclosed valuable portions of Washoe land while he continued to regularly harvest timber. Asbury explained to the Washoe individuals that in boundary disputes on allotted lands, normal procedure dictated that the allottee pay for a re-survey. He admitted to superiors that he had been apprised of the situation a number of years ago, but explained it had not been "practicable" for him to investigate. The complaints coming from southern Washoe families, and lack of response by federal agents, represent a discernible pattern of relations across Washoe country.[29]

In a similar case, a Pawalti couple, Spotted and Anna George, expressed their concerns regarding mining damage on their allotted lands. Upon investigation Asbury noticed that near their allotments, one mine had produced considerable wealth. Many non-Washoe miners continued to work the Georges' and neighboring allotments, often finding "good indications" and extracting valuable ore. Superintendent Asbury suggested the Georges "relinquish" their allotments for nothing in return.[30]

While Asbury investigated the Georges' land, he also tracked down the heirs of a deceased allottee, Gemima Maxwell. He provided an affidavit of heirship for her family and then requested relinquishment papers. Asbury described Maxwell's land as mineral rich but claimed the land held "absolutely no value" for Washoe families.[31]

Asbury obviously did not measure "value" the same way Washoe families did. For them, the pine nut lands were a connection to their past and their culture.

A year later, Dick Bender, who had accompanied Gumalanga to Washington in 1892, paid to have his allotment re-surveyed. Bender's survey turned up evidence of boundary tampering. Most Washoe landholders did not know the exact location of their allotment, and they generally calculated boundaries by landmarks like springs, mountains, trees, or rocky outcroppings. Boundary stakes that had been placed during the allotting process could be moved with impunity by unscrupulous newcomers.

Bender's surveyor discovered that the original allotment boundaries "had been moved a distance of some thirty rods" so that, conveniently, a strip of good timberlands fell just outside Bender's land. When questioned by the surveyor, Bender's non-Native neighbor claimed the boundaries had been that way when he purchased the land. Asbury determined to write the offending party and warn him of his trespass and told Bender the boundary could not be reestablished without the authority of the surveyor general's office.[32]

The growing cacophony of Washoe voices lobbying for protection of their pine nut claims emphasizes the unique priority that they placed on non-irrigable, but culturally significant lands. The process of determining what to do with Washoe allotments triggered a significant federal investigation. The agents assigned to the case determined it was finally time for the federal government to create reserved lands for Washoe families that they could live on year round. They also confirmed what Washoe allottees had been complaining about: trespassers and fortune seekers had degraded the already fragile ecosystem in the Pine Nut Mountains.

Based on the recommendations of the investigating agents in 1917 the federal government purchased lands for what would become three Washoe land bases, one for each ancestral Washoe region. As with the pine nut allotments Washoe individuals played a significant role in lobbying for lands and determining the general region where the lands should be.

Studying a brief period of history in the eastern Sierra from a transnational perspective reveals the unintended consequences of American federal actions. It reorients a region's past away from a linear narrative of conquest and capitulation toward a nuanced consideration of divergent priorities, customs, and beliefs. It also demonstrates the determination of a small Native community to remain in their homelands and to retain their traditions. Most importantly, it reminds residents of the American West that they share a past with people who shaped the region long before Europeans knew America existed.

Today, many Washoe families continue to maintain their pine nut allotments: some lease them, others have sold theirs. Despite years of struggle, dispossession, confusion, and assimilation, one thing remains constant: every fall the pinion forests around Simee Dimeh echo with the sound of Washoe voices. Those echoes remind those who listen that more than one nation has contributed to the identity of this region.

NOTES

1. For an account of the violent encounter, see Bernice Auchoberry, "An Interview with Bernice Auchoberry," interview by R. T. King (April 3, 1984), *A Contribution to a Survey of Life in Carson Valley, From First Settlement Through the 1950s* (Reno: Oral History Program University of Nevada Reno Library, 1984), 19.

2. Ibid., 13.

3. Eric Hinderaker's analysis of empire in the Ohio River Valley provides a useful concept for studying zones of intense colonization. He described encounters between French, British, Americans, Iroquois, and Algonquians as "negotiated systems." Colonization, when viewed this way, becomes "a mutable process, responsive to the choices of individuals and the contingencies of events." Eric Hinderaker, *Elusive Empires: Constructing Colonialism in the Ohio Valley, 1673–1800* (Cambridge: Cambridge University Press, 1997), xi–xii.

4. Frederick Jackson Turner "The Significance of the Frontier in American History," in *The Turner Thesis: Concerning the Role of the Frontier in American History*, ed. George Roger Taylor (London: D.C. Heath and Company, 1972), 4–5.

5. Alfonso Ortiz "Indian/White Relations: A View from the Other Side of the 'Frontier,'" in *American Indians in History: An Introduction*, eds. Frederick E. Hoxie and Peter Iverson (Illinois: Harlan Davidson, 1988), 3. Beginning in the late 1980s, a flurry of books and articles began to challenge the basic premise of Turner's thesis. Soon a corpus of scholarly literature came to constitute the "New Western History," characterized by the work of, among others, Patricia Limerick, Richard White, William Cronon, and Donald Worster. See Patricia Nelson Limerick, *The Legacy of Conquest: The Unbroken Past of the American West* (New York: W.W. Norton, 1987); Richard White, *"It's Your Misfortune and None of My Own": A New History of the American West* (Norman: University of Oklahoma Press, 1991); Donald Worster, *Rivers of Empire: Water, Aridity, and the Growth of the American West* (Oxford: Oxford University Press, 1985); and William Cronon, *Nature's Metropolia: Chicago and the Great West* (New York: W.W. Norton, 1991).

6. Colin Calloway's work, *One Vast Winter Count: The Native American West before Lewis and Clark* (Lincoln: University of Nebraska Press, 2003), provided a fantastic start for historians wanting to weave Native histories into the American experience. His work is of tremendous scope, although of necessity not all western Native communities were covered or even mentioned. Calloway's work serves as a clarion call to other historians; there is much work to be done. Particularly, there is a need to research and write the histories of small, typically overlooked communities.

7. Jesse T. Schreier summarized James C. Scott's analysis regarding American colonial practices and Indian people. Schreier suggested, "Colonizers initially found indigenous societies to be unintelligible." The process of colonizing Native peoples and land "made Native societies 'legible' and hence more understandable and more malleable to the colonial state." Nevertheless, Schreier, similar to Hinderaker, acknowledged that this "involved difficult and highly contested choices." See Jesse T. Schreier "Indian or Freedman? Enrollment, Race and Identity in the Choctaw Nation, 1896–1907," *Western Historical Quarterly* 42 (2011), 461.

8. See Elizabeth James-Stern, "Becoming a Community: The Nez Perces Confront the Dawes Act," in *American Indians in American History, 1870–2001: A Companion Reader*, ed. Sterling Evans (Westport, Conn.: Praeger Publishers, 2002), 37–44; and Emily Greenwald, *Reconfiguring the Reservation: The Nez Perces, Jicarilla Apaches, and the Dawes Act* (Albuquerque: University of New Mexico Press, 2002).

9. Warren L. d'Azevedo, "Washoe," in *The Handbook of North American Indians*, Vol. 11, ed. William C. Sturtevant (Washington, D.C.: Smithsonian Institution, 1986), 466–96; James F. Downs, *The Two Worlds of the Washo: An Indian Tribe of California and Nevada* (New York: Holt, Rhinehart and Winston, 1966), 1–3; and Jo Ann Nevers, *Wa She Shu: A Washo Tribal History* (Reno: Inter-Tribal Council of Nevada, 1976), 1–8.

10. For information on wegeléyu and shamans, see Stanley A. Freed and Ruth S. Freed, "A Configuration of Aboriginal Washoe Culture," in *The Washoe Indians of California and Nevada*, ed. Warren L. d'Azevedo (Salt Lake City: University of Utah Press—Anthropology Publications, 1963), 41–43; Downs, "Washoe Religion," 370; Edgar Siskin, *Washo Shamans and Peyotists: Religious Conflict in an American Indian Tribe* (Salt Lake City: University of Utah Press, 1983), 21; Don Handleman,

"Aspects of the Moral Compact of a Washo Shaman," *Anthropological Quarterly* 45 (1972): 84–98, 88; and Downs, *The Two Worlds of the Washo*, 55–59. For information of Cave Rock see Matthew S. Makley and Michael J. Makley, *Cave Rock: Climbers, Courts, and a Washoe Indian Sacred Place* (Reno: University of Nevada Press, 2010).

11. Interview with Amy James, Washo, Reno-Sparks Indian Colony, Reno, Nevada, Oct. 23, 1975, Interviewer Jo Ann Nevers (Reno: Inter-Tribal Council of Nevada Archives Project, file 100), as cited in Nevers, *Wa She Shu*, 6–10.

12. d'Azevedo, "Washoe," 473; Downs, *Two Worlds of the Washo*, 12–16; and Nevers, *Wa She Shu*, 9.

13. For a comprehensive treatment of Washoe plant management, see Darla Garey-Sage, "Washoe Women's Wisdom: Ethnobotany and its Role in Contemporary Cultural Identity," Dissertation, University of Nevada, Reno, 2003; see also: Nevers, *Wa She Shu*, 9–10.

14. Downs, in *The Two Worlds of the Washo*, 26–36, gives a comprehensive account of Washoe hunting practices; see also Nevers, *Wa She Shu*, 13–16. For information on the Da goom sa bye, see Nevers, *Wa She Shu*, 11–12; Matthew S. Makley "'These Will Be Strong': A History of the Washoe People" (Ph.D. diss., Arizona State University, 2007), 36–39.

15. For information on Smith's expedition, see Jedediah S. Smith, *The Southwest Expedition of Jedediah S. Smith: His Personal Account of the Journey to California, 1826–1827*, ed. George R. Brooks (Glendale Calif.: A.H. Clark Company, 1977; reprint, Norman: University of Oklahoma Press, 1989), 169–73. When I asked Beverly Caldera, chair of the language school committee for the Washoe Tribal council, she said that her grandsons use the word *mushege* when they refer to something scary or wild, like a monster or a large bear. John A. Price describes the Washoe use of *mushege* in "The Washo Indians: History, Life Cycle, Religion, Technology, Economy, and Modern Life," Nevada State Museum Occasional Papers 4, Carson City, Nevada, April 1980, 4. Also, James F. Downs represented a translation of the word *mushege* in *The Two Worlds of the Washo: An Indian Tribe of California and Nevada* (New York: Holt, Rhinehart and Winston, 1966). C. Hart Merriam in "Vocabularies of North American Indians" lists *mah se se* (pronounce "shush'h"), which he translated as "stranger," in folder "Washoshoo Vocabulary, 1923," box 5, Warren L. d' Azevedo, Washoe Indians Research Papers, Collection No. 99–39, Special Collections Department, University of Nevada, Reno. Edgar Siskin referred to *musegeu* as "someone to be feared," in Siskin's field notes, box 1, Edgar E. Siskin Papers, Collection No. 90–68, Special Collections Department, University of Nevada, Reno. For information on the word *da ba ah*, see Nevers, *Wa She She*, 45–46.

16. John C. Frémont, *Narratives of Explorations and Adventure*, ed. Allan Nevins (New York: Longmans, Green and Company, 1956), 344–47.

17. George D. Lyman, *The Saga of the Comstock Lode: Boom Days in Virginia City* (New York: Charles Scribner's Sons, 1939; reprint, New York: Charles Scribner's Sons, 1949), 13. Lyman wrote his history in grand fashion, sometimes stretching the limits of the historian's craft by inventing dialogue. Though a story-like history, Lyman's information is generally correct. He had access to sources because his father had been a mine superintendent on the Comstock.

18. Jacob T. Lockhart, Indian Agent Nevada, to W. P. Dole, Commissioner of Indian Affairs, March 12, 1862, *Letters Received, Nevada Superintendency 1861–1880*, NA microfilm publications 234, roll 538. The other observer was J. Ross Browne, author, reporter, and government agent for the Treasury Department. See J. Ross Browne, *A Peep at Washoe and Washoe Revisited, 1863, 1864, and 1869* (Balboa Island, Calif.: Paisano Press, 1959), 179.

19. Hubbard G. Parker, Superintendent of Indian Affairs, Nevada, to Dennis Cooley, Commissioner of Indian Affairs, Sept. 10, 1866, *Annual Report of the Commissioner of Indian Affairs* (Washington, D.C.: Government Printing Office, 1866), 117.

20. Nevers, *Wa She Shu*, 18–20, 68–69; Jane Green Gigli, "Dat So La Lee Queen of the Washoe Basket Makers" *Nevada State Museum Anthropological Papers* 3 (1967): 1–27.

21. Letter from Jefferson to Harrison as cited in R. David Edmunds, Frederick E. Hoxie, and Neal Salisbury, *The People: A History of Native America* (Boston: Houghton Mifflin, 2007), 177.

22. For information on the Dawes Act, see Frederick E. Hoxie, *A Final Promise: The Campaign to Assimilate the Indians, 1880–1920* (Lincoln: University of Nebraska Press, 1984), 70–76; Emily Greenwald, *Reconfiguring the Reservation: The Nez Perces, Jicarilla Apaches, and the Dawes Act* (Albuquerque: University of New Mexico Press, 2002); Heather Cox Richardson, *Wounded Knee: Party Politics and the*

Road to an American Massacre (New York: Basic Books, 2010) 96–98; Thomas R. Berger, *A Long and Terrible Shadow: White Values, Native Rights in the Americas Since 1492* (Seattle: University of Washington Press, 1991), 102–4; for an economic interpretation of the Dawes Act, see Leonard A. Carlson, *Indians, Bureaucrats, and Land: The Dawes Act and the Decline of Indian Farming* (Westport, Conn.: Greenwood, 1981); William T. Hagan "Private Property, the Indian's Door to Civilization," *Ethnohistory* 3 (1956) : 126–37.

23. For information on the government boarding schools, see Margaret Connell Szasz, *Education and the American Indian: The Road to Self-Determination Since 1928*, 3rd ed. (Albuquerque: The University of New Mexico Press, 1999).

24. Information on Gumalanga and reference to his meeting the president can be found in *Life Stories of Our Native People: Shoshone, Paiute, Washo* (Reno, Nev.: Inter-Tribal Council of Nevada, 1974), 13; see also Nevers, 60–61.

25. Heather Cox Richardson, *Wounded Knee*, 12–13.

26. Letter from H. F. Bartine on behalf of Dick Bender and Captain Jim, to The Washoe, April 27, 1892. Captain Jim Manuscript Collection, Nevada Historical Society, Reno, Nev.

27. Land Circular No. 320, Leasing Indian allotments free from Departmental Control, July 19, 1909, Robert G. Valentine, Commissioner of Indian Affairs, folder "61788–1909, Carson 313," box 57, Records of the Bureau of Indian Affairs Central Classified Files, 1907–1939, Carson, 22074–1909–313 part 2, 82772–1911–313, RG 75, National Archives and Record Administration (hereafter cited as NARA), Washington, D.C.

28. Calvin H. Asbury, Superintendent Carson Indian School, to the Commissioner of Indian Affairs, March 17, 1905, folder "19910–1910 Carson 313," box 57, Records of the Bureau of Indian Affairs Central Classified Files, 1907–1939, Carson, 22074–1909–313 part 2, 82772–1911–313, RG 75, NARA, Washington, D.C.

29. Letter from C. H. Asbury, Superintendent Carson Indian School, to Commissioner of Indian Affairs, March 4, 1910, folder "19910–1910 Carson 313," box 57, Records of the Bureau of Indian Affairs Central Classified Files, 1907–1939, Carson, 22074–1909–313 part 2, 82772–1911–313, RG 75, NARA, Washington, D.C.

30. Letter from C.H. Asbury to Commissioner of Indian Affairs, June 1, 1909, folder "42409–1908 Carson, 313," Box No. 56, Records of the Bureau of Indian Affairs Central Classified Files, 1907–1939 Carson, 17938–1908–313 to 22074–1909–313 part 1, RG 75, NARA, Washington, D.C.

31. Letter from C.H. Asbury, Superintendent Carson Indian School, to Commissioner of Indian Affairs, 1 June 1,1909 Folder "42409–1908 Carson, 313," box 56, Records of the Bureau of Indian Affairs Central Classified Files, 1907–1939 Carson, 17938–1908–313 to 22074–1909–313 part I, RG 75, NARA, Washington, D.C.

32. C. H. Asbury to Commissioner of Indian Affairs, May10, 1911, folder "Relief of Washoe Indians-197," Carson Indian School Administrative Files 1909–1923 [1925] Allotments Relief of Washoe Indians, Box 275, RG 75 NARA, San Bruno.

Chapter 11

Indigenous Resistance and Racist Schooling on the Borders of Empires

Coast Salish Cultural Survival*

Michael Marker

Histories of Indigenous education in North America have mostly focused on describing the policies and conditions of government and church-run residential schools. These schools, powerful agents of colonization and control, were the mechanisms by which British and American imperialism attempted to absorb Aboriginal communities into advancing nineteenth-century nation-state cultures. Although scholars have written extensively about these institutions, less attention has been paid to how schooling conditions evolved into mid- and late twentieth-century contexts of Indigenous cultural revival movements. These histories of the 1960s and 1970s, when Indigenous communities mobilized reclaimed languages and oral traditions toward self-determination, give us insights into the deeper realms of a continued struggle over contested cultural goals between nation-states and First Nations.

This paper reviews the experiences of Coast Salish people of British Columbia and Washington State as they responded to education for colonization in a borderlands region. Divided by two empires, the Coast Salish are one people who have resisted education as a tool of assimilation and cultural eradication. Indigenous communities that survived the racist policies of nineteenth-century empire building in the Pacific Northwest continued a struggle for cultural survival in integrated public schools in the 1960s and 1970s. Land claims, treaties, and fishing rights were at stake—and still are at stake—in contested versions of the region's histories. The schools

*This chapter originally appeared as an article in *Paedagogica Historica: International Journal of the History of Education*. See Michael Marker, "Indigenous resistance and racist schooling on the borders of empires: Coast Salish cultural survival," *Paedagogica Historica: International Journal of the History of Education*, (2009) 45:6, 757–772. DOI: 10.1080/00309230903335678. Reprinted by permission.

continued the colonial project of transmitting the official version of ethnic hierarchies and historiographies that defended the present social order and rejected Indigenous discourse on treaty rights. Coast Salish students were, in the late twentieth century, still resisting the same oppressive categorizations of identity that their grandparents had struggled against in the nineteenth century. Conditions had changed, and yet they had not changed in a century of colonization. The situation is resonant with Said's observation that "yet though imperialism implacably advanced during the nineteenth and twentieth centuries, resistance to it also advanced."[1]

This work is also an endeavor to avoid a strictly wide-angle lens comparative view and include aspects of a local Coast Salish imaginary in viewing conditions across the Canada-US border in the 1960s and 1970s. In order to understand what Indigenous communities have desired and still want from education, scholars must gain some recognition of how local people have read identity and meaning inscribed in oral tradition and landscape. Without this emphasis on how an Indigenous epistemology informs an alternate conception of place, the native emerges as simply a victim of colonialism's failed assimilationist project. The vibrancy of traditional Indigenous understandings of place must be merged with Fanon's call for an analysis of the colonial situation to understand the deeper structure of Indigenous resistance to empires.

Predicated on nineteenth-century racial and social evolution theories, Canadian and American policies operated across an elastic border to assign both conceptual and geographic space for native peoples in the Pacific Northwest. Education was the ultimate weapon of colonial conquest in this arena. Coordinated with the rise of anthropology and the belief in the universality of liberalism, government and church leaders regarded the residential schools as irresistible forces for change. Indian policy presumed that native children were pliable and could be transformed out of a savage past into a civilized present by being removed from the culture and family. Modernist, Christian interpretations of social reality were to replace the primitive Indigenous mind.

By the mid-twentieth century, integrated public schooling had replaced residential schooling as policy and practice in the United States. Canadian integration policy followed that of the United States a decade later, with residential schools continuing to operate until the 1980s. For Aboriginal people, the public schools, immersed in nation-state narratives of progress, were a continuation of the assimilationist residential schools. Schooling for colonization required not only that the natives be removed from the land, but that the place based consciousness of the land be removed from young Aboriginal minds. The present-day Indigenous decolonization movements are efforts to re-implant this place based consciousness, reorienting and healing the communities.

For the most part, Aboriginal scholars in North America have resisted the discourses of post-colonialism because, as Linda Smith observes, "post-colonialism is viewed as the convenient invention of Western intellectuals which reinscribes their power to define the world."[2] For Indigenous intellectuals, the counternarratives to those of the empires that invaded their territories must be constructed from an Indigenous place-based epistemology. Hence both the Indigenous understanding of the colonizers and the strategies for resistance are cast in local knowledge. Indigenous intellectuals have worked in a space of tension between the globalized knowledge of the academy and the local, intimate understandings of history and reality within the communities they come from. A decolonizing approach to historiography requires that Indigenous scholars reclaim the mental universe from pre-contact times and cause it to brush up against the official story from the center of the empire. Boundaries of nation-states often dissolve in the telling of an Indigenous history of place. Imperial geographies fade as shapes of reality from Indigenous languages and oral traditions push into these spaces of local landscape, driving out colonial categories of certainty.

To consolidate empires in the Pacific Northwest, both the United States and Britain needed to remove native people from the path of development and settlement. Treaties were made, and Coast Salish people were expected to stay within the borders of the empires and the borders of the reserves. Within the exclusionary discourse that assigned Aboriginal people to a category of primitive subordinate Otherness, there were also elaborate formulas and requirements for transformation and inclusion in society. The recipes for full participation in the Lockean social reality of the nineteenth century required that Indigenous people shake off the darkness of their premodern lifeways and fully embrace the cultural standards of their colonizers. The residential schools in Canada and the United States were designed as factories for cultural removal and for a quasi-cultural replacement. The government and church leaders saw the plan in reductionist terms; isolate children in institutions and punish any expression of their home culture while reformatting their cognitive maps, emphasizing the superiority of the empire.

The architects of these educational institutions set in motion multigenerational side effects from psychological trauma and abuse that continue to plague Aboriginal communities a century later. Rather than replacing Aboriginal culture with the template for participation in the broader colonial reality, the schools created shadowland personalities in the students, neither fully Indian nor fully white.

Makere Stewart-Harawira asserts that "education was the primary tool for the submerging of Indigenous peoples' highly developed 'inner' ways of knowing under a layer of colonizing ideologies."[3] State offensives to eliminate Indigenous ceremonial practices, such as the potlatch laws in British Columbia,[4] and the harsh punishments native children received for speaking their languages in the residential schools were coordinated efforts to eliminate the expression of Indigenous knowledge, of ancient understandings of identity and place.

The Coast Salish region of British Columbia and Western Washington State is an extraordinary case of both the invisibility of the nation-state—considering the fluidity with which Aboriginal people travel across the border—and the constant presence of two different nation-state policies in the Indigenous communities. Coast Salish identities are national, regional, and tribal. Historians of Indian education in North America have tended to stay focused on their own side of the Canada-US border and not look across for comparative analyses. In the case of Coast Salish educational histories, the border is a prominent signifier for the encounters with colonization and varieties of local and national policies. The border, for Coast Salish people, is saturated with the presence of empires and with the often invisible elements of local knowledge and place-based cultural understandings.

Both the residential schools and the mainstream public schools constrained and distorted Coast Salish views of land and history. In the 1960s and 1970s, integrated schools could be worse than residential schools for racism and psychological trauma. For the Lummi, a prominent Coast Salish tribe in Washington State, the government boarding school, designed for assimilation and cultural suppression, actually became a safe haven from the trauma of attending the local public schools where their culture was denigrated. My Ph.D. dissertation was an ethnographic study of the Lummi tribe and their relations with the white settler society that controlled the local schools in the 1970s. I interviewed both Lummis and non-Natives about their interpretations of the cross-cultural realities of the local high school. I have spent time in Coast Salish communities in both Washington State and British Columbia since that study was completed in 1995. I have come to recognize the community commonalities and also differences that have evolved from contrasting US and Canadian policies.

The problem in representing the Indigenous perspective and voice in these histories is denser than simply including testimony from Aboriginal students who attended the schools. Indigenous historiographies often place events and people in categories of meaning that are apart from western chronological and epistemological assumptions. Indigenous elders and traditional knowledge specialists make sense of the past by telling stories featuring ancestors and points of reference on the physical landscape. The

Coast Salish stories of Xa:ls, the creator-transformer, are the most significant for understanding the ways that people are reminded of ancient lessons as they remember the meanings of rocks, mountains, and islands in their world that is mapped by stories.

There is frequently a seamless blending of oral tradition, mythology, reflections on power, and a tracing of how the people came to be who they are today. Histories that center the ecology of the land as intimately and inextricably connected to Indigenous epistemology have arrived to find resonance with Indigenous language and cultural revival movements both in the academy and in the communities. Ethnographers such as Julie Cruikshank and Keith Basso have explained how languages and morality are formed by human interaction with the "sentient landscape."[5]

The comparative approach to understanding the ethnohistory of the region is messy and at times confusing because the colonial policies of Canada and the United States appear more similar than different for the most part. However, when we see differences across the border, we must avoid the tendency to "find out which country had the better Indian policy or the most positive relationship with its Aboriginal population, but should instead seek to understand the reasons for the similarities and differences in aboriginal history, and aboriginal-nonaboriginal relations, and Indian policies in the two countries."[6] Because the Coast Salish world is a borderlands reality, crossing the border for an analysis of the schooling histories is more congruent with an Indigenous historiography.

Throughout the late nineteenth and early twentieth centuries, as urbanization engulfed the Pacific Northwest, Coast Salish peoples were pushed into diminished geographic and social spaces in British Columbia and Washington State. Indigenous communities, to resist assimilation, maintained cultural boundaries, establishing complex spoken and unspoken rules for respecting conditions of privacy about the culture.[7] Coast Salish languages, forbidden in residential schools, were kept alive by elders who mentored one or two youths at a time. Outlawed winter spirit dancing and initiation rituals were kept secret or were performed in contexts that evaded surveillance and denouncement by government agents. A group of anthropologists in the 1950s and 1960s noted how Coast Salish communities were participants in the wage economy and selected elements of the mainstream societies in British Columbia and Washington State but dropped out of sight for ceremonies and traditional patterns of life.[8]

The schools were the places where Coast Salish people were most visible to the dominant settler society. It is important to note that the histories of Indigenous education are about *both* native and non-Native realities as people collided and cooperated with each other. Phillip J. Deloria has put it well:

> In the end, the search for common ground between distinctive historiographic traditions may yield insight into shared principles of history, bringing greater complexity into the creation of the stories we tell about the past. But encounters between deeply entrenched, coexisting worldviews are never easily negotiated. Where one observer sees common ground, another might see contested territory, a place of collision between imperialistic winners and victimized losers.[9]

In writing about the schooling realities of Indigenous peoples, we are also writing about the experiences of immigrant groups that framed and often constricted the cultural context for narrating the meaning of the schools. The educational histories of Coast Salish peoples are intertwined with oral tradition, genealogies, and portrayals of difference between the Indigenous and white world. Colleen Boyd, in a recent volume of *Ethnohistory*, has pointed to the efficacy of these traditions in narrating the past:

> In a rapidly globalizing and decolonizing world where the illusion of boundaries between "us" and "them" and past/present/future is effectively being collapsed, coeval indigenous historiographies are ripe with potential. In the wake of colonial ruptures, Coast Salish peoples use historical narratives to reemplace themselves and fashion a sense of continuity in a rapidly changing world.[10]

The Coastal Salish region of Western Washington State and British Columbia includes Puget Sound and the Fraser River system through the Straight of Georgia. As a culture region, it is an area that was connected by marriage, sharing of ceremonial practices, and common languages. The Coast Salish world was a multi-village universe in constant motion. Inter-village canoe journeys were necessary to preserve the complex social fabric of Coast Salish life. Potlatches, naming ceremonies, and other observances were required to affirm and maintain inherited rights and privileges. People remain connected in this way and travel throughout the region—almost as if there were no border—and yet the differences in Canadian and American educational policies have created diverse forms of resistance to colonialism across the border.

In many respects, the traditional Coast Salish world had nothing in common with the artificial border that was agreed to by the powerful nation-states of Canada and the United States. Paige Raibmon has explained, "When the Canada-US boundary sliced intervillage communities in two, many of the required journeys became border crossings. Coast Salish, who travelled from British Columbia to Washington, reentered a familiar orbit of extended kin more than they entered a foreign country."[11]

The border, although signifying the differences between two empires, made little sense to Coast Salish people who continued to travel between villages for ceremonies and to maintain the fabric of traditional cultural patterns. Anthropologist Bruce G. Miller emphasizes that "both the academic and popular literatures have commonly split the Coast Salish world in two, treating those living in Puget Sound and adjacent lands as constituting one world and those in British Columbia as constituting another. This practice fails to conform to the prior Aboriginal reality, before contact with whites and before treaties and borders."[12]

Coast Salish divisions of human geography are dissimilar to the borders drawn by empires. Saanich elder Dave Elliot, for example, made distinctions between communities based on whether a people's village was located where a river brought salmon every year or whether they had to devise technologies such as reef netting to get the fish out in the tidal salt water. Dave Elliot also explained how the Canada-US border had divided the Coast Salish people and kept them from fishing on the US side of the boundary. Saanich people lost reef net locations on the US side of the border and fell into poverty as a result.[13]

On the Washington State side of the border, Lummi elder Al Charles, during an oral history interview in 1973, explained how the border divided Lummi and Saanich families: "Our people lived right in the Islands across the boundary line. There was no boundary line between your people and other people. They put a boundary line and split us in half, and got us all balled up here."[14] He told a traditional story of Si'malh, a powerful young man who had raided villages and violated the laws. In the story, a group of warriors pursue him to Vancouver Island, where they decide to turn back. On the return trip, storms disperse the group to different islands and beaches, where they form the customary villages of the San Juan Islands and Gulf Islands. Listening to the recording, it becomes obvious that Al Charles is trying to get the interviewer to understand that the Lummi world is seamlessly connected to other Coast Salish communities across the border. His people are the people of the islands, and the Canada-US border has little meaning in this context. His traditional story of Si'malh is told in an effort to establish, in the mind of the listener, that the border is a conceptual impediment for understanding the Coast Salish sense of place. In short, the concept of the border is outside the Indigenous cosmology and belongs instead to the two colonizing empires that divided his people.

Schooling Policies across the Borderlands of Empires

While the Coast Salish traditional understanding of territory is without borders, Aboriginal people clearly recognize that their homeland is now a borderlands region. Families have been divided by the border. Meanwhile, the policies of keeping people separated based on the desires of nation-states to control Indigenous life has produced effects on both the colonized and colonizers. In this sense, the border is real and a marker of different trajectories through time for Coast Salish people who have arrived at the present moment on different sides of the border from each other under somewhat different colonizing conditions. Because schooling has been such a formidable apparatus to transform Indigenous Otherness into white expectations of acceptability, divergent histories of educational policy have shaped aspects of community life and discourses for cultural renewal. The assimilationist education policies directed at Indigenous communities were parallel at times and then divergent at other times across the Canada-US border. What follows is a brief overview of different conditions that evolved from different policies. The Coast Salish experience with education was a concurrent encounter with two different empires.

Both Canada and the United States established residential schools as a method to get Indians[15] off their traditional lands and assimilated into the margins of modern society. In Canada, the schools are referred to as residential schools while in the United States they were called boarding schools. In the United States in 1930s, commissioner of Indian Affairs John Collier, an ethnologist, set a new course for Indigenous education. The Indian Reorganization Act of 1934 was the centerpiece for a whole decade of progressive policies that focused on establishing tribally organized governments and economic development projects. Collier's goal was to reverse the failed assimilationist policies of the Bureau of Indian Affairs. Particularly, the boarding schools were highlighted as having been universally poor and unhealthy educational environments. Collier and his associates, expanding on the recommendations from the 1928 Miriam report, advanced a policy to renew traditional values through education and economic development. Many boarding schools were closed, and those that continued were guided by new policies toward supporting Indian cultural expression, including the teaching of native languages. Collier also supported Indigenous religious freedom and "issued new regulations forbidding the forced attendance of boarding school pupils at Christian religious services."[16] This more secular environment, supporting Indian identity and cultural expression in the United States, was in contrast to policies and conditions in Canada.

In British Columbia, during the 1940s, the church-run residential schools continued to advance the Canadian policy of assimilation. By the 1950s, the policy had shifted away from residential schools to integration into public schools. However, tuition agreements allowing Aboriginal students in public schools were stalled by the government's ambivalence about integration. The Department was under pressure from the churches to continue supporting residential schools. Because of Canadian ambiguity about changing policy, the residential schools continued to operate in parallel to a muddled approach to integration. As George E. Burns put it, the integration policy resulted in "tuition agreement schooling that was, and continues to be, paternalistic, coercive, racist, discriminatory, and assimilative."[17] Cole Harris commented on the larger picture of assimilationist policy:

> Assimilation was vigorously pursued in British Columbia from the colonial years before 1871 into the 1970s. Missionary teachings, school curricula, language training, even the reserve system, were deliberate instruments of social and cultural change. In sum, the transformative barrage was massive.[18]

Even though in Ottawa the official policy of the Department of Indian Affairs in the post-war era was integration, John Milloy notes, "The Department was given to understand that the children were 'not yet ready for integration' and that a segregated school would 'give better and more personal service to the Indian students.'"[19] The government explanation, "that the need for welfare and residential placement was not a product of economic circumstances but of parental moral shortcomings," was consistent with the Church perspective.[20] The Church asserted its influence on the government to continue the residential school policy—especially at the high school level. The dual policy of integration and residential schooling proceeded in an uncertain and jerky fashion into the 1950s.

Because church-operated residential schooling continued in Canada well into the 1970s, it has implanted itself into the public imaginary as a centerpiece of the discourse on Indigenous experiences with schooling. The residential schools in British Columbia, as J. R. Miller puts it, "were merely one important cog in a machine of cultural oppression and coercive change. The difficulty for the analyst is to separate out and weigh the influence of the residential school from this complex of interwoven forces."[21]

Although the residential schools were known to have horrific conditions, Coast Salish leaders in British Columbia recognized the problems in integrated schooling as well. Some traditional elders advised youth to elude schooling altogether as the only way to resist assimilation. Chief Simon Baker, Khot La Cha, who ran away from residential schools more than once, recalled a conversation with his grandmother as he told her about his plans to go to the white man's school. She said, "Son, I don't want you to go to white man's school because I have been teaching you our way of living and I want you to be the leader of our family here on the Capilano Reserve."[22] Elders in British Columbia presumed that school would dislocate the traditional cultural teachings in young people. On the Washington State side of the border, Coast Salish communities had been integrated into public schools for nearly twenty years longer than in British Columbia. The differences in schooling and the differences between settler state cultures across the Canada-US border produced different circumstances for Coast Salish students who attended school south of the forty-ninth parallel.

By the 1960s, Indian activism and treaty rights demonstrations were causing a backlash in American society. Coast Salish students in Puget Sound attended local public schools where they encountered a climate of institutional racism. The hostility toward Lummis, Swinomish, Upper Skagit, Tulalip, and other Coast Salish youth in classrooms was fueled by the public resentment over fishing rights victories in the courts in the 1960s and 1970s. This public outcry against "special rights" for Indians became part of the climate in the high schools in the Puget Sound region. A large number of teachers fished commercially in the summer and regarded Indian fishing rights, especially the controversial Boldt decision, as unfair government advocacy for Indians. Jim Egawa, a coordinator of Indian education programs for the Tacoma School District, explained in 1978 that "the Indian student meets open hostility from other classmates and even from teachers. He noted that children were being "accosted over fishing disputes . . ."[23] Some Coast Salish parents and students referred to the fishing rights backlash in the schools as a "spillover effect" from the tensions between whites and Indians in the broader society.[24]

The Boldt decision was based on interpretations of nineteenth-century treaties, notably the Point Elliot Treaty of 1855. Federal Judge George Boldt, after examining documents and hearing testimony from experts, including anthropologists, determined that Indians had originally reserved their right to half of the salmon. This reallocated the fishery and created waves of protest from angry whites who called the decision racist—or often "reverse racism." The Boldt decision brought economic renewal to impoverished Indigenous fishing villages that could now afford to improve boats and equipment with the increased incomes from more fish. However, tribal students, who already felt unwelcome in the schools, now had to endure a sustained assault on their right to be Indigenous as a result of the bitterness of the white teachers and administrators about the outcome of the Boldt decision.

Information about Coast Salish oral tradition and ethnohistory were key to the Indians winning in court.[25] Many white fishermen combined their outrage about the Boldt decision with a belief that the government and the Indians had invented a past reality. Those who opposed native fishing rights claimed that what truth might be contained in an Indigenous version of history was irrelevant to the present reality. On the fishing grounds, boats were rammed and guns were fired over the heads of Indian fishermen in the midst of escalating hostilities. As community and school life became saturated with open expressions of racism, Lummi, Nooksack, and other

Coast Salish families pushed more vigorously for their own separate schools. Native communities looked for education that was physically and culturally safe. Ironically, they turned to the government boarding school, formerly a tool of state control, as a way to evade racism and oppression.

The Boarding School as a Safe Haven for Cultural Expression

In the 1960s, tribal leaders from Western Washington State struggled politically for increased access to Chemawa Indian Boarding School in Salem, Oregon. Chemawa opened in 1880 to serve Northwest tribes. It was, until the Collier reforms of the 1930s, an authoritarian boarding school designed for assimilation. In the 1970s, however, many Indian parents saw the same boarding school as a possible safe haven for their adolescents who were experiencing psychological trauma in the racist classrooms of the local public schools. Coast Salish families, who had experienced cultural suppression at the boarding schools in the 1920s, now saw the boarding school as a way for their youth to gain educational opportunities and celebrate their cultural identity. Margaret Connell Szasz, in her classic history of American Indian education, wrote about Chemawa at the end of the 1960s: "Northwest tribes were once again permitted to send students to the school. These demands showed that Indians were not necessarily opposed to boarding schools; in many cases, they preferred to send their children to a school attended only by Indians."[26]

Coast Salish communities in the Puget Sound region were utilizing the boarding school, a government project intended for assimilation and colonization, and reclaiming it for cultural revitalization and protection from the racist conditions in the public schools. A former principal at Chemawa told me, "Lummis who came during that period quickly became the leaders of the school . . . it was common knowledge then that they had been pushed out of the public school by the Boldt decision stuff."[27] The Lummis, and other Coast Salish tribes in Puget Sound, were sending their children to Chemawa, a boarding school hundreds of miles from their home reservations, as a strategy for both cultural survival and educational opportunity. The grandparents of these students had a mixture of memories about attending Chemawa before the progressive era of the 1930s. Some of the memories focused on loneliness, neglect, and the suppression of language and cultural traditions. With this legacy in the forefront of their thoughts, the decision to send children and grandchildren to a boarding school far away from the community was a difficult one. Such choices were made based on the interpretations of the cultural and educational realities at the local high school in the midst of the "fishing wars."[28]

Religion and Schooling: Contrasts in Experience across the Border

The differences in the schooling and broader societal engagement for Coast Salish communities in British Columbia and Washington State had to do with the intensity of backlash against treaty rights in Puget Sound contrasted with the involvement of the churches in residential schools in British Columbia. The churches operated in partnership with the state in the coordinated tasks of nation building and assimilating Indigenous people. Religious authority merged with colonial authority to assert the superiority of Eurocentric cultural norms.

Although American government support for church-operated boarding schools was stopped by the 1920s, Canadian residential schools were run by the Catholic, Anglican, and other churches who fortified their control until the 1950s, when Aboriginal leaders challenged the church-state partnership. The churches in Canada were core to the entire Aboriginal schooling policy until the late 1940s. Because Canadian policy retained the goal of assimilation, a strong argument was made in Ottawa for the inclusion of religious values and moral instruction to expedite the solution to the "Indian problem." The discourse evolved with new words and phrases, but it retained the old foundational goals of dissolving Aboriginal people into mainstream Canadian society. J. R. Miller has written that

> like the Christian churches, and in marked contrast to the nearly unanimous views of the Indian communities, Ottawa still favoured the use of schooling for the assimilation of aboriginal peoples. In a presumably more enlightened age such as the late 1940s, Indian Affairs' rhetoric was stripped of its most obnoxious phraseology. Representatives of the branch were now more likely to advocate "educating for citizenship" than segregation. Native briefs and speeches might have emphasized schooling as a means to successful adaptation and economic development, but Indian Affairs continued to talk in terms of assimilation to Euro-Canadian ways through schooling.[29]

Coast Salish communities in British Columbia tell different kinds of stories than their relatives on the Washington State side of the border because the church-operated residential schools are such a significant focus for their experiences. Terry Glavin collected stories from Sto:lo and other Coast Salish individuals who attended St. Mary's school in Mission, British Columbia. The accounts show patterns that are similar to other studies of residential schooling in Canada.[30] A large number of former students tell of physical and sexual abuse at St. Mary's. The experiences of cultural suppression and trauma are pointed to as part of the legacy that Aboriginal people are trying to recover from. Glavin's work shows an educational experience in contrast to what Puget Sound Coast Salish students report from the same time period at Chemawa.

On both sides of the border, Native self-government movements were producing similar responses to the need for more culturally responsive education. In Canada, in 1972, the National Indian Brotherhood published *Indian Control of Indian Education.* This document spurred the push for local band control of schools. Coast Salish communities in British Columbia refined their critiques of residential school policy and began creating schools and curricula that brought elders in to teach language and traditional values. Such schools were slow to develop due to scarce funding. Although Native-controlled schools were beginning to enroll a few students, many Coast Salish students were still attending residential schools. The mixture of religion and abuse has left a dark legacy in Indigenous communities.

In a recent book examining the boarding school experience, David Wallace Adams asks, "In what ways and for what reasons did Indian youth sometimes come to look upon their years at boarding school as a rewarding and even joyful experience?" On the same page, he acknowledges that "most scholars who have studied the subject, however critical in their perspective, acknowledge that Indian communities and students alike saw redeeming value in the boarding school experience."[31] In this same book, the chapter that makes the sharpest departure from this assertion of the benefits of the boarding schools is the one on "The Catholic Experience at St. Boniface Indian School," by Tanya L. Rathbun. The forced Christianization is remembered by many of the former students as an overwhelmingly oppressive force. The church-operated schools were more brutal tools of empire than the secular boarding schools because they tended to be more militant about categorizations of Indigenous identity and inferiority. Historian Myra Rutherdale notes that this was "rooted in the philosophy of Christian mission, no doubt influenced by social Darwinism."[32] The differences between church-operated schools in British Columbia and government (Bureau of Indian Affairs)-operated schools in Washington State delineates some of the contrasts between colonial methods of conquest and control across the border.

For American Coast Salish students who attended Chemawa in the 1960s and 1970s, the school was a political and cultural institution that gave them space to frame identities that could be connected to the larger cultural and political struggles of their own landscape. It was a safe place to discuss fishing rights, treaties, and the connections between individuals and the vitality of their traditional values and beliefs. Because the US Indian boarding schools were more secularized institutions, and because the tribal communities had struggled to claim them as Indian educational space, Coast Salish people see them as institutions that evolved to spaces of resistance to colonization during the 1960s and 1970s. The writing from American historians such as Creek scholar Tsianina Lomawaima reflects an emphasis on the complexity of individual experiences with the schools. Additionally, the emphasis is placed on how "tribal and pan-Indian identities were reinforced, not diluted, in Indian schools."[33] In Canada, the power of the churches to influence policy confounded the efforts of both Native leaders and politicians to reform and transform the residential schools.

Indigenous Epistemology and the Politics of Local Knowledge

Expanding our field of vision to compare schooling across the Canada-US border allows us to de-center the history of residential schools and recognize that the deeper problems of cultural survival had to do with affirming Indigenous epistemologies in the midst of what Said called "the quotidian processes of hegemony."[34] Indigenous communities were not simply resisting racist schooling; they were also reaffirming and renewing their own traditional understandings of the uses of knowledge. Decolonization, from the Coast Salish perspective, meant distinguishing local cultural knowledge from the imported knowledge of the empires. Resistance to the hegemony of school-based knowledge often took the form of participation in those aspects of Coast Salish cultural life that had been kept as private ceremony and away from state surveillance.

To a large extent, the winter spirit dancing revivals during the 1960s and 1970s were re-orienting Coast Salish youth to traditional values; healing the psychological trauma from attending both residential and public schools. The dances are part of a complex cultural patterning or re-patterning that develops a place-based consciousness linked to ancestors, animal and guardian spirits, and oral tradition. The dances are private community events that, as anthropologist Pamela Amoss noted, "are so exclusively Indian that the surrounding white communities are often not even aware that such things are going on."[35] Wayne Suttles also noted the invisibility of Coast Salish cultural practices to the white community and especially the way winter dances were an expression of identity and Indigenous values, particularly for the youth. He noted the ways pressure to assimilate from the surrounding white society made the dances significant expressions of identity.[36] During the political backlash of the 1970s, Coast Salish students used the smokehouses, where the dances are held, as sites of cultural renewal and healing. They were away from schools for weeks at a time for fasting, ritual seclusion, and initiation. When these students returned to the schools, they returned with a transformed consciousness that reflected the intensity of their time away. Coast Salish students in both the residential schools and the public schools struggled to maintain a cultural and psychological strength that could withstand the degraded social assignments from church and state schooling. Spirit dancing and participation in ceremonial life became both an identity affirmation and a political assertion of continued resistance to colonization.

Conclusion

In examining the narratives from Coast Salish communities about their histories of schooling, it is clear that the conflicts over local, place-based knowledge are woven into explanations of how the schools worked to marginalize them. Not only are the political struggles for fishing rights and treaties predicated on Aboriginal communities' understandings of cultural claims to traditional resources, the oral traditions and languages contain the inherent statement "We are not you." Coast Salish communities have used traditional knowledge and ceremonies as a way of orienting youth to the values of the Aboriginal community and resisting the hegemony of modernity.[37]

The Coast Salish history of schooling contains multilayered tellings of local responses to colonialism in a borderlands region. The work of decolonization requires making distinctions about epistemic traditions and unraveling discourses regarding history and truth. Frantz Fanon pointed out:

> Colonialism is not satisfied merely with hiding a people in its grip and emptying the native's brain of all form and content. By a kind of perverted logic, it turns to the past of the oppressed people, and distorts, disfigures and destroys it. This work of devaluing pre-colonial history takes on a dialectical significance today.[38]

Indigenous communities are focused on assembling information about past cultural practices as a way to explore values that can be revived and reinserted into social reality. Leroy Littlebear has explicated how traditional Indigenous values frame an Indigenous educational imaginary:

> Aboriginal values flow from an Aboriginal worldview or "philosophy." Values are those mechanisms put in place by the group that more or less tells the individual members of the society that, "If you pursue the following, you will be rewarded or given recognition by the group," or alternatively, "If you pursue the following, you will be ostracized or punished by the group." Aboriginal traditions, laws, and customs are the practical application of the philosophy and values of the group.[39]

The values explicit in the education of present-day Coast Salish communities is a response to the histories of both residential schools and racist public schools. Historians of Indigenous education have been primarily interested in boarding schools and residential schools. Indeed, the effects of these institutions that removed children from their land, language, and values were devastating. But, as I have shown in this paper, focusing only on residential schools and their history of abuse and cultural genocide can miss the local complexity of both Indigenous voice and creative strategies for resistance.

For settler states such as Canada and the United States, Indigenous identity, inscribed and saturated with place-based knowledge, could not be truly assimilated into the imperial project; indigeneity had to be eradicated or confined to spaces, such as reserves, outside the empire yet remaining as a problem to be solved inside the empire. Elsewhere, I have pointed out that "there is a deep insecurity within the consciousness and conscience of settler societies that, when confronted by the Indigenous Other, is awakened to challenges about authenticity in relation to land and identity."[40] The nineteenth-century residential schools were a response to the nation-state's insecurity and ambivalence about Aboriginal people's relationship to the land. The schools, if they were successful it was thought, would erase the past from both native children and from the memory of the nation-state about a brutal invasion and colonization. The residential schools did not succeed in assimilating native peoples. However, the schools did produce widespread pathologies in both the Aboriginal communities and in the broader society that shudders at the mirror of this educational history. Decades after the boarding schools were closed on the US side of the border, Coast Salish students in racist public schools were still struggling to assert that they had not yet been assimilated. Indigenous decolonization movements have emphasized histories of resistance to schooling as an example of the resiliency of the people as they also emphasize a return to some forms of pre-contact and premodernist values. Eric Wolf has noted the ways that Indigenous communities "around the globe cling to their cultural forms and employ them to defend their own ways of life against capitalist encroachment."[41]

The Coast Salish region presents a powerful case study of how people divided by an international border developed different strategies for resisting various forms of colonizing education. A single-minded focus on residential schools as the core problem for Indigenous education has cemented a conflated telling of the past in public consciousness. In many ways, the experience of attending racist public schools was, for Coast Salish students in Washington State, as traumatic as attending the church-run residential schools for Coast Salish youth in British Columbia. As a way of explaining their goals for Aboriginal youth, elders often tried to explain to the colonizers how the land was sacred to them, how the land spoke to them and provided their values and education. These communities, divided by a border imposed upon them by powerful Others, are attempting to now use their own community-based, culturally responsive education as a way to reclaim, or reimagine a consciousness that returns them to the relationships their ancestors had with a sacred landscape.

Notes

1. Edward W. Said, *Culture and Imperialism* (New York: Alfred A. Knopf, Inc., 1993), xxiv.

2. Linda T. Smith, *Decolonizing Methodologies: Research and Indigenous Peoples* (Dunedin, N.Z.: University of Otago Press, 1999), 14.

3. Makere Stewart-Harawira, *The New Imperial Order: Indigenous Responses to Globalization* (London: Zed Books, 2005), 80.

4. See Paul Tennant, *Aboriginal Peoples and Politics: The Indian Land Question in British Columbia, 1849–1989* (Vancouver: University of British Columbia Press, 1990).

5. Julie Cruikshank, *Do Glaciers Listen? Local Knowledge, Colonial Encounters, and Social Imagination* (Vancouver: University of British Columbia Press, 2005); Keith H. Basso, *Wisdom Sits in Places: Landscape and Language Among the Western Apache* (Albuquerque: University of New Mexico Press) 1996. Cruikshank uses the term *sentient landscape* in her description of traditional ecological knowledge themes in the Yukon.

6. Theodore Binnema, "The Case for Cross-National and Comparative History: The Northwestern Plains as a Bioregion," in *The Borderlands of the American and Canadian Wests: Essays on Regional History of the Forty-Ninth Parallel*, ed. S. Evans (Lincoln: University of Nebraska Press, 2006), 35.

7. See Stacy M. Rasmus, "Repatriating Words: Local Knowledge in a Global Context," *American Indian Quarterly* 26 (2002): 286–307.

8. See Claudia Lewis, *Indian Families of the Northwest Coast: The Impact of Change* (Chicago: University of Chicago Press, 1970); Marian W. Smith, *Indians of the Urban Northwest* (New York: AMS Press, 1949); and Wayne Suttles, "Private Knowledge, Morality, and Social Classes Among the Coast Salish," in *Indians of the North Pacific Coast*, ed. Tom McFeat (Seattle: University of Washington Press, 1966), 166–79.

9. Phillip J. Deloria, "Historiography," in *A Companion to American Indian History*, eds. Phillip J. Deloria and Neal Salisbury (Oxford, UK: Blackwell, 2002), 17.

10. Colleen Boyd, "That Government Man Tried to Poison All the Klallam Indians: Metanarrative of History and Colonialism on the Central Northwest Coast," *Ethnohistory* 53 (Spring 2006), 350.

11. Paige Raibmon, Authentic Indians: Episodes of Encounter From the Late-Nineteenth-Century Northwest Coast (Durham, N.C.: Duke University Press, 2005), 109.

12. Bruce G. Miller, "Conceptual and Practical Boundaries: West Coast Indians/First Nations on the Border of Contagion in the Post-9/11 Era," in *The Borderlands of the American and Canadian Wests*, ed. Sterling Evans (Lincoln: University of Nebraska Press, 2006), 49–66.

13. Janet Poth, *Saltwater People, as told by Dave Elliot Sr.* (Victoria, B.C.: Saanich School District 63, 1983).

14. Al Charles, Interviewed by Jeff Wilner, College of Ethnic Studies professor April 26th Tape 23 (Northwest Tribal Indian Oral History Collection at Western Regional Archives, Bellingham, Washington, 1973).

15. In this paper, I use a range of names for broad categories of Indigenous peoples. In Canada, the terminology includes First Nations, Aboriginal, native, and Indigenous. In the United States, the term *Native American* is common, but *American Indian* is also used. The term *Indian*, is, of course, derived from fifteenth-century European confusions about both people and places in the Americas. Many tribal people refer to themselves as Indian and have, in many cases, reclaimed the term for their own purposes. My usage choice reflects tone and emphasis.

16. Lawrence C. Kelly, "The Indian New Deal," in *Indian-White Relation: A Persistent Paradox*, eds. Jane F. Smith and Robert M. Kvasnicka (Washington, D.C.: Howard University Press, 1976), 233.

17. George E. Burns, "Factors and Themes in Native Education and School Boards/First Nations Tuition Negotiations and Tuition Agreement Schooling," *Canadian Journal of Native Education* 22 (1998), 55.

18. Cole Harris, Making Native Space: Colonialism, Resistance, and Reserves in British Columbia (Vancouver: University of British Columbia Press, 2002), 298.

19. John S. Milloy, *A National Crime: The Canadian Government and the Residential School System, 1879 to 1986* (Manitoba: University of Manitoba Press, 1999), 229. Citing INAC file 6-21-7, Vol. 1, confidential, Memorandum to the Minister, March 12, 1959.

20. Milloy, 214.

21. J. R. Miller, *Shingwauk's vision: A History of Native Residential Schools* (Toronto: University of Toronto Press, 1996), 427.

22. Simon Baker, *Khot La Cha: The Autobiography of Chief Simon Baker*, Comp., ed. Verna J. Kirkness (Vancouver, B.C.: Douglas and McIntyre, 1994), 49.

23. State of Washington, "Are You Listening Neighbor?" report of Indian Affairs Task Force, 1978, 67.

24. Congress, *Indian Tribes: A Continuing Quest for Survival*, report of the United States Commission on Civil Rights, June 1981.

25. See Daniel L. Boxberger, "The Not So Common," in *Be of Good Mind: Essays on the Coast Salish*, ed. Bruce G. Miller (Vancouver: University of British Columbia Press, 2007) for reflections on the role of anthropologists and ethnohistorians in the Boldt decision.

26. Margaret Connell Szasz, *Education and the American Indian: The Road to Self-Determination Since 1928* (Albuquerque: University of New Mexico Press, 1974), 166.

27. Michael Marker, Lummi Stories from High School: An Ethnohistory of the Fishing Wars of the 1970s (Ph.D. diss., University of British Columbia, 1995), 90.

28. For description and analysis of the fishing wars, see Daniel L. Boxberger, *To Fish In Common: The Ethnohistory of Lummi Indian Salmon Fishing* (Lincoln: University of Nebraska Press, 1989); Fay G. Cohen, *Treaties on Trial: the Continuing Controversy Over Northwest Indian Fishing Rights* (Seattle: University of Washington Press, 1986); and Charles Wilkinson, *Messages from Frank's Landing: A Story of Salmon, Treaties, and the Indian Way* (Seattle: University of Washington Press, 2000).

29. J.R. Miller, *Shingwauk's vision*, 381–82.

30. See Celia Haig Brown, *Resistance and Renewal: Surviving the Indian Residential School* (Vancouver: Tillicum Library, 1988) for accounts from students who attended in the 1950s and 1960s.

31. David Wallace Adams, "Beyond Bleakness: The Brighter Side of Indian Boarding Schools, 1870–1940," in *Boarding School Blues: Revisiting American Indian Educational Experiences*, eds. Clifford E. Trafzer, Jean A. Keller, and Lorene Sisquoc (Lincoln: University of Nebraska Press, 2006), 36.

32. Myra Rutherdale, *Women and the White Man's God: Gender and Race in the Canadian Mission Field* (Vancouver: University of British Columbia Press, 2002), 153.

33. Tsianina Lomawaima, *They Called It Prairie Light: The Story of Chilocco Indian School* (Lincoln: University of Nebraska, 1994), 129.

34. Said, *Culture and Imperialism*, 109.

35. Pamela Amoss, "The Persistence of Aboriginal Beliefs and Practices Among the Nooksack Coast Salish," (Ph.D. diss., University of Washington, 1972), 209.

36. Wayne Suttles, "Spirit Dancing and the Persistence of Native Culture among the Coast Salish," in *Coast Salish Essays* (Seattle: University of Washington Press, 1987).

37. See Claude Denis, *We Are Not You: First Nations and Canadian Modernity* (Peterborough, On: Broadview Press, 1997); and Michael Marker, "That History is More a Part of the Present Than it Ever Was in the Past: Toward an Ethnohistory of Native Education," *History of Education Review* 28 (1999). Both of these works give examples of the use of Coast Salish winter spirit dancing for reorientation to traditional values and spiritual balance. The ceremonies counter the messages of mainstream society and the schools that are seen to dislodge youth from their Coast Salish identities.

38. Frantz Fanon, "On National Culture," in *Postcolonial Discourse and Postcolonial Theory: A Reader*, eds. Patrick Williams and Laura Chrisman (New York: Columbia University Press, 1994), 37.

39. Leroy Little Bear, "Jagged Worldviews Colliding," in *Reclaiming Indigenous Voice and Vision*, ed. Marie Battiste (Vancouver: University of British Columbia Press, 2000), 79.

40. Michael Marker, "After the Makah Whale Hunt: Indigenous Knowledge and Limits to Multicultural Discourse," *Urban Education* 41 (2006): 485–86.

41. Eric Wolf, *Envisioning Power: Ideologies of Dominance and Crisis* (Berkeley: University of California Press, 1999), 15.

Chapter 12

Indigenous Transnationalism and Alberta First Nations Gaming

Political Compromise or Negotiated Economic Advantage?

Yale D. Belanger

The October 2006 opening of the River Cree Resort and Casino located on the Enoch Cree Nation just west of Edmonton signaled Alberta's First Nations' entry into the provincial gaming industry. Four more First Nations casinos would open during the next two years to form an operational quintet that generates roughly $140 million annually for use by the province's forty-five First Nations.[1] The River Cree Casino's opening culminated a prolonged and frequently touchy period of provincial–First Nations negotiations dating to 1993, during which time First Nations representatives remained consistent in their claims to an inherent right to manage reserve gaming operations. This, it must be noted, countered Alberta's declared authority to dictate the terms of negotiations and revenue distribution formulas.[2] Observers have noted that the Tsuu T'ina Nation abutting Calgary and the Enoch Cree Nation pressing for reserve casinos eventually allied with interested provincial First Nations, leading to a collaborative relationship that guided negotiations with Alberta. Notably, First Nations leaders did not attempt to draw their historic treaty partner—the federal crown—into the dialogue, which, as discussed below, was a historically significant decision. By doing so, Alberta's First Nations embraced the spirit of what Ravi De Costa describes as Indigenous transnationalism "acts that form part of a long history in which First Nation peoples, or their advocates, have gone outside of or beyond the . . . nation-state, physically and ideologically, in order to pursue civil and indigenous rights to improve the lives of indigenous communities."[3] It further "indicates many indigenous peoples' commitment to a universal order of experience and justice; one in which indigenous and other peoples can co-exist."[4] But have First Nations advanced economically—or made political progress as a result? This chapter begins by assessing Indigenous transnationalism, after which the Indian

Association of Alberta's evolution is traced, emphasizing its transnational roots. The next sections elaborate the jurisdictional environment and establish a brief history of the negotiations leading up to 2001 implementation of the First Nation Gaming Policy. The final two sections offer an analysis of the policy's economic and political outcomes as well as conclusions.

Indigenous Transnationalism

Historically, the First Nations, located in modern-day Canada, pursued international support of their objectives by forming confederacies with neighboring First Nations, among other strategies, thereby enabling two or more nations to merge politically in furtherance of mutual goals. Later, this process was extended to allying with European powers such as the Huron with the French, or the Iroquois with the English.[5] Consistent settler population growth persuaded eighteenth-century First Nations leaders such as Joseph Brant (Mohawk) to maintain strong relationships with their European allies. In 1775, as an example, in anticipation of the outbreak of the American Revolutionary War, Brant travelled to Britain to determine the strength of the Six Nations–British relationship, and in the War's aftermath, returned, seeking redress for lost lands.[6] Similar episodes have been noted, one of the better known being the 1906 travels of three British Columbia (B.C.) chiefs to consult with Britain's King Edward VII about the Indian Land Question.[7] Chief Deskaheh traveled to Geneva, Switzerland, in 1924 to request the League of Nations to intervene in the ongoing battle of the Six Nation Mohawks of Grand River to contain the mounting territorial intrusion of the Canadian government.[8] It is impossible to trace the collection of events here, but evident in each instance were colonial promises to implement new policies to improve First Nations conditions and to renew the spirit and intent of previous nation-to-nation relationships. First Nations persistently reminded their historic allies, including Indigenous and European/Canadian/American representatives, of their responsibilities contained in pre- and post-contact treaties. Treaties can generally be defined as "formal agreements between two or more fully sovereign and recognized states operating in an international forum, negotiated by officially designated commissioners and ratified by the governments of the signatory powers."[9] In the late eighteenth century, the Swiss jurist Emmerich de Vattel had defined treaties in *The Law of Nations* as compacts "entered into by sovereigns for the welfare of the State, either in perpetuity or for a considerable length of time" by the highest state authority.[10] Treaty principles acknowledged First Nations as property owners with full dominion over their territories, which included the right to exclude others from those lands.[11] Further, Indigenous occupation conferred Aboriginal title, which could be extinguished only following formal negotiations and an agreed-upon treaty acknowledging a land sale.[12]

First Nations readiness to enter into treaties with neighboring First Nations, combined with the European willingness to negotiate treaties with Indigenous leaders amounted to an acknowledgment of Indigenous sovereignty. Internation norms of treaty making were forged on this understanding of the inviolable and binding nature of treaties, which Robert Williams illustrated were based on mutual reliance and trust.[13] Canada's colonial officers chose to ignore this history and instead asserted their self-identified capacity to structure "both political realities and subversive political imaginaries." Sovereignty could and was thus zoned in the Crown's favor.[14] A systemic dichotomy materialized that physically and ideologically situated groups of individuals that officials deemed uncultured in opposition to progressive colonials, a binary that in post-1867 Canada led to political and economic asymmetries and First Nations physical and ideological separation.[15] Policies and legislation such as the *Indian Act of 1876* guided this process by classifying Indians as wards to Canada's guardianship;[16] residential schools were created to "kill the Indian and save the child," justifying cultural genocide in the name of nation building;[17] and the treaties that previously guided cultural interface evolved into tools of extinguishment enabling Canada's settlement of the west by dispossessing First Nations.[18]

Despite their historic role as partners in confederation, First Nations in the post-1867 period, especially those in western Canada, were legally considered barriers to expansion and development. Canadian officials responded accordingly with laws and policies destined to compel Indian social assimilation that First Nations resisted. Notably underlying the resistance discourse were claims to independence—economic, political, and social.[19] All arguments aside, federal officials proclaimed First Nations sovereignty claims to be invalid and the historic nation-to-nation relationship, for all intents and purposes, an historic myth. In the wake of aggressive colonization, it was evident to almost all involved that it was necessary to adopt new strategies and adapt old ones in an effort to remain independent.

Indigenous Transnationalism in Alberta

First Nations' transnationalism in Alberta can be traced to England prior to the First World War's finish. On his way back to Canada from the European theater, Lieutenant Frederick Ogilvie (F.O.) Loft met with England's King George V in 1918. A Six Nations' Hereditary Council Pine Tree chieftain and long-time civil servant who worked as an accountant in the bursar's office at the Provincial Lunatic Asylum in Toronto, Loft's wartime experience confirmed his belief that non-natives were able, if unwilling, to treat First Nations as equals. During his audience, he informed King George of the inadequacies of Canadian Indian policies and how poorly non-natives treated First Nations. His message was clear: because Indian people had "fought, bled and died for the great cause the simple recompense they ask is a just and fair dealing for themselves at the hands of the governments, greater in the future than had [been] obtained in the past."[20] King George told Loft to organize Canada's Indians, after which he should return to England to rekindle the discussion.[21]

Loft sought to take advantage of the pan-Indian consciousness developing among First Nations veterans by immediately initiating his organizing drive. By December 20, 1918, a meeting was held at the Six Nations Reserve nearby Brantford, Ontario, which led to the creation of the League of Indians of Canada. Annual meetings were then held at Sault Ste. Marie, Ontario, in 1919; Elphinstone, Manitoba, in 1920; Saskatchewan's Thunderchild Reserve in 1921; and Hobbema, Alberta, in 1922. The League of Indians had, by the mid-1920s, grown both a national membership and reputation among First Nations for "political action on a national scale."[22] Preaching strength in numbers and stressing the centrality of First Nations–Crown treaty relationships, Loft and the League of Indians sought to renew old political connections as well as fashion new political relationships with Canada. The quick and influential evolution of the League of Indians aside, by 1934 (the year of Loft's death), it had collapsed into a scattering of regional groups. As the historian Hugh Dempsey reminds us, however, Loft engendered "an awareness of the possibilities of Indian associations as protest and pressure groups among bands on the Prairies and for this he has justly been called the 'Father of Western Canadian Indian Associations.'"[23]

The League of Indians represents an enlightened approach to First Nations organizing that Loft anticipated would penetrate parliamentary chambers to influence Indian policy and legislation. What he failed to fully appreciate, arguably, was that First Nations leaders were confronting unique regional, municipal, provincial, and federal political forces, all presenting exclusive notions concerning the First Nations' role in growing Canadian society. For instance, at this time, First Nations organizers in Alberta confronted an aggressive period of social restructuring that reduced them to a demographic and economic minority. The heart of this evolution was adopting farming and/or ranching, something many southern and central First Nations took up quite successfully. But they often found their efforts undermined by envious settlers and unresponsive Indian agents.[24] Greater access to natural resources was not sufficient to help the central and northern Alberta First Nations offset the negative effects of poorly developed federal economic development policies advocating reserve agrarianism.[25] The federal failure to consider the emergent industrial reality that promoted large-scale farming, mining and mineral exploration, and manufacturing was injurious. Aggravating matters were the seemingly unending federal attempts to compel land surrenders: First Nations leaders were in particular concerned that federal officials could use lucrative non-native leaseholds of reserve lands as proof of their inability to properly utilize agriculturally productive lands, thus justifying their seizure.[26] Arguably an infusion of financial capital from Ottawa would have benefited many of these communities, as would have suitable educational facilities and locating the reserves nearby regional economic hubs.[27] First Nations found themselves located on Canada's physical and social periphery and increasingly on an array of federal programs and policy alterations intended to mitigate deteriorating reserve socioeconomic development.[28]

Adding to the frustration were municipal norms advocating First Nations exclusion.[29] Early twentieth-century boosterism was a momentous barrier, as immigrant farmers drawn to Canada's western region staked illegal claims to the majority of arable land. An influx of European homesteaders followed; most found work in the burgeoning local sugar beet industry, which hindered First Nations attempts at securing meaningful wage labor.[30] A potent blend of ethnic prejudice and nationalism, termed Nativism, surfaced that promoted the physical exclusion of immigrants and First Nations.[31] In particular, the Protestant work ethic promoted community development that as a rule disregarded First Nations concerns.[32] When local officials did respond to First Nations concerns they tended to justify their draconian actions by citing popular attitudes equating 'Indians' as destined for disappearance, or at the very least cultural absorption.[33] These beliefs echoed seventeenth-century debates that guided a colonial project prescribing appropriate settler development processes.[34] By the early 1900s, these intersecting forces combined to shape state, civil, and market relations that effectively excluded First Nations participation.[35] It was socially complex and almost economically impossible for Alberta's First Nations to work with settler society at the municipal level, which made it virtually impossible to bolster failing reserve economies during this period. As a result, First Nations leaders turned their gaze to working with federal officials with whom they secured a treaty in 1877.

Those interested in organizing akin to the League of Indians discovered that contrary to its membership's common concerns based on a collective wartime experience, Alberta's First Nations had more difficulty finding common ground.[36] Considering the history of pre-contact confederacies and treaty relationships this was intriguing. Frequently overlooked in historical analyses was the intricacy of Alberta's cultural diversity being challenged by new social and economic forces. For example, beginning in the late eighteenth and early nineteenth century, amplified settler migration to what would become southern Alberta caused Cree-Blackfoot animosities to spike.[37] Following their famed 1885 resistance many Métis moved to northern Alberta leading to new political and economic allegiances, while the centrally located First Nations confronted similar pressures.[38] The collective need to replenish resources in rapidly diminishing territories drove each group's actions. It also led to an inevitable intrusion into neighboring lands resulting in elevated rates of warfare, bitterness, and fear.[39] Notably, hostilities did not always devolve into warfare as treaties and similar internation agreements helped to curb animosities. In an attempt to stem the tide of immigration and mitigate animosities and to help promote Indian alliances a League of Indians conference was held in Edmonton in 1922 attended by 1,500 Blackfoot, Sarcee, Cree, and Assiniboine delegates. Two more regional meetings followed at Fort Macleod in 1924 and 1925.[40] Several meetings occurred during the next decade and by 1939, the Indian Association of Alberta (IAA) had developed to represent "the combined and unified position of the Treaty Indians" of Alberta with 140 delegates representing twenty-seven bands.[41] As a sounding board for complaints and concerns, the IAA's "meetings gave members a sense of group strength and reaffirmed the importance of fighting for common goals."[42]

Laurie Meijer-Drees's (2002) exploration of the IAA confirmed how closely connected organizational leaders believed they were with Canadian federal politicians. It also demonstrated each participating community's resolve to preserve local autonomy, suggesting that the regional nature of organizing should not be conflated with political advocacy. Rather it is illustrative of Indigenous transnationalism. Alberta's First Nations—and all First Nations in Canada for that matter—considered neighboring First Nation communities to be politically unique, nations unto themselves operating according to internally crafted notions of sovereignty and economic development that sought cultural survival. This occurred by challenging normative social values grounded in a colonial history promoting First Nations social inclusion *vis-à-vis* assimilation *and* their political and economic exclusion.[43] Unfortunately, federal officials refused to acknowledge the IAA as anything more than a lobby group. When combined with municipal exclusion it left First Nations with limited options. The goal of organizing, as presented here, was utilized to reanimate old and establish new relationships with foreign powers be they First Nations, the British/Canadian Crown, or, as I argue below, the provinces.

By the 1940s the die was cast fostering a new period of Indigenous transnationalism in Alberta.[44] Federal and municipal ignorance of First Nations outreach temporarily derailed the IAA. However, the history of Indigenous interface and federal disinterest set the stage for the First Nations alliances established during the 1990s that resulted in the collective negotiations that enabled First Nations entry into the provincial gaming industry. It was also a process conspicuous in its lack of attempts to draw the federal crown into the negotiations.

Jurisdictional Environment

Prior to detailing the negotiations process, it is important to set the jurisdictional stage for, as suggested earlier, First Nations had to negotiate with the Province of Alberta if they were to have the right to build reserve casinos recognized. Provincial officials contended from the beginning that they alone would negotiate with First Nations, as they were constitutionally assigned jurisdiction for gambling. In one way this might suggest a lack of First Nations agency. Yes, First Nations' choices were limited, and recent scholarship demonstrates that Alberta utilized its favorable bargaining position to leverage the negotiations in its favor.[45] This is, however, also reflective of the risks associated with self-determination as identified by the Harvard Project on American Indian Economic Development. More specifically, the Harvard Project scholars would describe this decision as an act of *de facto* sovereignty whereby the First Nations consciously chose to negotiate the best deal possible with a foreign power.[46]

Canada's political model combines Britain's Westminster model of parliamentary government with a division of sovereignty popularly known as the division or distribution of legislative powers. The *British North America Act, 1867*, defines the federal government of Canada's scope of power and the powers of each individual provincial legislature or assembly. The federal government has powers and responsibilities in matters that concern all Canadians, most notably matters that cross interprovincial and/or international borders, whereas provincial governments have jurisdiction in matters of local interest and local well-being. Delegation must relate to a matter within the sovereign justice of the particular legislative body. As a result, the federal government is exclusively responsible for Indians' political, social, and economic well-being, a responsibility adopted in 1867 as confirmed by S. 91(24) of the *BNA Act, 1867*.

Historically, the provinces had little contact with First Nations, economically or otherwise, as they preferred to avoid challenging the federal responsibility for "Indians, and lands reserved for the Indians." These two worlds intersected in 1985 after the federal government and the provinces agreed to transfer authority for lotteries and other forms of gaming from federal to provincial jurisdiction.[47] Embedded in these new rights was the provincial authority to assign gaming licenses, even if previously "there would have been some who believed that a province could, in theory, license others to conduct lottery schemes using these mechanisms."[48] First Nations remained federal responsibilities, but community leaders seeking casino opportunities were now compelled to negotiate with the provinces. This split authority suggests that when parties sit down to consult, an inevitable overlap of constitutional authority will occur. As Colin Campbell has shown, "in the federal-provincial negotiations which led to the 1985 amendment and the corresponding transfer of jurisdiction over gambling, it is apparent that First Nations' interests were not considered" and that by disregarding these interests non-native governments were able to "consolidate jurisdiction over new forms of gambling and the revenues they would generate for private sector groups, for charities, and for provinces." Moreover, "the failure of Canadian legislators to consider First Nations' interests dramatically underscores the lack of foresight."[49]

Since then, the courts have determined that provincial legislatures have the authority to enact laws in the gaming area, subject to Parliament's supremacy in the case of a clash between federal and provincial legislation.[50] They have partially clarified this overlap of powers by refusing to acknowledge that First Nations have an inherent right to establish reserve casinos *ultra vires* provincial jurisdiction.[51] Alberta's First Nations could have challenged the federal government's abdication of its fiduciary duty to safeguard First Nations' interests, which would have been costly and time-consuming. However, as political sovereigns they consciously chose to bypass one foreign power (Ottawa) in lieu of establishing a legal relationship with another foreign power (Alberta) in pursuit of improved socioeconomic development.

Toward a First Nations Gaming Policy

Choosing to engage the Alberta government in negotiations was an innovative option, especially when one considers that historically the provinces had little contact with First Nations, economically or otherwise. As suggested, Ottawa's inability to help foster effective First Nations economic development also compelled provincial First Nations to organize to pursue casino operations. Casinos were consequently promoted as a catalyst to aid First Nation's socioeconomic development, not unlike how provincial officials promoted gambling.[52]

The Tsuu T'ina First Nation (southwest of Calgary), and the Enoch Cree First Nation (west of Edmonton) were awarded licenses in 1993 to hold superbingos guaranteeing jackpots exceeding $10,000. The Tsuu T'ina turned a $100,000 profit. Instantly, a myriad of First Nations voices were calling for the creation of an independent First Nations Gaming Commission.[53] First Nations leaders rallied and developed a policy model ensuring all bands would benefit equally from any reserve casino projects. At a chiefs' summit in November 1993, the policy model and any potential challenges associated with it were discussed with several provincial ministers and officials, the federal Minister of Indian and Northern Affairs Canada (INAC), and Alberta's First Nations chiefs. A second summit held in March 1995 resulted in the provincial minister of Family and Social Services, Mike Cardinal, encouraging First Nations leaders to "take a leading role" in determining "if a casino industry will exist."[54] The third summit was held in November 1995, which led to the *Understanding on First Nations–Canada Relations* signed by the federal Minister of Indian Affairs Ron Irwin, the chiefs of Alberta, and later Premier Ralph Klein and Minister Cardinal.

This was a surprising outcome considering that two months earlier the First Nations Gaming Congress, representing all Alberta bands, demanded $100 million from the provincial government in exchange for halting casino construction in what turned out to be a short-lived resistance. That December, Tsuu T'ina band members voted 73 percent in favor of a casino proposal, prompting a January 1996 meeting between Premier Klein, Alberta Lotteries Review Committee chair Judy Gordon, and Chief Roy Whitney and the Tsuu T'ina band council. All parties agreed that final arrangements about "casino size, location, construction dates, and revenue-sharing possibilities still needed to be discussed."[55]

At the outset, First Nation casinos offered two unique features that First Nations leaders prized. One, they were local businesses generating operating revenue and on-site employment. Two, partners absorbed a large part of the financial risk, thus mitigating community risk. First Nations who actively lobbied for permission to place casinos on reserves echoed the discourse of provincial officials who suggested that these casinos were a "legislative blessing . . . based on the premise that the social good of the activity outweighs any negative consequences."[56] In 1997, after several years of resistance and minimal consultation with First Nations, Alberta officials deemed the First Nations proposals worthy and announced a First Nations gaming policy. The new policy permitted the construction and operation of four casinos on First Nation reserves. With the exception of being located on reserves, the First Nations casinos were expected to operate under the same charity model with regards to the distribution of revenues (i.e., a significant portion going to the Alberta Lottery Fund rather than being retained by the First Nation community). First Nation leaders were stunned, especially those negotiating with provincial officials. Enoch and Louis Bull First Nations, for example, both had plans in place to develop large destination-type casinos, and ended their relationships with a Las Vegas developer when informed of the planned First Nations model. Their leaders reasoned that the established Alberta "charity model" would hinder the developer and the First Nations' ability to produce the revenues needed to justify the initial capital investment. Tsuu T'ina officials also temporarily halted their casino plans.

Enoch Chief Ron Morin challenged the province to revamp the revenue model to increase the First Nations share. "If you take a look at what First Nations had when we came into this province," Morin opined, "all of the oil and gas that has been produced, the revenues that non-First Nations people have got, those haven't been totally shared with us." He cryptically added, "I don't think I have to give a history lesson in Canada as to what First Nations agreed to share."[57] Initially, First Nation casinos would be expected to operate as any other provincial charity casino: half of the profits would go to the operator, and the other half would be redistributed to the province's forty-five First Nation communities. Non-native casino operators were free to spend their business revenue, as they deemed purposeful, whereas Alberta demanded First Nations leaders establish a charity to dole out revenues according to prescribed revenue-spending categories. Several First Nations reeled at this proposed model and threatened to build and operate their own casinos and bingo halls,[58] which was wasted effort as, in 1999, a twenty-month provincial moratorium on provincial casino construction was called in response to public concerns about unsustainable industry growth and demands for government accountability concerning gambling's social impact. The moratorium report released in 2001 led to the creation of new provincial gaming policies designed to "reflect this government's continued commitment to maintaining the unique charitable gaming model of this province."[59] First Nations remained in a holding pattern until 2002, when the moratorium was finally lifted.

In anticipation of the moratorium recommendations Alberta announced the First Nations Gaming Policy (FNGP) in 2001, touting a new revenue distribution formula. However, this model was simply an altered version of the old. Provincial officials again demanded First Nations register as charities prior to the release of gaming revenues and that successful First Nations hire independent management to oversee casino operations (other charities must do this as well), thus removing from First Nations any responsibility for daily operations (First Nations envisioned casinos through the dual lenses of economic and political sovereignty). A new provision insisted that 30 percent of slot machine revenue be divided between the casino operator and the host First Nation charity. The remaining 70 percent was to be divided between existing lottery programs and the proposed First Nation Development Fund (FNDF) to benefit all provincial First Nations. A systematic eight-step application process was established that ensured the provincial casino industry's controlled and managed growth. It also insisted that the First Nations ensure debt repayment to the key investor, which in this instance would be the casino operator, in turn privileging casino management's decision-making authority while simultaneously mitigating lender risk. The inverse relationship ordained amplified First Nations' risk.

By 2006, seven First Nations had applied to the AGLC according to the terms and conditions established for charitable casinos. Not unlike the mainstream process, the eight-step First Nations model considered various criteria, ranging from site selection to community support, to practical business plans properly evaluating alternate viewpoints. The FNGP was particularly restrictive, specifically those provisions aimed at First Nations spending practices, casino management composition, and, where casinos were placed on reserves, nearby regional municipalities, the rules compelling investment in municipal services, such as police and emergency medical services, to curb local fears about inevitable increases in gambling-related crime and societal breakdown. As the applications review proceeded, provincial officials worked with the First Nations, Alberta's satellite INAC office, and Alberta Community Development to establish the FNDF framework. To be funded by provincial revenues from electronic gambling in casinos on First Nations land, it was anticipated that the FNDF would provide opportunities for investment in reserve economic development as well as social, health, education, and infrastructure spending.[60] The River Cree Resort and Casino opened in 2006, followed in succession by the Cold Lake First Nation's Casino Dene and the Tsuu T'ina First Nation's Grey Eagle Casino in 2007; and the Eagle River Casino and Travel Plaza in Whitecourt and the Stoney Nakoda Casino on Stoney Nakoda First Nation in 2008.

Evaluating First Nation Gaming Success in Alberta

First Nations participation in the provincial gaming industry was prescribed by Alberta politicians embracing neocolonial politics aimed at ensuring substantial provincial jurisdiction over First Nation gaming operations. This

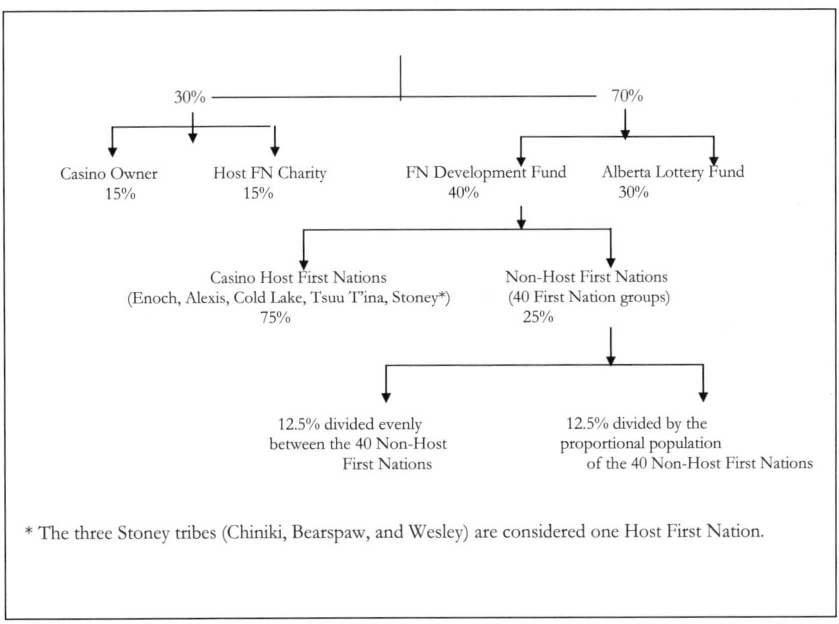

Revenue Distribution from Slot Machines in First Nations' Casinos.

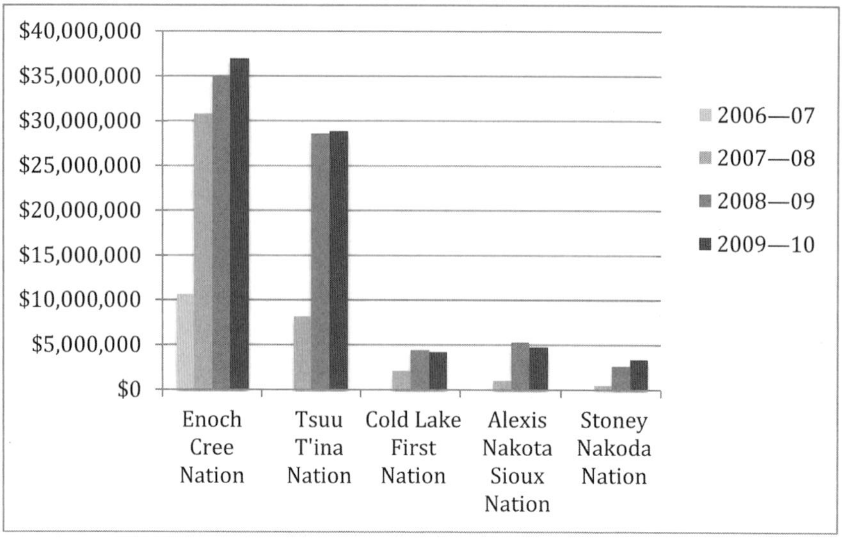

First Nations Development Fund (FNDF) revenue.

much seems evident. But what benefits do First Nations derive from casinos? And how does the Province of Alberta benefit? The remainder of this section is based on FNDF data gleaned from the AGLC's public website, Alberta Lottery Fund: Who Benefits.

First Nations Development Fund

Gambling revenue began to be deposited into the FNDF beginning in fiscal 2006/2007, with these amounts steadily increasing up to the present time. However, coincident with the general decrease and/or flattening of Alberta gambling revenue in 2009, the 2009/2010 deposits to the FNDF were only marginally larger than in 2008/2009 and dropped by roughly 1.9 percent in 2010–2011. From 2006–2010, the FNDF has been allocated a total of $379,096,100 for distribution to First Nations community development projects. The host First Nations are allocated 75 percent of FNDF funding and thus have been allocated $284,322,075 of the roughly $379 million generated. The remaining thirty-nine provincial First Nations divided the rest, which amounts to less than $2 million per community—or approximately $800,000 yearly.

The largest beneficiaries of the FNDF have been the five First Nations that host casinos. However, there is considerable variability within this group of five, with the Enoch Cree First Nation (River Cree Casino and Resort) and the Tsuu T'ina Nation (Grey Eagle Casino) being the main beneficiaries. This is almost certainly due to the fact that the River Cree Casino is just outside of Edmonton (pop. 1,034,945), and the Grey Eagle Casino is just outside of Calgary (pop. 1,296,000), whereas the other three casinos are located in what might be described as rural areas.

Enhanced First Nations infrastructure and community programming has resulted in the most important and positive benefits of legalized gambling in Alberta. All provincial First Nations are direct recipients of FNDF funding, although, to reiterate, the host communities are entitled to 81.8 percent of the available funding, leaving thirty-nine First Nations to divide the remaining 18.2 percent. The FNDF *does* provide additional revenue unavailable through federal programming. The main impact of legal gambling on First Nation's charities is that it provides consistent funds to support the five host First Nations local services, according to the seventeen FNDF project allocation categories.

Notwithstanding the prevalent concerns about potential social costs of installing casinos nearby First Nations residents, the difference in problem and pathological gambling rates between 2008 and 2009 is not statistically significant in three of the four First Nations for which data are available.[61] The number of problem gamblers at the Stoney Nakoda Nation did increase by a factor of 3.8 from 2008 to 2009. Consistent with prior research, First Nation prevalence rates are significantly and consistently higher than the general population prevalence rates across Alberta,[62] yet provincially, there is some evidence of decreased rates of First Nations problem gambling since 2000, coincident with the same trend that may be occurring in the general population.[63] This is despite further significant increases in gambling

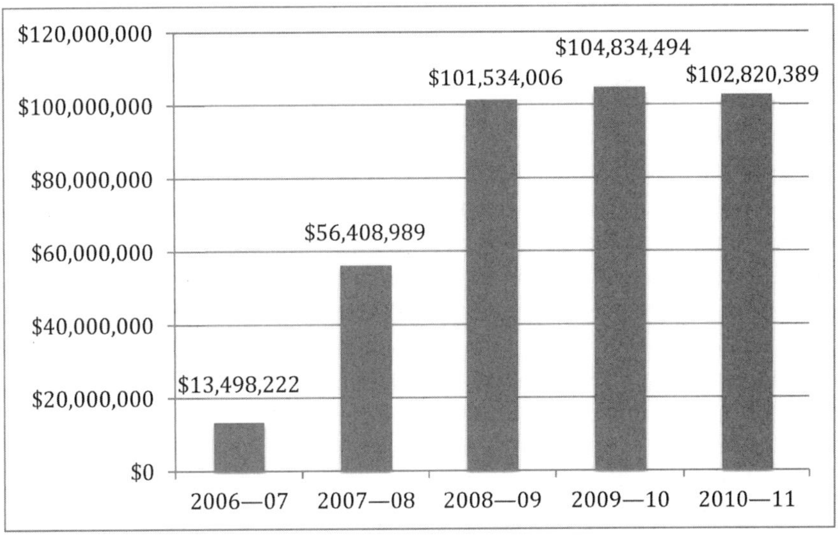

FNDF allocations for the five First Nations that host casinos.

availability and general population per capita expenditure during this time period. It is duly noted that these rates reflect Aboriginal populations across Alberta rather than Aboriginal populations in the immediate proximity of the five new First Nations casinos.

FNDF Revenue as a Proportion of Total Revenue

The primary source of First Nations revenue has traditionally been federal government payments through Indian and Northern Affairs Canada (INAC). The funding formula calculates individual First Nations funding levels based on per capita distributions.[64] In the case of these five host communities, these monies represent a significant portion of their overall revenue. For example, Enoch's FNDF disbursement of $35 million in 2008/2009 was 303 percent more than its INAC's budgetary allocation. Similarly, Tsuu T'ina received more than $28 million, which was 142 percent more than its INAC budget. Despite lower than expected returns, gambling revenues also contribute noticeably to the Alexis Nakota Sioux Nation's and the Cold Lake First Nations' overall budget. [*Note:* The Stoney Nakoda Resort was not operational long enough for inclusion in this list, nor are its INAC allocations available online.] In total, FNDF funding represented 83.3 percent of the four communities' collective INAC allocation.

Not surprisingly, the percentage of revenue accounted for by the FNDF is much less for non-host communities. During the same time period, twenty-one First Nations for which complete data sets were available received over $24 million in FNDF revenues, which averaged out to approximately $384,683 annually per community. Some smaller communities such as Smith's Landing First Nation supplemented their INAC budgets by 26 percent and 43 percent in 2007/08 and 2008/09 respectively. Fort McKay, Heart Lake, and the Athabasca Chipewyan First Nation also experienced double-digit gains. However, the FNDF supplemented non-host First Nations INAC budgets by, on average, 2.3 percent.

The FNGP has led to the redistribution of wealth to geographically removed First Nations. The casinos further function as conduits to solicit extra community revenues. From the outset, First Nations and provincial officials recognized that the majority of casino patrons would be non-Native. Arguably the 30 percent return to the provincial treasury for ALF use provides Alberta a safety net for reclaiming a portion of the gambling revenues leaking from the provincial economy vis-à-vis non-Native gamblers into the macro First Nations economy.

First Nation Development Fund Disbursements

First Nations Development Fund project allocations fall into seventeen categories. Non-gaming-related Debt Retirement (42%) has constituted the

FNDF Contributions to Host First Nations as a Percentage of Their Federal Payments			
	Federal Contribution	**FNDF**	**FNDF as % of Federal Contribution**
Alexis Nakota Sioux Nation			
2006–07	$13,478,803	$75,080	0.6%
2007–08	$13,478,803	$1,068,945	7.9%
2008–09	$11,663,635	$5,404,206	46.3%
Totals	*$38,621,241*	*$6,548,231*	*16.9%*
Yearly Average	*$12,873,747*	*$2,182,744*	
Cold Lake First Nation			
2006–07	$6,958,787	$80,073	1.2%
2007–08	$5,888,471	$2,187,136	37.1%
2008–09	$6,625,634	$4,527,365	68.3%
Totals	*$19,472,892*	*$6,794,574*	*34.9%*
Yearly Average	*$6,490,964*	*$2,264,858*	
Enoch Cree First Nation 440			
2006–07	$8,930,213	$10,665,047	119.4%
2007–08	$10,404,587	$30,808,226	296.1%
2008–09	$11,593,508	$35,147,872	303.2%
Totals	*$30,928,308*	*$76,621,145*	*247.7%*
Yearly Average	*$10,309,436*	*$25,540,382*	
Tsuu Tina Nation			
2006–07	$20,698,584	0	0%
2007–08	$22,401,884	$8,246,214	36.8%
2008–09	$20,067,719	$28,572,460	142.5%
Totals	*$63,168,187*	*$36,818,674*	*58.3%*
Yearly Average	*$21,056,062*	*$12,279,558*	
Total (4 Host First Nations)	**$152,190,628**	**$126,782,624**	**83.3%**
Yearly Average	***$12,682,552***	***$10,565,219***	
Total (21 Non-Host FNs)	**$1,056,942,912**	**$24,235,068**	**2.3%**
Yearly Average	***$16,776,872***	***$384,684***	

FNDF Contributions to Host First Nations as a Percentage of Their Federal Payments

largest portion of FNDF project disbursements since 2006. Almost all of this debt reduction (98.8%) has gone to reduce non-gaming-related First Nation debt incurred to build the casinos. The Cold Lake First Nations and the Stoney Nation largely used their own money and/or borrowed funds, whereas the other three First Nations had outside investors. Facility costs

FNDF Category Allocations (2006–2010)	
	Percentage Allocated
Debt Retirement (non-gaming related)	42%
Facility Costs	17%
Housing and Infrastructure	15%
Administrative Costs	7%
Community Development	4%
Community Safety Programs	3%
Education	4%
Equipment	2%
Cultural Events/Historical Resources/ Religion	2%
Wages, Salaries, Honoraria	2%
Other*	2%

* Like Skills Training, Addictions Treatment, Sports, Elders, Emergency Funds, Donations within Alberta, Aid of Distressed/ Children/Youth/Adults in Care.

FNDF Category Allocations (2006–2010)

at 17 percent and housing and infrastructure costs at 15 percent represent the next largest categories. Facility costs are for repairs or new construction on band-owned buildings and facilities. Housing and infrastructure costs are the costs associated with constructing new band housing and improving infrastructure such as water sanitation upgrades and road paving. Combined, these complementary categories amounted to $88,676,099, or roughly one-third of FNDF disbursements between 2006 and 2010. Infrastructure and housing are priority issues for most First Nation communities. At one time, it was documented that housing projects was the number-one allocation from charitable gambling proceeds, representing 28 percent of disbursements since 2006.

Employment

Original estimates suggested that the five First Nations casinos would employ 1340 people with an annual payroll of $37.8 million. Most First Nations indicated their preference to hire First Nations employees while acknowledging that a shortage of casino professionals and a limited Aboriginal labor pool would require that non-Native employees also be hired. The Enoch Cree Nation was the exception: it indicated that 125 First Nations individuals would be employed, representing only 17 percent of the work force (which included hotel and conference center employment estimates). Some Alberta First Nation leaders pointed to the Saskatchewan Indian Gaming Authority

(SIGA) as a model, where in 2009/2010 it was reported that 63 percent of employees were First Nations (down from 73% in previous years).

In fiscal 2009/2010, the five First Nations' casinos had a total 1030 employees. It is difficult to obtain precise payroll information, but it is known that the Grey Eagle Casino employ five hundred people for a payroll of $15 million, and the Stoney Nakoda Casino employ thirty-five individuals for a payroll of $1.025 million. The average wage per individual in both cases was just under $30,000 per year. Precise data were not available for the Enoch Cree Nation, the Alexis Nakota Sioux Nation, and the Cold Lake First Nations. However, if we assume the average wage is similar, then it is possible to project total payroll. Collectively, it is estimated that in fiscal 2009/2010, the five First Nations' casinos payroll was $31,025,000. The total number of employees and total payroll fell below initial projections. In total, current employee numbers represents 78 percent of initial projections, whereas the $31,025,000 payroll represents 82 percent of original projections. The River Cree Casino is the only facility that exceeded expectations.

The percentage of employees who are First Nation is also largely below expectations. The River Cree Casino and Resort employs a total of eight hundred people, three hundred at the casino and five hundred at the accompanying resort/hotel complex. News reports indicate that 25 percent of resort employees are First Nations, a total of two hundred people from which an estimated one hundred reside at the Enoch Cree Nation. Extrapolating for casino employment, fifty employees (25%) would be Aboriginal descent. An estimated 16 percent of the 500 Grey Eagle Casino workers are Aboriginal individuals. The majority of these are from the Tsuu T'ina Nation, residing both on reserve and in Calgary.

Similar to most casinos, 70 percent of the Eagle River Casino (Alexis) staff is full-time, and 30 percent part-time. Only 18 percent of the Eagle River Casino employees are Aboriginal, which might be a condition of geography,

Employment in the Alberta First Nations Casinos				
First Nations	Casino	Number of First Nations Employees	Total Casino Employees	Known or Estimated Payroll
Enoch Cree	River Cree	75 (25%)	300*	$9,000,000
Tsuu T'ina	Grey Eagle	80 (16%)	500	$15,000,000
Alexis	Eagle River	21 (18%)	120	$3,600,000
Cold Lake	Casino Dene	N/A	80	$2,400,000
Stoney	Stoney Nakoda	30 (100%)	30	$1,025,000
TOTAL		**206**	**1030**	**$31,025,000**

*Does not include an additional 500 employees in the hotel resort.

Employment in the Alberta First Nation Casinos

as the reserve casino site is located adjacent to Whitecourt, some 100 kilometers from the reserve community. The Alexis Nakota Sioux Nation, however, does have an employee bus shuttling employees twice daily to the casino. The percentage of Aboriginal employees in the Casino Dene is unknown. Only the Stoney Nakoda casino has a preponderance of Aboriginal employees, which is purported to be 100 percent. An important concern related to casino employee ethnicity is one of reservation economy. Because most of the employees are non-Aboriginal, most of the casino wages paid then leave the First Nations reservation community. Acknowledging the lack of Cold Lake First Nations data, the four host First Nations identified draw approximately $5,321,000 in earnings out of a total payroll of $31,025,000, which is 17.2 percent of the aggregate annual payrolls. Although 84.4 percent of First Nations employee wages is estimated to return to the host First Nations (i.e., a percentage of First Nation employees live off-reserve), annually an estimated $25,704,000 in wages leaves host First Nation communities, the majority into the municipal Edmonton and Calgary economies.

A significant percentage of the five First Nation casino *charities* employ First Nations people, however. Out of the approximately 170 employees, 90 percent (155) are believed to be Aboriginal. With the exception of the Northern Isga Foundation at the Alexis Nakota Sioux Nation, information is not available documenting full-time versus part-time charity employment or the percentage of First Nations employees who were also residents of the local First Nation community. The Northern Isga Foundation currently employs nineteen individuals with an annual payroll estimated at $400,000 (NIF News, 2009). Using $20,000 as an average wage, it is projected that the total payroll for the First Nations charities is roughly $3.4 million, with the First Nations themselves retaining $3.1 million of these wages.

In total, in recent years it is believed that 155 (charity casino employees) plus 206 (casino employees) plus 200 resort employees, are of Aboriginal heritage, for a total of 561 employees. To be clear, these 561 positions represent jobs that did not exist prior to the casino openings. Although prior employment status of these 561 individuals is not known, it can be expected that a portion of these individuals were unemployed or underemployed prior to their casino-related employment. Anecdotally, many of these people were said to represent the more skilled individuals in the communities who had been employed prior to the casino, thus potentially cannibalizing band administrations and local reserve businesses. In support of this supposition, there exists no clear evidence that these jobs significantly impacted overall employment levels within Alberta First Nations. According to the recently published Statistics Canada Aboriginal labor force analysis for 2008/2009, Alberta's Aboriginal population experienced a 5.6 percent *decline* in employment rate, now listed at 69.5 percent. This represents the lowest rate for

Aboriginal people in Canada. Alberta's Aboriginal unemployment rate rose by 5.8 percent to 12.9 percent. Although this time period did indeed represent the end part of a recession, Statistics Canada reports that the employment rate among the general population of Albertans fell by only 2.5 percent.[65]

Employment figures for each First Nations community are not available, which confounds any comparative analysis regarding casino openings and affected local employment trends. Statistics Canada and Indian and Northern Affairs Canada (INAC) utilize Canadian census data, the most recent report issued for the year 2006. Accordingly, because all of the First Nations casinos opened *after* 2006, we are unable to provide trends analyses at this time. First Nations have also cited an inherent right to self-government by either denying or greatly restricting the actions of Canadian surveyors, who attempt to gather information on reserve land. The Tsuu T'ina and the Enoch Cree Nations refused to participate in the 2006 federal census, and thus their community profiles lack vital data for employment, annual earnings, work force characteristics, and even gender and age. Considering these two communities host the largest casinos and benefit significantly from the projects, the lack of complete (or any) data hinders our analysis.

Provincial Benefits

First Nations have received significant benefits from gambling; however, these benefits have not been evenly distributed, which is directly attributable to the provincial FNGP. But what are the overall costs? We are able to evaluate what the Province of Alberta acquires from a process intended to provide communities with the "means to support economic, social and community development projects as well as use charitable gaming proceeds for initiatives such as infrastructure and life skills training."[66] Significantly, 30 percent of First Nations gaming revenue is assigned to the provincial government, specifically the Alberta Lottery Fund, which has been used to support thousands of local community initiatives each year through a granting process for interested "charitable" groups. To 2011, the Alberta Lottery Fund has received $284,322,077 from First Nations casino operations, which is subsequently used to fund provincial ministries and charitable grants. Simply put, First Nations casinos are in part driving provincial development despite the fact that First Nations casinos were touted as a means to aid First Nations development. Indeed, First Nations contribution to the ALF in total has amounted to 17.2 percent of the overall contributions to the fund since 2006.

It would appear that First Nations casinos benefit non-Native provincial citizens notably, even though casinos and their revenues were specifically earmarked to improve poor reserve socioeconomic conditions. Improvement in this case is, of course, also dependent on Alberta releasing FNDF revenues, which are held in trust until a First Nation satisfies provincial

First Nations' Contribution to Alberta Lottery Fund (2006–2011)			
Year	Alberta Lottery Fund	First Nations' Contribution to Alberta Lottery Fund	FN % Contribution
2010–2011	$235,698,855	$77,115,292	32.7%
2009–2010	$303,479,980	$78,625,871	25.9%
2008–2009	$443,898,329	$76,150,505	17.2%
2007–2008	$452,613,659	$42,306,742	9.3%
2006–2007	$215,062,997	$10,123,667	4.7%
Source: AGLC, Alberta Lottery Fund: Who Benefits?			

First Nations Contribution to Alberta Lottery Fund (2006-2011)

administrators' spending practices guidelines. Again, simply put, the monies will be released if they are to be spent according to provincially prescribed categories to assist in what outside administrators deem to be appropriate community development ventures. Alberta's reluctance to distribute the gaming revenue is disconcerting. To date 13 percent of all charity monies and a portion of FNDF funds, amounting to more than $13 million, remain undistributed and thus unexpended. These strict spending provisions dictate that provincial regulators are depriving First Nations of revenue generated in First Nations casinos. As Belanger and Williams have concluded, this process mirrors a combined neocolonial/neoliberal approach whereby provincial oversight is required to ensure appropriate First Nations spending while also directing what Harvey would describe as a *flow of tribute* to the provincial government, thus ensuring maintenance of both class structures and Alberta's political hegemony.[67] Reflecting again on Harvey's critique of neoliberalism, the Alberta model appears to confer rights and freedoms to those whose income, leisure and security, when compared to general provincial First Nations living conditions, need no enhancing.[68]

In sum, where a handful of communities have benefited significantly from Alberta's FNGP, most communities have experienced diminished financial returns. There would seem to be little prospect for this pattern to change without additional First Nations casinos. Perhaps most troubling is the restrictive nature of the funding arrangements, which the *Gambling in Alberta* authors commented on:

> It is unclear why this money is deposited into the ALF in the first place when the stated purpose of First Nations casinos is to "increase opportunities for [First Nations] participation in Alberta's economy" and provide "the means to support [First Nations] economic, social and community development projects as well as use charitable gaming proceeds for initiatives such as infrastructure and

> life skills training." For people uncomfortable with First Nations casino revenue going exclusively to First Nations people it needs to be remembered that First Nations people have disproportionately contributed to Alberta gambling revenue for the past 40 years (and Alberta revenue more generally) and have not received this back in terms of provincial services, as service provision for First Nations is a federal responsibility.[69]

It may be ethically suspect for an entity to benefit, even a little, from a venture designed to assist with mitigating First Nations' impoverishment.

Conclusion

In an attempt to foster reserve economic development, several First Nations in the early 1990s embraced Indigenous transnationalism to bypass the federal crown, which they had historically engaged in nation-to-nation relations, to take advantage of a Constitutional division of powers that assigned Alberta (a provincial crown) the authority to permit reserve casinos. One could argue that the federal refusal to negotiate, and the provincial refusal to compromise its authority over gambling-related concerns, left First Nations leaders with little choice in the matter. From a First Nations perspective, however, each entity was considered a foreign power and as such, approachable. Taking advantage of the division of authority enabled First Nations to pursue negotiations with the province. But it also permitted Alberta to leverage its Criminal Code of Canada-assigned authority to approve casino licenses while allowing officials to fashion a First Nations Gaming Policy almost completely independent of First Nations input. Belanger and Williams have illustrated the expansion of provincial gaming bureaucracy during a period of neoliberal reforms.[70] These actions guaranteed that Alberta retained the centralized authority to regulate First Nation casino operations while also restricting First Nations economic and political agency.

Perhaps most striking is how closely these negotiations processes duplicated past colonial relationships, which were characterized by First Nations subordination to a colonial power. This is not a trivial issue when one considers that Alberta's First Nations sought an equitable political and financial arrangement as they pursued improved living conditions that had been negatively impacted by previous federal and provincial colonial policies. Simply put, embedded colonial norms compelled First Nations acquiescence on several levels during and following negotiations. For one, First Nations must allocate Alberta roughly $75 million annually for the privilege of operating casinos despite the fact that provincial officials publicly stated their support for reserve casinos as an effective "means to support economic, social and community development projects as well as use charitable gaming proceeds for initiatives such as infrastructure and life skills training."[71] Consequently, despite becoming key players in a $25 billion provincial industry, First Nations have yet to exercise additional political influence.

Upon further reflection, several troubling trends are evident. At the national level, for example, Ottawa's steadfast refusal to permit First Nations to independently operate casinos on reserve lands clear of provincial oversight has compelled federally acknowledged self-governing First Nations to negotiate with the provinces for casino opportunities. This permitted Alberta's legislative and political penetration of a land base considered previously off limits to provincial authority. As the gaming regulator, Alberta is now free to enact gaming policies even to the harm of First Nations economic development.[72] The unfortunate reality is that First Nations accession to the FNGP is more indicative of impoverished First Nations' anxiety to promote and thus quickly secure benefits from a promising policy rather than as a rational choice predicated on a thorough assessment of best-anticipated outcomes. The first provincial First Nations casino opened in 2006, and further investigation has demonstrated that the FNGP has privileged a handful of reserve communities while inadvertently pitting non-host communities against casino communities; larger host communities against smaller, less lucrative host First Nations; and reserve populations accessing gaming revenues against urban Aboriginal populations that lacked similar access.[73]

The unique nature of Indigenous transnationalism, in this instance, is that it enabled Alberta's First Nations to bypass federal officials restrictive economic development programming, to operate their casinos under provincial jurisdiction. Upon final analysis, however, it would appear that this economic growth arguably occurred at the expense of political agency despite the fact that the adopted collective negotiating strategy was supposed to ensure negotiated leverage.

Notes

1. Yale D. Belanger, Robert J. Williams, and Jennifer N. Arthur, "Casinos and Economic Well-Being: Evaluating the Alberta First Nations' Experience," *Journal of Gambling Business and Economics* 5 (2011), 23–46.

2. Yale D. Belanger and Robert J. Williams, "Neoliberalism as Colonial Embrace: Evaluating Alberta's Regulation of First Nations Gaming, 1993–2010," *Business & Politics* 13 (2011), 1–34.

3. Ravi De Costa, *A Higher Authority: Indigenous Transnationalism and Australia* (Australia: University of New South Wales Press, 2007), 1.

4. De Costa, *A Higher Authority*, 2–3.

5. See, generally, Yale D. Belanger, *Ways of Knowing: An Introduction to Native Studies in Canada* (Toronto: Nelson Education, 2010), 185–89.

6. J. R. Miller, "Petitioning the Great White Mother: First Nations' Organizations and Lobbying in London," in *Reflections on Native-Newcomer Relations*, ed. J. R. Miller (Toronto: University of Toronto Press, 2004), 221.

7. The Indian Land Question can be described as the continued provincial and federal refusal to recognize First Nations claims to lands that had yet to be ceded by treaty or other legal mechanisms. See Keith Carlson, "Rethinking Dialogue and History: The King's Promise and the 1906 Aboriginal Delegation to London," *Native Studies Review* 16 (2005): 1–38; also Paul Tennant, *Aboriginal Peoples*

and Politics: The Indian Land Question in British Columbia (Vancouver: University of British Columbia Press 1990).

8. Yale D. Belanger, "The Six Nations of Grand River Territory's Attempts at Renewing International Political Relationships, 1921–1925," *Canadian Foreign Policy* 13 (2007): 29–43; Deskaheh, *The Redman's Appeal for Justice* (Brantford: D. Wilson Moore Ltd., 1924); Joelle Rostowski, "Deskaheh's Shadow: Indians on the International Scene," *European Review of Native American Studies* 9 (1995): 1–4; Douglas Sanders, "The Legacy of Deskaheh: Indigenous Peoples as International Actors," in *Human Rights of Indigenous Peoples*, ed. Cynthia Price Cohen (New York: Transnational Publishers, 1998); and Richard Veatch, *Canada and the League of Nations* (Toronto: University of Toronto Press, 1975).

9. Francis Paul Prucha, *American Indian Treaties: A History of a Political Anomaly* (Berkeley: University of California Press, 1994), 2.

10. Emmerich de Vattel, *The Law of Nations, The Classics of International Law*, ed. James Brown Scott (Washington, D.C.: Carnegie Institution of Washington, 1916), 160.

11. Writing in 1532, the Spanish jurist Francisco de Vitoria developed a set of principles that were eventually adopted as international law.

12. Sharon O'Brien, "Indian Treaties as International Agreements: Development of the European Nation State and International Law," in *Treaties with American Indians: An Encyclopedia of Rights, Conflicts, and Sovereignty*, ed. Donald L. Fixico (Santa Barbara: ABC-CLIO, 2008), 50.

13. Robert R. Williams, *Linking Arms Together: American Indian Treaty Visions of Law and Peace, 1600–1800* (New York: Oxford University Press, 1997).

14. Thomas Biolsi, "Imagined Geographies: Sovereignty, Indigenous Space, and American Indian Struggle," *American Ethnologist* 32 (2005), 240–41.

15. Yale D. Belanger, "Breaching Reserve Boundaries: *Canada v. Misquadis* and the Legal Evolution of the Urban Aboriginal Community," in *Indigenizing Modernity: Indigenous Identities and Urbanization in International Perspective*, eds. Evelyn J. Peters and Chris Anderson (Vancouver: University of British Columbia Press, 2013), 69–87.

16. See Pam Palmater, *Beyond Blood: Rethinking Indigenous Identity* (Saskatoon: Purich Publishing, 2011).

17. See J. R. Miller, *Shingwauk's Vision: A History of Native Residential Schools* (Toronto: University of Toronto Press, 1996); and John Sheridan Milloy, *A National Crime: The Canadian Government and the residential School System, 1879–1986* (Winnipeg: University of Manitoba Press, 1999).

18. See J. R. Miller, *Compact, Contract, Covenant: Aboriginal Treaty-making in Canada* (Toronto: University of Toronto, 2009).

19. See, generally, Sakej Youngblood Henderson, "Treaty Governance," in *Aboriginal Self-Government in Canada: Current Trends and Issues*, ed. Yale D. Belanger (Saskatoon: Purich, 2008); and for Treaty 7 Elders and Tribal Council, see Walter Hildebrant, Sarah Carter, and Dorothy First Rider, *The True Spirit and Intent of Treaty 7* (Montreal: McGill–Queen's University Press, 1996).

20. F. O. Loft, *Woman's Century* (ca. 1920), 6.

21. Yale D. Belanger, "Seeking a Seat at the Table: A Brief History of Indian Political Organizing in Canada, 1870–1951 (Ph.D. diss., Trent University, 2006).

22. See Brian Titley, "The League of Indians of Canada: An Early Attempt to Create a National Native Organization," *Saskatchewan Indian Federated College Journal* 1 (1984).

23. Richard R. H. Leuger, "A History of Indian Associations in Canada" (M.A. thesis, Carleton University, 1977), 148.

24. Robert N. Wilson, *Our Betrayed Wards: A Story of "Chicanery, Infidelity, and the Prostitution of Trust"* (Montreal: Osiris, 1973); also, Keith Regular, *Neighbours and Networks: The Blood Tribe in the Southern Alberta economy, 1884–1939* (Calgary: University of Calgary Press, 2009).

25. I have previously argued this position in more general national terms in "Labour Unions and First Nations Casinos: An Uneasy Relationship," in *First Nations Gaming in Canada*, ed. Yale D. Belanger (Winnipeg: University of Manitoba Press, 2011), 279–301.

26. See, for example, Peggy Martin-McGuire, *First Nations Land Surrenders on the Prairies, 1896–1911* (Ottawa: Indian Claims Commission, 1998).

27. Mark S. Dockstator, "Toward an Understanding of Aboriginal Self-Government: A Proposed Theoretical Model and Illustrative Factual Analysis" (Ph.D. diss., York University, 1993); and Anne-Marie H. Mawhiney, *Towards Aboriginal Self-Government* (New York: Garland Publishing, 1994).

28. See, for example, John Loxley, *Aboriginal, Northern and Community Economic Development: Papers and Retrospectives* (Winnipeg: Arbeiter Ring Publishing, 2011); Wanda Wuttunee, *Living Rhythms: Lessons in Aboriginal Economic Resilience and Vision* (Kingston and Montreal: McGill–Queen's University Press, 2004); and Robert Brent Anderson, *Economic Development Among the Aboriginal Peoples of Canada: The Hope for the Future* (Concord: Captus, 1999).

29. Sheila McManus, *The Line Which Separates: Race, Gender, and the Making of the Alberta-Montana Borderlands* (Edmonton: The University of Alberta Press, 2005).

30. John Campbell Lehr, "Mormon Settlements in Southern Alberta" (M.A. thesis, University of Alberta, 1971); also, Archie G. Wilcox, "Founding of the Mormon Community in Alberta" (M.A. thesis, University of Alberta, 1950).

31. Howard Palmer, *Patterns of Prejudice: A History of Nativism in Alberta* (Toronto: McClelland and Stewart Limited, 1992).

32. Benedict Anderson, *Imagined Communities* (London: Verso, 2006). On the Protestant work ethic, see Max Weber, *The Protestant Ethic and the Spirit of Capitalism*, trans. Talcott Parsons (New York: Dover Publications, 2003). For the local southern Alberta perspective, see, for example, William M. Baker, "Lethbridge: Founding the Community to 1914: A Visual History," *Occasional Paper No. 27*, Lethbridge Historical Society, 1992.

33. See for example John Maclean, *Canadian Savage Folk: The Native Tribes of Canada* (Toronto: W. Briggs, 1896).

34. Robert Berkhofer, *The White Man's Indian: Images of the American Indian from Columbus to the Present* (New York: Vintage Books, 1979); Olive P. Dickason, *The Myth of the Savage: And the Beginnings of French Colonialism in the Americas* (Edmonton: The University of Alberta Press, 1984); and Robert Williams, *The American Indian in Western Legal Thought: The Discourses of Conquest* (London: Oxford University Press, 1993).

35. See, for example, Roderick P. Neumann, *Making Political Ecology* (London: Hodder Arnold, 2005).

36. See John Snow, *These Mountains are Our Sacred Places*; and Theodore Binnema, *Common and Contested Ground: A Human and Environmental History of the Northwestern Plains* (Toronto: University of Toronto Press, 2004); Mike Mountain Horse, *My People The Bloods* (Calgary: Glenbow Museum, 1979); Joseph F. Dion, *My Tribe The Crees* (Calgary: Glenbow Museum, 1979); John S. Milloy, *The Plains Cree: Trade, Diplomacy and War, 1790–1870* (Winnipeg: University of Manitoba Press, 1988); and Patricia McCormick, *Fort Chipewyan and the Shaping of Canadian History, 1788–1920s* (Vancouver: University of British Columbia Press, 2010).

37. See generally Hugh A. Dempsey, *Maskepetoon: Leader, Warrior, Peacemaker* (Calgary: Heritage House Publishing Company Ltd., 2010); and Binnema, *Common and Contested Ground.*

38. Catherine Bell, *Alberta Metis Settlements Legislation: An Overview of Ownership and Management of Settlement Lands* (Canadian Plains Research Center: 1994).

39. See, for example, Dempsey, *Maskepetoon.*

40. Yale D. Belanger, "'An All Round Indian Affair': The Native Gatherings at MacLeod, 1924 & 1925," *Alberta History* 53 (2005), 13–23.

41. NAC, RG10, vol. 6811, file 470–3–6, part 1 (1945), Indian Association of Alberta, *Memorial on Indian Affairs.*

42. Laurie Meijer-Drees, *The Indian Association of Alberta: A History of Political Action* (Vancouver: University of British Columbia Press, 2002), 38.

43. See, for example, Alejandro Rojas, Lorenzo Magzul, Gregory P. Machildon, and Bernardo Reyes, "The Oldman River Dam Conflict: Adaptation and Institutional Learning," *Prairie Forum* 34 (2009): 235–60; and Eldon Yellowhorn, "Heritage Protection on Indian Reserve Lands in Canada," *Plains Anthropologist* 44 (1999), 107–16.

44. Murray Dobbin, *The One-and-a-Half Men: The Story of Jim Brady and Malcolm Norris* (Vancouver: New Star Books, 1981); Belanger, "Seeking a Seat at the Table"; and Meijer-Drees, *The Indian Association of Alberta.*

45. See Belanger and Williams, "Neoliberalism as Colonial Embrace."

46. For this general discussion, see "Harvard Project Lessons on Self-Government: Improving Aboriginal Self-Government in Canada," *Frontier Center for Public Policy: Backgrounder.* [online]

http://www.fcpp.org/main/ publication_detail.php?PubID=517 (last accessed Dec. 16, 2008). See also Stephen Cornell and Joseph P. Kalt, *Two Approaches to Economic Development on American Indian Reservations: One Works, the Other Doesn't* (Cambridge, Mass.: Harvard Project on American Indian Economic Development and the Native Nations Institute for Leadership, Management, and Policy, on behalf of the Arizona Board of Regents, 2006); Stephen Cornell, Miriam Jorgensen, Joseph P. Kalt, and Katherine A. Spilde, *Seizing the Future: Why Some Native Nations Do and Others Don't* (Cambridge, Mass.: Harvard Project of American Indian Economic Development, 2005).

47. See generally Michael Labrosse, *The Lottery . . . From Jacques Cartier's Day to Modern Times* (Montreal: Stanke, 1985).

48. Hal Pruden, "An Overview of the Gambling Provisions in Canadian Criminal Law and First Nations Gambling," *Journal of Aboriginal Economic Development* 2 (2002), 38.

49. Colin Campbell, "Canadian Gambling Legislation: The Social Origins of Legalization" (Ph.D. diss., Simon Fraser University, B.C., 1995), 250.

50. *R. v. Furtney*, 1991.

51. *St. Mary's Indian Band v. Canada*, 1995; *R. v. Gladue*, 1986.

52. Yale D. Belanger, *Gambling with the Future: The Evolution of Aboriginal Gaming in Canada* (Saskatoon: Purich Publishing, 2006).

53. Monte Stewart, "Natives seeking own gaming commission," *Calgary Herald*, Aug. 29, 1993, A4.

54. "Klein Nod Given to Reserve Casinos Already, Says MLA," *Edmonton Journal*, March 17, 1995.

55. "Tsuu T'ina Open to Some Changes," *Calgary Herald*, Jan. 30, 1996, A6.

56. Garry Smith and Harold Wynne, *A Review of the Literature in the Economic and Policy Domains* (Edmonton: Alberta Gaming Research Institute, 2000), 32.

57. Tom Arnold, "Natives Seek Bigger Chunk of Gaming Profits," *Edmonton Journal*, Nov. 21, 1996, A7.

58. Ibid.

59. Alberta, "Government Approves Policies to Effectively Manage Growth of Gaming: Community Support Required for New Casinos; VLT cap to remain," http://www.gaming.gov.ab.ca/news/20011022.asp (last accessed June 2, 2005).

60. Alberta Gambling and Liquor Commission (AGLC), *Annual Report: Protecting the Integrity of Alberta's Gambling and Liquor Industries* (Alberta: Alberta Gambling and Liquor Commission, 2003).

61. Robert J. Williams, Yale D. Belanger, and Jennifer N. Arthur, *Gambling in Alberta: History, Current Status, and Socioeconomic Impacts* (Edmonton: Alberta Gaming and Liquor Commission, 2011).

62. Robert Williams, Rhys Stevens and Gary Nixon. "Gambling and Problem Gambling in North American Indigenous Peoples," in *First Nations Gaming in Canada*, ed. Yale D. Belanger, (Winnipeg: University of Manitoba Press, 2011), 166–94.

63. Williams, Belanger, and Arthur, *Gambling in Alberta*, 283–84.

64. Because there is no stipulation about what percentage of INAC funding bands should provide to off-reserve residents, in most cases these monies are spent exclusively on reserves to the detriment of off-reserve members. For a more in-depth discussion, see Yale D. Belanger, "First Nations Gaming and Urban Aboriginal Peoples: Does an Economic 'Fit' Exist?" in *First Nations Gaming in Canada*, ed. Yale D. Belanger (Winnipeg: University of Manitoba Press, 2011), 140–64.

65. Daniella Zietsma, *Aboriginal People Living Off-Reserve and the Labour Market: Estimates from the Labour Force Survey, 2008–2009* (Ottawa: Statistics Canada, 2010).

66. Williams, Belanger, and Arthur, *Gambling in Alberta*, 275.

67. David Harvey, *A Brief History of Neoliberalism* (Oxford: Oxford University Press, 2009).

68. Harvey, *A Brief History of Neoliberalism.*

69. Williams, Belanger, and Arthur, *Gambling in Alberta.*

70. Belanger and Williams. "Neoliberalism as Colonial Embrace."

71. Yale D. Belanger and Robert J. Williams. "Urban Aboriginal and First Nations Perspectives on Casinos and the Alberta First Nations Gaming Industry." *International Gambling Studies* 11, (2011): 1–16; and, Alberta. "Government Approves Policies to Effectively Manage Growth of Gaming."

72. See Belanger and Williams, "Neoliberalism as Colonial Embrace."

73. See Belanger, Williams, and Arthur, "Casinos and Economic Well-Being."

Contributor Biographies

Clarissa W. Confer is an associate professor of history and the director of the Ladonna Harris Native American Institute at California University of Pennsylvania. She is the author of *The Cherokee Nation in the Civil War*, which explores the social history of Cherokee Indians during the turmoil of internal and external division; *Daily Life in Pre-Columbian Native America*; and *Daily Life in the Indian Wars*.

Yale D. Belanger is an associate professor of political science studies and adjunct associate professor, Faculty of Health Sciences, at the University of Lethbridge, Alberta. He published *First Nations Gaming in Canada* and *Gambling with the Future: The Evolution of Aboriginal Gaming in Canada*.

José Angel Hernández is an associate professor at the University of Houston. He has published articles in *Aztlán: A Journal of Chicano Studies* and *Mexican Studies/Estudios Mexicanos* as well as *Landscapes of Violence: An Interdisciplinary Journal Devoted to the Study of Violence, Conflict, and Trauma*. He recently published an award-winning monograph, *Mexican American Colonization During the Nineteenth Century: A History of the US–Mexico Borderlands*.

Kristin Hoganson is a professor of history at the University of Illinois, Urbana-Champaign. She is the author of *Fighting for American Manhood: How Gender Politics Provoked the Spanish-American and Philippine-American Wars* and *Consumer's Imperium: The Global Production of American Domesticity, 1865–1920*. Her book-in-progress reframes the history of the US heartland by centering on mobility and connections.

Matthew S. Makley is an associate professor of history at Metropolitan State University of Denver. He co-authored *Cave Rock: Climbers, Courts, and a Washoe Indian Sacred Place*. His current manuscript, *The People of Tahoe: A History of the Washoe Indians*, is under review with the University of Nevada Press.

María Cristina Manzano-Munguía is a research professor at the Institute of Social Science and Humanities "Alfonso Vélez Pliego" at the Benemérita Universidad Autónoma de Puebla. She has published on issues related to aboriginal-state relations, Indian policy and legislation, Indigenous diaspora, and aboriginal leaders in urban centers. Her current research interests include Indigenous forced transnationalism across borderlands and the transpacific relations between Mexico and China. She is member of the National Research System (SNI 1) CONACYT in Mexico.

Andrae Marak is a professor of history and political science and the chair of the Division of Humanities and Social Sciences at Governors State. He has authored, co-authored or co-edited *At the Border of Empires: The Tohono O'odham, Gender and Assimilation, 1880–1934*, with Laura Tuennerman; *Smugglers, Brothels, and Twine: Historical Perspectives on Contraband and Vice in North America's Borderlands*, with Elaine Carey; and *From Many, One: Indians, Peasants, Borders, and Education in Callista Mexico, 1924–1935*. He is currently working on a book about the Seri Indians.

Michael Marker is an associate professor and director of Ts"kel Indigenous Graduate Studies at the University of British Columbia. His publications have concentrated on historical and ethnological approaches to education and culture change in the Coast Salish region. His recent work is focused on the politics and social context of traditional ecological knowledge in classrooms and in research methodologies.

W. Dirk Raat is a SUNY Fredonia Emeritus Professor and an adjunct professor at ASU West. His most recent book publication is a study he did with photographer George Janeçek, entitled *Mexico's Sierra Tarahumara: A Photohistory of the People of the Edge.* He is currently working on a book project with Navajo artist Steven Yazzie and Heard Museum curator Janet Cantley on the nineteenth-century experiences of several Native American groups in the Greater American Southwest.

Ian Stacy teaches history and geography at Whatcom Community College in Bellingham, Washington. He has published in *Environmental History* and *Journal of the West.* His research interests include environmental politics and Pacific Northwest history.

Laura Tuennerman is a professor of history at California University of Pennsylvania. She is the author of *Helping Others, Helping Ourselves* and co-author, with Andrae Marak, of *At the Border of Empires: The Tohono O'odham, Gender, and Assimilation, 1880–1934*. She co-authored chapters in *Smugglers, Brothels, and Twine: Historical Perspectives on Contraband and Vice in North America's Borderlands*, eds. Andrae Marak and Elaine Carey; and in *En la encrucijada. Historia, marginalidad y delito en América Latina y los Estados Unidos de Norteamérica, siglos XIX y XX*, ed. J. A. T. Bretón. Her current work focuses on the Seri and popular historical memory.

Gary Van Valen is an associate professor at the University of West Georgia. He is the author of *Indigenous Agency in the Amazon: The Mojos in Liberal and Rubber-Boom Bolivia*, 1842–1932, and has contributed to the *Diccionario histórico de Bolivia*, the *World History Bulletin*, the *SECOLAS Annals*, the *Anuario de Estudios Bolivianos, Archivísticos y Bibliográficos*, *The Middle Ground Journal: World History and Global Studies*, and *Voices: The Journal of New York*

Folklore. He is currently researching the Pueblos of New Mexico in the period of Mexican rule.

Tony Ward is an associate professor in the Department of Economics at Brock University. He has written a variety of journal articles and book chapters, primarily on peoples' histories during the period of European settlement, examining issues concerning both the Indigenous population and also the incoming settlers.

Index